INSIGHT GUIDES

SOUTH INDIA

INSIGHT GUIDE
SOUTH INDIA

Editorial
Managing Editor
Maria Lord
Editorial Director
Brian Bell

Distribution
UK & Ireland
GeoCenter International Ltd
Meridian House, Churchill Way West,
Basingstoke, Hampshire RG21 6YR
Fax: (44) 1256 817988
United States
Langenscheidt Publishers, Inc.
36–36 33rd Street 4th Floor
Long Island City, NY 11106
Fax: 1 (718) 784 0640
Australia
Universal Publishers
1 Waterloo Road
Macquarie Park, NSW 2113
Fax: (61) 2 9888 9074
New Zealand
Hema Maps New Zealand Ltd (HNZ)
Unit D, 24 Ra ORA Drive
East Tamaki, Auckland
Fax: (64) 9 273 6479
Worldwide
Apa Publications GmbH & Co. Verlag KG (Singapore branch)
38 Joo Koon Road, Singapore 628990
Tel: (65) 6865 1600. Fax: (65) 6861 6438

Printing
Insight Print Services (Pte) Ltd
38 Joo Koon Road, Singapore 628990
Tel: (65) 6865 1600. Fax: (65) 6861 6438

First Edition 1990
Second Edition 2006
Updated 2006

CONTACTING THE EDITORS
We would appreciate it if readers would alert us to errors or outdated information by writing to:
Insight Guides, P.O. Box 7910, London SE1 1WE, England.
Fax: (44) 20 7403 0290.
insight@apaguide.co.uk

www.insightguides.com

ABOUT THIS BOOK

This guidebook combines the interests and enthusiasms of two of the world's best-known information providers: Insight Guides, whose many titles have set the standard for illustrated travel guides since 1970, and Discovery Channel, the world's premier source of nonfiction television programming.

The editors, writers and photographers of Insight Guides (www.insightguides.com) provide a visual document, practical advice and general understanding about a destination's history, culture, institutions and people.

Discovery Channel and its popular website, www.discovery.com, help millions of viewers explore their world from the comfort of their own home and encourage them to explore it firsthand.

Insight Guide: South India is structured to convey an understanding of the state and its people as well as to guide readers through its sights and activities:

◆ The **Features** section, indicated by a yellow bar at the top of each page, covers the natural and cultural history of the state in a series of informative essays.

◆ The main **Places** section, indicated by a blue bar, is a complete guide to all the sights and areas worth visiting. Places of special interest are coordinated by number with the maps.

◆ The **Travel Tips** listings section, has been completely revamped and divided into easy-to-use sections on Transport, Accommodation, Eating, Activities, an A–Z directory and Language and Further Reading.

The contributors

This book was edited and revised by **Maria Lord**, an Insight Guides editor and writer. She wrote the Travel Tips and substantially updated and reworked all of the Features and Places chapters, especially those on music, cinema, Kerala and Andhra Pradesh.

This second edition builds on the valuable work of previous contributors. Starting with the Features section, the Geography and Wildlife chapters were written by **Dr Kamala Seshan** (lecturer at the National Council for Educational Research and Training) and **Nirmal Ghosh** respectively. The extensive History chapters were supplied by **Dr D.B. Chattopadhyaya,** of Jawaharlal Nehru University, Delhi, and **Sushila Ravindranath**.

Society and Culture were dealt with by one of India's most acclaimed writers and anthropologists, **Dr M.N. Srinivas**. The food chapter was contributed by food writer **Ummi Abdullah**, while Art and Architecture were covered by **Dr Shobita Punja**. The crafts section was written by **Jaya Jaitly**. The chapter on Music and Dance was initially written by the highly respected **Dr N. Pattabhiraman**, founder of the Sruti Foundation. Cinema was covered by the Malayalam film maker **V. Abdullah**, who also wrote on his native Northern Kerala in the places section.

Other places were covered by a variety of writers. **S. Muthiah**, aided by **S. Krishnan**, covered much of Tamil Nadu, including Chennai, the area to the south of Chennai, the Hill Stations, and Pondicherry. He also wrote many of the Kerala chapters: on Thiruvananthapuram, the Backwaters and Kochi, and the Western Ghats. The Kaveri Delta and Madurai were covered by **Rajam Krishnan**, while **Shobita Punja** contributed the feature on Tanjore Painting. **K.S. Padmanabhan** wrote the article on the Lakshadweep Islands. Andhra Pradesh was covered by **Uzra Bilgrami**, a native of Hyderabad. Parts of Karnataka were written on by **John Abraham**, including the sections on Bangalore, Mysore, and the sites around Bijapur and Badami. The rest of the state was covered by **Prasad Bidapa**, who wrote on Sravanabelagola, Hampi, the Northern Deccan, the coast, and his native homeland of Kodagu. The introductory sections to the states were written by **Ashok Ranganathan**.

The book was proofread by **Jan McCann** and indexed by **Helen Peters**.

The main places of interest in the Places section are coordinated by number with a full-colour map (e.g. ❶), and a symbol at the top of every right-hand page tells you where to find the map.

INSIGHT GUIDE

SOUTH INDIA

CONTENTS

Maps

Introduction

History

People

Features

Dusk falls at Kovalam beach

Travel Tips

♦ Full Travel Tips index is on page 325

Information panels

Places

The Best of South India

South Indian temples, wildlife, beaches, palaces and hotels... here, at a glance, are some highlights to help you plan your journey

Temples

Some of the most spectacular temples in the world are found in South India.

- **Aihole, Karnataka** *(see page 281).*
- **Badami, Karnataka** *(see page 280).*
- **Brihadesvara temple, Thanjavur, Tamil Nadu** *(see page 149).*
- **Chennakesvara Temple, Belur, Karnataka** *(see page 255).*
- **Ekambaresvara temple, Kanchipuram, Tamil Nadu** *(see page 140).*
- **Guruvayur, Kerala** *(see page 215).*
- **Hoysalesvara Temple, Halebid, Karnataka** *(see page 257).*
- **Krisna temple, Udipi, Karnataka** *(see page 263).*
- **Lepaksi, Andhra Pradesh** *(see page 320).*
- **Minaksi temple, Madurai, Tamil Nadu** *(see page 157).*
- **Mukhalingam, Andhra Pradesh** *(see page 308).*
- **Nataraja Temple, Chidambaram, Tamil Nadu** *(see page 147).*
- **Pattadakal, Karnataka** *(see page 283).*
- **Ramalingesvara temple, Tadpatri, Andhra Pradesh** *(see page 322).*
- **Ramanatasvami temple, Ramesvaram, Tamil Nadu** *(see page 165).*
- **Shore Temple, Mamallapuram, Tamil Nadu** *(see page 138).*
- **Simhachalam, Andhra Pradesh** *(see page 307).*
- **Somnathpur, Karnataka** *(see page 251).*
- **Srirangam, Tamil Nadu** *(see page 154).*
- **Tirumala, Andhra Pradesh** *(see page 319).*
- **Tiruvannamalai, Tamil Nadu** *(see page 169).*
- **Vadakkunnathan temple, Thrissur, Kerala** *(see page 215).*
- **Vittala Temple, Hampi, Karnataka** *(see page 269).*

ABOVE: one of the spectacular *gopurams* in Madurai.

Beaches and Resorts

South India has some superb beaches and resorts, offering wildlife, ayurvedic treatments and diving.

- **Bangaram, Lakshadweep** *(see page 225).*
- **Gokarna, Karnataka** *(see page 263).*
- **Green Magic Nature Resort, Vythiri, Kerala** *(see page 335).*
- **Kadmat, Lakshadweep** *(see page 225).*
- **Kovalam, Kerala** *(see page 191).*
- **Lagoona Davina, Pachallur, Kerala** *(see page 334).*
- **Mamallapuram, Tamil Nadu** *(see page 137).*
- **Surya Samudra Beach Garden, Kerala** *(see page 333).*
- **Taj Garden Retreat, Coonoor, Tamil Nadu** *(see page 336).*
- **Varkala, Kerala** *(see page 193).*

MUSEUMS AND GALLERIES

- **Art Gallery, Thanjavur** *(see page 151)*.
- **Government Museum, Bangalore** *(see page 239)*.
- **Government Museum, Pudukkottai, Tamil Nadu** *(see page 155)*.
- **Napier Museum, Thiruvananthapuram** *(see page 190)*.
- **Pariksith Thamburam Museum, Ernakulam** *(see page 205)*.
- **Pondicherry Museum** *(see page 178)*.
- **Salar Jung Museum, Hyderabad** *(see page 292)*.
- **Sri Chitra Art Gallery, Thiruvananthapuram** *(see page 190)*.
- **State Government Museum, Chennai** *(see page 131)*.
- **Victoria Jubilee Museum, Vijayawada, Andhra Pradesh** *(see page 203)*.

PALACES

The hereditary rulers of South India did not stint themselves when it came to building residences.

- **Bangalore Palace, Karnataka** *(see page 235)*.
- **Chandragiri, Andhra Pradesh** *(see page 320)*.
- **Faluknuma Palace, Hyderbad, Andhra Pradesh,** *(see page 292)*.
- **Mattancherri Palace, Kerala** *(see page 202)*.
- **Mysore Palace, Karnataka** *(see page 246)*.
- **Padmanabhapuram, Tamil Nadu** *(see page 167)*.
- **Puttan Malika Palace, Kerala** *(see page 188)*.
- **Tippu Sultan's Palace, Bangalore, Karnataka** *(see page 237)*.
- **Tirumalai Nayaka Palace, Madurai, Tamil Nadu** *(see page 161)*.

HILL STATIONS

One of the more civilised legacies of British rule is this network of cool, elevated retreats.

- **Coonoor, Tamil Nadu** *(see page 170)*.
- **Horsley Hills, Andhra Pradesh** *(see page 318)*.
- **Idukki, Kerala** *(see page 209)*.
- **Kodaikanal, Tamil Nadu** *(see page 172)*.
- **Kotagiri, Tamil Nadu** *(see page 172)*.
- **Kuttalam, Tamil Nadu** *(see page 173)*.
- **Lakidi, Kerala** *(see page 218)*.
- **Madikeri, Kodagu, Karnataka** *(see page 260)*.
- **Munnar, Kerala** *(see page 210)*.
- **Nandi Hills, Karnataka** *(see page 241)*.
- **Palani, Tamil Nadu** *(see page 172)*.
- **Ponmudi, Kerala** *(see page 207)*.
- **Thekkady, Kerala** *(see page 208)*.
- **Udagamandalam, Tamil Nadu** *(see page 171)*.
- **Yercaud, Tamil Nadu** *(see page 169)*.

LEFT: Munnar, Kerala.
ABOVE: Padmanabhapuram in Tamil Nadu.
BELOW: a fishing boat at Gokarna, Karnataka.

Forts

Successive empires and waves of invaders have left spectacular forts all over South India.

- **Bekal, Kerala** *(see page 219).*
- **Bidar, Karnataka** *(see page 278).*
- **Chitradurga, Karnataka** *(see page 241).*
- **Dansborg Fort, Tranquebar, Tamil Nadu** *(see page 144).*
- **Fort St David, Cuddalore, Tamil Nadu** *(see page 142).*
- **Gandikota, Andhra Pradesh** *(see page 322).*
- **Gingee, Tamil Nadu** *(see page 142).*
- **Golconda, Andhra Pradesh** *(see page 295).*
- **Palakkad, Kerala** *(see page 215).*
- **Penukonda, Andhra Pradesh** *(see page 322).*
- **Srirangapatnam, Karnataka** *(see page 249).*
- **St Angelo's Fort, Kannur, Kerala** *(see page 219).*
- **Sulthanbathery, Kerala** *(see page 218).*
- **Tiruchirappalli, Tamil Nadu** *(see page 153).*
- **Udayagiri, Andhra Pradesh** *(see page 323).*
- **Vellore, Tamil Nadu** *(see page 141).*
- **Warangal, Andhra Pradesh** *(see page 311).*

Best Times to Go

Mid-September to March is the best time, between the major monsoon season in June to September and the onset of summer in April. Summer is extremely hot, and the rains can make getting around difficult.

Above: the Keralan backwaters, Alappuzha.
Below Left: the Lalitha Mahal, Mysore.

Wildlife Sanctuaries

- **Bandipur, Karnataka** *(see page 347).*
- **Eravikulam, Kerala** *(see page 348)*
- **Indira Gandhi, Tamil Nadu** *(see page 349).*
- **Kolleru, Andhra Pradesh** *(see page 346)*
- **Mudumalai, Tamil Nadu** *(see page 349).*
- **Nagarahole, Karnataka** *(see page 348).*
- **Periyar, Kerala** *(see page 349).*
- **Point Calimere, Tamil Nadu** *(see page 349).*
- **Pulicat, Andhra Pradesh and Tamil Nadu** *(see page 347).*
- **Silent Valley, Kerala** *(see page 349).*
- **Srisailam-Nagarjunasagar, Andhra Pradesh** *(see page 347).*
- **Sri Venkatesvara, Andhra Pradesh** *(see page 347)*
- **Thattekkad, Kerala** *(see page 349).*
- **Waynad, Kerala** *(see page 349).*

Best Places to Stay

- **Brunton Boatyard, Kochi, Kerala** *(see page 333).*
- **Emerald Isle Heritage Resort, Alappuzha, Kerala** *(see page 332).*
- **Green Hotel, Mysore, Karnataka** *(see page 332).*
- **Le Dupleix, Pondicherry** *(see page 335).*
- **Kovalam Hotels, Kovalam, Kerala** *(see page 333).*
- **Lalitha Mahal, Mysore, Karnataka** *(see page 332).*
- **Malabar House Residency, Kochi, Kerala** *(see page 333).*
- **Taj Connemara, Chennai, Tamil Nadu** *(see page 335).*

FESTIVALS

- **Pongal/Sankranti** *(see page 344)* January.
- **Tiruvaiyaru Music Festival** *(see page 345)* January.
- **Masi Magam, Pondicherry** *(see page 176)* February–March.
- **Ugadi, Andhra Pradesh** *(see page 287)* March–April.
- **Ana Puram, Thrissur** *(see page 214)* April–May.
- **Minaksi and Sundaresvara Festival, Madurai** *(see page 157)* April–May.
- **Onam** *(see page 197)* September.
- **Ganapati Chaturthi** *(see page 344)* September–October.
- **Navaratri/Dussera** *(see page 344)* September–October.
- **Dipavali** *(see page 344)* October–November.
- **The Chennai Festival** *(see page 345)* December–January.

ABOVE: waiting for the bus, Mysore.
LEFT: canopies for the god, Tiruvannamalai.

JOURNEYS

Many journeys across South India are worth taking in their own right; here is a selection.

- **By train to Udagamandalam** *(see page 170)* A delightful "Toy Train" winds its way up to the hill station from Coonoor.
- **To Ramesvaram and Danushkodi** *(see page 165)* A storm ravaged sand spit that is a revered pilgrimage destination.
- **The Keralan backwaters** *(see page 195)* A dreamy boat ride between Kollam and Alappuzha.
- **Up to Munnar in the Western Ghats** *(see page 210)* Beautiful views of the mountains and tea gardens.
- **Travel along the Karnatakan coast by the Konkan Railway** *(see page 263)* This spectacular railway line is one of India's great engineering triumphs.
- **From Vijayawada to Visakhapatnam** *(see page 301)* The railway along the east coast passes through the beautiful deltas of the Krishna and Godavari rivers.

THE CITIES

Chennai The South's largest city and capital of Tamil Nadu. A bastion of Tamil culture and location of one of India's finest museums. *See page 121.*

Thiruvananthapuram The capital of Kerala is charming and easy-going, with a superb temple and interesting colonial architecture. *See page 187.*

Kochi-Ernakulam The economic powerhouse of Kerala is both a booming port city and historical centre with fascinating palaces, synagogues and churches. *See page 199.*

Bangalore Said to be South India's most pleasant city, Karnataka's capital has a mild climate and a laid-back feel. As well as a thriving software industry it is also, unusually for India, known for its pub culture. *See page 231.*

Mysore Elegant and regal, Mysore is dominated by its ornate royal palace and the nearby Chamundi Hill, location of an impressive temple and one of India's largest Nandi statues. *See page 243.*

Hampi The ruined and deserted capital of the Vijayanagara Empire is one of India's most atmospheric archaeological sites. *See page 265.*

Hyderabad The vibrant capital of Andhra Pradesh is known for its Muslim heritage, a superb museum and one of South India's most impressive forts, Golconda. *See page 289.*

A POTPOURRI

The South, with its distinct and deep-rooted identity, is as diverse and endlessly fascinating as the rest of India

The Vindhya and Satpura mountain ranges form the geographical divide between northern and southern India. Politically, South India had earlier been thought of as the former Madras Presidency and the adjoining princely states of Hyderabad, Mysore, Travancore and Cochin. With the integration of the princely states and the redrawing of the map of India on a linguistic basis in 1956, this area was carved, with some additions and subtractions, into the modern states of Andhra Pradesh, Karnataka, Kerala and Tamil Nadu.

The real divide between these states and the Indo-Gangetic plain is twofold: firstly, the Dravidian languages spoken in them – Telugu, Kannada, Malayalam and Tamil – have little connection with the dominant languages of the north, though all of them have in varying degrees a linkage with Sanskrit; secondly, the South, though exposed through the ages to international maritime and trade contacts, remained relatively isolated from the successive invasions that periodically convulsed most of India. Even at the zenith of the Islamic empires, large parts of South India remained out of their orbit (though Andhra Pradesh and Karnataka had enclaves of Muslim domination for centuries). Given this history of isolation, it is one of Indian history's ironies that the most extensive conquest, the British subjugation of India, should have started in the mid-18th century in the southernmost state of Tamil Nadu.

This relative isolation led to distinct styles of architecture and different forms of music, dance and drama than found elsewhere in the country. Even among the four southern states there are physical and cultural diversities. It is hard to overplay the role language plays in South Indian identity. Tamils in particular have long resisted the pan-Indian use of the Indo-European Hindi as a "National Language" and rioting has sporadically broken out when central government has tried to impose it for official documents and in education. This battle, it seems, is being won with the state government insisting on Tamil as a major component in the school curriculum and with central government recently declaring Tamil a classical language, recognising its long history and putting it on a par with Sanskrit. The Tirupati hills, in the south of Andhra Pradesh, form the boundary between the central and southern Dravidian languages, the former being the closely linked Telugu (spoken in Andhra Pradesh) and Kannada (from Karnataka), and the latter being Tamil from Tamil Nadu and Malayalam, spoken in Kerala and in many ways a Sanskritised dialect of Tamil.

PRECEDING PAGES: elephants decked for the *Ana Puram* festival in Thrissur; the annual celebration of the marriage of Siva and Minaksi, Madurai; Lambadi women celebrate the arrival of spring.
LEFT: a young Jain at Sravanabelagola, Karnataka.

It is not only with regard to language that identity is seen in terms of opposition to the North. The post-Independence Pan-Dravidian Movement sought to forge a South Indian identity based on a shared cultural history, rejecting Brahmanised and Sanskritised versions of Hinduism. Indeed, the epic *Ramayana* was reinterpreted as a tale of northern domination, whereby the light-skinned, and therefore northern, Rama was seen as the tyrant attacking the darker-skinned Ravanna, King of Lanka in the South. As an overwhelmingly Hindu region, this religious identity not only imprints itself on the landscape (in terms of distinctive temple architecture and networks of local shrines and pilgrimage sites) but also in traditional music, which is largely centred around devotional song, and theatre in depictions of the tales of gods and goddesses.

Lying below the Tropic of Cancer, and separated from the rest of India by a high plateau and ranges of hills, geography also contributes to the South's distinctiveness. Most of Karnataka and large parts of Andhra Pradesh, including the capital cities of Bangalore and Hyderabad, lie in the region of the Deccan plateau. Tamil Nadu and Kerala consist mainly of tropical coastal plains, though both of them share the Western Ghats, the fractured and uplifted rim of the plateau. Kerala, which bears the brunt of the southwest monsoon, has verdant tropical vegetation and some of the only surviving primary rainforest in India. Andhra Pradesh, Karnataka and Tamil Nadu are largely dependent on man-made irrigation, particularly on the series of barrages and dams which have been built on the Krishna, Godavari and Kaveri rivers.

Scenically, the southern states have all the variety that a visitor could wish for: dramatic coastlines both on the Arabian Sea and on the Bay of Bengal, meeting at Kanniyakumari on the Indian Ocean; many isolated beaches, dense forests and game reserves with a bewildering array of flora and fauna; swift flowing streams and large rivers meandering lazily towards the sea; and the beautiful Nilgiri and Anamalai mountain ranges. ❑

RIGHT: a Keralan lorry driver.

GOD IS
TRUTH
MANOJ
SWAGATH

GEOGRAPHY

South India covers a huge area, taking in forest-covered mountains, tropical beaches and the high Deccan Plateau

The Deccan peninsula, lying between 8° and 15°N, and 75° and 86°E, is the remnant of a once large and stable plateau. Parallel to the west coast and close to it lie the Western Ghats, a series of step-like terraces and weather-worn hills stretching from the Tapti river valley in the north to Kanniyakumari on India's southern tip. They form the high western edge of the Deccan plateau, which slopes gently eastwards to the Eastern Ghats on the other coast of peninsular India. The Western and Eastern Ghats unite in the Nilgiri Hills in the extreme south, like a grand knot in a necklace around the Indian peninsula.

The landscape of South India is varied. Along the west coast, from North Kanara district in Karnataka to the tip of the peninsula, lie some of India's oldest ports and harbours, many of them now in disuse. One that survives is Karwar, at the head of a narrow inland area, now a shipbuilding harbour and fishing port. Small, swift-flowing rivulets cross this region.

The Malabar Coast

The coastal strip broadens out southwards, providing some of the finest beaches in the country along this coast. Inland, up into the Western Ghats in Kerala and Karnataka, extensive rainforests are still found, protected from human depredation by the inaccessible scarp and dissected landscape of the hills. There is an abundance of flora and fauna, particularly exotic butterflies and the wild elephant, and it is the only home of some species, like the lion-tailed macaque. The plant life in some of these forests has yet to be properly catalogued and studied. This is also a region rich in plantation crops such as cardamom, tea and coffee.

The coast of Malabar on the southwestern tip has numerous and extensive mud-banks. Laterite soil forms the foothills of the plateau, and behind these areas are highlands of glistening gneissic rock. The alluvial lowlands are cut across all the way inland by interconnected creeks from the sea. Life in these areas – from transportation and soaking coconut husk to stringing out the day's catch of fish and prawns – revolves around these picturesque backwaters.

Lying some 200–300 km (120–190 miles) off the Keralan coast are the Lakshadweep islands, a low-lying archipelago, the only true coral islands owned by India. Surrounded by reefs, which enclose shallow lagoons, and set in glitteringly clear seas, the islands are part of the same chain as the Maldives which lie further to the south. Lakshadweep is home to many species of sea bird, with a number of important nesting sites on uninhabited islands, while the surrounding seas are an important habitat for turtles, reef fish and manta rays. The flora of the islands is dominated by coconut palms, which contribute a significant part of the islands' economy.

LEFT: this Dravidian temple sets off a landscape of rocky outcrops and orderly fields.
RIGHT: Kerala's backwaters.

The Western Ghats

Inland of the coastal strip lie Vembanad Lake and the Annamalai Hills. Cutting across this mountainous rib is the Periyar river which empties its headwaters across the Palakkad Gap. These low gaps of Palakkad and Shencottah are the main inroads from the Coimbatore plateau to the west coast.

The hills to the north of these gaps, the cloud-covered Nilgiris, form part of the long line of the Western Ghats; reaching 1,800 to 2,440 m (6,000 to 8,000 ft), these are the highest in the peninsula. The dense forests in the tropical region have a variety of ferns and wild berries, along with the aromatic Nilgiri lily. These hills, situated in the path of the southwest monsoon, are the catchment areas for the Vaigai and Periyar rivers.

Plateaux and gorges

The interior of the peninsula has several distinct plateau regions which belong to the Deccan lava region and the older Archaen gneisses. The Telengana plateau to the north is a dry, desiccated terrain with only the Godavari flowing across it. To its south, between the Bhima and the Godavari, lie broad, much-eroded valleys heaped with rocks "as if giants had amused themselves with childish games" (*Hyderabad Gazetteer*, 1909). The vegetation here is mostly savannah-type with thorny scrub, while in the more moist areas date palms are found. Southwestwards is the "trap dyke land" along the tributaries of the Pennar, which drains into the sea near Nellore, through laterite plains characterised by fertile land dotted with large tanks, which are man-made reservoirs.

The gorges of the rain-fed Krishna and Pennar rivers and their tributaries form long valleys, like silver threads on a broad spread of rock, with white sand and shingle beds. It is along these long valleys that the big tanks are found – mostly on the Chennai–Mumbai rail route – and the great pilgrimage centres of Renigunta and Tirupati. The landscape here is grey and the plains are dotted with mango groves.

Lakes, deltas and valleys

The upper part of the eastern coast is dominated by the vast deltas of the Krishna and Godavari rivers, which irrigate some of the most productive lands in the region, known as the "rice bowl of southern India". The two rivers rise almost at the western coast, high up in the ghats, and flow eastwards across the Deccan. Mangrove coasts with sand dunes are to be found where the rivers meet the sea. The

Kolleru Lake lies between the two deltas and is ideal for fish cultivation. It is in this section that the large ports of Machilipatnam and Kakinada are situated. Once they exported India's famous printed cloths; today they are used mainly for the export of bauxite. Andhra's rich coastal land is frequently lashed by cyclones and is often flooded during the monsoons.

Overlooking Renigunta along the Tirupati escarpment is the Nellore plain, which marks the beginning of the Coromandel coast extending south into Tamil Nadu. It is well known for its rich paddy fields and the high-yielding Nellore cow with its distinctive swept-back horns.

The saltwater lagoon at Pulicat just north of Madras is an interesting feature of this region.

The coast of Tamil Nadu, the land of the Cholas, is a lowland dipping into the sea. From narrow streams in the large open valleys of the Adyar, Cooum and Korteliyar rivers, the coastal plain runs along a narrow path of marine and river sand deposits, backed by casuarina, lime quarries and saltpans.

Westwards lies the Coimbatore plateau, bound by the Bhavani, Amravati and Annamalai tributaries of the Kaveri. From the Krishnarajayar reservoir the Kaveri flows over several rapids to enter the plains at Sivasamudram. The Thanjavur plain is a gift of the Kaveri, where the Chola kings constructed a grand anicut to control its waters. The huge Kaveri delta is approximately 10,350 sq km (4,000 sq miles) and fans out between Porto Novo and Point Calimere. It is, in essence, the source of Tamil Nadu's prosperity, and this is reflected in the majestic temple towers of Thanjavur.

Southeastwards from the delta is the cotton belt of Madurai, Ramanathapuram and Tirunelveli districts, almost entirely supported by tank irrigation (artificial lakes and ponds). In the northwest are the Palani Hills from where the Vaigai starts in the Varshugrad valley.

In terms of irrigation, the entire peninsula is a monsoon-dependent area. Separated from the northern plains by the Satpura and Vindhya ranges, the peninsula has a variety of landforms – plains, plateaux and hills – and rivers that may not be as wide as the northern rivers of the Ganga and Brahmaputra, but are almost as long. It is a geographical area with distinct characteristics, home to a rich and varied culture and civilisation. Dravidian culture flourished in this fertile land and is still evident in its distinct architecture. ❑

LEFT: the Tungabhadra river near the Vijayanagara site at Hampi.

ABOVE: deforestation is evident in the hills.

WILDLIFE

South India is home to some of the country's most impressive species, including herds of wild elephants, tigers and the powerful gaur

South India is a land of rolling hills and lush plains, dry scrub-forested plateaux, deep valleys of moist evergreen forest and one of the most beautiful coastlines in the world. The weather in much of the peninsula is governed by the two seasonal monsoons; the southwest monsoon from late May to August and the gentler northeast monsoon in the winter months. The amount of rainfall varies regionally, with much of the interior receiving substantially less than the coasts and the hills which flank it.

The natural vegetation is mainly dry tropical forest with patches of moist evergreen and rainforest such as the Silent Valley and the *sholas* of the Western Ghats. Lush and diverse montane subtropical forest also exists at high altitudes, ranging from 1,000 to 1,700 metres (3,300 to 5,500 ft), in the Western Ghats. The flora and fauna of peninsular India form part of the Indian bio-geographic subregion (within the Oriental Region), with remnants of the vegetation of East Africa harking back to the ancient connection with Gondwanaland.

The Eastern and Western Ghats also support many unusual species which show a close affinity to those found in India's northeastern hill tracts. The small populations of these endemic species in the Ghats are relicts of forms that must have once been distributed across the country. The humid upland forests of the Ghats act as faunal refuges for forms that have been severely affected by ecological impoverishment in all except the least disturbed and accessible habitats of their former ranges.

The states of Karnataka and Tamil Nadu boast some of the largest intact jungle tracts south of the Vindhyas. In the early years, these extensive jungles were the private hunting preserves of former rulers, notably of Mysore. It is only because of the protection extended by the princes that the jungle has survived; much of these areas are officially protected today, and form a contiguous chain of national parks, reserves and sanctuaries.

Two large herbivores characterise the forests of South India, the majestic Asian elephant and the formidable gaur *(Bos gaurus)*, a large wild ox. The contiguous jungles of Nagarhole National Park, Bandipur Tiger Reserve, Mudumalai National Park and Wynad Wildlife Sanctuary, together with the beautiful Periyar Tiger Reserve further south in Kerala on the Kerala-Tamil Nadu border, support the largest population of elephants outside of India's northeast. Easily accessible from Mysore, these reserves provide accommodation for visitors. However, one of the most comfortable stays would be that provided by Kabini Lodge at Karapur in Nagarhole National Park (see the state government-run www.junglelodges.com).

PRECEDING PAGES: elephants grazing at Bandipur National Park, Karnataka.
LEFT: a tiger gazes out from the undergrowth.
RIGHT: an egret in breeding plumage.

Nevertheless, the reserves are definitely the best areas for observing elephants as they drink, bathe and play with their young in lakes and waterholes. Ivory poaching has taken a great toll on bulls, but some large tuskers can still be seen, single or dominating their herds. It is in these forests that the elephant-capturing method known as *Khedda* was practised until 1974.

Khedda involved the building of a large, strong stockade in a strategic location in the jungle. Several domestic elephants and "beaters" over days or even weeks would herd wild elephants towards the stockade and entrap them. Thereafter two of the strongest domestic elephants with experienced *mahouts* would enter the stockade, subdue the wild elephants individually and frogmarch them out. They would be shackled to trees and trained to accept human company and finally to obey commands. *Khedda* was a frequent practice in areas which required large domestic elephant stables for logging.

The gaur is the largest plains-dwelling bovid in India. Young bulls are coffee-brown in colour and older ones jet black, with characteristic white stockings. Mature bulls are compact, up to 1.8 metres (6 ft) tall at the shoulder and up to a tonne in weight. They are not averse to hilly terrain and are largely forest-dwellers, but emerge into open meadows to graze.

South India supports the most concentrated populations of wild dog and gaur in India, and perhaps of elephants as well. It is also endowed with larger virgin jungle tracts than those found anywhere else in the country, with the exception of the northeastern tracts, northwestern Uttar Pradesh and parts of Madhya Pradesh. The diversity of forest types is unique to the region, as is its climatic diversity, so that it supports a wide range of plant and animal life, often in settings of pristine beauty.

Tamil Nadu

The Nilgiris are the region's most attractive feature, forming the southern limit of the main Western Ghats system. The Palakkad Gap, an area of dry lowlands, separates them from the Anamalai ranges located further south.

The western slopes of the main plateau of the Nilgiris rise abruptly from levels of 100 to 300 metres (330 to 1,000 ft) through a steep escarpment to about 1,800 metres (6,000 ft). A similar steep rise on the southern slopes makes the Nilgiris a sharply defined geological feature. The plateau is undulating, with valleys at 1,600 metres (5,000 ft) or so and peaks rising to more than 2,500 metres (8,000 ft). Temperature variations during the year are modest, but there are significant differences according to altitude. Habitat types include rainforest, wet evergreen, mixed deciduous, and thorn forest where rainfall is less than 1,000 mm (39 in). This last type is not dissimilar to parts of the East African savanna and even supports typically African tree species such as the acacia. The blackbuck *(Antilope cervicapra)*, India's most elegant (and fastest) antelope, is found here.

The montane zone is characterised by *sholas* or sheltered, very dense evergreen forests, and open grasslands, home of the Nilgiri tahr which the eminent American wildlife biologist George Schaller describes as an "evolutionary link between primitive goat-antelopes and true goats". Once extensively hunted, the tahr is now making a comeback after strict protection, and can be best observed south of Coimbatore in the Eravikulam National Park in Kerala. Temperatures rarely drop below freezing point even in the higher reaches of the tahr's typical habitat, but the atmosphere is often misty, rain-swept and quite cold.

LEFT: an impressive gaur.
ABOVE: a common langur.
RIGHT: the rare lion-tailed macaque.

Mudumalai Reserve, established in 1940 in the Nilgiris, is the oldest sanctuary in the state of Tamil Nadu. It is contiguous with Karnataka's Bandipur Tiger Reserve (a Project Tiger Reserve) and the Wynaad sanctuary of Kerala. Mudumalai's habitat is moist and dry deciduous forest, with teak *(Tectona grandis)* dominating. The teak forests of this and adjoining areas are both natural as well as of plantation origin. Elephants and gaurs are of course very visible. Predators include the tiger *(Panthera tigris tigris)*, leopard *(Panthera pardus)* and the wild dog or dhole *(Cuon alpinus)*.

Indian wild dogs, or dhole*s*, are the most visible of the predators. Once remorselessly hunted and driven to near-extinction in large parts of their range (which covers most of the country), they have made a comeback in Bandipur and Mudumalai. Moving around in packs, their hunting method is to run down a deer to the point of exhaustion, then close in for the kill. They keep in touch with each other by making peculiar whistling sounds, especially when the pack is trying to reassemble after a hunt. Of a rust or sand colour, dhole*s* weigh about 15 kg (33 lb) and are generally 38 cm (15 in) high at the shoulder. The females are slighter than the males, and both have bushy tails.

The largest wildlife refuge in Tamil Nadu is the Anamalai Wildlife Sanctuary. It has a sizeable population of Nilgiri tahr and is also an important habitat for the lion-tailed macaque, a handsome, black, maned monkey. The lion-tailed macaque can also be found in the Kalakadu Mundanthurai sanctuary in Tamil Nadu and the Silent Valley National Park in Kerala. The former constitutes one of the few tropical rainforests in India left quite undisturbed by human development. Apart from great floral diversity, its striking range of animal life is apparent from the fact that it holds five species of primate: the nocturnal slender loris, the bonnet macaque, the Hanuman or common langur, the Nilgiri langur and the lion-tailed macaque.

A sanctuary of particular note is Point Calimere, projecting into the Bay of Bengal on the southeastern coastline just north of Sri Lanka. Blackbucks and chital deer *(Axis axis)* inhabit the coastal forest and plains, and after the northeast monsoon the shoreline comes alive with shorebirds, ducks and waders, mostly migratory. Dolphins are occasionally seen in the lagoon.

Up in the southern reaches of the Western Ghats, the Peppara Wildlife Sanctuary, near Ponmudi, covers around 50 sq km (19 sq miles) of land and protects elephants, leopards, sambar, lion-tailed macaques and a number of rare bird species.

There are also several small waterbird sanctuaries in the state, with large populations of cormorants, grey herons, open-bill storks, spoonbills and others. One of India's few patches of mangrove swamps outside the Sunderbans of West Bengal can be found at Pichavaram: it is rich in marine life and waders.

Karnataka

Neighbouring Karnataka state, with a coastline on the Arabian Sea, is endowed with striking climatic – and hence habitat – variations. An annual rainfall of about 600 cm (230 in) at its western edge declines eastwards to less than 80 cm (32 in) within 150 km (90 miles) of the coast. The coastal plains rise steeply to the ridges of the Western Ghats at about 1,500 metres (5,000 ft); eastwards the Ghats slope gently onto the Deccan plateau. Natural habitats range from montane *sholas* to wet evergreen, semi-evergreen, moist deciduous, dry deciduous, dry evergreen, thorn scrub and wetlands, including mangroves. Again, as in

Tamil Nadu, four species of primate are found occurring together in the Brahmagiri hills.

The dwindling numbers of tigers are concentrated in the sanctuaries of Bandipur, Nagarhole and Bhadra. Leopards are sometimes visible, especially in Nagarhole, and have increased in population.

Elephants and gaur are the most prominent herbivores. Sambar *(Cervus unicolor)*, chital, barking deer *(Muntiacus muntjak)* and the nocturnal, rarely-seen mouse deer *(Tragulus memmina)* are present. The forests of the state also support chinkara *(Gazella gazella)* and blackbuck on the northern plateau. There are about 2,000 blackbuck roaming the grounds of the Ranebennur sanctuary. The four-horned antelope *(Tetra-cerus quadricornis)* can be seen in the drier parts of Nagarhole, Bandipur and Biligirirangans.

Wolves are normally seen in scattered small packs on the northern and southern plateaux, in scrub and plantation habitat interspersed with fields. The most prominent predator is again the dhole, found mainly in protected forest areas.

The sloth bear *(Melursus ursinus)* is found almost throughout Karnataka's wild habitat range and in fact is widely distributed throughout South Indian forests in general. The mugger, or marsh crocodile *(Crocodylus palustris)*, is found in the Kaveri river, which is also famous for the large *mahseer* fish. The Government is active in the conservation of sea turtles, mainly Olive Ridleys *(Lepidochelys olivacea)*; several hatching areas are found on the coast.

Birdlife is extensive and includes a number of rare species, most notably the endangered great Indian bustard at Ranebennur. The sanctuaries at Ranganathittu and Kokkare Bellur are well known for waterbirds and waders.

LEFT: the slender loris is largely a nocturnal animal.

ABOVE: the Indian porcupine.

Kerala

The southwestern state of Kerala is a lush green land, dotted with plantations of pepper, rubber, tea and cardamom. The most characteristic tree apart from the ubiquitous coconut palm is the jackfruit *(Artocarpus heterophyllus)*. The most well known of Kerala's sanctuaries is Periyar Tiger Reserve, located on the crest line of the Western Ghats. The forest consists of grasslands, deciduous and evergreen habitats, and, in fact, was once the private hunting preserve of the erstwhile princely state of Travancore. A 26 sq km (10 sq mile) lake near Thekkady was formed in 1895 by a masonry dam. This expanse of water forms the fulcrum of an ecosystem that supports, among other species, the elephant, gaur, sambar, wild boar, tiger, leopard, dhole, Nilgiri langur, lion-tailed macaque and the Malabar giant squirrel. The dead trees raising ghostly branches skywards from the lake's surface make it a surreal, other-worldly sight. This is one of India's more successful Project Tiger Reserves (with over 35 individuals) and has attracted praise following the discovery of the dire state of tiger populations elsewhere in the country. This is due to its enlightened work in involving local peoples in access and conservation policies which may be adopted as a model for other reserves.

Two species of squirrel are found in Periyar and throughout much of South India. The Malabar giant squirrel (*Ratufa indica*) is found in deciduous to evergreen forest. It feeds on a large variety of fruit, bark, leaves and seeds, especially the seeds of the teak tree which is prominent in many of South India's lowland jungles. The smaller flying squirrel *(Petinomys fuscocapillus)* is a more nocturnal species, although it can sometimes be observed at dusk.

The Silent Valley National Park is a 90 sq km (35 sq mile) pocket of rainforest of undisturbed beauty. Its name was written in conservation history when a nationwide campaign in the early 1980s prevented it from being inundated by a proposed reservoir. It is a virtual genetic storehouse of rare plants and herbs, and apart from the elephant, lion-tailed macaque and tiger it is also the typical habitat of the spectacular king cobra or hamadryad *(Ophiophagus hannah)*. These two reserves, along with Eravikulam and Waynad, ensure that representative forest areas of Kerala are well protected.

Andhra Pradesh

Further north, Andhra Pradesh – as befits South India's largest state – has India's largest Project Tiger Reserve, Nagarjunasagar Sri Sailam. The state is endowed with diverse habitats such as the wetlands of Kolleru and Pulicat – rich in birdlife – the mangroves of Coringa, lush coastal lands, dry grassland and scrub of the Deccan plateau, the humid moist deciduous forest of the northern Eastern Ghats and the dry deciduous forest of the Nallamalais. There is a corresponding diversity of flora and fauna. Climatically, the coastal belt is humid, while the Deccan plateau is semi-arid or arid.

The abundant and varied birdlife includes rare species such as the great Indian bustard and the lesser florican. Jerdon's or double-banded courser *(Cursorius bitorquatus)*, believed extinct since 1900, was rediscovered by the Mumbai Natural History Society in Cuddapah district in 1986, to the jubilation of naturalists.

The elusive, nocturnal slender loris takes refuge up on the treetops with the birds, deep in the forests of Chittoor district. The wolf *(Canis lupus)* is the main predator of the dry lands. Waiting and watching on the Deccan plateau, it generally pounces on its victim without the help of its fellow mates, although it lives in pairs or in scattered packs and occasionally organises cooperative hunting. More common is the dhole, the Indian wild dog, particularly in the Eastern Ghats.

Gaur are found in forested tracts, and chinkara, four-horned antelope, blackbuck and nilgai *(Boselaphus tragocamelus)* in drier habitats. Until the 1960s the wild buffalo roamed parts of Visakhapatnam district, but these have now retreated to Bastar in Madhya Pradesh. A small herd of elephants has appeared, having migrated from the jungles further south. The mugger (Indian crocodile) is widely present, and the estuarine or saltwater crocodile *(Crocodylus porosus)* is present in the Coringa sanctuary, in the delta region of the Godavari river. The saltwater crocodile has apparently earned a special reputation, mainly because it consumes cows, goats or even human beings to vary its diet. The stocky, medium-sized fishing cat *(Felis viverrina)* and an Indian sub-species of the common otter *(Lutra lutra)* can also be easily spotted at Coringa.

Nagarjunasagar Srisailam consists of tropical dry deciduous forest, with an average elevation of 600 metres (2,000 ft), the highest point being 917 metres (3,000 ft). It is dissected by the Krishna river and two large dams, Nagarjunasagar and Sri Sailam. Parts of this region are inaccessible, while other areas have been, and still are, overrun by tourists, vehicles and cattle. This enclosure is, in many respects, India's most unwieldy Tiger Reserve because of its size (3,568 sq km/1,300 sq miles) and these pressures. The tiger population, though, has recently been reported to comprise over 60 individuals, and the leopard population is almost as large. ❑

LEFT: pangolins are found south of the Himalaya and in Sri Lanka.

ABOVE: a sambar deer.

Decisive Dates

Early History

c. 2000–1000 BC: The domestication of animals, settled cultivation of millet and gram, and the beginnings of organised settlement in the South.

c. 1500 BC: Copper and bronze tools begin to supplant those made of stone, followed later by the introduction of iron.

6th century BC: The proto-state of Asmaka exists in the Godavari Valley.

3rd–4th century BC: The Magadha Empire occupies the Deccan.

c. 1st century BC: The Satavahanas rule over the Deccan from Maharastra. Although Vedic they encourage the patronage of Buddhist monuments, including the *stupa* at Amaravati. The Tamil areas to the south are controled by groups such as the Cholas and Pandyas; present-day Kerala is under the control of the Cheras. The Tamil *sangams* (anthologies of poems) date from this period. Trade networks are extensive, bringing in merchants from as far as Rome.

4th–6th century AD: The Pallavas and Chalukyas emerge as regional powers in present-day Tamil Nadu and Karnataka. Buddhism and Jainism decline in popularity with the rise of *bhakti* (Hindu devotional religion). *Bhakti* teachings are spread though the wanderings of itinerant singer-saints.

7th–8th century: The temples at Badami, Aihole and Pattadakal in Karnataka, and the Shore Temple at Mamallapuram in Tamil Nadu are built. The Pallavas come into conflict with the Chalukyas to the north and Pandyas to the south.

The Cholas

c. 850: The Cholas begin to assert their dominance from their heartland in the Kaveri Delta.

1012–44: The reign of the great Chola king Rajaraja I. He conquers all of present-day Tamil Nadu and extends the Chola Empire to Orissa and Sri Lanka.

12th century: The Chola Empire dominates South India, trading widely and building many temples. During this time small kingdoms, notably the Pandyas in southern Tamil Nadu and the Kulasekharas of Kerala, struggle to maintain their independence.

1110–1342: In Karnataka the Hoysalas establish a powerful kingdom. Like the Cholas they build many temples, including those at Halebid and Belur.

12th–14th century: The Kakatiyas of Andhra break free from Chalukya rule and establish a kingdom around Warangal in the north of present-day Andhra Pradesh. This period sees South Indian peoples consolidate many of their patterns of social organisation that have continued up to the present day.

The Arrival of Islam

13th–14th century: Many of the large state structures that dominate South India begin to collapse.

1303–11: The Muslim Delhi Sultanate sends raiding parties south under Malik Kafur to plunder the Kakatiya, Hoysala and Pandya kingdoms.

1347: The creation of the Bahmani kingdom on the Deccan. This is set up by Hasan Gangu, a renegade official of Muhammad-bin-Tuglaq in the North. The Bahmani's rule over northern Karnataka until the early 16th century, leaving many fine monuments. The kingdom eventually splits into five separate states: Bijapur, Golconda, Ahmadnagar, Bidar and Berar.

Vijayanagara

1336: Two brothers, Harihara and Bukka, break away from the Kakatiyas and found the Hindu Vijayanagara kingdom at Hampi.

15th century: The Vijayanagara Empire expands and acquires much of South India, and legendary wealth.

1509–29: The reign of the greatest Vijayanagara king, Krisnadevaraya. He wins important victories against the Bahmanis and, under him, Vijayanagara attracts traders from far afield.

1565: The Deccani sultanates form an alliance and attack Vijayanagara, leaving it in ruins.

THE MUGHALS

1556–1605: The reign of Akbar, arguably the greatest of the Mughal emperors. He sends raiding parties into the Deccan and annexes part of Ahmadnagar.
1627–1707: The reigns of Shah Jahan and Aurangzeb. Shah Jahan conquers all of Ahmadnagar, Bijapur and Golconda. Aurangzeb, Shah Jahan's son, is made governor of the Deccan. Under Aurangzeb the Deccan is subjected to plundering raids by Sivaji's Maratha armies.
1724: Nizam-ul-Mulk, a high-ranking noble of the Mughal court, founds the independent state of Hyderabad, which rules central Andhra until just after Independence in 1947.

THE BRITISH

1498: Vasco da Gama lands near Kozhikode.
15th and 16th century: European powers attempt to break the Venetian and Arab monopoly of trade with India by opening up trade routes to the South.
Mid-17th century: Fort St George in Madras (present-day Chennai) is founded by the British, from where they fight the French for control of southern trade. By the mid-18th century the French are confined to Pondicherry. The British East India Company, however, is unable to expand its influence quickly due to the resistance of Haider Ali, and then Tippu Sultan, of Mysore.
1797: The British defeat Tippu Sultan at Seringapatinam (present-day Srirangapatnam) and establish the Wadiyars on the throne of Mysore as a client state.
1850: By the mid-19th century the British East India Company has firmly established its grip over South India, either ruling directly or through pliant local rulers.
1857–8: The Indian Uprising ("Mutiny") breaks out in Meerut. The campaign spreads across India. The British defeat the insurgents and the East India Company is abolished. In 1858 the British Crown imposes direct rule and Queen Victoria is proclaimed Empress of India.
Late-19th century: The rise of nationalist consciousness. Indian cultural societies are established in Madras (Chennai). Uprisings occur among the Moplahs of Kerala and peasants in the hill tracts of Andhra Pradesh.
1885: The formation of the Indian National Congress marks the start of the freedom struggle.
1920: The Non-Cooperation Movement is launched.
1920–42: The freedom movement gathers pace with acts of civil disobedience, culminating in the Quit India Movement.

PRECEDING PAGES: Visnu, Devi and Siva on a Madurai *gopuram*.
LEFT: the Brihadesvara temple, Thanjavur.
RIGHT: Nehru displays the Indian tricolour.

INDEPENDENCE (1947–PRESENT)

1947: India gains independence at midnight on 15 August. Jawaharlal Nehru becomes its first prime minister with Dr Rajendra Prasad as president.
1948: Troops are sent into Hyderabad state to force the Nizam to accede to India.
1940s and 1950s: A pro-Dravidian and anti-Brahman movement gathers pace in Tamil Nadu.
1953: Potti Sriramulu dies after a hunger strike demanding a separate Telugu state. The state of Andhra Pradesh is formed out of the former state of Hyderabad.
1956: The States' Reorganisation Act divides the South along linguistic lines into the present-day states of Tamil Nadu, Kerala, Karnataka and Andhra Pradesh.

1957: The first democratically elected Communist government in Kerala, under E.M.S. Namboordiripad.
1967: The DMK are elected in Tamil Nadu under C.N. Annadurai; this is the first major success for a South Indian regional political party. He is replaced 10 years later by the film star M.G.R. Ramachandran.
1969–72: Riots break out in Andhra Pradesh over the possible creation of a new state of Telengana.
1982: Film star N.T. Rama Rao is elected Chief Minister of Andhra Pradesh with his Telugu Desam Party.
1991–7: Narasimha Rao (INC) from Andhra becomes prime minister, then Deve Gowda (JD(S)) of Karnataka.
1998: The Konkan Railway opens.
2004: A huge tsunami hits the Tamil Nadu and Andhran coasts, killing and displacing many people. ❑

PREHISTORY TO INDEPENDENCE

The South has been dominated by powerful Hindu empires, interspersed with later Muslim kingdoms, all of whom have left monuments and a cultural legacy

In 1863 Robert Bruce Foote chanced to pick up a palaeolith from a laterite pit at Pallavaram near Chennai (Madras); since then, Early Stone Age tools have been found in various parts of the South. The discovery of hand axes and other stone tools from Attirampakkam near Chennai points to the existence of a similar cultural pattern in the South during prehistoric times. Here, hunter-gatherer cultures eventually began agriculture and the domestication of animals, resulting in profound changes in living conditions and social relations. This transformation began in the Neolithic and progressed steadily through different stages of use of metal technology, initially of copper or bronze and then of iron. It is possible to reconstruct the stages of this change from excavations carried out in Karnataka, Andhra and Tamil Nadu. At the initial stage of this culture change, tools were still made of stone but with a different kind of technique. Domestication of such animals as cattle, goats and sheep had begun; handmade coarse pottery and terracotta figurines were produced, and settlements on granite hills, on levelled terraces or on plateaux were constructed.

If the beginnings of this kind of culture change can be traced back from the end of the third millennium to the beginning of the second millennium BC, further progress was slow, despite the introduction of metal around the middle of the second millennium BC. Nevertheless, new cultural elements made their appearances: circular huts, very similar to those still made by local Adivasis, were built; varieties of gram and millet were cultivated; the horse was probably added to the list of domesticated animals; and metal tools came into use.

Beginnings of history

In the north, particularly in the Ganges basin and certain outlying areas, *janapadas* and *mahajanapadas* (proto-states) had already emerged with their villages, marketplaces and urban centres. There had developed an extensive network of routes connecting different regions and providing Magadha, a *mahajanapada* of south Bihar, with enough stimulus to build an almost pan-Indian empire by the 4th–3rd century BC. The megalithic South was

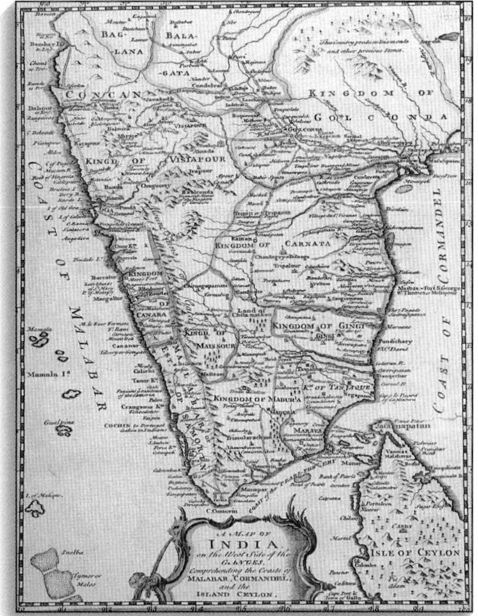

not totally outside the orbit of these changes; the *mahajanapada* of Asmaka in the central Godavari valley is believed to have been in existence in the 6th century BC. However, interaction with regions to the north was slow, and the Magadhan empire's interest in the South may have been motivated by the desire to acquire resources. Kautilya, author of the political treatise *Arthasastra,* parts of which date back to this period, highlighted the advantages of *dakshinapatha*, the term denoting the southern route as well as the region. The Magadhan emperor Asoka Maurya wrote edicts for the Deccan, which was part of his empire, and for a major centre, Suvarnagiri (Hill of Gold).

LEFT: the Kambesvara temple, Kanchipuram.
RIGHT: an 18th century map of peninsular India.

Beyond the Deccan, Asoka mentioned the Cholas, the Pandyas, the Cheras and the Satyaputras; the references were not to established states but to dominant communities, and one can see in the distinction between the Deccan and the southern region of the Cholas, Pandyas, Cheras and Satyaputras some essential differences in the manner in which the early history of the two regions developed.

The inclusion of the Deccan in the Magadhan empire was not merely a political phenomenon; it also resulted in movements of people and ideas, and thus new cultural elements were incorporated in the already changing structure of South Indian society. For the Deccan, two significant developments derived from the idea of a state headed by a monarch and from ideas associated with Buddhist and Brahmanical social and religious ideology. Initially, in several localities of the Deccan, there emerged local ruling elites known from their coins which were fashioned after coins originating in the north. They called themselves *rajas*, *maharathis* or by other designations, and the centres of their power also became urban centres in which commercial exchange took place and religious monuments, particularly Buddhist *stupas* and *viharas*, were constructed. Since the end of the 1st century BC these small centres of power came to be integrated into the empire of the Satavahanas. At the height of their power the Satavahanas, whose main base was in Maharashtra, called themselves *Dakshinapathesvaras* (Lords of *Dakshinapatha*). They had, by the 2nd century AD, expanded throughout the entire stretch of the Deccan to coastal Andhra in the east and Vidarbha in the north. The Satavahanas performed Vedic sacrifices, conformed to Brahmanical norms, defended the *varna-dharma* (the principle of the division of society into four *varnas*) and, at the same time, patronised Buddhist *bhikshus* (monks) by constructing rock-cut *viharas* or monasteries for them and giving them land. The Satavahana officials were present in different parts of their empire and performed similar acts of religious patronage. It was the different strata of ruling elites, merchants and lay devotees of this period who, by their acts of patronage, created magnificent *stupa* sites such as Amaravati in coastal Andhra and the rock-cut caves located near the passes connecting the western coast with the Deccan plateau. In both Karnataka and Andhra, there also emerged urban centres such as the early historical site of Nagarjunakonda of coastal Andhra, which were centres of commerce and religion.

Dravidadesa (Tamil country) lay outside the orbit of both the Magadhan empire of the north and the Satavahana empire of the Deccan, but the early anthologies of Tamil poems, *Sangam*, speak of the crowned kings of the Cholas, the Pandyas and the Cheras in addition to tribal chiefs in Tamilaham or Tamil country which would comprise the modern states of Tamil Nadu and Kerala. The state apparatus was yet to develop, but the authority of the crowned kings, who were more like chieftains, was recognised in their respective regions. The Cholas ruled in Cholamandalam, the Coromandel region, which included the Kaveri basin; the Pandya domain comprised the Madurai, Tirunelveli and Ramanathapuram region, drained by the Vaigai and the Tamraparni; and the Chera domain was in Kerala. The *Sangam* poems present to us the picture of a society in transition; there were Brahmanic elements present, and the virtue of making gifts to bards and Brahmins was lauded. Some short inscriptions, written in what is called the Tamil-Brahmi script and dated to this period, refer to donations to Jainas who formed an influential ideological group in Tamil Nadu during the early Christian era.

The picture is very different in the Tamil epic *Cilapattikaram* and its sequel *Manimekalai* which refer to Madurai in the Pandya country and the port city of Kaverippattinam or Puhar in the region of the Cholas. These texts reveal a society very prosperous through trade. The wide network of trade which had developed both in the Deccan and the far south in the first few centuries of the Christian era was both in land and littoral. Magadhan expansion drew traders and other social groups from the north in their quest for local resources.

From the end of the 1st century BC, a new boost came when knowledge of the southwestern monsoon winds for purposes of navigation brought in merchants from the Roman world to the Indian coasts for spices. Local literature mentions the phenomenon of Indo-Roman trade; Tamil texts refer to the settlements of Yavana merchants in the port city of Puhar and to Yavanas at Musiripattinam in Kerala. But by far the most important records on this trade come from the writings of Western authors and from evidence provided by archaeology. An unknown Greek sailor who must have sailed along the western coast left a logbook, *The Periplus of the Erythraen Sea*, which not only lists the important trading posts on both coasts and the items of merchandise but also refers to the transport of goods across the Deccan to the ports of the west coast. Ptolemy's *Geography*, written about a century later in the middle of the 2nd century AD, supplements this evidence and suggests that by his time trade on the east coast had become both much more numerous and important than before. Archaeological evidence on Indo-Roman trade is provided not only by many Roman coin hoards, the majority of which have been found in peninsular India, but also by other objects of Roman association such as pottery and art objects which turn up regularly at excavations at the early historical sites of peninsular India. Excavations conducted at Arikamedu, near Pondicherry, have shown it to be an Indo-Roman trading station. The period also witnessed the beginnings of commercial and cultural relations with Southeast Asia, as trade with the west gradually dwindled.

LEFT: a Buddha at Sankaran near Visakhapatanam.
RIGHT: a tortoise-shaped bath at Nagarjunakonda.

The Pallavas and the Chalukyas

The peninsular cities and the kingdoms of which they were important foci faced decline after the 3rd–4th centuries AD, as did urban centres in other parts of India, but this does not mean that peninsular society broke down. From about the 6th century, but with modest beginnings earlier, there emerged two major regional kingdoms with large agrarian bases: that of the Pallavas in Tamil Nadu and of the Chalukyas in Karnataka. The Pallavas were first known from their Prakrit inscriptions of south Andhra and Tamil Nadu, but at the height of their power they used both Sanskrit and Tamil in their documents. The nucleus of the kingdom was Tondaimandalam in the Palar basin with its centre at Kanchipuram. The growth of Kanchi as a major political and religious centre, with its temple-building activities through centuries, is closely linked with the rise of Pallava power. So was the case with Mamallapuram, or Mahabalipuram, a great centre of Pallava period art, which was a littoral centre of Pallava power. Beginning with the reign of Simhavishnu in the 6th century and through the reigns of his successors Mahendravarman I, Narasimhavaraman I and Paramesvaravarman, Pallava power rose to great heights in the 7th and 8th centuries and brought them into repeated conflicts with the Pandyas of south Tamil Nadu and the Chalukyas of Badami in Karnataka. By the middle of the 7th century the Chalukyas, who were the builders of the rock-cut caves at Badami and of the temple complexes at Pattadakal and Aihole in Karnataka, had consolidated their power to the extent that the Chalukyan ruler Pulakesi II (610–42) could claim to have defeated Harshavardhana, undoubtedly the most powerful ruler of North India at that time.

Notwithstanding the constant conflicts between the kingdoms and depletion of resources, the period of Pallava-Chalukya ascendancy saw some significant developments in peninsular India. In the political sphere, the monarch was the head of the state but had to function with subordinate rulers or feudatories. Both the Pallavas and the Chalukyas had feudatories who wielded autonomous power in their own localities, and in the conflicts between kingdoms such feudatory families as the Gangas and Kadambas in Karnataka or the Banas in Andhra and Tamil Nadu played key roles. Secondly, this period witnessed donations of land to Brahmans (*brahmadeya*) and to temples (*devadana*) as a regular pattern. They assumed a much grander scale and significance in later periods of South Indian history. The emergence of *agrahara* settlements, where Brahmans were the dominant community, and of large estates owned by South Indian temples can thus be traced back to this period. It resulted in the expansion of Brahmanical ideas and institutions on a significant scale. This advance can also be seen in juxtaposition with the general decline of Buddhism and Jainism, and although there were sporadic cases of patronage extended to them even in later periods, at least Buddhism suffered an overall decline. Jainism survived in Karnataka, though not without opposition from other religious sects, and contributed substantially to the development of Kanarese literature.

In Tamil Nadu, the decline of Buddhism and Jainism is directly associated with two factors. One was the growing importance of Puranic Hinduism, with its accent on worship of deities with sectarian affiliations such as Saivism (worship of Siva) or Vaishnavism (worship of Vishnu). In the Deccan too, in the temple structures or the rock-cut caves built by the Chalukya rulers, it is the Saivite or Vaishnavite deities which predominate. Secondly, in Tamil Nadu, this period coincided with the emergence of the Bhakti movement which underlined total devotion to a personal god. The Nayannars (Saivite saints) and Alvars (Vaishnavite saints) were composing devotional hymns in praise of their respective gods and making the temple centres their bases. Tradition has it that Pallava Mahendravarman, who is credited with the composition of the Sanskrit farce *Mattavilasaprahasana*, originally professed Jainism but discarded it in favour of Saivism under the influence of the Saivite saint Appar. The hymns of the Saivite and Vaishnavite saints became popular because they were composed in Tamil, and even in official documents, as in land grants, the beginnings of the use of Tamil and Kanarese, along with Sanskrit, date from this period.

The Cholas

Dynastic changes in South India were rapid; so were alignments between local powers entrenched in their respective regions for centuries. In this respect, South Indian history represents a trend which is typical of Indian history in general. There was rapid succession in Karnataka and western Deccan from the Badami Chalukyas to the Rashtrakutas to the Chalukyas of Kalyana and so on. But there also arose large state structures which provided political cohesion to the macro-regions for centuries and shaped their cultural pattern. In the period following the Pallava-Chalukya ascendancy, there arose several such state structures, among whom the most prominent were those of the Cholas in Tamil Nadu, of the Hoysalas in south Karnataka and of the Kakatiyas in Andhra.

The Cholas, originally feudatories of the Pallavas, started by gaining control of the Kaveri basin by the middle of the 9th century and then by expanding into other regions. Thus Parantaka I in the first half of the 10th century conquered the land of the Pandyas in south Tamil Nadu and called himself *Maduraikonda* (the conqueror of Madurai). Further expansion took place under Rajaraja I (AD 985–1016) and Rajendra I (AD 1012–44), best known of the Chola rulers. Rajaraja not only brought the whole of Tamil Nadu under his control but also undertook expeditions to Andhra, Kerala, Sri Lanka and the Maldives. Rajendra despatched an expedition to North India which reached the interior of Bengal; this was not designed to achieve permanent territorial expansion, but more as a symbolic act which would give the Chola monarch the status of a *Chakravarti* (universal monarch). Chola power gained further ascendancy under Kulottunga I (1070–1122) who united the Chola family with the Vengi Chalukya family of coastal Andhra, and by the 12th century the Chola state was unquestionably the strongest state structure in South India.

LEFT: the Pallava Shore Temple at Mamallapuram.
RIGHT: Hoysala carving at Halebid, Karnataka.

One remarkable feature of Chola expansion was the recognition by rulers like Rajaraja and Rajendra of the need for a strong navy. Overseas trade had by then revived, and the demand for textiles, spices and precious stones had resulted in the establishment of a number of Arab mercantile settlements along the coast of India. Overseas trade also extended to south China through Southeast Asia; Chola interest in this trade is suggested both by the number of emissaries sent to China and by Chola naval expeditions to Southeast Asia. In fact, the emergence of a wide network of trade, not only in the Chola kingdom but also in the Deccan and in Kerala, is suggested by numerous inscriptional documents of merchant groups across the peninsula and beyond, from as distant an area as Sumatra. Chola naval expeditions were also sometimes in the nature of plundering raids bringing in immense booty, and inscriptions record in detail the treasures gifted by the Chola rulers and other members of the royal family to temples built by them. The Brihadisvara temple at Tanjore built by Rajaraja and the Gangaikondacholapuram temple built by Rajendra received substantial donations of land, cash, gold ornaments and other precious items.

Although it is argued by some that the Chola state was a segmentary state, with the king exercising only ritual sovereignty in the empire, the four centuries of Chola rule gave a new political and cultural cohesion to the far South. Many of the patterns of administration and cultural life which were crystallised in the Chola empire had parallels in other parts of the peninsula as well. The Chola empire, despite the growing commercial network, rested on a solid agrarian foundation. The smallest agrarian units of administration, comprising several villages, were the *nadus*. The Cholas integrated the *nadus* with bigger administrative units like the *valanadus* and the *mandalams* and through the hierarchical administrative structure ensured a flow of resources to the State.

The Hoysalas and Kakatiyas

The Hoysalas of south Karnataka came up from a tribal base in the hills of southwestern Karnataka. Initially feudatories of the Chalukyas of north Karnataka, they rose to prominence by displacing the Western Gangas from south Karnataka, and from the period of Vishnuvardhana I (1110–52) to the period of Ballala III (1291–1342) were a major political power in South India, centred in the Hassan district. Despite repeated conflicts with other contemporary powers like the Cholas and the Chalukyas, the Hoysala region experienced agrarian expansion. Like the Cholas, the Hoysalas were great builders. At their capital at Dorasamudra, also known as Halebidu (old settlement) or Halebid, they built temples in addition to a majestic Saiva temple. The Vaisnava temples were at Belur and Somanathapura, and they too received large donations from the royalty and subordinate rulers.

The Kakatiyas, also originally feudatories of the later Chalukyas of Karnataka, made the comparatively barren tract of Warangal to the north-east of Hyderabad the base of their independent power from about the beginning of the 12th century. Under some able rulers the Kakatiyas became a major power in Andhra from the 12th to the early 14th century, not only through a sustained policy of agrarian expansion and support provided to overseas trade, but also through repeated administrative reorganisations.

In addition to these major powers, there were a number of other ruling families in different localities who either aligned themselves with the major powers or, like the Pandyas of southern Tamil Nadu and the Kulasekharas of Kerala, fought them to retain their autonomy. However, these repeated political struggles should not obscure the fact that, as in the period of Pallava-Chalukya ascendancy, between the 9th and the 13th centuries, many of the key institutions that characterised South Indian society attained considerable maturity. Regular grants of various kinds show temples and Brahman settlements to have been major integrating factors in society. Construction of irrigation tanks on a large scale, not necessarily undertaken by the royalty alone, also drew different segments of society together. Such old tanks still dot the landscape of South India and some are of such dimensions as to be called *samudram* (ocean).

The processes of social integration notwithstanding, there were conflicts at various levels. Within the Brahmanical ideological framework, the period witnessed intense philosophical debates, as reflected in the works of such proponents of different schools as Sankaracharya, Ramanuja and Madhavacharya. Conflicts and cases of persecution arising out of religious sectarianism were not infrequent. The overall domination of Brahmans in society and the overarching presence of the caste system led to the emergence of such protests as Virasaivism or the sect of the Lingayats, originally in Karnataka but gradually spreading to other parts of South India. Many of the tensions which characterised South Indian society in later times had their origin in this period.

LEFT: the temple complex at Tiruvannamalai.
RIGHT: the Qutb Shahi tombs, Hyderabad.

Islamic expansion

By the close of the 13th century, the large state structures were beginning to collapse. This was not a direct result of invasions by the Islamic powers of the North; however, many of the major powers of the South did face invasions and suffer defeats. The establishment of Turkish rule in Delhi by the close of the 12th century had created a new type of political regime, and

in the beginning of the 14th century, during the reign of Alauddin Khilji, the first inroads were made into the Kakatiya kingdom, the Hoysala kingdom and the Pandya kingdom of Mabar (south Tamil Nadu). Undertaken by Malik Kafur between 1303 and 1311, these forays yielded a huge amount of plundered wealth and promises of tribute to the Delhi Sultanate. Such raids continued, but Islamic influences started becoming an integral part of the Deccanese culture only with the establishment of the Bahmani kingdom. Created in 1347 by Hasan Gangu, a rebel official of Muhammad-bin-Tuglaq, and lasting till early 16th century, the kingdom included the whole of the northern

Deccan down to the river Krishna. One well-known Bahmani ruler was Firoz Shah Bahmani who was acquainted not only with Islamic literature and Turkish, Arabic and Persian languages but with various branches of science as well, and who was conversant with local languages like Marathi, Telugu and Kannada. By inducing learned scholars from Iran and Iraq to settle in his kingdom, he transformed it into a major cultural region of the Deccan.

Another major phase of Bahmani history is represented by the close of the 15th century when Mahmud Gawan, an Iranian merchant, became the prime minister. Besides enhancing

the political status of the state, he reorganised its administrative structure.

The Bahmani kingdom was indeed a cultural bridge of that time between the North and the South, but internal weaknesses ultimately broke it up into five kingdoms: Bijapur, Golconda, Ahmadnagar, Bidar and Berar. With the annexation of Berar by Ahmadnagar and of Bidar by Bijapur, the remnants of Bahmani rule were ultimately represented by Bijapur, Ahmadnagar and Golconda. Because of the eclectic character of their rule, the Bahmanis have left a rich cultural heritage in the form of surviving religious, military and civil architecture in which many elements were synthesised.

Vijayanagara

To the south of the Krishna was the empire of Vijayanagara – the arch rival of the Bahmanis – with its centre at Hampi (near Hospet in Karnataka), a sprawling and magnificent capital built on the bank of the Tungabhadra in a granite rock area traditionally identified with Kiskindha of the early Sanskrit epic *Ramayana*. Tradition again traces the foundation of the empire to two brothers, Harihara and Bukka, originally feudatories of the Kakatiyas. They aligned themselves with the Muslim power in the Deccan and were even converted, but finally, as followers of the sage Vidyaranya, founded Vijayanagara in 1336 and became upholders of Hindu interests in the Deccan.

The empire of Vijayanagara, which lasted through four dynasties – Sangam, Saluva, Tuluva and Aravidu – was of a multiethnic composition, and despite the growing importance of Bahmanis in its administration, it employed both Muslims and Europeans in various services. The Vijayanagara capital attracted visitors like Abdur Razzak, Nuniz and Paes who came from distant countries. In fact, much of what is known about the pattern of life in the capital is derived from their accounts.

The greatest monarch of Vijayanagara was Krisnadevaraya (1509–29), who not only achieved military victories against the Bahmanis, against Orissa and other powers but was also an able administrator and realised, like other contemporary powers, the importance of trade, both internal and overseas, for enhancing the wealth of the country. The multiethnic population of Vijayanagara included Jews and Parsis. Judging from the accounts of 16th-century travellers like Varthema, Barbosa, Ralph Fitch and others regarding the extent of commercial activities in Kerala, Golconda, the Andhra coast and the Vijayanagara and Bahmani kingdoms, Mughal expansion from the North and European commercial expansion into South India was inevitable.

The Mughals

The consolidation of Mughal power in the North began to affect the political regions of South India only from the period of Akbar (1556–1605), the greatest of the Mughal rulers, who conquered parts of Ahmadnagar, though it was fully annexed only during the reign of Shah Jahan. Bijapur and Golconda also submitted to the authority of the Mughals, and Aurangzeb, Shah Jahan's son, was appointed governor of the Deccan. However, it was never fully integrated into the Mughal empire, and the growing strength of the Marathas in the west aggravated the problems of the Mughals in the Deccan. When Aurangzeb became emperor, he had to send a large army to the Deccan to curb the activities of the Maratha chief Sivaji, whose father was originally a feudatory of the Bijapur sultan. For the Deccan, as for many other parts of India, Maratha plundering raids were a constant menace and the imposition of *Chauth* and *Sardesmukhi*, taxes which people living outside the Maratha region had to pay, worsened the condition of the people of the Deccan. However, one important consequence of Mughal expansion in the Deccan was the creation by Nizam-ul-Mulk, a powerful noble at the Mughal court and erstwhile *vazir* of the Mughal emperor, of the independent state of Hyderabad in 1724, which lasted until the middle of the 20th century.

The arrival of the Europeans

A major development was the penetration of European commercial interests into India, which had started towards the end of the 15th century. Attempts to establish direct trade relations with India were necessary for new European powers in the 15th–16th centuries; they had to break the Arab and Venetian monopolies in trade with India, and to bypass the Ottoman empire of the Turks. Alternative routes were desperately being sought, and the arrival of the Portuguese Vasco da Gama at the port of Calicut (Kozhikode) in Kerala in 1498 heralded a new era, not only in the history of South India but in the entire East.

Although the Portuguese had the virtual monopoly of eastern trade for about a century, the English, the Dutch, the French and others finally followed them. Initially their trade was carried on from "factories" at certain centres, with small settlements around them, and was dependent on concessions obtained from local rulers and from the Mughals. Gradually, however, there arose fierce competition among the European trading companies which began contending for territorial control. Portuguese power soon came to be restricted to several centres on the west coast. Similarly the Dutch East India Company, which had extensive interests in Southeast Asia and trade depots at Kochi, Nagapattinam, and Masulipatam on the Andhra coast, as well as in other places, could not survive

LEFT: a fresco in the Brihadesvara temple, Thanjavur.
RIGHT: a 19th-century view of Bijapur.

competition from the British East India Company and shifted its major interests to Indonesia.

The fiercest competition was between the French and the British, and from their bases in the Deccan and the South, particularly Fort St George in Chennai (then Madras; established around the middle of the 17th century), the English kept harrying French interests. Despite the brilliant manoeuvres of Dupleix, the French Governor-General of Pondicherry, French power after the mid-18th century was virtually confined to Pondicherry.

The British attempts at territorial expansion were initially not very successful, but with the

occupation of Bengal in 1757 and with secure bases in Chennai and Mumbai (then Bombay), they advanced rapidly, particularly as the Mughal empire was crumbling away. In the Deccan and the South, protracted struggles against Haider Ali and Tippu Sultan of Mysore and against the Marathas ended in victory for the British. The fall of Srirangapatnam (Seringapatam), the capital of Tippu Sultan, in 1797 of course brought back the original family of Rajas to Mysore, but like other rulers of "native" states they too were completely subservient to the British. By the middle of the 19th century the British, starting as merchant adventurers, had become rulers of India, and despite the continued existence of many local *Rajas* brought South India too under their complete hegemony.

Imperialism and after

In trying to understand the impact of British imperialism from an all-India perspective, one needs to keep a few general points in mind. Firstly, the British economic exploitation of India changed in nature over time. Since the end of the 18th century, the British gradually converted India into a market for their own products, while using the country as a quarry for raw materials. This spelt doom for traditional indigenous industries. Secondly, after the great revolt of 1857, India ceased to be ruled by the East India Company and passed on to the British crown, enabling the British to rule their most prized colony directly. Thirdly, imperialism did not mean economic exploitation alone but also ideological domination.

The growing resentment against the stranglehold of the structure created by the British found expression at two levels, not always directed against the British themselves: spontaneous popular rebellions and movements, and middle-class participation in what became pan-Indian nationalism. Examples of popular movements are varied in space and time; from the series of formidable Adivasi rebellions in the forest and hilly areas of Andhra Pradesh from the late 19th century to the early 20th century; to the peasant uprisings of the Moplahs of Malabar in Kerala from the first half of the 19th century to the beginnings of the 20th century; and to the massive Telengana uprising in Andhra from 1946 to 1951, involving at least 3,000 villages spread over 25,600 sq km (16,000 sq miles) and drawing on the ideological support and participation of the communists.

The nature of South India's participation in the mainstream national movement is related to the emergence of an English-educated middle class. After the great revolt of 1857, British enthusiasm for introducing social reforms in India ebbed considerably, but the universities of Madras, Calcutta (now Kolkata) and Bombay had already been established. The British education policy of creating a subservient literate social class produced surprising results. The Indians' response to Western education and ideas began to foster national consciousness, a critical concern at the evils of their own society and an effort to rediscover their own cultural heritage.

Initially, the articulation of this consciousness took the form of various regional associations and regular publications, in both English and regional languages. For example, the Madras Native Association, already established in the middle of the 19th century, was followed in 1881 by the Madras Mahajan Sabha. In 1886 the headquarters of the Theosophical Society was located in Madras (now Chennai), and under the leadership of Annie Besant the Society wielded considerable influence, as did her Home Rule League at a later stage. The publication of such journals as the *The Hindu*, the *Swadeshmitran*, *Andhra Patrika* and *Kerala Patrika* did much to disseminate nationalistic ideas, as did the writings of people such as Subrahmanya Bharati. Active efforts at social reforms were widespread. In Andhra Pradesh, Virasalingam's Rajahmundri Social Reform Association (established in 1878), Natarajan's publication, *Indian Social Reformer*, and the Hindu Social Reform Association, which was started in Chennai in 1892, testify to concerted efforts to deal with what were considered evils in contemporary society.

The formation of the Indian National Congress in 1885 drew enthusiastic response from the South; prominent southerners like Subrahmanya Aiyar and Ananda Charlu participated in its early sessions. The various stages of the freedom struggle – the Noncooperation Movement, the Civil Disobedience Movement and the Quit India Movement, despite uneven intensity of participation, were indeed mass movements, bringing to prominence leaders such as Pattabhi Sitaramayya, Sarojini Naidu and Chakravarti Rajagopalachari.

It would, however, be wrong to consider the national movement as a unilineal or unified movement even in its South Indian context. Its regional ramifications took diverse shapes, for example in the anti-Brahman movements spearheaded by the Justice Party in the 1920s and 1930s in Tamil Nadu, or in the demand for a separate state for Telugu-speaking people put forward by the Andhra Mahasabha. Independence came in August 1947, and the integration of independent princely states like the Nizam's Dominions or the State of Travancore in Kerala with the Union of India was also achieved; but the new leaders of India still had to find solutions to the problems which the long-drawn history of British imperialism and the many-hued struggles against it had generated. ❑

LEFT: Tippu Sultan's tomb, Srirangapatnam.
RIGHT: the British Governor-General of Madras.

AFTER INDEPENDENCE

Since Independence the South has experienced a reassertion of its Dravidian identity, through language, regional politics and ideology

On 15 August 1947, the political map of South India was very different; it consisted of the huge Madras Presidency, the princely states of Cochin, Travancore, Mysore and Hyderabad, and a number of smaller principalities. While the rulers of all these states accepted the reality of India and acceded to the Indian Union, the Nizam of Hyderabad resisted.

The Nizams, descendants of a governor appointed by the Mughal emperor Aurangzeb, ruled over nine dominions with Hyderabad as their capital. In 1947, the then Nizam, known to be one of the richest men in the world and also the most miserly, held out for almost a year. In 1948, following popular resistance to the Nizam's rule, the troops of the Government of India entered and occupied his dominions and Hyderabad finally became a part of the Indian Union.

The post-Independence period saw a resurgence in regional pride in the South. There were some cultural differences among the people of the South and, besides, they did not speak the same language. Tamil, Telugu, Malayalam and Kannada were the major languages of the region. The demand for reorganising the country on the basis of language gained momentum, especially in the South. The process was hastened in 1953 when Potti Sriramulu, a Telugu patriot, died on an indefinite fast demanding a separate state for the Telugu-speaking people. In the same year, Andhra Pradesh came into being with Telugu as its language, the first state in India which was formed on a purely linguistic basis. The former state of Hyderabad, where the majority spoke Telugu, and with a significant minority of Muslim Urdu speakers, was incorporated into the new state.

In 1956, the States' Reorganisation Act was passed and the Indian states were reorganised on the basis of language. The South was divided into four states. The Telugu-speaking districts formed Andhra Pradesh, the Kannada-speaking parts became the Mysore state (later called Karnataka), those areas where Malayalam was the principal language became Kerala, and the Madras Presidency reduced in area with Tamil as its predominant language. The name of Madras state was later changed to Tamil Nadu.

Jawaharlal Nehru, the visionary first Prime Minister of India, disapproved of linguistic states because he felt that this would lead to factionalism and fragmentation of the country. His fears have been justified to a certain extent; however, it is doubtful whether in the long run it would have been possible to prevent this reorganisation. At the time when the four southern states were formed, the Congress was firmly in power in all of them except Kerala.

The half-century since the new states came into being have seen great political changes in the South. The most noticable development has been in the rise of regional parties, notably the DMK in Tamil Nadu and TDP in Andhra *(see below)*. The south has largely escaped the tide of Hindu chauvanism that swept the country after religious extremists destroyed the Babri Masjid (mosque) in Ayodhya in 1992. However, Chandrababu Naidu's TDP did prop up the right-wing, Hindu nationalist BJP (Bharatiya Janata Party) government elected in 1999. Although allegedly secular the TDP did share the BJP's passion for neo-liberal economics, which sought to "disinvest" (privatise) much of the Indian economy. The BJP itself has not had much of a power-base in South India, although it gained ground in Karnataka in recent elections.

The BJP and its allies were unceremoniously booted out of power in 2004 after a misjudged election campaign that tried to sell the supposed success of the middle classes to a population that had seen very little improvement in its standard of living. Government was taken over by Congress and its allies (including the DMK), supported from the outside by the left, which includes numerous Communist MPs from Kerala.

Initially, as the leader of Congress, Sonia Gandhi (widow of the former prime minister Rajiv Gandhi) was expected to take up the premiership, but she declined in favour of a former finance minister, Manmohan Singh. He has appointed a centrist Tamil economist, P. Chidambaram as finance minister

LEFT: Nehru (left) and Gandhi (right) confer at a Congress meeting.
RIGHT: Manmohan Singh and Sonia Gandhi.

The economy

At Independence the South was, in general, not industrialised. However, Tamil Nadu did have some small-scale industry and Chennai (Madras) had a fairly well developed port, and many

British trading houses had their headquarters in the city. Mysore state also had small-scale industry, but Andhra Pradesh and Kerala at the time of Independence had virtually no industrial base.

In the 1950s, the government of India took a decision to develop indigenous industry and impose import restrictions. To accelerate industrialisation, the government set up plants to provide basic materials like iron and steel required by the new industries, and, in spite of repeated droughts and a grim power situation, much progress was made in the four southern states.

Despite this industrialisation drive much of the South remains rural, with pockets of great deprivation. Recently much has been made of the South's hi-tech industries, particularly in Bangalore and Hyderabad, with many Western companies "outsourcing" routine tasks, such as those carried out by call centres. However, it seems that in the near future these jobs might go to even cheaper destinations in Africa.

Myth or reality?

Although they have been at the centre of much recent political discourse, it is notoriously hard to try and pin down exactly who the Indian middle class are. In general they comprise that urban 10 percent of the population that has enough disposable income to afford consumer durables such as a washing machine or car. However, according to the World Bank, India's national annual per capita income is US$460, which works out at around 1,670 rupees a month at current rates of exchange (about £22) and a recent report from the National Sample Survey Organisation revealed that little has changed for the vast majority of people (72 percent of the population) who live in the countryside.

Not all of it is bad news; 89 percent of households now get sufficient water (in 1992 only 19 percent of rural households received enough water). In urban areas 74 percent of this comes from the tap, while in rural areas 51 percent of water comes from tube wells and hand pumps, with 18 percent still drawn from wells. There is, however, a greater disparity in the distribution of electricity supply – 91 percent of urban households have access to electric lighting but this drops to 53 percent in rural areas. In terms of consumer durables, only 29 percent of rural households have a television (as opposed to 66 percent in towns). Even more stark divisions are seen with goods such as fridges (present in 28 percent of urban households but only 4 percent in rural areas) or washing machines (11 percent of urban households have one but fewer than 1 percent of rural ones), let alone a car, which only 4 percent of urban households have access to (the figures for rural areas are negligble).

Even more telling are the figures for telecommunications and information technology, allegedly the great saviour of the Indian economy. Of urban households 26 percent had a phone (this includes mobiles) while in rural areas this was only 6 percent. The figures for computers are even more stark; only 1.4 percent of urban households had a computer with internet access (another 1.7 percent had a computer with no internet), while in rural areas household computers with internet access were "practically non-existent", while only 0.6 percent of rural households had access to a computer at all.

Tamil Nadu

In the early days of post-Independence industrialisation, Tamil Nadu came into its own. What is particularly striking about the state's progress is that Tamil Nadu as a manufacturing location has very little to recommend itself. It has no raw material or mineral base, and the markets for its products are spread far and wide. However, thanks to state government support , both the public sector and the private sector did well for almost two decades. Large public sector projects included setting up the Neyveli Lignite Corporation, the Integral Coach Factory, Madras Refineries Limited, a unit of BHEL (Bharat Heavy Electricals, a public sector conglomerate set up to manufacture power plant equipment), and Madras Fertilisers Limited.

Its leaders during the two decades after Independence made quite an impact on the national scene, such as K. Kamaraj, R. Venkataraman (the former President of India) and C. Subramaniam. However, all was not wholly idyllic. In reaction to centuries of Brahman rule, a pan-Dravidian and anti-Brahman movement gathered pace after Independence, claiming that Brahmanical rule

and influence were a symbol of northern domination and a continuing Sanskritisation of Dravidian culture (leading to Dravidian readings of epics such as the Ramayana in which Rama is seen as the oppressor of the darker-skinned Ravanna). In 1967, a party championing the lower castes, the DMK, won power under C.N. Annadurai, the right-hand man of the great Dravidian campaigner Periyar E.V. Ramaswamy. The DMK was a breakaway party from the DK of P.E.V. Ramaswamy which initially campaigned for an independent *Dravida Kazhagam*; a separate country of "South India". The film star M.G. Ramachandran (known by his initials as MGR) took over as chief minister a decade later, con-

LEFT: Indira Gandhi.
ABOVE: NTR, founder of the Telugu Desam.
RIGHT: the Andhran prime minister Narasimha Rao.

trolling the splinter-party AIADMK (the split was due to differences of opinion betwen the scriptwriter-turned-politician Karunanidi, still leader of the DMK, and MGR) and attracting a huge level of support. On his death he was succeeded by his former co-star, and "companion", Jayalitha Jayaram. Voted out in 1996 over allegations of corruption, undaunted, and still attracting fierce loyalty from her supporters, she entered parliament and led her party into coalition with the BJP in 1998. This relationship soon soured, and when she withdrew her support the central government fell. Her party, the AIADMK, was trounced by its bitter rival, the DMK under M.

Karunanidi, in the 2004 general election, who also took control of the state during the elections to the legislative assembly in 2006.

Language was an important element in the pan-Dravidian movement and today it remains a vital part of Tamil politics. The adoption of Hindi as the "national language" (another manifestation of northern arrogance) was greeted with horror in the South, and its official imposition can still spark off riots.

Andhra Pradesh

Andhra Pradesh also set up a few public sector industrialisation projects after it was formed. The public sector giant BHEL started a unit in Hyderabad, the Electronics Corporation of India (ECIL) was established, the Singareni coal mines were developed, and a steel plant was built in Visakhapatnam with improved harbour facilities at its port. However, Andhra is principally an agricultural state. Although parts of the state are exceptionally fertile many areas are very dry in summer and the environment is extremely harsh. Liberalisation of agricultural markets and the scrapping of income protection to farmers has led many into huge debts, which, coupled with failing crops, have made life unbearable for many. Since 1998, more than 4,350 farmers have taken their own lives, often by drinking pesticides. It is not only farmers who have faced the collapse of their markets and have been led into despair. The state's handloom weavers have received no help and, like the farmers, hundreds have committed suicide.

Up until the early 1980s, Congress remained in power in Andhra. However, the state was constantly rocked by rumblings of discontent. This is mainly because Andhra consists of three distinct regions– the coastal region, made up of eight districts generally called Andhra, the interior region consisting of four districts collectively known as Rayalaseema, and the Telengana region comprising the capital Hyderabad and nine districts surrounding it – each with its own loyalties. Between 1969 and 1972 there were riots in Telengana and Andhra over the issue of a further division in the state. To resolve the issue, a six-point formula was suggested by the prime minister, Indira Gandhi. This was accepted (and incorporated into the Constitution) and peace was restored. However, partly due to this crisis, and in part to extreme levels of poverty in many rural areas, an armed leftist movement, the Naxalites, has become very powerful in many northern districts. The Telengana issue was revived at the 2004 general election with the Telengana Rashtra Samiti winning five seats.

On the political front, the 1980s were a turbulent period. The chief minister was changed four times between 1980 and 1982 by Central Government and the increasing disgruntlement lead to the emergence of a new leader – N.T. Rama Rao (NTR) another popular filmstar turned politician. He founded the Telugu Desam (TDP) in 1982 to champion Telugu identity and became a major national political figure. He was succeeded by his son-in-law N. Chandrababu Naidu, who envisioned Andhra Pradesh as a model capitalist state, Hyderabad earned a nickname, Cyberabad, because of his wooing of hi-tech industries (Naidu referred to himself as the state's "chief executive officer").

Just how far he wanted to push these ideas can be seen in "Vision 2020", a plan which claimed that "the private sector… is better able to provide efficient, rationally priced and high-quality services in many areas", to be achieved by slashing subsidies and the privatisation of government agencies. Services were to grow from 49 to 67 percent of the economy, with agriculture falling from 33 to 12 percent. With services already employing 45 million people across India, this seemed wishful thinking.

The effect on farming would have been drastic. Farms would be "rationalised"; i.e. smallholdings would be consolidated into large, corporate farms and monoculture cash crops sown, many of them GM. The reforms would have displaced some 20 million rural workers, who would have been forced to migrate to the cities in search of work. With India's jobless total estimated at between 41 and 42 million, their chances would have been bleak. Naidu's vision was rejected overwhelmingly by Andhran voters (his party, the TDP, won only five out of 42 seats in 2004, down from 29).

Andhra is now controlled by Congress, under chief minister Y.S. Rajasekhara Reddy.

FAR LEFT: R. Venkataraman.
LEFT: finance minister P. Chidambaram.
ABOVE: young middle-class women in Bangalore.

Karnataka

If any southern state received the bounty of the central government, it was Karnataka. Bangalore grew into a city dominated by public sector units. In part because of its temperate climate, major electronics units, such as Bharat Electronics Limited and the Indian Telephone Industries were set up in Bangalore. Over the years Karnataka has built up a strong industrial base, especially in the machine tools and electronics industry. Its base in electronics was to make Bangalore a boom town when the electronics explosion occurred in industry in the 1980s, and the city remains one of India's high-tech capitals.

Politically, Karnataka was very much a pro-Congress state till the 1980s. However, the 1980s proved to be a period of political change. The state turned against the Congress in 1982 and elected the Janata Party to power. Its leader Ramakrishna Hegde became the chief minister of the state. Hegde, who was considered to be one of the most sophisticated and shrewd politicians in the country, remained there for 6 years. He was succeeded by Deve Gowda, still head of the Janata Dal (Secular), who became Prime Minister in 1996–7 after the resignation of the Andhran Congress politician P.V. Narasimha Rao. Currently the state is ruled by a Congress-Janata Dal (S) coalition under a JD(S) chief minister, ex-film producer H.D. Kumaraswamy.

Karnataka benefitted greatly from the construction of the Konkan Railway, the longest line constructed in India since Independence. Work began in 1990, but it was fraught with difficulties due to the terrain it had to pass over or through. It crosses over 179 major bridges, and runs through 92 tunnels, including the longest tunnel in India at 6.5 km (4 miles). The 760-km (475-mile) line was finally opened in 1998.

Apart from its industrial base, Karnataka accounts for much of the silk produced in the country. Among food crops, Karnataka produces around half the country's *ragi* crop and is, particularly in the Kodagu region, the major coffee producer in the country.

Relations with neighbouring Tamil Nadu tend to be uneasy, particularly over water-sharing. When the notorious Tamil bandit and ivory and sandalwood smuggler Veerappan (who had terrorised large parts of the Tamil Nadu-Karnataka border, often closing off the two states' large national parks to visitors) kidnapped the Kannada film star Rajkumar, there were anti-Tamil riots in Bangalore. It took a joint Tamil Nadu-Karnataka police operation many years before he was finally tracked down and killed in 2004.

Kerala

Kerala made its impact on modern India when, in the state's first elections in 1957, it formed the world's first democratically elected Communist government – controversially dismissed by the Congress government in Delhi after intense lobbying by Indira Gandhi. The CPI(M), which soon regained power with a huge popular mandate, was led by the great E.M.S. Namboodiripad (known simply as "EMS"), who pushed through sweeping land reform, educational and health care programmes. As a result, Kerala has the most equitable land distribution in India, near total literacy (claimed to be around 95 percent) and low rates of poverty – all in the Indian state with the least natural resources.

This high level of literacy (which was also due in great part to the enlightened educational policies of the hereditary rulers of Travancore), coupled with few employment opportunities in Kerala itself, has led to Keralites finding work all over India and in the Gulf states. Gulf workers in particular have proved an important source of income for the state, sending much of their money home to their families. Evidence for this can be seen in the proliferation of "Gulf houses", some of them extraordinary fantasies built of concrete in defiance of the climate and environment.

Women in Kerala have traditionally had a higher profile than elsewhere in India. Some communities, predominantly the Nairs, practised matrilineal inheritance and women were in charge of family property. Although this has now largely ended, its legacy and high literacy rates have empowered Keralan women and they tend to have more freedom than their counterparts in other states. This is also one of the very few Indian states where women outnumber men as, unlike elsewhere in India, female foeticide is practically unknown.

For historical and climatic reasons, the state is a major producer of cash rather than food crops. Kerala produces around 45 percent of India's spices but this once lucrative trade is now seriously under threat from cheaper exports from Vietnam. The subsequent crash of the world market and rise in debt has seen, as in Andhra, a number of Keralan farmers commit suicide.

Keralan politics are complex, with around 32 political parties, and the state has been alternately ruled by the faction-ridden Congress or the Marxists. At present the LDF (Left Democratic Front) is in power under Communist chief minister V.S. Achuthanandan. ❑

LEFT: modern offices housing Bangalore's hi-tech industries, and, **ABOVE:** how the poor majority of Bangalore's people live.

SOCIETY AND CULTURE

Similar but different, the South shares cultural and social patterns with the rest of India while recasting them in its own, unique fashion

South India and North India share similarities as well as differences. The institutions of caste and the joint family, and beliefs regarding the relative purity and impurity of persons, places, things, diets and occupations, are found all over India, but they assume different forms in different regions. This phenomenon finds expression in a political cliché, India's "unity-in-diversity". The cliché, however, fails to take note of the linked phenomenon that instances of apparent "unity" often conceal differences.

Thus, in the traditional caste system of India, both the barber and washerman occupy a low rank, but in parts of North India the barber is also the matchmaker for the high castes and hence has a relatively higher status, while the washerman is assigned a low rank because of his washing of the highly "polluting" menstrual, birthing and funeral clothes.

South India is a plateau fringed by plains in the east and west. The mountains of the Western Ghats skirt the plateau in the west while the lower, more broken Eastern Ghats are dotted about different parts of South India. The Nilgiris, which form the highest range in the south, are the meeting point of the two mountain ranges. The Nilgiris were a frontier region, as it were, until a century ago, peopled by Adivasi groups such as the Badaga, Toda, Kota and Kurumba. Today, though, it is much more an agricultural and tourist area.

In the South, the landscape is generally undulating, except in the coastal plains and the deltaic areas of the principal rivers, the Godavari, Krishna and Kaveri. Some parts of South India are endowed with tanks or artificial lakes which serve both as reservoirs and as sources of irrigation. Generally, each tank forms part of a system whose waste waters flow into a stream.

PRECEDING PAGES: guests at a Syrian Christian wedding in Kottayam, Kerala.
LEFT: a village shrine to Skanda, Tamil Nadu.
RIGHT: a family sit down to a meal, Tamil Nadu.

One of the pleasures of travelling in the South is the frequent occurrence of these tanks near which are grown millets, paddy and sugar cane, and also mango, coconut and other fruit-bearing trees. Indeed, the traveller is often startled by the sight of a majestic temple tower rising sheer from an expanse of green paddy fields.

Since the reorganisation of Indian states on the basis of linguistic homogeneity (November 1956), South India has had four states: Andhra Pradesh (population 76.2 million, area 275,600 sq km/106,000 sq miles), Karnataka (population 52.8 million, area 202,800 sq km/78,000 sq miles), Tamil Nadu (population 62.4 million, area 130,000 sq km/50,000 sq miles), and Kerala (population, 31.8 million, area 39,000 sq km/15,000 sq miles), as well as the small Union Territories of Pondicherry (population 974,000, area 5,200 sq km/2,000 sq miles) and Lakshadweep (population 60,600, land area 32 sq km/12 sq miles), of which each is a separate political entity with its own Chief Minister.

Pondicherry was a part of France until November 1954, when it became a political unit of India under a Lieutenant Governor.

Language

All the Dravidian languages – Tamil, Telugu, Kannada and Malayalam – derive from a Dravidian root language, the closest modern language to this being Tamil, the classical language of the South. All are more or less influenced by Sanskrit, even as far back as the age of *Sangam* literature (*circa* 2nd–4th century AD). All Indian languages, including Tamil and Malayalam, have derived their alphabet

from the Brahmi script. In addition to the main languages, there are many regional dialects.

Each of the Dravidian languages has a rich literature, Tamil perhaps being the richest, and in proverbial literature perhaps even superior to Sanskrit. The epics, *Ramayana* and *Mahabharata*, and a few of the more popular *Puranas* (mythological literature celebrating a god or goddess or a centre of pilgrimage) all have their regional linguistic versions. The epics are also rich in poetry. Each language also has a body of traditional songs and tales which are now being written down as part of a process of increased awareness of group, regional and linguistic identity. All these languages have also experienced "purity" movements, particularly Tamil, under which they have tried to expunge "foreign" words – which has meant the discarding of Sanskrit, Persian and, of course, English words and phrases.

Traditionally, Sanskrit has been the language of philosophy and religion, and of prayer and ritual. However, under the influence of the powerful *Bhakti* movement, which started in the 6th–8th century AD in Tamil Nadu and spread to other parts of South India before moving north, there was a determined effort to use the spoken language of the people for communicating religious and ethical ideas. Caste, untouchability and Vedic ritualism were all attacked and, on the positive side, members of the so-called "lower" castes, including women, were encouraged to join the movement. The importance of performing manual work was stressed, which was something quite new if not revolutionary, considering the low status which it had in the caste system. Thanks to the *Bhakti* movement, the Dravidian languages have a body of protest literature as part of their heritage.

Urdu, which is popularly associated with Muslims and North India, actually originated in the Deccan. It started as the language of Mughal armies in the Deccan, and was even called "Dakhni". As the language spread, a literature was created in it using Arabic script, and the language and ethos of Islam and the Middle East as a source of sustenance. Urdu was used extensively in the North by both Muslims and Hindus, but in recent decades it has increasingly become identified with Muslims.

Significant changes have occurred in each of these languages during the last 70 years or more. The need to mobilise a mostly illiterate people for the national struggle for independence from the British led to the development of a style of speaking and writing which was intelligible to one and all. The development of journalism in the regional languages also facilitated the evolution of a clear prose style. Modern literary forms, the short story and the novel, plays and essays, and literary and social criticism, became popular in the regional languages. The post-Independence years witnessed a sharp increase in the number of magazines and novels catering to increasing numbers of people who wanted information and entertainment in their own mother tongue.

Rural society

Traditionally, the village community has been the fundamental unit of economic, political and social organisation. There were two major types of villages in South India, the nucleated and dispersed. The nucleated type prevailed everywhere except on the west coast. In the latter area, collections of discrete farms were grouped together for administrative purposes and called a village. In the nucleated village, on the other hand, the houses and huts lay huddled together in a small area surrounded by fields cultivated by the villagers. But however tiny the settlement area, the village was internally differentiated, each caste occupying a street or segment. In the fertile Thanjavur delta in Tamil Nadu, the street occupied by Brahmans was called *agraharam* while the street occupied by the Dalits was called *cheri*, and each caste group avoided the other's street.

The most frequent form of land revenue obtained in South India was the Ryotwari system, in which the landowner paid rent on the land directly to the government. This did not mean, however, that the landowner cultivated the land. There may have been a tenant, sharecropper or bonded labourer, or all three. In another system, a group of landowners, generally related by paternal kinship, owned all the arable land in the village, and the head of the lineage paid the rent on behalf of all the shareholders in the estate. This system, which existed in parts of Andhra Pradesh and Tamil Nadu, was perhaps more widespread in the past. Land was occasionally given at a concessional rent to those who had rendered distinguished service to the state, or to learned and pious Brahmans to earn religious merit for the donor. All concessional and hereditary tenures were abolished in the land reforms following Independence.

Left: back-breaking work; women plant out rice seedlings in Karnataka.
Right: a bullock cart in the streets of Mysore.

Payment in land occurred at all levels: it was customary to endow a temple with a few acres of land so that the crop could maintain the priest and also make possible daily offerings of food to the deity.

Traditionally, each large village had a headman and an accountant. The headman looked after law and order while the accountant kept the land records, and the two were responsible for collecting the land tax and remitting it to the government treasury. Each was paid a share of the total amount collected as tax. These offices, mostly hereditary, were abolished in the post-Independence years, and nowadays the task of collecting revenue is entrusted to an official appointed by the government.

Arable land was generally owned by the higher castes except in areas where hereditary village servants, drawn from the very lowest castes, were paid in perpetuity with grants of small quantities of land. However, the bulk of the land was generally owned by the members of the peasant castes, referred to as "dominant castes" in the literature on Indian villages. The smaller landowners worked on their own land while the bigger landowners employed tenants, share croppers and hereditary servants to do the manual work for them. The owners only supervised the work.

Producing a crop necessitated cooperation with members of other castes. The blacksmith, who also did carpentry work, made and repaired ploughs and other agricultural implements, the potter, the oilman, the barber, and the washerman were all paid by the landowner with quantities of grain at harvest. Besides these, some grain was given to the village temples, and to the mendicants and poor who generally gathered round the threshing yard.

Ritual and religion

All over South India, every village has a shrine to a goddess (commonly referred to as Mari but also called by other names such as Kali, Bhagavati, Chamundi and Ellamma), associated with a wide variety of important functions such as protecting the village from epidemics of plague, cholera and smallpox and often also with the protection of infants. With the disappearance of epidemics over the years, the deities have lost their *raison d'être*, but their worship continues.

The Nandi bull, the vehicle of the great god Siva, is worshipped in parts of South India and is supposed to look after the rain, fodder and agriculture. The Sanskritic gods of Hinduism and their various manifestations are worshipped generally by the higher castes, especially Brahmans. They are supposed to look after the general welfare of the people, and do not have specific duties like the village deities.

Sometimes shrines are erected to the deity of a caste or a cluster of paternally linked lineages. The Dalits traditionally worshipped a form of Mari, and at her periodical festival fowl, goats and even male buffaloes were sacrificed. Animal sacrifices were commonly made by non-vegetarian castes but, since Independence, state governments have discouraged them. Also, the spread of education, increased urbanisation and better living conditions have all favoured the emulation of the culture and religion of the highest castes, Brahmans, Lingayats and some trading groups. This has increased the popularity of Siva and Visnu and their manifestations, who are propitiated with offerings of fruit, flowers and vegetarian food.

Weekly markets, a feature of rural South India, were far more important economically and socially before the rapid development of roads and transport following Independence. Peasants were also partial to pilgrimages. The annual festivals of deities in the post-harvest season provided them with reasons for travel and relaxation. Cattle fairs were also frequently held at these festivals. In recent years, the religious field of the South Indian peasantry has widened enormously to include pilgrimages to the great temples at Tirupati, Madurai, Srirangam, Ramesvaram, and Sabrimala, and even Varanasi, Allahabad and Haridwar in the North.

The village *panchayat* comprising several elders maintained law and order in the village: physical assault, theft, encroachment, failure to return a loan, all went to the *panchayat* for settlement. But there were offences against caste, custom, diet and morality which sometimes went to the elders of the concerned caste or castes, or directly to the elders of the dominant caste. In this connection, it is essential to mention that the burden of maintaining the social and cultural order devolved on the dominant castes. The latter are ubiquitous in rural India, and generally account for a sizeable percentage of the village population. The other group usually represented in some strength are the low-caste Dalits (literally "oppressed") who perform manual labour on the land.

Members of minority religions such as Muslims and Christians accepted the power and authority of the dominant castes, and the latter in turn felt bound to protect minority culture and religious practices. In some Karnatakan villages Hindus have animals slaughtered in the *halal* way in order for their Muslim guests to partake of the festival (or wedding) dinner. Similarly, Muslims occasionally make votive offerings at Hindu temples. Hindu-Muslim conflict is largely an urban affair, and in any case it is generally muted in South India.

Radical changes have occurred in rural India since Independence with the introduction of land reforms, with making the practice of untouchability in any form a cognisable offence, with the introduction of adult franchise, with the strengthening of local self-government agencies, and with the spread of education to groups and sections which did not have access to it before. Rapid population growth has resulted in land becoming scarce, forcing an increasing number of men to become landless labourers or migrants to urban areas in search of jobs. The growing penetration of money into rural areas, particularly the more prosperous ones, is leading to the erosion of the multi-stranded relationships between landowning patrons and clients, in favour of cash-based particular transactions. This has been compounded by the tremendous development of roads and transport which are diminishing the difference between urban and rural areas. Finally, the popularity of television and the radio has reduced the isolation of villages and brought them within the ambit of the wider, encompassing society, polity and culture.

LEFT: the *dargah* of the Muslim saint Hazaret Syed Shahul in Nagore, Tamil Nadu.
RIGHT: traffic on the roads of Chennai.

South Indian kinship practices are not only different from those in the North but may be described as opposed to them: South Indians prefer to marry close relatives, such as the mother's brother's daughter, father's sister's daughter and, except in Kerala, even an elder sister's daughter. These practices are common to all the castes, with the result that members of a local caste group are usually related to one another in many ways. Until Independence, the marriage network of an endogamous caste in the rural areas rarely exceeded a radius of 32 km (20 miles). It was only the rich, educated and Westernised members of the upper castes in rural areas who ventured beyond and married into a different endogamous group (but part of the same caste). This practice has spread especially to the dominant peasant castes whose sub-groups were spread over a wide area and divided from each other on differences in some detail of ritual or custom. Thanks to this process of "horizontal stretch", the marriage field has in recent decades expanded significantly for many castes.

All sections of the population have a rich religious life: daily life is marked by prayer to the domestic deities and, among the higher castes, bathing and eating are also at least partly ritual acts. The year is marked by festivals, among which the more important are the birthday of

Krisna, the festival of the elephant-headed Ganesha, *Navaratri* (nine nights), *Dussera*, *Dipavali* (festival of lights), *Sankranti* (harvest festival), *Sivaratri* (worship of Siva) and finally, the new year. Karnataka and Andhra Pradesh follow the lunar calendar, while Tamil Nadu and Kerala follow the solar. The solar new year falls usually a month after the lunar new year. The harvest festival of Kerala, *Onam*, precedes the harvest festivals of other regions by over three months: *Onam* has now assumed the character of a "national" festival of Kerala, marked by magnificent boat races.

Hindu astrology is inextricably mixed up with Hindu religious beliefs, but it is popular with all the other religious groups as well. There is a minority of Western-oriented rationalists who denounce astrology and many of the other beliefs and practices of the Hindus, but who may not be above consulting an astrologer during a crisis.

The Hindu-Buddhist ideas of *samsara* (rebirth), *karma* (fruit of action), *dharma* (moral and religious order) and *moksa* (salvation – differently conceived in different sects) are popular and do continue to influence behaviour; but in post-Independence India the sudden access of large numbers to education and employment, and the increase in purchasing power, has resulted in a sharp rise in consumerism and materialist values. The urge of mobility, personal, familial and caste, drives people in all directions. Religion, astrology and godmen all provide invaluable support for mobility and, more importantly, a cushion against failure.

Religious minorities

Religious minorities are represented in strength in South India with the Muslims at the top followed by the Christians and Jains. Traditionally, the minorities lived like distinct castes. One of the positive features of a caste society is its capacity to accommodate diverse groups within the local community.

In each linguistic area, Muslims were divided into distinct groups, though marriage and commensality cut across these barriers. By and large, Muslims did not have a close nexus with land except perhaps in areas of the former rulers like the old Hyderabad state and Mysore. The bulk of the Muslims were traders and artisans while the educated members entered the professions, the bureaucracy and the army, police and forestry service, at different levels.

But with the progress of the freedom struggle, a large number of Muslims gradually came to believe that their interests were different from those of the Hindus. In independent India they are an articulate minority, determined to assert their right to have access to education and government jobs, on the one hand, and to lead their own cultural and religious life, on the other. In cities like Bangalore, Chennai and Hyderabad, while the majority are poor a number of Muslims have become wealthy through trade and commerce.

Most of those who converted to Christianity hailed from the lower castes to try and escape the stigma associated with their social position. (In Karnataka there is a significant population of Dalits who, following the great low-caste hero Dr B.R. Ambedkar, converted to Buddhism for the same reason.) However, on the west coast of India many converts have been high-caste, almost from the first century after Christ. They are again divided by language, sect and caste, and caste differences have proved particularly resistant among them. In fact, in many South Indian churches different castes occupy distinct pews. Marriages usually occur within the caste, except among the educated. While conversion to Christianity has improved the living conditions of the converts and provided them with access to education, health and employment, it has failed to dissolve the stigma of their previous caste status. There is a move among converts from the Dalits to demand that they be treated as on a par with Hindu and Sikh Scheduled Castes so that they may get the benefits of job reservation.

Mention must also be made of the Syrian Christians of Kerala who are divided into several sects and have their own churches in Kerala. Syrian Christians claim to have been converted to Christianity by the Apostle St Thomas during his visit to India in the 1st century AD. They are an integral part of Kerala society like the patrilineal Nambudri Brahmans and the matrilineal Nayars and Izhavans. Many Syrian Christians retain a tradition of being descended from Brahmans (like some converts to Catholicism during Portuguese rule on the west coast). Syrian Christians constitute a powerful minority in Kerala, and educated members of the community are prominent in the professions and government service all over India. The community has contributed nurses to hospitals throughout India as well as overseas.

The Jains may not be a numerically significant minority, but they are culturally important. Jain kings ruled parts of Karnataka till the 12th century AD and Jain writers were pioneers in Kannada literature. The Jains are also known by the great statue they erected for one of their *tirthankaras* (great sages), Bahubali, on top of a hill in Sravanabelagola in Hassan District in Karnataka. At Karkala, in South Kanara District, huge stone statues continue to be carved for export to different parts of the country.

LEFT: temple elephants at a festival in Alappuzha, Kerala.
RIGHT: a Christian procession on Vypeen Island, Kochi.

Traditionally, it was not uncommon for the members of one religion to worship the deities and sacred objects of another faith. Thus, Hindus visit the graves of Muslim *pirs* or saints, particularly at their *urs* (festival on the date of their death). Hindus also visit, for instance, the Church of Mother Mary at Velanganni ("Our Lady of Velanganni") in Tamil Nadu, and many converts to Christianity continue to worship Hindu gods. Perhaps Hindus are more amenable to syncretism than the others, but other faiths not totally free from it. Thus the modern Hindu godman, Sri Satya Saibaba, has devotees from all religions and from every part of the country. ❑

FOOD

Delicious and varied, South Indian regional food ranges from the delicate vegetarian cuisine of Udipi to the spicy meat dishes of Hyderabad

No account of the culture of South India should miss the richness, variety and sophistication of the cuisine in different parts of the region. Rice is grown in the irrigated areas of South India, and also in the heavy rainfall areas on the west coast (but without irrigation). Millets such as *ragi (Eleusine coracona)* and *jowar* (sorghum) are grown in the dry areas and form the staple diet of the poor, along with a gruel made of rice, *ragi* or *jowar*. Rice is the staple of the landed classes. In Kerala parboiled rice is used by all, though the very poor often eke it out with cooked tapioca flour. Along the west coast, the various products of the banana, coconut and jackfruit *(Artocarpus integrifolia)* are used in a variety of ways in cooking. For non-vegetarian groups, fish and other marine products are an indispensable part of the diet.

The bulk of the population of South India, with the exception of Brahmans, is non-vegetarian, though the upper Hindu castes generally keep away from beef and pork. But even those who eat non-vegetarian food do so once a week or fortnight and only certain better-off groups in urban areas are able to afford meat daily.

However, eating habits are beginning to change, particularly in the urban areas. Modern bakeries are popular, even among the poorer members of society. The preparation of pickles, *papads* and snacks is rapidly becoming a non-domestic activity employing wage labour. Tea and coffee shops serving beverages and snacks are popular in South India, and are rapidly spreading to the villages. Freshly prepared South Indian coffee is excellent. Unfortunately, traditional filter coffee is quickly being replaced by a variety of nasty brand-named instant coffees.

LEFT: a woman sells bananas at a local market near Tiruchirapalli, Tamil Nadu.

RIGHT: a biryani stall – a speciality of Hyderabad – on the streets of Bangalore.

Rice and dal

South Indians are by and large rice eaters, but the familiar image of a mound of rice and a couple of pungent curries to go with it is all wrong. The crisp *dosai* and the white fluffy *idli* (made of fermented rice and *dal* batter) are well known and appreciated by many. It is not as if

the four South Indian states serve the same type of food; each region has its variations, though a common bond is apparent.

Rice is common to all four, with a distinct preference for what is called raw rice in most regions, except in Kerala where parboiled rice is generally preferred. The Tamils and the Karnatakans prefer to have their rice with *sambar*, made of *dal* (lentils) and vegetables, with plenty of tamarind for taste, *rasam*, a thin, peppery soup, assorted vegetables called *kutus*, perhaps a *pachadi* (vegetables mixed with curd), followed by a generous helping of curd (yoghurt) to be mixed with rice as the last course. This is usually the menu for both lunch and dinner. The meal is traditionally served on fresh banana leaves which are thrown away afterwards – a hygienically sound custom.

The Telugus, the inhabitants of Andhra Pradesh, prefer more chillies with their curries, and as a first course they may mix a powder made of ground lentils and chillies with rice, adding a generous helping of *ghi* (clarified butter). An unwary visitor who tries the savoury Andhra dishes might find their eyes watering for the rest of the evening. The Keralan rice meal includes, in addition to sambar, many bland curries, such as *olan* (a thin gravy made of pumpkin and coconut) and *kalan* (made of yam with yoghurt and coconut). Among the more delectable vegetable dishes is *kutus*, a thick stew of assorted vegetables.

Bananas, both raw and ripe, are used in various types of curries and crisps in Keralan cuisine. The banana chips made in Kozhikode are a class apart, the wafer-thin round slices made according to recipes handed down through the generations. *Pappads*, big and small, made with various combinations of ground grain but without *masala* (spices), and fried in oil, are part of an authentic South Indian meal. The *pappad* is known as *pappadam* in Kerala and *appalam* in the other southern states. The two have distinct flavours because of their different ingredients.

Though the South Indian meal is basically curry and rice, *chapatis* and *puris* are available as tiffin. So are *dosais* (pancakes made of rice and lentils), *idlis* (steamed rice cakes) and *vadais* (fried doughnuts made of lentils), which make a good breakfast. Other items are *pongal* and *uppuma* (made of rice or semolina) and a variety of savoury snacks in various shapes and sizes, ranging from the concentric *murukkus* to *omapodis* and savoury *bundis*. All these snacks are made of rice and gram flour, and fried in oil. *Bhajis* and *pakoras*, vegetable or onion fritters dipped in a batter of ground gram flour, are also very popular. Karnataka's *bisi bele bath* (rice seasoned with lentils, tamarind and spices) is a great delicacy.

Non-vegetarian dishes

It is certainly not vegetables all the way in South India. The majority of South Indians are non-vegetarians and they cook meat, chicken and fish in a variety of ways. Although the basic combination of spices is the same to those used in vegetarian dishes, there are sharp variations which provide regional flavour. Chillies dominate Andhran food while coconuts are essential in Keralan cuisine.

Hyderabad boasts a Muslim cuisine of its own, somewhat similar to the Mughlai dishes of North India. The Deccani or Hyderabadi *biryani* or *pilauf*, long-grained Basmati rice cooked with meat or chicken masala in its own stock, is a delight. So are the *kababs*, of barbecued meat, hot and succulent from the glowing charcoal burners. Other Hyderabadi specialities include a delicious aubergine dish called *baghara baingan* and the distinctive *halim*, made from mutton and wheat cooked very slowly for a long time.

The Tamils have their Chettinad style of cooking, in which a variety of meat and fish dishes are cooked with chillies and ground coriander. This style of cooking has undergone a renaissance and is available in many restaurants in Chennai. The Tamils make tasty, pungent curries with tender shark. The *sora puttu*, shark meat scrambled with masala, is considered a great delicacy. The smaller non-vegetarian restaurants that abound in Chennai go by the name of "military restaurants/hotels". An age-old distinction in Tamil Nadu cities is the one between non-vegetarian and vegetarian "civil" food. Udupi restaurants serve good vegetarian food.

In Kerala, non-vegetarian food is prepared in a *masala* in which coconut predominates. Seafood is plentiful in this small state with its long coastline. A typical meal of Keralans consists of rice and fish curry. Fish is cooked in a variety of ways – fish *moilli*, fish curry, *min varattiyathu* (fish in a thick masala sauce), *masala* fried fish, *min mulagittathu* (fish in a thin sauce made of chillies and tamarind or raw mangoes) and *min vattichathu* (fish in a thick coconut gravy with tamarind and a little chilli), to mention just a few.

The Christians of central Travancore cook the delicious *min pollichathu* (a special kind of baked fish curry). A local variety of tamarind called *kodampuli* or *minpuli* has medicinal qualities and is popular in central Travancore. It gives the "Christian" style of fish-based dishes a unique taste. The duck preparations of the region and the pork curry of Thrissur are also a delectable experience. Traditionally a food of the poor, tapioca and fish, boiled together with tumeric and chillies, is both filling and nourishing. Steamed rice cakes, called *puttu*, are a popular breakfast item, eaten with boiled gram in *masala* or with fish.

LEFT: a street stall selling *idlis, parathas, bhajis* and curries.
ABOVE: the vegetable market, Thiruvananthapuram.

Muslims, especially in the northern Malabar area, cook a variety of delicious, often non-vegetarian, dishes. The Malabar Muslims or Moplahs make rice *chapatis* called *pathiri* and a number of special chicken and meat dishes. Stuffed chicken, stuffed fish, *min pathiri* (a kind of steamed rice pie filled with fish *masala*) and mussels stuffed in their shells, steamed and later fried, are a few of the items worth mentioning. Many may not be available in the restaurants attached to hotels in Kerala but they are available in smaller eating houses in Kozhikode, Thelasserri and Kannur, as well as in people's homes.

Appams and pickles

Two special dishes from Tamil Nadu and Kerala are the *appam* (called *vellappam* in Kerala) and the *idiappam*. An *appam* is made of ground rice and coconut with no oil used in the cooking. It is eaten with coconut milk or with any vegetarian or non-vegetarian curry. The steamed *idiappam* is made of rice flour and looks like vermicelli. It can also be accompanied by either vegetables or meat. *Appams* have an anglicised name in Sri Lanka where they are also called "hoppers"; *idiappam* are referred to there as "string hoppers".

The South has a plethora of chutneys and pickles with local variations. Andhra boasts a large variety of pickles, mainly based on the mango. They are generally preserved in oil and are extremely sharp in flavour. The Andhra *avakka* pickle and *gongura* chutney are most appetising, but they cannot be recommended for those not used to chillies. The Tamil and Karnatakan pickles are a little milder. The Keralan *kadumanga* pickle, tender mangoes mixed with powdered chillies and mustard, is tasty and mild.

Sweets and fruit

The common sweet after a meal, particularly on special occasions, is *payasam*, a liquid milk-based pudding with either rice or vermicelli, and a little aromatic spice for flavour. This is common to all the four states, though there are regional variations. Kerala has its *ada prathaman* which is also milk-based, and the *chakka prathaman* made of ripe jackfruit and *gur* (jaggery). Boiled ripe banana or candied banana chips go with the meal. A Tamil speciality is the *chakkara pongal* made of rice, *gur* and spices. There is also *athirasam*, made of rice flour and *gur*, and deep fried like a *puri*; this is common in some parts of Tamil Nadu. Karnataka has many desserts which would appeal to anyone's sweet tooth. Its *polis*, pancakes made of flour and rolled with different types of sweet fillings, are well known. So is the Mysore *pak*, a cube-shaped cake made of ground gram, sugar and *ghi*. Apart from these Southern specialities, the sweets commonly seen all over India are also relished in the South: the spherical *laddu*, made of gram flour and sugar; the *jalebi* and *jangri*, made of fermented flour or lentils, deep fried in circular patterns and soaked in sugar syrup; *gulab jamuns* made of dried milk and drenched in syrup; and a variety of *halvas*.

The South produces a large variety of fruit that is sold either at the local fruit and vegetable market or peddled by vendors from carts or at roadside stalls. Chief among these is the tender, green coconut, prized for both its refreshing drink and the cream which is scooped out and eaten as a snack. The yellow flesh of the ripened jackfruit is considered a delicacy and is sold in little leaf bowls. There are many varieties of banana such as the red bananas and mini-bananas, which have a distinct flavour. Mangoes, guavas, pineapples and papayas are just some of the delicious fruits available throughout the region.

LEFT: a breakfast of *puris, idlis* and *dosais* on a stall in Thanjavur.
ABOVE: *murukku* for sale in Tirupati.

Where to eat

When looking for a place to eat in South India, a glance at the signs placed near the entrance will indicate whether it is a snack bar or "meals" restaurant. Look out for words such as "Tiffins", "Meals", "Pure Veg" etc. Coffee houses serve fresh coffee and tea and snacks. The tiffin places are good for breakfast dishes. The "meals" establishments offer what in the North would be called a *thali* – rice served on a round, steel tray (literally a *thali*) with little steel bowls of vegetable dishes and curd (yoghurt). *Pappads*, *chapattis* or *parathas* will also be on offer.

Meals revolve around rice, eaten with dal-based soups, thin and spicy *rasams* and the thicker *sambars*, often flavoured with tamarind. To these are added "*sambar* powder", made up of spices such as coriander, *methi* (fenugreek) seeds, cumin and the pungent asafoetida. Often they are finished by "tempering", chillies and whole spices heated in oil until the important black mustard seeds "pop"; the whole lot is then poured on the top of the dish. Dry vegetable dishes (and in certain places, notably Andhra Pradesh and Kerala, spicy meat and fish preparations) are also served with the rice, to which is added copious quantities of curd (yoghurt) and fiery pickles. ❑

ART AND ARCHITECTURE

Early Buddhist sculpture, Chola bronzes, towering gopurams and Deccani Muslim tombs are just some of the wonders produced by South Indian artists

Several factors have influenced the development of South Indian architecture. Among them are the hot tropical climate, the dramatic monsoon rains, the availability of good tropical wood and a wide variety of stone for building, and frequent contact with foreign influences. All these combined to shape several different styles of architecture, sculpture and painting. Each style was linked with the other by the course of political and economic development and the movement of ideas and philosophies over the land and its people.

The study of architecture in South India is often restricted to religious architecture, which was built in materials such as stone and brick. Secular buildings in this region, being constructed from perishable materials such as bamboo, wood and mud, often escape historical mention. Yet it was from these structures that religious architecture drew inspiration and ideas.

Buddhist architecture

As Buddhism travelled southward to Andhra Pradesh, Tamil Nadu, Karnataka and on to Sri Lanka, several religious structures were erected on the way. At Amaravati and Nagarjunakonda in Andhra Pradesh, large *stupas* (burial mounds) were constructed around the 2nd century BC. These are solid rubble hemispherical structures with a huge stone railing, ornamental carved gateways and pillars. These celebrated monuments are unfortunately in ruins. The few remaining sculptures from these locations are now housed in the Government Museum in Chennai, the Site Museum at Amaravati, the museum at Nagarjunakonda and in the British Museum in London.

The Amaravati stupa, though similar in design to those constructed in Central and North India, seems to have evolved unique features which in turn influenced later trends in the region. Its limestone sculptured panels are good examples of the superior craftsmanship of the region during the early years of the Christian era. Human figures carved within the panel are crowded together, each shown in movement and exhibiting a variety of perspectives, costumes and headgear. A mood of joy and exuberance pervades these sculptures.

Similarly, the image of Buddha in Amaravati is unique in style and form. The figures of Buddha found in the northwestern provinces of Gandhara have distinctive Greco-Roman features with sharp aquiline noses, and thick wavy curling hair. In Amaravati, the Buddha's figure is delicately proportioned, slim and youthful, and the oval-shaped face is smooth with half-closed meditative eyes and almost no eyebrows. These figures are among India's finest early Buddhist sculpture, and their diminutive scale does not hint at the gigantic figures of Buddha that are to be found in later sculptures in Sri Lanka, Nepal, Burma, Thailand, China and Japan.

PRECEDING PAGES: designs are made on the Kathakali stage and swept away before each performance.
LEFT: sculpture at Gangaikondacholapuram.
RIGHT: intricate Teyyam makeup, Kerala.

Jain architecture

Jainism, like Buddhism, also travelled to the southern states leaving its architectural heritage in Orissa, Andhra Pradesh, Karnataka and Tamil Nadu. The prosperity of the mercantile Jain community and several rulers provided sustained patronage for artistic achievements for more than 2,000 years in this area. In Sittannavasal near Pudukottai in Tamil Nadu are rock-cut Jain temples excavated from the hillside which date to the 8th century AD. These caves contain mural paintings similar in style to those at Ajanta in the Aurangabad district of Maharashtra.

In Karnataka, the Jain temple designs draw their inspiration from secular wooden architecture, with its sloping tile roofs and pillars, as in the case of the Mudabidri Jain temple in Udupi (AD 1000). Other Jain temples followed the plan of Hindu religious architecture with pillared halls or *mandapas,* flat roofs and pyramidal towers.

Sravanabelagola *(see page 253)* has a colossal monolithic image of Gomatesvara, one of the largest freestanding statues in India and the most spectacular Jain site in the South. The site was established as a pilgrimage spot around the 9th century AD and remains to this day an important one for the Jain community.

Early Hindu temple architecture

Village temples and shrines marking spots sacred to the Hindus scatter the length and breadth of South India. Famous temples have grown around such sanctified locations as Chidambaram, where Siva challenged his consort Parvati to a dance competition, and Madurai, where Siva as Sundaresvaran married Minaksi ("the goddess with fish-shaped eyes").

The reign of the Pallava kings (6th–9th century AD) ushered in an age of experimentation in art in South India. At Mamallapuram, the Pallava sea port, about 35 km (22 miles) from present-day Chennai, huge granite boulders and parts of the hillside were carved into temples with rooms, pillars and sculptured walls. It is here that one can study the experimental designs for temple architecture. The *pancha rathas* (five chariots) at Mamallapuram are five rock-cut temples, each one carved out of the living rock. The Draupadi Ratha is a simple temple consisting of a square room for the deity (the *garbha griha* or sanctum) and a roof fashioned out of the stone to resemble an ordinary village hut, a copy of wood and thatch construction. It rests on a platform supported by tiny carved elephants.

The concept of the temple as a chariot of the gods is derived from an ancient practice, still prevalent, of carrying the image in procession through the streets of the city during festivals. The chariots were made of wood with huge wheels, and were drawn by animals or by the devotees themselves. Many temples in India, therefore, have a border of elephants and horses near the base.

The architect-artist's next problem was designing the roof for the stone temple. At Mamallapuram the Draupadi Ratha has a village hut roof, but the Arjuna Ratha has a roof carved in two distinct horizontal levels with miniature hut roof designs along the edge and topped by a many-sided cupola called the *sikhara*. The Dharmaraja Ratha has a roof of three levels with tiny roof motifs, while the Bhima Ratha also has a roof designed on the thatch principle, its sides forming a curved gable-like arch over a rectangular room. This design was later used as the roof design for gateways or *gopurams* to the temples. This experiment seems to have pleased the South Indian artists; it became the accepted form of the Dravida temples, and was codified in the *Sastras* or canons.

Each temple was built on mathematical formulas of exacting precision. The square or rectangular sanctum containing the deity was the dark centre of the temple. Above it rose a roof made up of many receding horizontal levels, with miniature roof designs, ascending in a pyramidal shape with the aim of creating an octagonal *sikhara* that would carry the *kalasa* (or sacred water-pot of plenty) and the emblem of the god enshrined within the temple.

While northern and eastern Indian temples evolved a curvilinear or conical *sikhara*, the South Indian temple roof is predominantly pyramidal. This ingenious temple design was used to construct the shore temple at Mamallapuram, and the magnificent Kailasnath temple in the Pallava capital of Kanchipuram. The roof in the latter is larger and higher, and the *vimana* (outer walls) are decorated with elegant sculptured panels. As rituals and religious functions developed, there was need for more space in front of the sanctum, for the assembly of devotees. *Mandapas* were erected beside the temple for special functions – the Kalyana Mandapa or marriage hall, Natya Mandapa or hall for recitals of devotional music and dance.

LEFT: beautifully carved elephants at Mamallapuram.
RIGHT: painting from the Brihadesvar temple, Visakhapatnam.

The Kailasnath temple at Kanchipuram is an important landmark in South Indian architecture, for it perfects the proportions of the building plan. Its massive pyramidal *sikhara* suggests Mount Kailas in the Himalayas where Lord Siva is said to reside. The *vimana* walls are adorned with Pallava stone sculptures of gods and goddesses, each set in their appropriate cardinal positions. Pallava figures are rendered with great elegance – long, slim limbs, narrow waists and minimal jewellery. Siva, to whom the temple is dedicated, is depicted in many manifestations – as Nataraj, the Lord of Dance, accompanied by musicians; as Dakshinamurti, the Sage of Learning, teaching his devotees, both human and animal, with his beautiful consort Durga; and as Gangadhara, who bore the might of the descending Ganges on his head, subduing the powerful river as it meandered through his matted locks to fall gently to earth.

Although the Chalukyan kings threatened Pallava power in several battles from their centres at Badami, Aihole and Pattadakal, the supremacy of Pallava art was never in doubt. The Kailasnath temple provided the inspiration for the Virupaksha temple, built in the 8th century in Pattadakal, Karnataka. The Chalukyan empire, because of its central geographical location in peninsular India, served as the meeting place for several formative styles of architecture. The major Chalukyan sites seem almost workshops or laboratories for experiments in temple architecture. On the magnificent cliffs of Badami, early rock-cut caves have been carved out with sculptured pillars, ceilings and walls similar to those at Ajanta and Ellora in Maharashtra. At Pattadakal, one can see within a comparatively small area, temples with plans and roofs that were later to be adopted in eastern and central India, along with temples in conformity with the Dravida or South Indian styles.

The quality of stone sculpture from these temples is also outstanding. There are carved narrative and decorative panels on pillars, walls and ceilings, figures of deities in their various manifestations and episodes from the *Ramayana*, bracket figures and architectural mouldings with floral motifs. Research in this area has suggested that artisan guilds worked together, the master craftsman providing the plan, while artisans cut and shaped each rock to be assembled at the temple site. The master craftsmen lent an overall perspective, maintaining unity of style in all parts of the building and the sculptures.

With the break-up of the Chalukyan empire, ideas from Badami, Aihole and Pattadakal spread to different areas. The Rastrakutas took the design of the Kailasnath temple to Ellora in Maharashtra for their magnificent sculptured rock-cut Kailasa temple. It was in this way that ideas spread across the length and breadth of India, suggesting an underlying unity amidst regional diversity in temple architecture.

The Cholas and bronze casting

Back in South India in the 9th and 10th centuries, the Chola dynasty was gaining a foothold. The wealth amassed from agricultural prosperity and trade with the Far East stimulated patronage of the arts. The Chola capital in Thanjavur was the centre of activity. The great Brihadesvara temple took 15 years to build and was consecrated around 1009–1010 AD. It follows the standard Indian temple plan with a *garbha griha* and a *mandapa*, set within a walled enclosure. The tower of the Brihadesvara is 63 metres (210 ft) high, the largest and tallest in India, a big step upward from its origins at Mamallapuram. The *sikhara*, made from a granite block 25.5 metres (77 ft) square, is thought to weigh 80 tonnes. It is said that a huge wooden ramp was built several kilometres long to roll the *sikhara* up to its position 61 metres (200 ft) above the ground.

In 1930 a series of paintings was uncovered along the internal circumambulatory passage of the Thanjavur temple. The murals of Siva and of the Chola patrons are exquisite, similar to the ones found at Kanchipuram in the Kailasnath temple. The colours, subdued by age, are muted earth mineral hues of rust, red, ochre and white. The Brihadesvara temple has a large collection of metal images gifted by various patrons. Bronze masterpieces of the Chola period are known for their superb quality and the mastery of the technique of casting. The best collections can be seen at the Thanjavur Art Gallery and the Chennai State Museum and Art Gallery, which has the largest collection of bronzes in India with several fine images of Siva and Visnu. There is another superb example of a Chola bronze at the National Museum in Delhi, the *Kaliya Mardan Krisna* shows Krisna dancing on the hood of the five-headed giant serpent known as Kaliya: Krisna as a cowherd discovered that his cattle were being poisoned by the serpent, who upon realising Krisna's identity worshipped him, while Krisna held up its long tail in triumph.

These bronzes were first modelled in wax with all details and the image was then coated in mud paste. When the mud mould dried, it was heated, and the melting wax was allowed to escape through a hole at the base. Into the hollow mud mould a hot molten mixture of five metals was poured in. When it cooled, the mould was broken and the bronze image was given some final touches and polished. This technique of *cire-perdue* or lost-wax process is still practised in Thanjavur today in the city workshops.

Metal images were installed in minor shrines in temples, and since they were movable, they represented the main temple deity in processions on festival occasions. The bronze images were clad in silk, decked with sandal paste and floral garlands, and ceremonially taken out in procession in temple chariots or *rathas* for devotees to receive *darsan*.

A sculptured figure was conceived according to a set of basic principles set down in the Shastras. The form is divided into 9 to 13 parts, the stone block into 16 squares, with *apsaras* or divine sky nymphs in the corners, consorts beside the figure, and the *vahana* (animal mount) of the deity below, along with devotees. The figure was identified by iconographic details of form, composition, hand gestures, weapons, *vahanas*, costumes and others. In the vast Hindu pantheon, Brahma the Creator is represented as a sage with long flowing beard and five heads that enable him to observe the universe. Visnu holds a conch signifying the sound of creation in one hand and the wheel of time in the other, for he is both Creator and Preserver. Visnu has 10 incarnations that saved the world from destruction – the most popular being Varaha, the boar that saved the earth from the floods, Rama, the hero of the epic poem *Ramayana*, and Krisna, the child god, the cowherd and divine lover.

Siva holds a trident, with a leaping deer in one hand; he is called Pasupati, the Lord of Creation and Protector of the animal world. Female deities, referred to as *Devis*, such as Durga, Kali or Parvati, the female principal of Siva, are equally powerful. Each deity also has an animal symbol that manifests their qualitative aspects. Siva, the upholder of Dharma, rides the bull Nandi, Visnu the Garuda or regal bird of virtue, while Durga, the mighty destroyer of evil, rides on a tiger.

The Chola artists seemed to have taken these guidelines and interpreted them to their advantage, elongating the figures to achieve longer limbs, slim waists and slender oval faces. Chola bronzes are recognisable by iconographic details and the sheer elegance of their presence.

The dancing Siva, or Nataraja, carries in one hand a drum beating the rhythm of life, in the

LEFT: a 16th century fresco from the Virabhadra temple in Lepaksi.
RIGHT: a Chola bronze of Bharata.

other a small flame symbolising destruction, which is a part of creation. His third hand is raised in the gesture of protection from ignorance and darkness, which is personified as a dwarf demon being trampled underfoot by him. The dance of Siva is framed by a circle of flames, for in Hindu philosophy the metaphor is of wisdom and light dispelling darkness and ignorance.

Interestingly, the Thanjavur Brihadesvara temple has many copper plates that record temple management, finance and donations. The temple in South India grew from its humble origins as the home of village deities into the centre of village or city life. It acquired produce

from the land, cattle and donations for upkeep of the building, payment to Brahmans, and oil to feed the lamps. It was also the cultural centre for music, dance, literature, sculpture and painting. As in centres like Kanchipuram, the Brahmans associated with the temple ran *gurukuls* or schools where young students were taught the holy scriptures, and ancient manuscripts were copied and preserved. Markets grew up around the temple, where pilgrims from neighbouring villages could come not only to pray, but to collect supplies and sell their wares. The whole town came to be enclosed within the many consecutive walls of the temple, each one added to accommodate the growing town.

Later temple architecture

During the later Vijayanagara, Pandya and Nayaka periods (13th–17th century) temple expansion continued with the addition of *mandapas*, tanks for bathing, and walls to encompass the township. Several tall gateways or *gopurams* were erected at cardinal points on these boundary walls that could lead the pilgrim's eye to the heart of the city. The temple cities of Chidambaram, Madurai, Srivilliputtur, Srirangam and many others grew with additions made by several ruling dynasties and patrons. The *gopurams* rose high into the sky, often more than 30 metres (100 ft), towering edifices of stucco figures and sculptured embellishments, painted today in gaudy enamel colours, while the main *sikhara* of the temple diminished in size, often lost in the maze of additional buildings of the temple complex.

Today, as you wander through the city streets of Madurai, you will see rows of shops and florists near the main temple, residential houses for Brahmans, metalware shops, all in distinct areas, each marked by locations prescribed by caste rules laid down in the texts for town planning and temple architecture.

In Karnataka, the Hoysalas came into power around present-day Mysore and Hassan after the fall of the Chalukyas in the early 11th century. In the Hoysala temples the square *garbha griha* prescribed in the *Silpasastra* has been rotated to form a star shape, and instead of a single sanctum two or three cellas have been added to form a complex star-shaped plan, which is carried through from the platform to the *sikhara*.

The temples of Belur, Halebid and Somnathpur are built on raised star-shaped platforms. The wall surface of the *vimana* in these temples is broken into horizontal bands of sculptural motifs, the lowest band consisting of elephants, horses and foliage, and above, at eye level, narrative panels with depictions of the *Ramayana* and *Mahabharata* and stories of Krisna. Further above are rows of *yalis* (mythological creatures) and *hamsas* (legendary birds), surmounted by larger vertical panels of gods and goddesses in various poses. At Belur the overhanging eave of the temple roof is supported by single stone brackets superbly carved with frames and lace-like foliage. These figures are all in movement and sport an abundance of heavy jewellery. The stone used in these temples differed from the hard granite of the Pallava temples and the sandstone of Badami and Aihole. Here a heavy textured black chlorite schist was used which could be carved in intricate detail and set free from the stone bases.

In Kerala, the Dravidian stone temple design coexisted with local forms of wood and tile construction. The temple plan was often circular instead of square or rectangular, and the walls were adorned with sculptured wooden pillars and brackets and with murals. The circular *garbha griha* was given a tiled conical roof, often extended to a two-tiered *sikhara*, forming a pagoda-like structure. The whole temple was enclosed in a courtyard with an elaborate gateway. In Kerala the earliest mural is dated to the 16th century at a temple at Ettumanoor in Kottayam district. Later murals are in Padmanabhapuram Palace, now in Tamil Nadu, and the Mattancheri Palace in Kochi, Kerala.

In the Central Deccan region, around the Krishna river, the Vijayanagara empire was established with its capital at Hampi (now in Karnataka). Here lies an important example of a Hindu pre-modern capital city, and excavations are still in progress to reveal the buildings, temples and city plan. Hampi is set amidst lush river and plains, hills and huge granite boulders that provided natural protection as well as building material. Between the 13th and 15th centuries the Krisna, Virupaksa, Vitthala and the Hazara Rama temples were built. In front of the Vitthala Temple is a remarkable small temple chariot complete with turning stone wheels.

All Hindu architecture was based on the engineering principle of beams and pillars. Where stone was used, the space between pillars could not be very wide for fear that the stone roof beam would collapse. Hence, temple doors are narrow and halls or *mandapas* are crowded with pillars supporting the stone beam above. Nomenclature for *mandapas* refers to this phenomenon in such terms as "hall of 500 pillars", or "1,000-pillared hall". The pillar design changed with each dynasty in a manner similar to the "orders" of Greek and Roman columns. The Pallava royal emblem, the lion, is to be seen at the base of many Pallava pillars, while the Vijayanagara and Nayak dynasties of later centuries employed the motif of the rampant horse and rider in their pillared halls at the Madurai and Vellore temples.

The Hoysala temple pillars within the *mandapa* are monoliths, fashioned with circular mouldings, presumed to have been produced on a lathe. How the huge stone pillars were rotated or abrasives applied to erode the stone is still not fully understood.

LEFT: a Chola bronze of Siva as Nataraja.
ABOVE: the pillared *mandapam* of the Simhachalam temple near Visakhapatnam.

Islamic architecture

While the temples of South India were being built, a fresh influence entered northern India in the 9th, 10th and 11th centuries. With Islam came a new architectural and engineering principle that transformed the history of building in India: the use of the arch in building, instead of pillars and narrow beams, and the construction of domes instead of diminishing *sikhara* tiers. There is archaeological evidence of trading contact with Greece and Rome in Arikamedu in Pondicherry, and Indians were familiar with Roman sculpture, pottery and coins. However, the principle of the arch was as the Jama Masjid and the Gol Gumbaz, the tomb of Sultan Mohammed Adil Shah who died in 1657.

The plan of a mosque consists of a large open courtyard, where the congregation assembled for prayer. The *mihrab* or facade demarcating the direction of Mecca is framed with arches, calligraphic designs and often a dome. A minar or tower was placed on one, two or four sides of the courtyard, and was used by the priest to call the faithful to prayer five times a day.

The Indian artisans soon adapted to the new architectural challenges. The use of the arch enabled the architect to span wide areas without

not introduced to India until some time in the 11th century when the the first mosque in India with built with wide arches at the Qutb complex in Delhi.

Under an official of the Tughlaqs, the Bahmanis in the South established an independent kingdom, building forts and palaces at Gulbarga and Bidar in Karnataka in 1425 with several elements derived from their Islamic heritage. Under the Qutb Shahi dynasty, a huge fortress was built on the rocky hills of Golconda in 1512 and tombs with bulbous domes were constructed in many places. Bijapur became a stronghold of the Deccani Sultanate and here Islamic monuments were erected, such

the obstruction of "a hundred pillars". Expansive doorways and windows offered an airy lightness to the building. The rooms thus created were bridged by squinches to convert square rooms into circular bases for the huge domes which were constructed. The Gol Gumbaz in Bijapur in Karnataka is the largest single-chambered building in India, with a dome measuring 43 metres (144 ft) in diameter. In decoration, too, where Hindu temples are peopled with figures of gods and goddesses, Islamic buildings are embellished with stone screens or *jalis*, verses of the Quran in calligraphy, geometric designs in inlaid stone work, and stucco and plaster painted decorations.

European architecture

While many of the Deccani kingdoms were brought under Mughal rule, the 17th and 18th centuries saw the building of the first European structures on Indian soil. It must be remembered that Greeks, Romans and Arabs were well established on the west coast by the 2nd century AD, and Christian and Jewish settlers had made their home in Kerala, building modest churches and synagogues for their use.

Vasco da Gama landed on the site of the Roman settlement at Kozhikode in Kerala in 1498. By the mid-16th century there were three settlements of the Portuguese, at Daman, Diu and Bassein. The first English factory was established at Surat in Gujarat in 1613. In 1639 a new station was established in Chennai, and work began the following year towards building a new fort called Fort St George and a factory, and the "white" or Christian town with residential areas. St Mary's Church at Fort St George was consecrated in 1680 and is the oldest Anglican Church in Asia. The church is simple in plan, but contains an interesting record of the early East India Company in the gravestones of the cemetery. Other secular buildings of this period are the old Secretariat in Chennai, the old Banqueting Hall, now Rajaji Hall, and the former Ice Factory on Marina Beach. These buildings are characterized by their classical style, making full use of Indian masons, local *chunam* (whitewash) and building materials.

From the territory of Hyder Ali and Tippu Sultan of Mysore came the greatest resistance to British expansionist policies. The fort of Srirangapatnam, where Tippu Sultan fought his last battle and died in 1799, and the Summer Palace are a curious mixture of Islamic, Hindu and European ideals.

Apart from official and religious buildings, by the 1800s European residential houses too acquired a distinct style. The English "bungalow" originated in Bengal from the term *bangla* or "big house in the village" with a long rectangular plan and open verandahs suitable for the hot summer, set in gardens with organised flower beds. The homesick Englishman and family sent for many things from England to decorate their Indian homes, including seeds for roses, dandelions, honeysuckles, oak, fir, pear and chestnut. Bangalore, with its soothing climate, and the southern hill stations of Udhagamandalam (previously Ooty), Coonoor and Kodaikanal offered the British a "home away from home". Little cottages with English gardens called "Spring Haven", "Swiss Cottage", "Gorse House" and "Three Elms" were built as summer retreats and residential houses. In Ooty St Stephen's Church was consecrated in 1830, the building timber for the church being obtained from Tippu's Lal Bagh palace at Srirangapatnam. Residential houses in Bangalore were characterised by wooden trellis-work canopies or "monkey tops", tiled gabled roofs and wide-roofed porches.

LEFT: a carved bracket from the Minaksi temple in Madurai.

RIGHT: Church of the Sacred Heart, Pondicherry.

Soon after 1857, the attitude of the British in India changed drastically, and all concentration was directed away from the South to building the cities of Kolkata (previously Calcutta), Mumbai (previously Bombay) and finally the new capital city of New Delhi.

Today, in any South Indian village or town, you will see how the past coexists with the present, the ancient with the new, buildings of different religions beside one other: a saga of history, continuity and change, affirming the contribution of the South Indian artists to the mosaic of Indian culture. ❑

CRAFTS

The South has been famous since Greek and Roman times for the superb quality of its textiles, wood- and stone-carving and metalwork

The deep-rooted traditions of India intricately knit together its religious and social system with its vast and widespread community of artisans and weavers. Within this all-encompassing umbrella there are immense variations and differences which create the diversity of its cultural heritage. This is vividly displayed in the crafts and textiles of South India where, in Tamil Nadu, Kerala, Andhra Pradesh and Karnataka, towns, villages and hamlets have been known for hundreds of years for their special and distinct craftsmanship.

The caste structure, set out centuries ago, placed the craftsman within an ordained pattern of existence. Potters, cobblers, blacksmiths, weavers and basket-makers lived as professional groups within the rural community, passing on their skills to their children and working according to the needs of a well-defined market. Generations of experience and a deep relationship with religion dictated both the form and the norms of work. Creativity was the prerogative of the individual, but craftsmanship was guided by certain canons set out in the *Silpasastras*, Sanskrit treatises on the various art forms.

Tamil Nadu

In Tamil Nadu most metalwork, handloom and jewellery-making traditions drew their patronage and sustenance from the many famous temples in the state. Stone and metal images and vessels for religious use had to be cast and the images then draped and ornamented. This created a concentration of metal workers, weavers and goldsmiths who were wholly dedicated to serving the temple and the surrounding community, besides the thousands of pilgrims who would throng the holy centres. Each temple complex became a beehive of religious, commercial and artisanal activity with flower markets, temple processions, music and dance alongside each other.

Kanchipuram was famed as the capital of the Cholas and Pallavas between the 7th and 13th centuries. Over 150 temples with all their gods and goddesses created a tremendous demand for the artefacts and accessories that go with festivals dedicated to the various deities. Weavers were required to provide skirts, *lungis* and

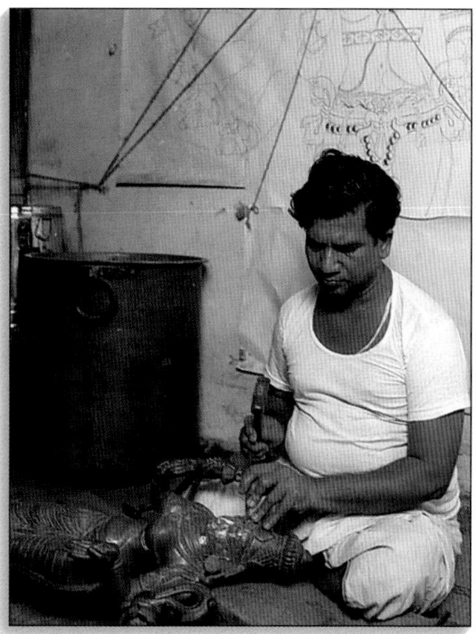

angavastrams or shawls to cover the upper portion of the torso. Curtains, veils and turbans with special ornamentation all formed part of the fabric needs of each temple.

The creation of any metal figure or vessel had since early times been imbued with spiritual significance as the substance was solid and permanent. The *cire perdue* or lost-wax method meant that when the molten metal was poured into the earthen or waxen mould in order to take its shape, there were some crucial moments when it seemed that it was a divine presence rather than the artisan's hand that controlled the creation of the artefact. The metal was also presumed to absorb the energy of the cosmic body it represented, so that

LEFT: making ritual canopies in the Pudu Mandapam in the Minaksi Temple, Tamil Nadu.
RIGHT: contemporary Tamil bronzes are worked according to ancient principles and proportions.

when an icon was installed in the inner sanctum of a shrine, the energy was believed to be lodged there. If the image was carried out during festivals and processions, the shrine was considered empty of power and energy. Various acts of propitiation were thus necessary to render the entire process both auspicious and successful, necessitating the physical and aesthetic purification of the craftworkers.

The main centre where solid casting of metal is done is Swamimalai in Thanjavur. Madurai, Salem, Chingelpet and Tiruchirapalli are other metalwork centres producing a variety of temple lamps, from tiny single-wick pieces to elaborately ornamental 1.5 metre- (5 ft-) high creations which can hold enough oil to light up a stage performance all through the night.

Metalsmiths claim descent from Visvakarma, the architect of the gods, who governs the hands and tools of all artisans, and each metal is said to have its own alchemic and healing properties. Specific prayers are normally recited before work begins, for the gods must come to dwell in the artisan's fingertips and mind as well as the artistic creation.

The high quality of skill in Tamil Nadu's basket and mat-weaving is evident. The simple basket is made in palm or palmyra leaf, dyed or given raised textures to produce a variety of shapes and sizes of boxes, trays, mats, bags and screens. Tirunelveli, Ramanthapuram and Kanniyakumari are the main basketry centres.

Tamil Nadu excels in handlooms, too, both silk and cotton. The weavers who congregated around temples made Kanchipuram a household word for the traditional silk *sari* in bold colours with broad contrasting borders and *pallus* and gold threads forming lines, checks and motifs. Kanchipuram weavers also produce the most brilliant cottons in India. A typical Kanchipuram, whether in silk or cotton, is recognisable by its border design of the *gopuram* or temple spire pattern, broad contrast borders and distinct elegance. A special feature of some of the *saris* is the difference in colours of the upper and lower border, termed Ganga-Jamuna, signifying two of the holiest rivers of India.

The city of Chennai abounds in goldsmiths, many of whom live and work around the Mylapore temple *(see page 127)*. Another important centre is Nagercoil.

Kerala

The skills of the craftspeople of Kerala, as in most of South India, are directed by religious requirements as well as simple utilitarian needs, and its beautiful coastline lays it open to a variety of influences from other parts of the world.

The bell-metal vessels made by the Musaris are huge vessels almost 2 metres (6 ft) in diameter in an alloy of copper and tin and are cast by the *cire perdue* technique after invocatory rituals are performed. Some of the more classic pieces are the *urli, charakku* and *varpu*, generally used for cooking food on a mass scale. It is fascinating to see rice being cooked in these to feed the elephants at the Guruvayur temple. Oil cans, jugs, drinking glasses, ladles and jewellery boxes are some of the smaller items made for household use. Hanging lamps, *changalavelakku* and *kuthuvelakku,* spouted water jugs, rounded gourd-shaped water containers and smaller temple lamps in the soft yellow tones typical of bell-metal are seen all over Kerala.

The town of Aranmala is known for its long-handled metal mirrors.The mixing of herbs with molten metal produces a highly reflective surface. According to legend the technique was revealed to a woman of the Visva-karma community from whom the Musaris of the Kammala caste (makers of eye-pleasing objects) claim descent.

Keralan designs of necklaces in gold are distinctive and have never been copied by artisans in other parts of the country. Very fine and highly skilled work is required to create the delicate *puthali* and the green-stoned *pachakalluthali*. The goldsmiths of Thrissur are well known, and the best shops for both gold ornaments and bell-metal vessels are around the Vadakkumnath temple in the heart of the town.

Wood carving, particularly in the old traditional homes of Kerala and on the ceilings of temples scattered all over south Malabar, demonstrates rich techniques and a variety of subjects. Deities, elephants and floral and geometric patterns cover large panels and pillars. Dark ebony, rosewood or teak are used for carving in Kerala. Grand old architectural woodwork can be seen at the Padmanabhapuram palace and Sri Padmanabhasvami temple.

Kodungallur, the historic port town of Malabar, is famous for its Sri Kudumba temple. The making of palmyra and screwpine mats is a widespread craft here. These, along with articles made out of coconut shell, keep the women actively involved in cottage industry. It is a secondary income-generating activity, with the men being occupied in traditional work like fishing and toddy-tapping. Screwpine mats are woven by hand on the ground into sleeping mats or as wrappings for fish or for light machinery. The finer version is seen in table mats, handbags, sun hats and other objects for commercial markets.

Kerala handlooms are typical of its people – restrained, dignified and austere. Traditionally men and women wear the white *mundu* or cloth with a narrow coloured border. A touch of gold thread with a *chutti*, an arrow-like design at the upper and lower corners, is the most traditional style. For marriages and special occasions the *kasavumundu* in unbleached cotton is worn. Here the border is an 8–11 cm (3–4 in) broad strip of pure *zari* or gold thread which sets off the fine 100 x 120 count cream-coloured handloom cotton body of the fabric. The upper garment or *angavastram* is another cloth of the same kind, which when worn together looks like a *sari* without the frontal pleats. Weaving areas are around Palakkad and Thiruvananthapuram.

LEFT: village crafts range from elaborate stiching and embroidery to brick making.
RIGHT: a female potter, Karnataka.

Andhra Pradesh

Andhra is predominantly a textile-producing state where a variety of silk and cotton fabrics are woven by more than 600,000 weavers. The number has dwindled considerably for economic reasons, but the handloom weaves are still vibrant and plentiful. Three decorative processes connected with textiles are very much a part of the Andhran tradition. The first is the patterning done by resist-dyeing or tie-dyeing the yarn prior to weaving. The pre-conceived pattern emerges as the yarn is woven, and the edges of the motifs and figures have a "spread" or "flame" effect. Chirala and Pochampalli are the best-known

areas for these *ikat saris*. Bold geometric designs of birds, animals and flowers set in squares with borders and end pieces are woven in both cotton and silk. The *rumal,* square like a scarf, in red, black and white, is a well-known loom product of Andhra Pradesh. There is an old tradition of pre-soaking the yarn in oil and alkaline earth for some days which gives to the scarf a distinctive aroma and also the local name of *telia,* or oily, *rumal.*

The second and most common form of ornamenting textiles is to create a pattern by changing the colour of the yarn during weaving, and by elaborate forms of placement of the warp and weft to create motifs and varied textures. Siddipet, Dharmavaram, Narayanpet and Gadwal *saris* are among the rich and vivid textiles embellished with gold thread at the borders and end panels. In a variety of counts from thick to superfine, in checks, stripes and solid colour, these *saris* emerge from the small huts and worksheds dotted across the countryside. Men sit at the loom for over 8 hours a day, while the women and children assist in pre- and post-loom tasks such as stretching or dyeing the yarn, or washing and finishing the yards of fabric. The click and clatter of the loom, the brilliant hanks of yarn hanging about them, and the confidence in the skill at their fingertips are the more beautiful moments of their otherwise harsh existence.

Kalamkari is a hand-painted fabric which derives its name from the word *kalam* for pen and *kari* for work. Outlines of birds, trees, creepers and flowers are block-printed and then painted in with a "pen" made of a bamboo stick padded at one end with cotton cloth. Kalamkari is produced in Machilipatnam and Kalahasti; the latter is well known for its temple hangings depicting scenes from religious epics and legends. Here, too, the outlines are hand-painted with pigments from local plants and flowers. The traditional colours of ochre, soft pink, indigo, madder red and iron black are the characteristic tints of Kalamkari fabric. The traditional temple cloths are more ornate and exquisite and serve as decorative items, while the repeat-design fabric is used for furnishings and garments.

Nirmal is the name of both the location and the craft practised in a part of Adilabad district. Using dyes made of local ingredients to create scenes from the *Mahabharata* and *Ramayana*, ornate table tops, boxes and trays are produced. A deep and attractive coloured wood found in the Tirupati area is red sanderswood, locally known as *raktachandan*, from which dolls and household articles like bowls and dishes are now made, as well as religious figures. Venkatesvara, the deity of the nearby Tirupati temple (a famous centre of pilgrimage), and Krisna in his most popular and recognisable attributes are some of the figures carved in this tough but elastic wood. Special chisels such as the *valu uli* and *gubba uli* are used to carve the different features of the body. The man-woman pair of dolls with distinct clothes and ornaments are among the more whimsical toys.

Kondapalli, a little village in Krishna District, produces a fascinating range of wooden toys depicting the lives of the people. Village life is captured in scenes of a variety of fruit and vegetables, a woman cooking or pounding grain, a washerman at work, a man climbing a palm tree and an incredible range of weavers carrying out 13 different weaving processes.

Ettikopakka in Visakhapatnam District creates bright lacquer toys made on hand- or machine-operated lathes. A lac stick is pressed against the wooden toy as it turns on the lathe; the friction created produces enough heat to melt the lac and make the colour stick.

Art and craft forms in local idioms usually developed as adjuncts to different modes of worship of local temple deities, as in shadow theatre using ornamental painted leather puppets, locally called *tolu bomalatta*. Made of translucent skin (goat, cow or deer), coloured with bright dyes in red, pink, brown, green and black and ornamentally perforated, the two-dimensional puppets take the shape of mythological characters from the *Ramayana* and *Mahabharata*. They are manipulated by bamboo sticks against a cloth screen behind which flickering oil lamps create a vibrant backdrop. Drum-beats and narration complete the setting for this traditional theatre. The theatre puppets can be as tall as 1.5 metres (5 ft).

In their appearance and attire the Lambadis make a striking contrast to the rural Telugu people in the areas surrounding Bijapur. Their bright red, black and yellow skirts, blouses and head cloths, richly decorated with Banjara embroidery and flashing mirror pieces, resemble the style of the nomadic peoples of Rajasthan and Gujarat. Strips of coloured fabric are joined together in a patchwork, with white thread, and embellished with glass beads and shells. Banjara embroidery is being adapted to bags, cushions, belts and quilts for the urban market.

Carpet-weaving has come to be generally associated with Kashmir and other parts of northern India; but the South has its own tradition in the Deccan rugs of Eluru and Warangal, established in the 17th century when artisans moved south with the Mughal army. They are a type of flat-weave *durri* with geometric designs of Persian origin known by the old Mughal name of *shatrangi*, with other names of local origin used for central and border designs. Some are named after Telugu patrons of the carpet industry such as Ramchandra Khani and Gopalrao Khani. This comes from the old Persian practice in which designs were given poetic names like "Shah Nawaz" and "Gulbanthi". The colours are light, with a later introduction of delicate floral patterns on a cream-coloured ground. Carpet-making survives in this area as it has a twin tradition of weaving and cotton-growing to support it.

Karimnagar is known for its fine silver filigree work, in which silver is pressed or moulded into trellis, creeper and leaf patterns to produce jewellery with a lacy effect. It needs deft fingers to twist and set the tiny components together, for which Karimnagar's silversmiths have devised an interesting method. The late Kamaladevi Chattopadhyay, the most prominent leader of the crafts revival movement in India, has described how little strips are cut "from a sheet of alloy of silver and copper known as *tankam*, that are spread to make up the entire design, then placed on a furnace. Then well-heated dry paddy husk is sprinkled on it and it bursts into flame and melts the *tankam* pieces. The molten *tankam* penetrates into crevices and ensures the firm binding together of the little bits that form the components. The block is then cooled in cold water." The most well-known item of Karimnagar filigree work is its perfume containers.

Pembarthi in northern Andhra Pradesh has long been the home of a special kind of repoussé brasswork from the Kakatiya dynasty. The styles and forms are similar to the work seen in the temples of Lepakshi and Ramappa. Large vases, pots and wall panels are distinctive of its products.

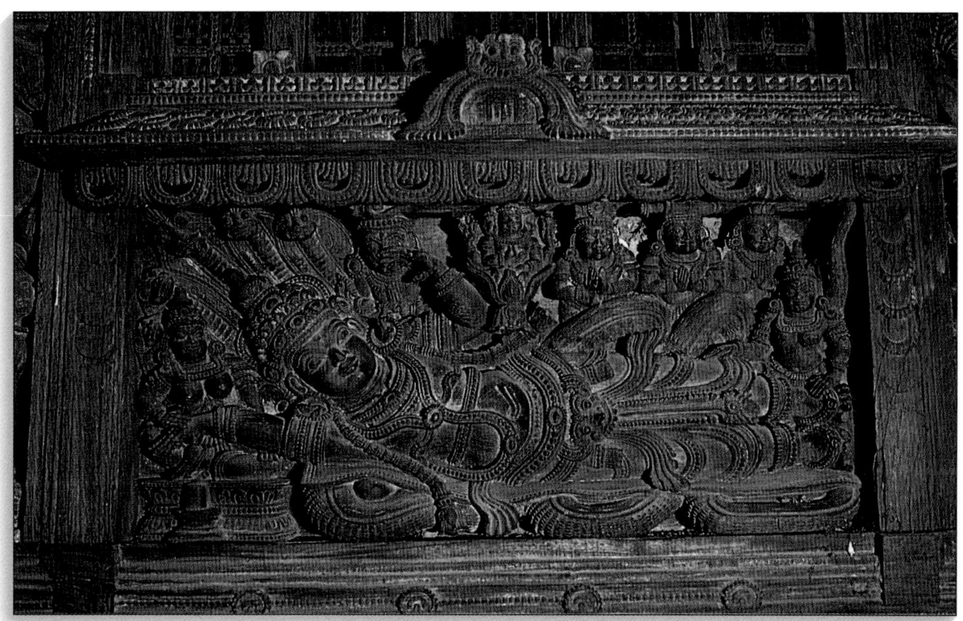

LEFT: repousse work.

ABOVE: the wood carving tradition of Karnataka is very fine, as seen on this throne from Mysore.

The pearl market flourishes to this day in Hyderabad, and Hyderabadi jewellers often use uncut stones in their jewellery, giving it a distinct appearance. Also popular here are glass bangles set with glass stones and mirrors.

Bidriware (named after Bidar in Karnataka where it originated) is a craft of the Deccan and consists of an alloy of zinc, copper, lead and tin with an inlay of fine silver wire on its blackened surface. This technique dates back to the Bahmani dynasty and was patronised by the Mughal rulers whose Persian heritage accounts for the floral and geometric patterns. Popular articles include vases, boxes and decorative plates.

Karnataka

The Belur and Halebid temples are exquisite examples of the tradition of stone-carving developed during the Hoysala period. The quiet atmosphere of these old temples accentuates the images prolifically carved on their walls. There is symphony of movement and music, as gods, goddesses, musicians, dancers, chariots and charioteers swarm across the walls of dark grey stone which glistens almost black, after a light drizzle of rain.

Karnataka's present-day stone workers have neither kingdoms nor patrons to work for, so they turn to carving facsimiles of old statues. Oil lamps for prayer rooms, spice containers and miniature kitchen utensils as toys for children are still made. But unfortunately the old glory has gone, since stone friezes have a limited market in today's world.

Among artisans, wood and stone carvers are considered of the same status and caste. The *Shilpasastras* prescribe the kind of wood required for a particular image, the auspicious time and season for felling a tree and for propitiating the resident spirit. Religious significance is imbued in those crafts which require a high degree of skill.

Karnataka wood carvers of the Visvakarma community use ebony, rosewood and sandalwood for precise and elaborate work. Once the visitor has passed the ubiquitous trail of wooden elephants that invariably emerges as the most typical example of Karnataka's crafts, they will see the versatility of woodcraft trays, boxes, statues, fans and other objects. The charm of sandalwood is in its aroma, golden colouring and velvety feel. It is possible to be duped by counterfeit pieces – ordinary wood dipped for a while in sandal perfume – but the real thing is well worth the high price tag. Sandalwood artisans, called *gudigars*, obtain their wood from the forests of Karnataka. Rosewood is dark brown, with a deep red glow. This is inlaid with pieces of lighter coloured wood to form geometric or pictorial decoration. Dwindling forests put up the costs of raw materials, posing a problem for many woodworkers, who turn to lower-quality substitutes and plastic inlay. The past glory of the woodcarver can be seen on the doorways and wall panels of old temples and in coastal Karnataka, where wooden figures are worshipped by local communities.

Toy making is an important part of Indian handicrafts. Festival toys, educational toys, religious toys and toys of pure whimsy are all part of the widespread and varied toy tradition. On the way to Mysore from Bangalore is the small township of Chennapatna, a flourishing centre for lac-painted wooden toys. It was the capital of the region in the 16th century and the Chitragar artisan community excelled in the manufacture of delightful sets of miniature cooking vessels complete with mortar, pestle and rolling pin. That this is not a static tradition can be seen in the toy aeroplanes and telephones, and the balls, rattles and other toys made for a growing export market.

Saris in silk with gold thread are a speciality of Bellary. The *irkal sari* and blouse pieces in bright coloured handlooms are produced in the villages of Irkal and Galedgudda in Bijapur district. The Dharwar *sari* is an earthy cousin in cotton with distinct contrasting borders, sometimes in silk. The borders have the *rudraksha* pattern imitating the pitted dark red seed used to make necklaces of auspicious significance. Tiny spokes or spires representing temples are also frequently used to define the edge in border designs.

A special embroidery called *kasuti* is done on deep blue, green and brown Dharwar *saris* in the Hubli area. A fine and distinctive stitch used to create peacocks, elephants, temples, the *tulsi* plant (basil) and even cradles, *kasuti* consists of cross and zigzag running stitches using only single or double threads. The motifs spread themselves sparsely on the main body of the *sari* and collect in a close cluster nearer the *pallu* or end border.

Thick cottons with broad borders in brilliant reds, ochres, greens, blues and browns reflect the heritage of the everyday *sari* which, for convenience in the fields, must be of a colour and width that does not soil easily. These are the styles most popular among those who belong to the movement for the revival of handlooms. Apart from the fine fabrics, flat-woven floor rugs in brilliant primary colours and geometric designs are produced in Navalgund.

LEFT: a silk *sari* being woven in a workshop in Kanchipuram.
RIGHT: the finished result.

Silk

The silks of Karnataka are lustrous and vivid, emerging, as everywhere else, from the tiny huts where handloom weavers repeat patterns embedded in their aesthetic memory. During the Vijayanagara Empire the prosperity of weavers reached its zenith. The community known as

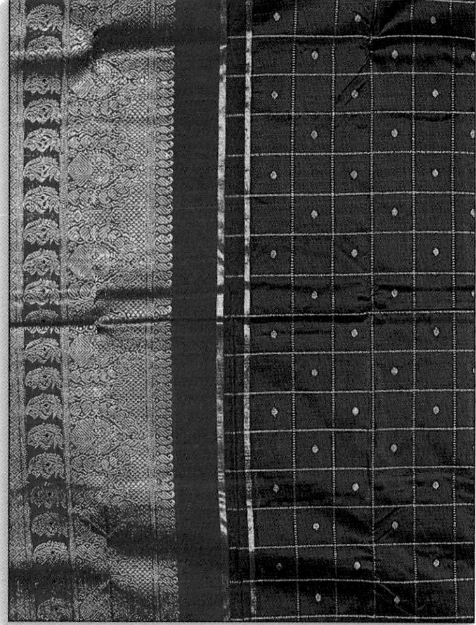

Saliya weavers have a lullaby which describes the child's forefather as creating his weaves on a loom that had a silver plank and a rope made of a costly bronze alloy. The range of silks, both in *saris* and in fabric length, attracts many trousseau shoppers from the country.

Silk was considered a pure fabric, most appropriate for use on ceremonial occasions. Its lustre, softness and the richness of its natural colour gave it precedence over all other fabrics. Either white or natural coloured silk was worn by the Brahmans. Women wore bright colours and the darker hues were reserved for the Sudras, the lower castes. Silk was worn for rites of passage such as births or marriages, and offerings of finely woven silks were made to deities in temples. Silk has been woven in India for at least 3,500 years.

For generations before the advent of the powerloom and chemical dyes, the sons of the silk weavers of Bangalore would be taught to develop a feel for the fabric. The elders would show them how to fashion strings for their kites from leftover silk warp threads tied in weavers' knots. As they grew up, they learnt to make colours from vegetable dyes: yellow from powdered jackfruit wood, red from sandalwood tree bark, indigo from the indigo plant. Without graph paper to plot their designs

on, they learnt to weave the traditional motifs of elephants, peacocks, trees and flowers, in the traditional repeats.

Today weavers still use the traditional handloom, though dyes have moved on from their natural origins and are often chemical. Designs are no longer woven from memory (many are modern prints – especially on chiffon), and cotton weavers are switching to silk, since it pays much better and Karnataka silk is treasured all around the world, and over 7 million sq. metres (8.4 million sq. yds) are exported each year.

The beginnings of Karnataka's silk industry lie with Tippu Sultan, although silk had been used by the nobility for centuries before he cultivated it on any scale: there are references to silk clothing in the *Mahabharata* and *Ramayana*. Tippu Sultan was enamoured of its tactile opulence, its shimmering tones, its seductive fluidity. He recognised the potential of sericulture, with its high value and low volume, and as an export commodity which could be exchanged for arms and ammunition to fuel his war machine.

After much searching, his envoys found a South Chinese species of silkworm producing a yellowish yarn, which they brought home to cultivate. Under the Sultan's supervision sericulture flourished in Bangalore, Kollegal, Channapatna and Dodballapur, and Mysore.

The Depression of the 1930s hit sericulture. The industry recovered during World War II, when Karnataka's silk was suddenly in demand again, this time for parachutes. Since the War, the silk industry has grown to the extent that today Karnataka produces about 5,317 tonnes of yarn annually, about 65 percent of India's total output. About 70 percent of this is consumed by the other states, so that many of the splendid *saris* from Varanasi, Kanjivaram and Lepakshi are in fact woven from Karnataka yarn.

There are basically five kinds of silk: soft silk, crepe, georgette and chiffon, dupion and spun silk. The first three are distinguished on the basis of the twist count of their yarns. Twisting of fibres strengthens yarns and varies texture. Yarns used for soft silk bestow a smooth finish and are more lustrous than the high-twist yarns which create the textures of crepe and georgette. Dupion yarn is reeled from two cocoons, which gives the fabric its coarse, slubbed surface. It is often erroneously referred to as raw silk. Spun silk is spun like cotton from the waste left when yarn is reeled. It figures a great deal in furnishing fabrics, like the Channapatna variety woven into carpets.

Traditional *saris* are still woven from soft silk. These have an appeal that goes beyond the beauty of the fabric; it derives from colours and motifs particular to each style. Geographical and climatic circumstances shaped the evolution of most regional styles. Molkalmuru in north Karnataka is one area where the environment has played its part in how the craft developed. In the arid region where the village is situated, frequent drought compelled many farmers to look to other livelihoods; weaving, already a part-time occupation, was the natural choice. This combined with other factors formed the nucleus around which weavers from other areas were drawn to settle down in Molkalmuru.

The silk weavers of Bangalore come from the Devanga community which traces its origins to the Vijayanagara period. They once wove angavastrams, the mantle used to clothe temple deities – hence *dev* (god) and *anga* (body). Traditional colours, designs and patterns prevail, although amidst them can be seen concessions to modernity. The Molkalmuru *sari* is one of contrasts in deep colours – red, indigo, snuff and pink.

The motifs used are to some extent general, such as the sacred *rudraksha* bead, the mango (familiar to us as paisley) and the lotus. Another symbol of veneration is the temple design where an architectural detail of the temple itself becomes a motif. Ornamentation is enhanced by gold thread, *zari*, used in the motifs and in various configurations on the *sari* body, border and *pallu* (the end piece of the *sari*), of stripes of diverse widths, checks, and the *butas* (dots).

In a craft with products so geographically diverse, what distinguishes one type of silk from another, apart from the motif and colour, are features like the way patterns are repeated, how the *pallus*, borders and bodies are connected, and even the way a *sari* is folded. Known as the silk capital, Kanchipuram is famous for the superb quality of its handmade silk *saris*.

The price of these *saris* is determined by weight and the content of gold or silver thread, used mainly in the intricate border and the *pallu* or the head piece. A *sari* usually weighs between 400–600 gms (15–21 ounces). The silk is dyed using natural pigments and woven into intricate but subtle patterns featuring motfis of birds or fruits.

The spinning process can be observed by visitors at a weavers' service centre. Weavers, once employed by royalty, still use many of the traditional methods. The inspiration that goes into every metre of silk in an age of mass production gives it a universal appeal.

The Coromandel coast, known for its trade in spices, was the doorway for the import and export of silks. Shimoga, Arasikere and Halebid were the great silk-producing areas in earlier times. Silk yarn produced here is supplied to weavers who have their own specific range of colours, border design and motifs according to the district and area of work. ❑

LEFT: a man makes coir mats in Kochi.
ABOVE: coir (coconut fibre) being spun into rough yarn for weaving.

MUSIC AND DANCE

The distinct and fascinating performing arts of the South range from exciting temple and concert musics to vibrant dance-dramas

South India offers a variety of performing arts for the visitor to savour. It has a great tradition of classical music and dance and is home to rich local traditions as well.

The classical music of South India is known as Karnatak music, sometimes written as Carnatic music, which may give the wrong impression that it is the music of Karnataka. Karnatak music has grown from the same roots as the classical music of the North, known as Hindustani music, but has developed on distinctly different lines over the last several centuries.

The fundamentals

The classical musics of South Asia use a basic collection of seven notes *(svara)* within an octave – *sa, ri, ga, ma, pa, dha, ni, (sa)* – which roughly correspond to the Western doh, re, mi etc., and which also have upper and lower ("sharp" and "flat") variants. However, they differ radically from Western pitches by not having a fixed value; for example, *sa* is fixed at a convenient level (higher or lower) for each individual musician, to suit an instrument, or his or her voice. Also essential to an understanding of Karnatak music are the twin concepts of *raga* and *tala*.

Raga (from the Sanskrit for "colour") designates which notes it is permissible to play during the performance of a piece, and also (as different *ragas* share the same collection of notes) characteristic phrases and "ornamentations". In the South, *ragas* are classified according to their place in a scheme of 72 *melakartas*, or "parent *ragas*", from which all other *ragas* are derived. Often misrepresented as merely a "scale" or "mode", a *raga* is more than a lineally arranged group of pitches (although this is often the most convenient way of notating them), but also implies the approach the musician should take towards the *svara*.

LEFT: a *Teyyam* dancer from northern Kerala with elaborate face make-up.

RIGHT: a dancer accompanied by female musicians, from Srirangapatnam.

Tala (from the Sanskrit for "clapping") is the name for the repeating rhythmic cycles that underpin the metred sections of any Karnatak performance. Different *talas* consist of different numbers of beats *(aksaras)* which are classified as either "weak" or "strong", and the first beat of a cycle provides a reference point, not

only for the musicians, but also the audience. At a performance of Karnatak music it is common to see the audience collectively marking the cycle through claps and waves on strong and weak beats respectively.

Although sharing similar basic concepts of *raga*, *tala* and *svara*, Karnatak music differs quite considerably from the concert musics of the North, perhaps most evidently in its performance of fully composed pieces, a lesser degree of improvisation and an important tradition of devotional song. Also, Karnatak music has tended to be a Brahmanical tradition, as opposed to that of either the Muslim or lower-caste musicians of the North.

Compositions

The first Karnatak compositions are generally held to be those of the Tallapakam composers, Annamacharya, Peda Tirumalacharya and Chinnanna (father, son and grandson), of the 15th–16th century. They are remembered for their Telugu *kirtanas* (devotional songs), written in the tripartite form of *pallavi*, *anupallavi* and *caranam* (ABC) – the basic structure of much present-day Karnatak music. Although none of their actual melodies survive, many of their texts, which indicate the *raga* in which they are to be performed, have been preserved on copper-plate inscriptions.

At around the same time, Purandaradasa (1484–1564), known as the "father of Karnatak music", was writing his *kirtana*, following the old two-part form of *pallavi* and *caranam*. Some of his melodies have survived and are still sung in concerts. However, he is chiefly famous for composing the basic exercises that all students of Karnatak music still learn.

These early composers were followed by the great "trinity" of Karnatak composers, Tyagaraja (1767–1847), Muttusvami Diksitar (1775–1835) and Syama Sastri (1762–1827), all of whom were born in the temple town of Tiruvarur in the Kaveri delta. Their compositions are generally thought by Karnatak musicians to be the finest in the repertory. They were primarily responsible for transforming the *kirtana* form into the *kriti* through the addition of composed variations known as *sangati*. Of the three, Tyagaraja was the most prolific and his compositions are the most popular. Each year, in honour of Tyagaraja, one of the largest South Indian music festivals is held on the banks of the River Kaveri near Thanjavur.

Karnatak music is overwhelmingly oriented towards vocal performance, especially with its emphasis on devotional texts. Other vocal forms often included in concerts include the *varnam* and *ragam-tanam-pallavi*. The latter form, in contrast to the devotional *kirtana* and *kriti*, stems from the musical traditions of the South Indian courts and is considered a great demonstration of technical skill. Comprising three sections, the *ragam* and *tanam* are unmetred and present the *raga* in a discursive manner, the third section takes a short composition, the *pallavi*, through a demanding series of melodic and metrical variations, all improvised.

Although Karnatak music differs greatly from that in the North by being dominated by through-composed songs, an improvisational element to the music is dominant during *alapana*, which is the elaboration of the *raga* prior to the start of the song proper; the *niraval* which consists of musical variations linked to the lyric; the *svara prastara*, which is the use of combinations of the *svara* syllables that are used especially to highlight the character of the song and the *raga*; and *tala vinyasa* or the segment of the concert handed over to the accompanying drums and idiophones.

Instruments

A Karnatak ensemble usually consists of a soloist, usually a singer but who may also be a *vina* (long-necked, plucked lute) player, accompanied by violin (introduced into Karnatak music in the 18th century by Muttusvami Diksitar's brother, Balusvami), *mrdangam* (double-headed barrel drum) and *tambura* (drone lute), now sometimes replaced by an electronic drone known as a *sruti*-box. The ensemble may be augmented by a *ghatam* (clay pot used as an idiophone), *kanjira* (small framedrum) and a *morsing* (jew's harp).

Within the ensemble the violin tracks the vocal line of the singer, providing what is akin to a melodic shadow to, and commentary on, the soloist's *svaras*. The *mrdangam* player performs a similar function in terms of rhythm, not merely giving form to the *tala* but also picking up and elaborating on rhythmic patterns provided by the soloist. If present the *ghatam*, *kanjira* or *morsing* player will tend to follow the lead of the *mrdangam*. The *tambura* not only provides a pleasing background wash of sound but is also essential in establishing the tonic, *sa*, for both the musicians and audience.

Violinists and flautists (playing the South Indian *venu*) often appear as a soloist, occasionally in a pair, and various other more unusual instruments (such as mandolin, saxophone and guitar) have also gained acceptance as solo instruments as Karnatak musicians explore new avenues. However, traditionally the principal solo instrument of Karnatak music is the *vina*. This fretted lute (which also has an unfretted version known as a *gottuvadyam*) is considered a "complete" instrument as it is able to provide its own accompaniment and sense of *tala* through a series of drone strings that are played with the little finger on the right hand and which mark the major divisions of the *tala*.

LEFT: a *centa melam* ensemble of oboes *(kuzhal)* and drums *(centa)* from Kerala.

RIGHT: a young *vina* player in Thiruvananthapuram.

Local, temple and popular musics

Local performance traditions in South India are usually associated with life-cycle and calendrical rituals, and also village festivals, often for local goddesses. Although they might be thought of as "rural" genres, they can still be encountered in urban areas. Births, deaths and weddings are all accompanied by music, particularly by women singing. Marriage processions are usually accompanied by bands, traditionally playing oboes and drums, but now more commonly by brass bands playing covers of film songs. Funerals have traditionally been accompanied by low-caste drummers.

Music and dance play an important part in local religion and ritual and are used to accompany festivals such as *Pongal* and the yearly *Ganapati puja*. At other times people gather in temples to collectively sing *bhajans* or *kirtana* (devotional songs).

In South Asia musical sound, *nada*, is considered to be intrinsically auspicious, and hence its widespread use in ritual and to accompany religious festivals. In South Indian temples, processions of the deities are accompanied by the *periya melam* ensemble of *nagasvaram* (oboe) and *tavil* (barrel drum). The Minaksi temple in Madurai is a good place to hear *periya melam* music.

Special mention should be made of Keralan temple music traditions. Temple festivals and processions are accompanied by either the *pancavadyam* (literally "five instruments") or the *centa melam* ("*centa* ensemble"). The *pancavadyam* is a large ensemble made up of five different instruments: *maddalam* (barrel drums), *timila* (hourglass drums), *itaykka* (tension drums), *kompa* (large, curved trumpets) and cymbals. The *centa melam* includes *centa* (cylindrical drums), *kompa*, cymbals and *kurum kuzhal* (small oboes). Performances can last a long time and consist of loud ensemble sections interspersed with solos and duets.

The popular music of South India most commonly encountered by visitors, indeed almost constantly, is *filmi*, or film, music. Following the conventions of traditional theatre the action in films is broken up by songs and dances that serve to push the action forward and represent the passing of time. These songs quickly gained great popularity.

The singers in the early films were the actors and actresses themselves, but when recording technology allowed the songs to be dubbed in the late 1930s, most songs became prerecorded and specialists, known as "playback singers", took over. Film song is phenomenally popular and playback singers have become musical superstars. Music directors (film song composers) draw on an eclectic range of sources, from traditional *bhajans* (devotional songs), to South American genres, to modern Western rock and pop.

Dance

There is a great variety in the dances performed in the South. *Bharata-natyam*, now almost a symbol of Tamil culture, predominates, but other dance forms have achieved classical status and varying degrees of popularity in recent decades, these include *Kuchipudi*, *Kathakali* and *Mohini Attam*.

The classical dances of southern origin are, of course, complemented by a variety of local traditional dances. Like local musical traditions, many of these dances are linked to the passage of the seasons and the celebrations of key events in community life such as harvests and religious festivals.

Classical dance is broadly divided into *nrtta* and *nrtya*. *Nrtta* refers to abstract movement to music, while *nrtya* is the use of movement and facial expression to convey emotion. Movement is also divided into two types, *anga*, the movement of the torso, head, arms and legs, and *upanga*, facial expression. The close relationship between dance and sculpture can be seen in the shared system of poses, based on *sutra* (the vertical and horizontal planes) and *bhanga* (the bending of the body).

Bharata-natyam

This is the most popular South Asian dance style, which, although originating in Tamil Nadu, is now taught and performed across India as well as overseas. Its origins lie in Tamil temple dance and it has been a concert form since the early 20th century.

Until the early 1930s, this dance form was known as Sadir or Dasiattam and was virtually the preserve of a caste or community of musicians and dancers in the service of temples. The men were musicians or dance masters. The female hereditary temple dancers *(devadasis)* took part in rituals in praise of the temple deity and were considered "married" to the god. This made them auspicious women as they could never become widowed. They would also be the sexual partners of the temple priests and local king (sponsor of the temple). It was this aspect of their duties that outraged Victorian sensibilities and an "anti-nautch" (from the Sanskrit *naca*, "dance") was started – largely by middle-class Indians who had taken on the social mores of the colonial power. This culminated in the 1947 *Madras Devadasi (Prevention of Dedication) Act*, which effectively banned temple dancing.

At the same time as the anti-nautch campaign sought to ban dance in the temples, growing Indian nationalism was seeking to legitimise claims for independence by presenting elements of South Asian culture as evidence of a strong national identity. Tamil temple dance was seized on as a perfect example and, led by the Brahman dancer and teacher Rukmini Devi, moves were made to establish a "pure" form of the dance on the stage – the result was present-day *Bharata-natyam*. The dancer who first helped Bharatanatyam to acquire international stature and conferred pride on the community of traditional dancers was the late T. Balasaraswati, known widely and simply as Bala. In its present form, the dance largely follows a format developed by four brothers, known collectively as the Thanjavur quartet. Like the musical "trinity", they were natives of the Thanjavur district in the delta of the river Kaveri.

A traditional recital always begins with an invocation or a floral offering to a deity, usually the elephant-headed Ganapati, the god who removes all obstacles. The sequence that follows consists of *alarippu, jatisvaram, sabdam, varnam, padams* and *javalis, tillana* and *sloka*.

Alarippu, based on rhythm alone, is pure dance. The concentration on rhythm helps to free the dancer from distractions and prepare her for the presentation ahead. In *jatisvaram*, a melody is added to the rhythm, but without words or syllables. *Sabdam*, with lyrics added to the melody and rhythm, represents the next stage in the performance. The dancer now seeks to interpret the words and their meanings as well. The *varnam* is the central section of the recital. According to Bala "This is the place which gives the dancer scope to revel in the rhythm, moods and music of the dance." In *padams* and *javalis* and other compositions which follow the *varnam*, the emphasis lies on the interpretation of mood through *abhinaya*. In the *tillana*, the dancer reverts to pure rhythm, prior to concluding the programme on a note of prayer. However, not all *Bharata-natyam* artists today follow this sequence, although the majority still do.

LEFT: a temple *periya melam* ensemble consisting of *nagasvaram* (oboe) and *tavil* (drum).
RIGHT: a *Bharata-natyam* dancer.

Kuchipudi and Yaksagana

Kuchipudi had its origin as a temple dance in a village of the same name in Krishna-Godvari Delta in Andhra Pradesh. Historically it was – and to some degree continues to be – a vehicle for presenting scenes from Hindu epics and mythological tales through dance-dramas combining music, dance and acting. It is said to have been invented somewhere between 1350–1450 by Sidhyendra, a Telugu Brahman. It takes its themes from the *Parijatapaharana*, the story of Krisna and his consort Satyabhama, and the *Golla Kalapam*, a philosophical discussion between a milkmaid and a Brahman. Traditionally, all these parts were played by male dancers though today women also dance Kuchipudi. Over the years, teachers and choreographers – among them Vempati Chinna Satyam – have changed the presentations a great deal and-*Kuchipudi* dance dramas and recitals now generally consist of a series of solo dances.

The lyrics used in *Kuchipudi* are usually in Telugu, though Sanskrit verses are also not uncommon. While *Kuchipudi*, like *Bharata-natyam*, comprises pure dance and mime, it is the use of speech as well that distinguishes its presentation as dance-drama. Also, while the basic technique of *Kuchipudi* is similar to that of *Bharata-natyam*, it does have a distinct identity. According to one observer, *Bharata-natyam* is "restrained and perhaps geometric", while *Kuchipudi* is "freer, more flexible".

Kuchipudi dance-dramas each present a particular episode or a series of episodes. A solo recital, on the other hand, typically consists of such items as the *sabdam*, *bhama kalapam* which is the main item, *padams* and *tarangams*. In *bhama kalapam*, the dancer has enormous scope for the dramatisation of characters. The main character is Satyabhama, a beautiful but arrogant queen who goes through the process of discovering the path of true love and devotion. In the *tarangam*, the dancer frequently balances the feet on the edge of a brass plate.

Like *Kuchipudi*, the *Yaksagana* of Karnataka also fulfilled a social purpose. A musical play in form, it has traditionally served – and often extent still does – as a popular vehicle for tales drawn from myths and legends and presenting a moral, generally the victory of good over evil. With songs and verses employed for the narration of the themes, it is dramatic in nature. Yet, in contemporary presentations, the lyrics are often lost with the words of the songs are virtually drowned by loud drumming.

An interesting feature of *Yaksagana* is that the characters can speak, unlike, say, in *Kathakali*, giving experienced performers an opportunity to improvise and develop the dialogue. The dance element is less prominent than in some other genres. What is likely to capture the attention of a visitor are the costumes and make-up, which reflect the essential traits of the characters. The *Yaksagana* repertoire consists of the new as well as the old and there are more than 300 plays in existence, dating from the 16th century. The best plays of *Yaksagana* are performed by a few temple troupes.

Kathakali and Kutiyattam

Kathakali is to Kerala what *Bharata-natyam* is to Tamil Nadu. It has been described as "one of the most magnificent theatres of the imagination". While owing much to ancient Sanskrit drama, it has during its history absorbed many other elements of ritual, some local such as *Teyyam*, and of Keralan martial arts (specifically *Kalaripayattu*). *Kathakali* is a highly stylised dance-drama which presents stories from the *Ramayana*, the *Mahabarata* and other Hindu epics, myths and legends. The dance aspect consists of pure dance as well as mime.

What is striking about *Kathakali* is the emphasis given to *aharya-abhinaya*, the use of elaborate costumes, ornaments and facial makeup. This, according to one observer, helps to transform the dancer into a type rather than a character. According to the qualities that they represent, the characters fall into five main types, and the makeup illumines these types (green stands for good, red for evil and white for a deity). Because of the heavy make-up the *Kathakali* dancer has to use his eyes very expressively to convey even the most subtle expressions.

Kathakali makes strenuous demands on its exponents, dance critic Sunil Kothari notes this is because "it is the only dance form in which the entire body, both skeleton and muscles, down to even the smallest facial muscle, are used to portray emotion."

The same noted commentator, Kothari, observes: "The actor in *Kathakali* never speaks except with his hands. The text of the drama is sung for him and is the baseline for his interpretation. It is in histrionics or interpretive dancing that the *Kathakali* artist excels, the spectator's experience enhanced by the thrilling drum beats."

Allied to *Kathakali* is the Sanskrit drama *Kutiyattam*. This is the only continuing performance art that adheres closely to the precepts laid down in Bharata's *Natyasastra* (*circa* 4th century AD), the earliest extant treatise on music and drama. A temple art performed traditionally by a specific community, *Kutiyattam* embraces elements of music and dance as well as pure spoken drama. The performers use makeup similar to *Kathakali* but are permitted speech, albeit in a stylised manner. Because it is theatre committed to deep interpretation, it is often several days or even weeks before a *Kutiyattam* drama cycle is completed.

LEFT: a *Kuchipudi* dancer.
RIGHT: *Kathakali* involves the use of elaborate makeup and costumes.

Mohini Attam

Mohini Attam, also called the Dance of the Enchantress because it emphasises the seductive and graceful aspects of movement, was resurrected in the 1930s from virtual oblivion, A devotional dance form, *Mohini Attam* is not widely performed outside of Kerala although some leading performers today include those who are not natives of Kerala. Unlike other Keralan classical dances which are restricted to men, it is a solo female dance in which the striking feature is the rhythmical swaying of the dancer from side to side and the smooth and unbroken flow of body movement. The dance is focussed essentially on mood and emotion. ❑

CELEBRITY FILMS PVT.LTD.
PRESENT
RUSH HOUR
2
OSCAR FILMS (P) LTD.

CINEMA

The four South Indian states have collectively the largest film industry in the world, with a host of dedicated and adoring fans

The South Indian cinema, which began a generation after the first film was made in India, comprises the Tamil, Telugu, Kannada and Malayalam cinema.

For a long time Chennai – with the film studios at MGR Film City, famously entered through the jaws of an enormous shark *(see page 132)* – was the centre of film production in South India, and films in all four South Indian languages as well as some in Hindi were produced here. Chennai was next only to Mumbai in film production; in some ways, the studios in the South have a lot more to offer producers by way of technical facilities such as well equipped studios and organised production schedules. Generally speaking, today Telugu films are produced in Hyderabad, Kannada films in Banglore and Mysore, and a large number of Malayalam films in Thiruvananthapuram at the Chitranjali Studios. The largest of the South Indian industries is now in Hyderabad at the huge complexes of Ramanaidu Studios and Ramoji Film City. At times Telugu production has even beaten that of Bollywood (overall the South Indian film industry is larger than that of Hindi cinema).

The early years

The first film made in Tami Nadu was a silent movie called *Kicaka vadam*, by R. Nataraja Mudaliar in 1917. This proved to be a catalyst and there was soon a small but thriving industry in Chennai. These early silent films tended to be fairly racy, especially compared with what came later on. There was censorship, but this was mostly concerned with any political content, and there was plenty of flesh on display and "lip to lip" kissing. Notable male actors and directors included A. Narayanan and R. Prakash. Female actors tended to be drawn from the Anglo-Indian community though one Tamil-speaking actress, T.P. Rajalakshmi, went on to become a very successful producer and director, working up to the 1950s. The films were generally acompanied by two musicians, a harmonium player and a drummer, and the plot was explained by a speaker, who often became a star in their own right, who stood to the side of the screen.

LEFT: this towering movie advert in Chennai is handpainted.
RIGHT: a woman walks past a movie poster in Bangalore.

Silent film production was initially restricted to Tamil Nadu and the studios at Saidapet. However, *Marthanda Varma*, completed in 1928 and based on a well-known novel, was the first film to be made in Kerala. This is now the only surviving South Indian silent film.

The arrival of the talkies

In 1931 the first sound films were made in India: *Alam Ara* in Hindi, *Kalidas* in Tamil and *Bhakta Prahalada* in Telugu. All three were produced in Mumbai (then Bombay), the South had to wait until 1934 before A. Narayanan built the Srinivasa Cinetone sound studio in Chennai. *Kalidas* (directed by H.M. Reddi) was not completely in Tamil – the female star, Rajalakshmi, sang and spoke in Tamil, while the male lead used Telugu.

H.M. Reddi also directed *Bhakta Prahalada*, which is all in Telugu; in both films are the two essential ingredients of Indian cinema, namely music and dance. This also marked the beginning of the rise of the music director (composer and song writer) as a star (the music for *Bhakta Prahalada* was written by Chantala Kesava Das and H.R. Padmanabha Sastri). The first completely-Tamil talkie *Galavarisi* (1932, directed by Badami and T.C. Vadivelu Naicker) was the first film that famous music director G. Ramanathan worked on, while *Sitakalyanam* (1933) not only saw the Karnatak musician Papanasam Sivan make his debut as music director but also the 6-year-old S. Balachandar make his acting debut (he later went on to become one of the greatest of all Karnatak *vina* players).

It was not at all unusual for famous singers trained and working in the "classical" world to sing for the movies. The great Telugu music director S. Rajeswara Rao wrote the music for the 1930s hit *Illalu* in which the songs were performed by R. Balasaraswati. While one of the greatest singers of the 20th century, M.S. Subbulakshmi, started her career singing for the 1938 Tamil film *Sevasadanam*.

The "golden age"

Once the talkies had been established in the South there was an explosion of film making, with some films and stars earning huge amounts of money. In 1934 the Tamil *Bhama Vijayam* by Mani Lal Tandon was the first film to gross 1 million rupees, while K.B. Sundarambal, star of the 1935 film *Nandanar*, was the first actor to be paid 100,000 rupees, an enormous fee in those days. Other important Tamil stars of the 1930s include K. Subramaniam, who became a very successful film maker, and the husband and wife team, N.S. Krishnan and T.A. Maturam, who appeared in many films. However, perhaps the greatest Tamil star of the period was Thyagaraja Bhagavathar, both as an actor and singer. His 1937 hit *Chintamani* (directed by Y.V. Rao, who also directed a number of hit Telugu movies, and with music by Papanasam Sivan) ran for over a year.

Along with emerging superstar directors, actors and music directors, this period also saw the rise of the "movie moghul". The two most important of these were S.S. Vasan and A.V. Meyyappan who were to dominate Tamil cinema for decades. Meyyappan was responsible for the first instance of "dubbing", a technique that revolutionised the Indian cinema industry. Although the Kannada film industry (at this time based in Chennai) was still comparatively small, it was a popular Kannada film *Harichandra* (1943) that V.S. Raghavan and Meyyappan used to replace the original soundtrack with a Tamil one. With so many regional languages this proved to be phenomenally successful and films are routinely dubbed from one language into another.

Throughout the 1940s and 1950s the South Indian cinema industry continued to grow and important studios outside of Chennai began to develop, particularly with the building of Saradhi Studios in Hyderabad. Although mythological and straightforward, family-based love stories still dominated the studios' output, a number of action movies achieved considerable success, a trend that was to come to fruition in the 1970s and 1980s. Notable among these was the Tamil *Malaikkallan* (1954) which starred M.G. Ramachandran *(see below)*. This film was so successful it was dubbed into Telugu, Kannada, Malayalam and Hindi. Another very important film was *Parasakti* (1952) which launched the career of the Tamil superstar Shivaji Ganesan, who has starred in an huge number of films.

Politics and cinema

Cinema has had such a hold on the South Indian population that a number of actors have used it as a springboard into regional and national politics. M.G. Ramachandran, popularly known as "MGR", who acted in a large number of Tamil films as a swashbuckling conquering hero, later became the Chief Minister of Tamil Nadu. Jayalalitha, another famous actress, was his protege and later his successor.

Tamil cinema grew along with the Dravidian movement, a powerful political force that swept away the Indian National Congress from the state. The first Dravidian Party (the DMK) chief minister, the late C.N. Annadurai, as well as his immediate successor, M. Karunanidhi, were film scriptwriters with large followings within the cinema-going public. The political animosity between Jayalitha (of the splinter AIADMK) and Karunanidhi (of the DMK) is still the driving force in Tamil politics.

The situation has been similar in Andhra Pradesh, where N.T. Rama Rao (known as "NTR") was chief minister for 10 years for his Telugu Desam Party (the TDP). His film roles – usually Hindu gods in devotional films called "mythologicals" – were, and continue to be, extremely popular with Telugu audiences. He first made his mark in the 1940s in *Manadesam*, while his later movies, such as *Sri Krisna Pandaveda*, were enormous hits. As in Tamil Nadu, NTR has spawned a dynasty with his son-in-law, Chandrababu Naidu, becoming his heir in the TDP, ruling the state as chief minister before being voted out of office in 2004.

The "New Wave"

Malayalam film-makers have tended to follow India's "New Wave", inspired by the great Bengali director Satyajit Ray. Significant landmarks in the history of Malayalam cinema include *Nilakukil*, based on a story by the novelist Urub. The film, by P. Bhaskaran and Ramu Kariyat, had beautiful shots of the Keralan countryside. This was followed by *Chemin* in 1965, directed by Ramu Kariat, and based on a well-known novel. The writer M.T.Vasudevan Nair has not only written screenplays but also directed films, including the superb *Nirmalayam* of 1973 starring P.J. Antony. Other notable Malayalam films include *Utharayanam*, on India's freedom struggle, and *Chidambaram* (1985) by Aravindan. His films, with their subtle interplay of human emotions, have won a number of Indian and foreign awards. Films by directors Adoor Gopalakrishnan – *Swayamvaram* (1973), *Elipathayam* and *Mukhamukam* – and Shaji (*Piravi*, 1988) are also highly regarded. Kannada film-makers have also contributed to the New Wave, including films by B.V. Karanth. More recently the Kannada film *Shanti*, by Baragur Ramachandrappa has achieved considerable success.

LEFT: a street scene in Goa is recreated in the Chennai studios.
RIGHT: a Telugu cinema in Hyderabad.

Contemporary faces

The contemporary South Indian film industry now challenges the hegemony of Bollywood, partly on the back of such countrywide successes as the Telugu *Sankarabharanam* (1979). Kolly- and Tollywood (as the Chennai and Hyderabad industries are known) have seen stars such as the actors Sri Devi and Aishwarya Rai and music director A.R. Rahman achieve great success in Hindi cinema. South India cinema is dominated by the phenomally succesful music director Ilayaraja. Current superstar female actors include Sharada, Roja, Simran and Meena, while male actors include Rajanikant, Ajith Kumar, Prasanth and Kamal Hassan. ❑

PLACES

A detailed guide to the entire region, with principal sites cross-referenced by number to the maps

All four states of South India and the westerly Lakshadweep Islands lie within the steamy Tropic of Cancer. Perhaps that explains the slightly languid pace of life. Coconut palms lash the monsoon sky, coconut chutney quenches the fire of the curries, and coconut oil gleams in the hair of passers-by.

South Indian women twine fragrant jasmine blossoms into their hair. Patterns made from flower petals or crushed and coloured rice enhance the entrances of temples and households. Rice is the staple grain here, and people devour gargantuan heaps of the stuff from clean banana leaves. Sweet coffee rather than *chai* is normally offered, and pouring it dramatically at arm's length ensures a delicate foam.

Phrasebook Hindi, perhaps known to travellers familiar with the North, won't get you very far here, where the languages are Dravidian. Linguists would need Telugu in Hyderabad, Kannada in Bangalore, Tamil in Chennai, and Malayalam in Thiruvananthapuram. However, English is widely understood. English is an official government language, so that southern politicians who are loath to speak Hindi, a symbol of northern domination, can communicate with each other.

The vast Deccan plains, the stepped rainforests of the Ghats, and two long coastlines distinguish the south. With an overwhelmingly Hindu population, temples are truly colourful here: each deity is brushed with a vibrant hue and the steep templetops look as chaotic and crowded as a bazaar. Traces of pigment have been found on venerable carved stone temples, which used to be painted in the same way. Christian churches are especially numerous in the South, and the 16th-century Jesuit missionary Francis Xavier was surprised to find a thriving Christian congregation with links to the apostle St Thomas.

Kerala is noted for its elephants and a unique martial arts tradition. Hyderabad, the gateway to South India, has been famous since Marco Polo's time for the skills of its Islamic craftsmen and the grandeur of Golconda Fort. This glory is almost surpassed by Hampi, a deserted stone city in Karnataka. Bangalore's pubs are a meeting place for men in India's most forward-looking city. And Chennai, formerly Madras, values its heritage of music, dance and commerce. While it has retained its charm, the South has thrown off part of its slightly dreamy traditional image and is the driving force behind India's new technology and software industries. ❑

PRECEDING PAGES: the deserted Vijayanagara city of Hampi in Karnataka; Chinese fishing nets in Kochi, Kerala; the brightly painted *gopurams* of the Minaksi temple, Madurai, Tamil Nadu.

LEFT: a bullock cart makes its way through the countryside of Karnataka.

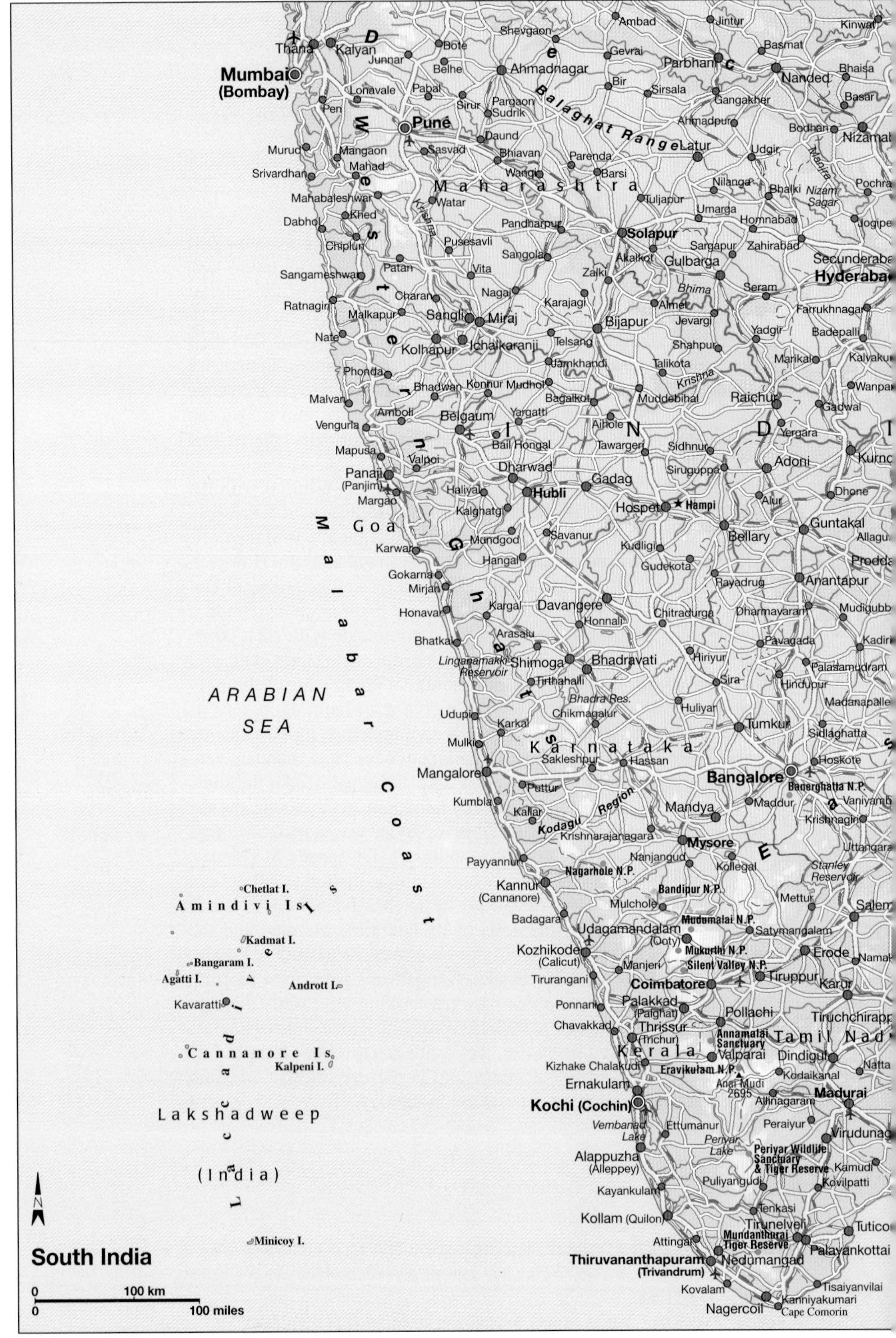
South India
Mumbai (Bombay)
Thana
Kalyan
Puné
Maharashtra
Western Ghats
Deccan
Balaghat Range
Ahmadnagar
Solapur
Gulbarga
Hyderabad
Secunderabad
Bijapur
Kolhapur
Sangli
Miraj
Belgaum
Dharwad
Hubli
Gadag
Hospet
Hampi
Bellary
Panaji (Panjim)
Margao
Goa
Karwar
Malabar Coast
Shimoga
Bhadravati
Davangere
Tumkur
Bangalore
Mysore
Mandya
Mangalore
Udupi
Karnataka
Kodagu Region
Kannur (Cannanore)
Kozhikode (Calicut)
Udagamandalam (Ooty)
Coimbatore
Palakkad (Palghat)
Thrissur (Trichur)
Kerala
Ernakulam
Kochi (Cochin)
Alappuzha (Alleppey)
Kollam (Quilon)
Thiruvananthapuram (Trivandrum)
Kovalam
Nagercoil
Kanniyakumari
Cape Comorin
Madurai
Tamil Nadu
Dindigul
Tirunelveli
Salem
Erode
ARABIAN SEA
Amindivi Is.
Chetlat I.
Kadmat I.
Bangaram I.
Agatti I.
Andrott I.
Kavaratti
Cannanore Is.
Kalpeni I.
Laccadive Is.
Lakshadweep (India)
Minicoy I.
Nagarhole N.P.
Bandipur N.P.
Mudumalai N.P.
Mukurthi N.P.
Silent Valley N.P.
Annamalai Sanctuary
Eravikulam N.P.
Anai Mudi 2695
Periyar Wildlife Sanctuary & Tiger Reserve
Mundanthurai Tiger Reserve
Banerghatta N.P.
0 100 km
0 100 miles

Bay of Bengal
INDIAN OCEAN
Coromandel Coast
Orissa
Madhya Pradesh
Andhra Pradesh
Eastern Ghats
Chennai (Madras)
Visakhapatnam
Vijayawada
Brahmapur
Vizianagaram
Srikakulam
Rajahmundry
Kakinada
Machilipatnam
Guntur
Ongole
Nellore
Tirupati
Vellore
Kanchipuram
Pondicherry
Cuddalore
Kumbakonam
Mayuram
Jaffna
Palk Strait
Palk Bay
SRI LANKA
Anuradhapura
Wilpattu National Park
AFGHANISTAN
PAKISTAN
CHINA
NEPAL
BHUTAN
BANGLADESH
BURMA (MYANMAR)
INDIA
Jammu and Kashmir
Himachal Pradesh
Punjab
Uttaranchal
Haryana
Delhi
Rajasthan
Uttar Pradesh
Bihar
Sikkim
Arunachal Pradesh
Assam
Nagaland
Meghalaya
Manipur
Tripura
Mizoram
West Bengal
Jharkhand
Gujarat
Madhya Pradesh
Chattisgarh
Orissa
Daman and Diu
Dadra and Nagar Haveli
Maharashtra
Andhra Pradesh
Goa
Karnataka
Tamil Nadu
Kerala
Lakshadweep (India)
Andaman and Nicobar Islands (India)
ARABIAN SEA
INDIAN OCEAN
SRI LANKA

TAMIL NADU

Huge temple complexes, cool hill stations and sandy beaches are just some of the attractions of this state

Tamil Nadu is situated at the southeastern end of the Indian peninsula. With an area of 130,000 sq km (50,000 sq miles) and a population of over 62 million, it is one of the country's larger states. The official language is Tamil, an ancient classical language with a rich body of literature.

Tamil Nadu has three distinct agro-climatic zones: the mountainous ridge of the Nilgiris that runs along its western boundary; semi-arid plains dependent on the monsoon and on tank and tube-well irrigation; and the alluvial Kaveri basin. Paddy, millet, sugar cane, pulse and bananas are the main crops, besides extensive coconut groves and tea and coffee plantations in the hills. The state has a long coastline with many beaches, estuaries and lagoons. The Marina beach in Chennai is reputed to be the second widest in the world. South India's major hill stations – Udagamandalam, or Ooty, Kotagiri and Coonoor – are all located in Tamil Nadu.

Tamil Nadu, as its official emblem indicates, is the temple state of India. The history of South Indian temple architecture and sculpture begins with the Pallavas who ruled large parts of South India from the dawn of the 5th century to the last quarter of the 9th century. The Cholas, who supplanted them and ruled till the middle of the 12th century, were also great temple builders. They added the concept of the *gopuram* or gateway to Dravidian temple architecture. In later years the ornate *gopurams* in the enclosed temple premises increased in number and size and sometimes overshadowed the main shrine. In addition, pillared halls and long colonnades were added to the temples built by the later Cholas and their successors, the Pandyas and Nayaks who ruled the far south from Madurai.

The British, too, left Tamil Nadu a rich architectural legacy in structures like Fort St George, and several Victorian Gothic buildings such as the Egmore railway station, the High Court, the Senate House and the San Thome church in Chennai. Since the British were longer in Tamil Nadu than anywhere else in India, there is a widespread familiarity with the English language, a convenience to visitors. Tamil Nadu is a rapidly changing state where the old and the new dwell harmoniously together: modern factories and offices along with Karnatak music and dance forms and a flourishing tradition of art and literature. ❑

LEFT: the Sucindram temple and tank, Kanniyakumari.

Map on page 122

CHENNAI

The South's largest city, a centre of Tamil identity, with early colonial architecture, a thriving music scene, and one of the largest and best museums in India

Chennai, formerly Madras, capital city of Tamil Nadu and "Gateway to the South", is many things to many people. One of India's four leading metropolises, this city of 180 sq km (70 sq miles) and 6.5 million people has been variously described as "The Queen of the Coromandel", "The First City of Empire", "City of Shrines", "City of Tradition and Culture", "City of Graciousness and Spaciousness", and even as "A Withered Beldame Brooding on Ancient Fame". It is this variety that makes Channai one of the most fascinating cities in India.

As Indian cities go, Chennai is not ancient. It was founded only 350 years ago, the first of the cities of Britain's Age of Empire. But as it grew, it took within its bounds many an ancient town and port of the Coromandel, and is today a curious amalgam of Coromandel – ancient, imperial and modern.

The Coromandel is India's southeastern coast. But in the past, when the Arabs, the Chinese, the Romans and the Greeks came to trade in its ports, and when Chola and Pallava kings took the culture of Hindustan from here to the lands now called Southeast Asia, there was no Chennai. That city was born in the age of modern trade where Vasco da Gama's explorations led.

The Portuguese and the Dutch, the British, the French and the Danes all sought the riches of Coromandel, its textiles and cordage, its dyes and timbers and spices, and the wealth of its hinterland. In fact, it was the quest for "excellent long cloath better cheape" that led to the founding of Chennai.

When British trading posts north of the area now called Chennai came under pressure from the Portuguese and the Dutch, Francis Day, an East India Company trader, and his local broker, the *dubash* Thimanna, sailed south to prospect for a better settlement. What the local governor of the declining Vijayanagara Empire was willing to part with was a sandy spit of surf-wrecked beach, 3 km (2 miles) long and 1.5 km (1 miles) across at its widest, protected on two sides by rivers and on the third by an angry sea. It was on that land grant of July 1639 that Day and his superior, Andrew Gogan, and their *dubashes* built a fortified "factory", which they christened on St George's Day, 23 April 1640 – Fort St George.

The tiny settlement, Britain's first Indian bastion, was the nucleus from which an empire grew. And Chennai played a central role in that growth. The city has contributed much to modern India and exploring the history of Chennai

LEFT: the Indo-Saracenic court buildings. **RIGHT:** school girls at the Kapalesvara temple, Mylapore.

makes that evident. As the circumstances of history have changed the face of a nation, the city has returned to its beginnings as the "Gateway to the South".

The relics of British rule in India are not all that remain in Chennai. Here are ancient legends and symbols of much older faiths, of cultural traditions and ways of life that have changed little over the centuries. Here is also a graciousness and a spaciousness that few metropolises in India possess. But that does not prevent Chennai from being a vibrantly alive city where the bustle of industry and commerce, politics and modern entertainment vie equally for the attention of the traveller. Chennai is rewarding for both its history and contemporary life.

Fort St George

Fort St George Ⓐ, where the city began, is perhaps the best place to begin an investigation of Chennai. Like most other forts in India, this one too is an ancient monument. But unlike in most of them, life flourishes within its walls during the day and even on Sundays – government and the military, the administration and churchgoers, all have something to do within its precincts.

A stroll through the Fort's walls reveals that its buildings look almost the same as when Clive and Pitt, Wellesley and Hastings lived and worked there. Much of Fort St George as it is today was built over 125 years, growing from one small rhombus-shaped building named Fort House by Cogan and Day, fortified by four walls into 17 hectares (42 acres) of streets, buildings and parade grounds. Outside its fortifications, the Fort developed another 23 hectares (58 acres) for its field of fire, much of which is parks and quarters now.

When the first major construction in the Fort began, a few years after its foundation, the designation of **Fort House** was conferred on another building constructed to the east of the original Fort House. That second Fort House, where the earliest governors of Chennai lived, is the oldest

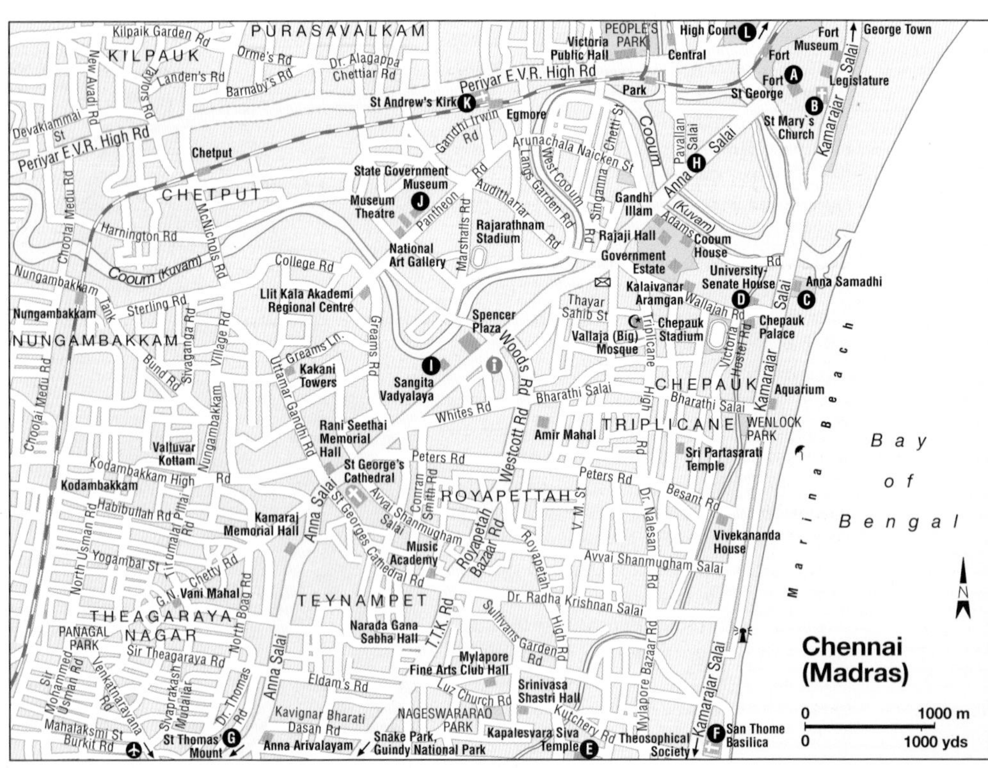

Map on page 122

surviving British construction in India. However, it survives as the core of a building that was expanded several times over the years. The last great additions in the early 20th century provided the **Secretariat** and **Legislature** of the Tamil Nadu Government with their handsome classical appearance, facades embellished with gleaming black pillars.

The main gates of the Fort today open on the Secretariat and the Legislature, whose splendid **Assembly Hall** may be visited with the permission of the Speaker's office. To the south of this handsome symmetrical block is the second oldest surviving British building in India and the oldest Protestant church in Asia, the historic **St Mary's Church** Ⓑ. Constructed in 1680, it is now an ancient monument tended carefully by both the Archaeological Department and an enthusiastic congregation.

It was first built as a rectangular box with an arched, cannonball-proof roof; the towers, steeples and curved flights of steps were added over the years to make it the St Mary's of today – in its tree-shaded setting, one of the loveliest monuments of the British rule in India. Part of its courtyard is paved with tombstones brought here from the British cemetery in Chennai, just north of the Fort. Amongst them is the tombstone of Elizabeth Baker, its inscription of the date of her death in 1652 making it the oldest British tombstone in India.

Within the wood-embellished, multipillared St Mary's are records and registers, tombs and memorials, paintings and silver plate, many commemorating key figures in British Indian history: Elihu Yale, the founder of the eponymous university, helped found the church, and was married in the building; Robert Clive married Margaret Maskelyne here; Job Charnock had his three daughters, of an Indian mother, baptised here before he went on to found Calcutta (present-day Kolkata); Arthur Wellesley was best man at a wedding here; and Warren Hastings and his future wife Marian worshipped here before they married. Everywhere in St Mary's are reminders of the men and women who put in place the conditions that led to 200 years of British rule.

Across the road and to the west of it is **Clive House**, an imperially handsome building in which Clive, one of the heroes of the Carnatic Wars, lived in 1753 with his bride. Next to it, and also part of government offices now, is what was known as **Writers' Building**, once lodgings for newly arrived writers (clerks) from England. Among them was Clive, and it was in this building that he made the first of his many attempts at suicide. Just a little to the south of these two handsome buildings is **Wellesley House**, its crumbling state a sad memorial to the man who was responsible for consolidating much of the British Empire in India.

Northwards are the Parade Grounds where many magnificent parades and rallies were held, before and after Indian Independence, as well as a multistorey, glass-and-concrete modern building. To the east is the later **Fort House** which the army maintains in 18th-century splendour,

RIGHT: the Valluvar Kottam.

and the **Fort Museum** (open Sat–Thur 10am–5pm, entrance charge).

Just by the museum and overlooking its cannon is the **Cornwallis Cupola**, moved from the Parade Grounds. A statue of Cornwallis greets visitors entering the museum. The museum, a treasure trove of British South Indian memorabilia, is housed in what was built as the **Public Exchange**. Warehouses and the city's first bank occupied the ground floor. On the first floor, what is now a wooden-floor art gallery was once the coffee shop where the merchants and officials of Chennai met daily for gossip, coffee and trade. Other items on display include coins, weapons and books.

To the southeast of the museum is the country's tallest flagpole, about 46 metres (150 ft) high, which goes back to 1687 when Governor Elihu Yale hoisted the first Union Jack over the first British settlement in India. Today the Indian tricolour flutters over its classically designed bastions and ramparts, with towering walls and massive wooden gates – a memorial to impregnability.

The Marina

One of the best ways to see Chennai is to follow the four roads that lead out of the Fort. First take the road south, to "ancient Meliapor" of which Camoens sang. Then move westwards to Anna Salai. Still further west is the ancient road running through Egmore to Poonamallee, whose governor deeded Chennai to "John Company". Finally, move north, to the newest of the four parts of the city.

The road south begins at **Fairlands**, by the War Memorial. Then begins **Marina** promenade with the beach drive which was developed 150 years ago by a Governor. Marina begins with the **Anna Samadhi** ❸ commemorating C.N. Annadurai, who led the Dravidian movement to political power and changed the social and political structure in Tamil Nadu. Beside it is a memorial to M.G. Ramachandran, a film star beloved of the

Map on page 122

masses, and Annadurai's main vote-getter. Almost a decade after his mentor's death, "MGR" came to power himself, the first film star to make it to the leadership of a state in India.

Another important aspect of Chennai begins across the road from the memorials. This part of the Chennai skyline is mainly made up of the buildings of the University and those further south, of Chepauk Palace, designed by a British architect and built in 1768 for Muhammad Ali of Arcot. Both display an architectural style termed the Indo-Saracenic, where Hindu and Muslim elements were amalgamated by Britons brought up on the Gothic, Classical and Regency architectural styles. The results, as in the case of **Senate House** **D** (undergoing restoration), the oldest university building dating from 1873, can be spectacular. No less striking is the tower that links the two halves of **Chepauk Palace**, now used by the state government to house part of its administration. Close by is an 1887 statue of Queen Victoria.

Presidency College, the first collegiate educational institution in South India, is the last of the Indo-Saracenic contributions to this skyline. Then come more Victorian contributions: the **Ice House**, now a women's hostel called Vivekananda House, but once an intriguingly circular-styled storehouse for ice imported from Boston, and **Police Headquarters**, which was earlier a vast, Regency-style Masonic hall.

Across from Marina is Governor Grant-Duff's promenade of walks, newly replanted gardens and drives, now embellished further with sculpture and lighting. Beyond it is one of India's most magnificent beaches, washed by the dangerous Chennai surf. Bathing is not advisable here, neither is sunbathing, though getting one's feet wet is everyone's favourite dare when strolling along the beach. Although few signs remain, Marina beach was part of the coast hit by the 2004 tsunami. The Marina, as usual, was full of people when the wave hit. Over 200 people were killed, and silt and mud were dumped on the beach.

LEFT: Fort St George.
BELOW: the Ice House.

Triplicane and Mylapore

Marina ends where San Thome begins. But a little before them, off the Marina, is Triplicane, Mylapore's suburb of "the sacred lily tank". The ancient tank is still there, though the lilies are few. But its Vaisnavite temple, dedicated to **Lord Partasarati**, is very beautiful. Dating to the mid-8th century, it is the oldest building in the city with much of its original construction intact.

Not far from the Partasarati Temple is the beautiful **Vallaja** (Big) **mosque** which the Nawabs of the Carnatic bequeathed to Chennai 200 years ago. Nearby is **Amir Mahal**, the home of the Nawabs, visitable by invitation.

Beyond Triplicane and the Marina lie Mylapore and San Thome. **Mylapore** was one of the great ports of the Pallavas in the 7th and 8th centuries, but its traditions go back 2,000 years and more as one of the South's leading cultural and religious centres. The Portuguese arrival in the 16th century pushed Mylapore back far from shore, and the great **temple of Kapalesvara** **E** had to be rebuilt where it now is. The magnificent sculptures within the temple and all over its towering *gopuram* are among the most spectacular sights in Chennai. The temple is dedicated to Siva in the form of a peacock *(mayil)* from which the town receives its name (*mayil-puram*, "peacock town", which became Mylapore). The central shrine has a Siva *lingam* (phallus), behind which is the large temple tank.

All around the Kapalesvara Temple, in narrow lanes and bylanes, life is little changed from the traditional. The clothes and some of the comforts may be contemporary, but customs, household worship, food habits and festive occasions go back centuries.

Mylapore is one of the busiest parts of the city, with its tiny old houses built in traditional style, Hindu religious organisations, and busy bazaars selling traditional "temple jewellery", floral decorations and the glittering silks that adorn Bharata

LEFT: San Thome Cathedral. **BELOW:** a *pujari* in the Kapalesvara temple.

Map on page 122

Natyam dancers. Chennai's best goldsmiths live around the Kapalesvara Temple. Jewellers can also be seen sitting in the doorways of their tiny shops making gold-plated "dance jewellery sets". Silver ornaments are dipped into a gold solution. A bright pink tissue paper is then placed into pre-moulded grooves before being capped with a pale pink stone. The result mimics the ruby-studded gold traditional patterns required for classical dance.

The classic headpiece comprises a *rakodi*, worn just above the flowers in the hair, flanked by a stylised sun and moon. Ear ornaments come in three parts: a chain, a dangler, and a support for the lobe. Around the neck is a choker, plus a half-moon-shaped pendant *(padakkam)* suspended from a longer chain. A *vanki* bracelet grips the upper arm and is heavier than the standard gold bangles jingling at the wrist. A broad ornamental belt, called an *odyanan*, completes the costume. Sometimes a *sarpam* hair ornament snakes around the long plaited hair.

San Thome

The Portuguese may have appropriated Mylapore's shore and called it San Thome, but long before them Mylapore had a connection with Christianity, and the "Town of Thomas" was what it was called by the ancient Nestorians. One of the most enduring legends of South India is the story of Thomas Didymus, the Apostle who doubted the resurrection of Christ. So much is this legend an article of faith for most South Indian Christians that Thomas was decreed the Apostle of India in 1972. The culmination of that legend can be seen in **San Thome Basilica** **F**.

Much of the evidence for the existence of Saint Thomas is in Mylapore where, legend has it, he preached every day. Thomas is said to have lived in a cave on **Little Mount**, at one end of Mylapore. From there he would walk every day to the beach at Mylapore, resting a while and preaching in the groves where the Portuguese later built **Luz Church** and **Descanco Church**. But the biggest crowd would wait on the beach to hear him, and it was on this site that it is believed he was buried after his martyrdom. The Portuguese found an old Nestorian church on the spot and the tomb of Thomas within. Moving the Apostle's remains further inland, they built another church over the new crypt. In 1896–8 a magnificent neo-Gothic basilica was built on the ruins of the first Portuguese church; Portuguese priests remained in charge of the cathedral throughout British rule. The church's towering steeple, its ornate interior, its magnificent stained-glass windows telling the story of Thomas. The newly renovated crypt is said to have once held the saint's body, although this is considered unlikely and his remains are now in Ortona, Italy.

To the southwest is **St Thomas' Mount** **G**, just outside the city and near the airport. It was to here that he fled from the cave in Little Mount and where he later died. The lovely little Portuguese church here, with its relics of the saint and its steps for the faithful, is one of the most serene in Chennai. The view of Chennai from here is spectacular.

RIGHT: walking around the Kapalesvara temple.

Adyar

Originally the road south reached the city limits at the Adyar River estuary. Dry for most of the year but occasionally in spate during the monsoons, the Adyar is little noticed except by historians, nature lovers and washer-people. To historians it is the river at which a handful of French-trained troops stopped the Nawab's army, demonstrating the possibilities of Empire for any small but disciplined army. To bird-watchers the **Adyar Estuary** is a protected area of river, dunes, islands and woods that is home to small animals and bird life, much of it migrant during the winter.

The city has, however, now spread way beyond the Adyar River and takes in Adyar and Guindy. Adyar is the headquarters of the **Theosophical Society** (open Mon–Fri 8.30–11.30am, 2–5pm), founded in 1882, and dedicated to the quest for truth through the interaction of all faiths. It is a major Indological research centre, set in hundreds of acres of garden and scrub forest. The Society boasts some magnificent buildings, houses typical of Chennai of another age, shrines of all faiths and an internationally famous library with a priceless collection.

However, the greatest attraction for the public is in the gardens of the Society – the second biggest banyan tree in the subcontinent, 200 years old and more, and with its spreading branches shading 4,180 sq m (5,000 sq yds) of space. It is often used for meetings and discourses. The main trunk of the tree was uprooted during a freak storm in 1989, but was replanted and has begun to revive.

The Society's acres stretch from the main road south to **Elliot's Beach** on the Coromandel shore. Once an exclusive beach for the sahibs of colonial Chennai, it is now a stretch of fun and leisure for the new colonists who occupy Adyar and beyond. By the beach is the **Ashtalaksmi temple**, one of the country's only two shrines on the shore dedicated to the goddess Mahalaksmi.

LEFT: the Theosophical Society headquarters.

Guindy

The road south branches left at the Theosophical Society to lead to the beach and the road to Mamallapuram. To explore the rest of the city, keep going straight on until you reach Guindy, once the country homes of the squires of urban Chennai. Today, Guindy's only retreat is **Raj Bhavan**, the Governor's mansion, to the east of which stretches its private forest reserve, the only National Park within a city anywhere in the world. Permission is needed to view Raj Bhavan even from the outside, but **Guindy National Park** may be driven through on payment of a fee. This protected sanctuary is home to herds of spotted deer and blackbuck, monkeys and a wealth of bird and small wildlife. Several acres of this vast wooded estate of the Governor have been taken over, rather sadly for conservationists, for a variety of purposes. The **Indian Institute of Technology**, one of the premier educational institutions in the country, has a spacious wooded campus.

Next door is the **Snake Park** (open daily 8.30am–5.30pm, entrance charge).

Map on page 122

The Snake Park is the only major reptilium in India. It was founded by herpetologist Romulus Whitaker, who has worked towards educating visitors on the types of snakes in India, and on preventing the thoughtless killing of reptiles.

Also here are **memorials** to **Gandhiji**, **Rajaji** and **Kamaraj** – respectively the Father of the Nation, the Chennai Prime Minister who became free India's first Indian Governor-General, and the first Tamil political leader from the grassroots.

Anna Salai

Anna Salai **H**, previously called Mount Road, Chennai's main thoroughfare, was once the mall to the Mount of St Thomas and the cantonment, bungalows and sanatoria that surrounded it. On either side, until well into the early years of the 20th century, were the "garden houses" of the elite of Chennai. Today it is a modern commercial road where the expansive homes of the past are fast giving way to multi-storey blocks. Snaking out of the city past St Thomas' Mount, the road leads past the airports and then, as National Highway 45, into the heartland of Tamil Nadu.

Leading out of the Fort, Mount Road crosses the man-made island watched over by the statue of Sir Thomas Munro and begins to veer southwest at **Government Estate**. The mansion where Chennai's governors once lived in regal splendour is beginning to fall apart, but connected to it by a courtyard is the handsome banqueting hall built by the second Lord Clive to commemorate his father's victory at Plassey and the Chennai Army's victory at Seringapatnam (now Srirangapatnam) a generation later. Now called **Rajaji Hall**, the building has lost its imperial glitter but is still the venue for important official functions.

Anna Salai now becomes a commercial stretch till it reaches the suburbs, and along its early reaches are some of the city's oldest commercial landmarks and vestiges of the age of empire. Here are the offices of *The Hindu*, a paper as indis-

BELOW: Anna Salai.

pensable to the educated inhabitant of Chennai as a cup of morning coffee. Then there are **Higginbotham's**, a long-established bookshop, and **Spencer Plaza**, a large, air-conditioned block full of shops (a useful place to pick up Western comfort food and toiletries), fast-food restaurants and with **Landmark Books**, said to be the largest bookshop in Asia. Almost next door is the Art-Deco **Connemara**, one of the city's finest hotels and distinguished by its blend of tradition with urbane modernity. The coffee shop and restaurants here are very pleasant.

To the south, the **Sangita Vadyalaya** ❶ (759 Anna Salai, behind the Tamil Nadu Handicrafts Centre) has an interesting collection of musical instruments (open Mon–Fri 9.30am–5pm).

Wherever commerce was in the past, clubland was never far away. More or less across the road from these three landmarks are the vestiges of the first buildings of the **Madras Club**, the "Ace of Clubs", a memorial to the British elite's desire to unwind amidst splendour and spaciousness, and the Ionic lineaments of the **Cosmopolitan Club**, where Indians followed the track the British pioneered. Not far from these splendid buildings is a school and college, some of whose buildings and grounds were part of the estate where the Begums of the Carnatic lived. Bringing this busy stretch to an end are the **Horticultural Gardens**, a riot of colour during the season for a hundred years and more, and **St George's Cathedral**, a magnificent replica of St Martin's-in-the-Fields, London.

The Government Museum

To the north of the busiest part of Mount Road are many of the newer landmarks of the city, most of them 100–150 years old. On Pantheon Road, where the **Pantheon** was home to public entertainments in Arthur Wellesley's day, are Chennai's magnificent Museum, rich in bronzes, Buddhist antiquities and arms, the **Connemara Public Library**, one of India's four national libraries to which every

BELOW: a Chennai *sabha* (music society) concert hall.

Map on page 122

book published in India must be sent, and the **National Art Gallery** with a permanent exhibition of Indian painting. In the newer wings is a gallery of contemporary art where temporary shows are held.

The **State Government Museum** **J** (open Sat–Thur 9.30am–5pm, entrance charge; www.chennaimuseum.org) was established in 1846 and has one of the finest collections in the country. The archaeological galleries are particularly fine. They house a rare collection of sculptures from Amaravati in Andhra Pradesh, belonging to the Buddhist period, 2nd century AD. The white limestone sculptured medallions and panels tell the story of the life of the Buddha. The **Bronze Gallery** has a superb collection of Chola bronzes (9th–13th century AD). Some are hardly 4 cm (1½ ins) high and others are over half a metre (1½ ft) tall, all iconographically sophisticated. The dancing Sivas, Durgas and Ganapatis and the famous Rama, Laksmana and Sita group are the pride of this museum. Other collections include displays of South Indian ethnographic artefacts, prehistoric finds and galleries of zoological and geological specimens.

Not far from here is the campus of the Director of Public Instruction with its magnificent gateways, dating back to when it was the college of Fort St George, where the officials of the Company learnt language and governance. The campus houses the handsome Indo-Saracenic building of the **Madras Literary Society**, a treasure house of old books. Next door are **Doveton House**, where Tippu Sultan's sons may have been held hostage but which they certainly visited when they were wards of Sir John Doveton, and the **Meteorological Centre**, whose commemorative pillars and benchmarks are the oldest in Asia.

Nearby are **Valluvar Kottam** and the **Archives**. The former is a huge auditorium dominated by a 31-metre (101-ft) tall temple chariot, in whose construction the ancient skills of Chola and Pallava artisans were revived. It is a memorial to Thiruvalluvar, the great philosopher-saint who laid down in verse a code of ethics for the Tamil people.

Egmore

Beyond the Archives is the Indo-Saracenic splendour of **Egmore Railway Station** and the lively **Kirk of St Andrew's** **K** with its towering steeple, domed roof and many-pillared circular nave built in 1818–21. Other colonial buildings worth seeking out are the **College of Arts and Crafts**, the gleaming white of the Municipal Corporations's splendid **Ripon Buildings**, a vivid contrast to the striking red of **Victoria Public Hall** (an auditorium out of the gaslight era), the **Central Station**, the imperial *hauteur* of **Memorial Hall** and the palatial magnificence of the **Southern Railways Headquarters**. This area was once called "Black Town", the Indian town that existed outside the walls of the first "White Town" in Fort St George, and it is now the commercial heart of Chennai.

Perhaps the most magnificent Indo-Saracenic complex in the city is the **High Court** **L** and **Law College** campus. The pillar of the city's first lighthouse and the

RIGHT: the Armenian Church interior.

obelisk marking the grave of Elihu Yale's son David, the last memorial of the first European cemetery, are landmarks that tend to get lost amidst the handsome pillars of justice. This campus was the site of the Fort's very first Indian settlement in what was the new town of Madras. When it was razed to create an esplanade providing the Fort's guns with a clear field of fire, the new Black Town began to develop. The boundary of that esplanade is still to be seen in a pillar at the southeast corner of George Town, by **Dare House** where 200-year-old E.I.D. Parry (India) Ltd has its headquarters. **Parry's Corner** at the junction of what was Esplanade Road and North Beach Road is dedicated to the man who founded the company that is the second oldest modern business house in India.

George Town

Behind North Beach Road is a 344-hectare (850-acre) warren, almost square in shape, which is **George Town**, the banking and wholesale trading centre of Chennai. Developed in the classical gridiron pattern, George Town's narrow streets were meant for a more leisurely age. Today they are by day one of the busiest parts of the city; however, by nightfall, George Town empties and, as the shops on roadsides close, lights go on above them in what are veritable mansions behind shabby exteriors.

In George Town are the oldest temple and mosques of British Madras and the churches of the first Protestant missionaries. The twin **Chennakesavara** and **Chennammallikesvara** temple, the first "Town temple", and the beautifully maintained **Armenian Church**, are also well worth a look.

On the eastern boundary of George Town are the handsome Indo-Saracenic buildings of the **State Bank of India**, successor to the first modern bank in the country, and the **General Post Office**. Beyond is the handsome Regency **Bentinck's Building**, built for the first Su-

Map on page 122

preme Court of the Presidency, their eastern bastion **Clive Battery**, now providing homes for harbour officers, and the earliest railway buildings in the city at Royapuram. On this stretch too, abutting the harbour, is **Burma Bazaar**, a row of tiny shops. Another engrossing experience is **Kothawal Chavadi** at dawn, when the trucks begin to arrive with the day's supplies of fresh fruit and vegetables for sale and distribution throughout the city.

To the north of the city

A day trip north of Chennai to **Durgarayapatnam** is worthwhile. This is an ancient port by the northern end of Lake Pulicat, known to Francis Day, founder of Chennai, as Armagaon. It was while he was serving as a factor here that Day began to search the coast further south for a better site. At the opposite end of the lake from the ruins of this early British settlement and the inevitable cemetery nearby are the better preserved ruins and cemetery of Fort Geldria, established by the Dutch in 1609 at **Pulicat**.

The tranquil Lake Pulicat, and the backwaters which join it, are connected by the southern and northern reaches of the **Buckingham canal**. The lake itself is home to many species of water birds, including flamingos, pelicans and spoonbills, as well as welcoming many migratory species. The 650-km (400-mile) long canal connects Kakinada in Andhra Pradesh with Markanam in Tamil Nadu and was once navigable along its entire length, but today the high cost of desilting makes this possible only on some stretches. One such span is from the northern reaches of Chennai to the rice-bowl town of Nellore in Andhra Pradesh, about 200 km (125 miles) by slow boat.

On the road back to Chennai is the ancient village of **Tiruvottiyur** with its several temples dating to the 8th and 9th centuries, among them the **Adipuresvara temple**, a splendid example of Chola architecture. ❑

LEFT: these enormous shark's jaws lead into MGR Film City.
BELOW: Marina Beach.

THE COROMANDEL COAST

South of Chennai and along the coast lie some of Tamil Nadu's most important sites, including the Shore Temple at Mamallapuram, while inland lies the temple city of Kanchipuram

Within easy reach of Chennai are two of South India's greatest attractions, Mamallapuram (formerly Mahabalipuram) and Kanchipuram. The roads from Chennai that lead due south to Mamallapuram and southwest to "Kanchi" offer variety and stimulation every few miles. Moving further south along the coast are further treasures, including the old Danish settlement at Tranquebar and the rich bird life of Point Calimere.

The coastal road

Just outside Chennai lies the village of **Tiruvanmiyur ❶**, which houses **Kalakshetra**. When the celebrated dancer and scholar Rukmini Devi Arundale took the ancient dance form of Bharata Natyam out of the temple and gave it a new "respectability", she went one step further: she made up her mind that others who followed her would learn the art in a school that would be world-renowned. Today, students from all over the world come to Kalakshetra not only to learn *Bharatanatyam* but also Karnatak music and those ancient crafts of the Coromandel, namely weaving and dyeing. The age-old *gurukulam* system of education is still followed, and many classes are conducted in wooded surroundings.

Also in Tiruvanmiyur is the ancient **Marundiswarar temple**. Built by those great temple-builders, the Cholas, in the 11th century, it has a wealth of stone sculpture. About 10 km (6 miles) beyond it is **Cholamandalam** with its **Artists' Village**, an experiment in cooperative living. Within this artists' commune by the sea, some of South India's best painters live and work. The art gallery exhibits contemporary art all year round, but visitors are likely to find the prices of the craftwork displayed separately more alluring. The income from craftwork is what allows many of these artists to keep on painting. An open-air theatre among the sand dunes stages plays, poetry readings and dance recitals from time to time.

The next stop, a few kilometres further along, is the **VGP Golden Beach Resort**. Its cottages amidst casuarina groves have made it one of the most popular weekend outings for residents of Chennai. The groves and beach have had film decor from South India's famed "historicals" and "mythologicals" imposed on them, and every corner is a cinema set replete with creations in wood, granite, metal and plaster of Paris. Practically every Tamil film-maker is eager to shoot at least one scene in these picturesque gardens to ensure a successful film.

LEFT: touching carvings at Mamallapuram. **RIGHT:** a dance class at Kalakshetra.

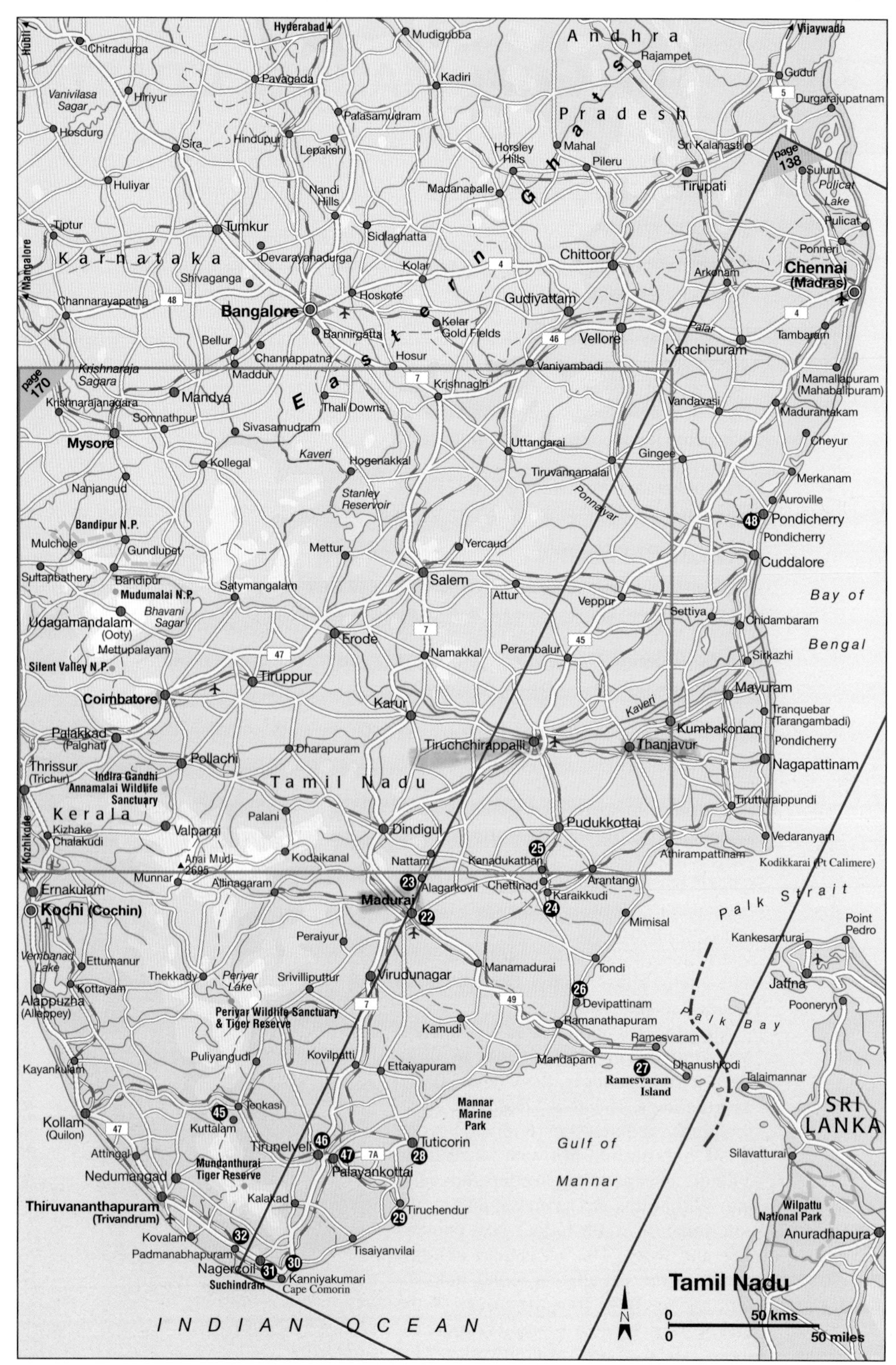
Hubli
Hyderabad
Mudigubba
Andhra
Vijaywada
Chitradurga
Rajampet
Gudur
Pavagada
Kadiri
Vanivilasa Sagar
Hiriyur
5
Durgarajupatnam
Pradesh
Palasamudram
Hosdurg
Hindupur
Sira
Lepakshi
Horsley Hills
Mahal
Sri Kalahasti
page 138
Pileru
Suluru
Pulicat Lake
Huliyar
Nandi Hills
Madanapalle
Tirupati
Pulicat
Tiptur
Tumkur
Sidlaghatta
Mangalore
Karnataka
Devarayanadurga
Chittoor
Ponneri
Kolar
4
Chennai (Madras)
Shivaganga
Arkonam
Hoskote
Channarayapatna
48
Bangalore
Gudiyattam
Eastern Ghats
Kolar Gold Fields
Bannirgatta
4
Palar
Tambaram
Bellur
46
Vellore
Channapatna
Kanchipuram
Hosur
Maddur
Vaniyambadi
page 170
Krishnaraja Sagara
7
Krishnagiri
Mamallapuram (Mahabalipuram)
Mandya
Krishnarajanagara
Thali Downs
Vandavasi
Madurantakam
Somnathpur
Sivasamudram
Mysore
Cheyur
Kaveri
Uttangarai
Kollegal
Hogenakkal
Gingee
Tiruvannamalai
Merkanam
Nanjangud
Stanley Reservoir
Ponnaiyar
Auroville
Bandipur N.P.
Pondicherry
Pondicherry
Mulchole
Yercaud
Mettur
Gundlupet
Cuddalore
Sultanbathery
Bandipur
Salem
Mudumalai N.P.
Satymangalam
Attur
Bay of Bengal
Bhavani Sagar
Veppur
Udagamandalam (Ooty)
Settiya
Chidambaram
7
Erode
Mettupalayam
45
Perambalur
Namakkal
47
Sirkazhi
Silent Valley N.P.
Tiruppur
Coimbatore
Mayuram
Karur
Kaveri
Tranquebar (Tarangambadi)
Palakkad (Palghat)
Kumbakonam
Tiruchchirappalli
Thanjavur
Pondicherry
Dharapuram
Thrissur (Trichur)
Pollachi
Nagapattinam
Indira Gandhi Annamalai Wildlife Sanctuary
Tamil Nadu
Tiruturaippundi
Kerala
Palani
Kozhikode
Kizhake Chalakudi
Valparai
Dindigul
Pudukkottai
Vedaranyam
Anai Mudi 2695
Kodaikanal
Nattam
Kanadukathan
Athirampattinam
Kodikkarai (Pt Calimere)
Munnar
Allinagaram
Alagarkovil
Chettinad
Arantangi
Ernakulam
Madurai
Karaikkudi
Palk Strait
Kochi (Cochin)
Mimisal
Point Pedro
Peraiyur
Kankesanturai
Vembanad Lake
Ettumanur
Manamadurai
Tondi
Jaffna
Thekkady
Periyar Lake
Srivilliputtur
Virudunagar
Kottayam
Devipattinam
Pooneryn
Alappuzha (Alleppey)
7
49
Periyar Wildlife Sanctuary & Tiger Reserve
Ramanathapuram
Palk Bay
Kamudi
Rameswaram
Puliyangudi
Kovilpatti
Mandapam
Dhanushkodi
Kayankulam
Ettaiyapuram
Ramesvaram Island
Talaimannar
Tenkasi
Mannar Marine Park
SRI LANKA
Kollam (Quilon)
47
Kuttalam
Gulf of Mannar
Tirunelveli
Tuticorin
7A
Attingal
Palayankottai
Silavatturai
Mundanthurai Tiger Reserve
Nedumangad
Kalakad
Thiruvananthapuram (Trivandrum)
Tiruchendur
Wilpattu National Park
Kovalam
Anuradhapura
Padmanabhapuram
Tisaiyanvilai
Nagercoil
Kanniyakumari
Cape Comorin
Suchindram
Tamil Nadu
INDIAN OCEAN
N
0 50 kms
0 50 miles
22
23
24
25
26
27
28
29
30
31
32
45
46
47
48

Map on page 138

A few miles beyond Golden Beach, the backwaters of **Muttukadu** offer a variety of boating facilities as well as a luxury hotel, Fisherman's Cove, on **Covelong Beach**, built on the remains of an old Dutch fort whose walls have been landscaped into the hotel grounds. Covelong offers a fairly safe bathing beach (except during the monsoons, June–August, October–January) as well as water sports.

Also in Muttukadu is **Dakshina-Chitra** (open Wed–Mon, 10am–6pm, entrance fee; www.dakshinachitra.org). This exemplary museum has a number of rescued examples of South Indian village architecture and aims to preserve and promote traditional crafts.

Crocodiles and tigers

About 5 km (3 miles) further along is the **Crocodile Bank**, run by Romulus and Zai Whittaker. Romulus Whittaker, founder of the Snake Park in Chennai, is attempting to save the vanishing crocodile of India and has more than 3,000 muggers and gharials in the Bank, all of them bred on the premises, as well as several other crocodile and lizard species from other countries as exhibits. He has also brought elements of the Snake Park here, and the Adivasi snake-catchers' cooperative he promoted has a corner where hundreds of cobras, kraits and vipers are reared in pots and regularly "milked". The venom, sent to anti-venin institutes to be made into vaccines, provides the cooperative with a handsome income; the small fee to watch "milking" operations at fixed times daily also helps swell their income.

Silver Sands, another beach resort, is close by. Then comes the very briefest of introductions to Mamallapuram *(see below)*, **Tiger Cave**. Left unfinished, like much of Mamallapuram, Tiger Cave was obviously meant to be the stage for a regal open-air amphitheatre; the cave has remarkable acoustics which has led to speculation that it was meant for musical performances. Sculpted tiger heads frame a tiny stage in a casuarina grove which must have been in the first stages of being chiselled out of the rock when work was interrupted. The rest of the theatre is as unfinished, but the exquisite details of the tigers' faces offer the best possible preview of what awaits the visitor in a few kilometres.

Mamallapuram

As well as being a beach resort, **Mamallapuram ❷**, a tiny village by the sea, is an extraordinary showcase for Tamil art. Here is an open-air museum of sculpture which has few parallels in the world.

The star exhibit is undoubtedly **Arjuna's Penance** or the **Descent of the Ganga**, the world's largest bas-relief, 27 by 9 metres (764 by 288 ft) and one of the major masterpieces of Indian art. It is a beautiful composition of hundreds of celestial beings, humans and animals, all hurrying to a natural rock cleft that divides the giant stone canvas. Dominating the scene is a 5-metre (16-ft) long elephant leading a procession of elephants to the scene of the penance by the cleft, where Arjuna stands on one leg to propitiate Siva to help him win back the kingdom of the Pandavas.

RIGHT: salt workers on the coast.

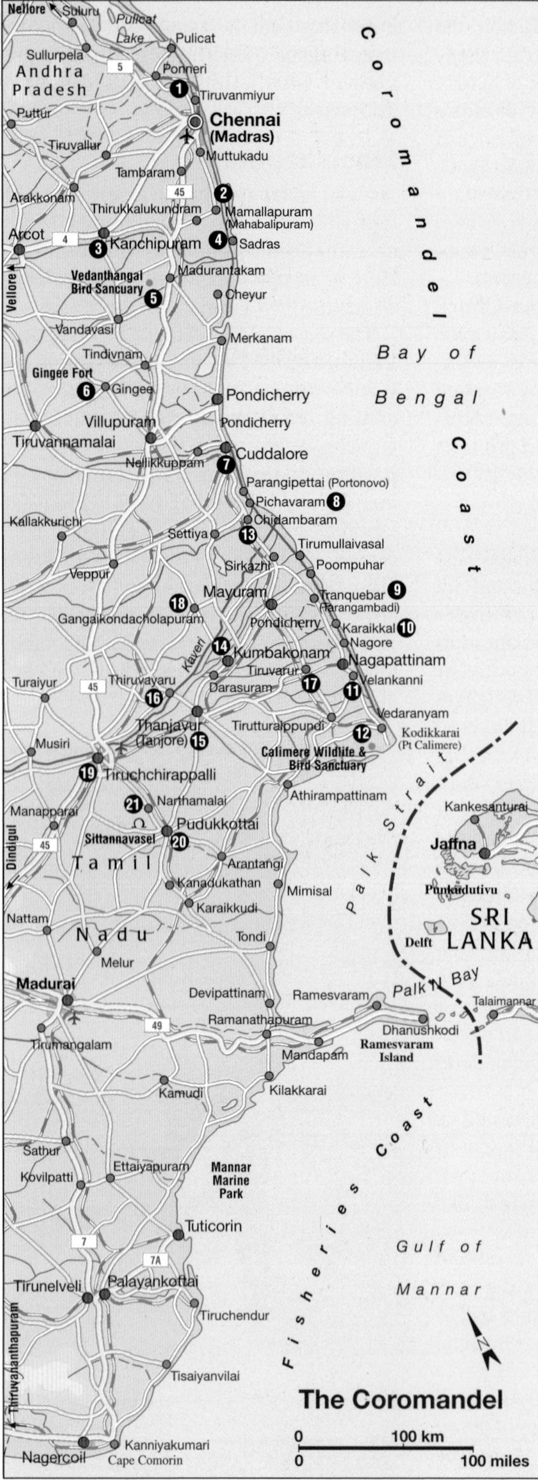

The best-known landmark of Mamallapuram, however, is the **Shore temple** (entrance charge). Standing by the sea, now protected by a wall that hides its facade but saves it from the elements that are fast eroding it, this twin spire is pure poetry in granite in its perfect proportions and wealth of sculpture. It is also unique in that it includes shrines for both Siva and a Visnu in repose. The temple's architectural importance has been recognised by UNESCO, which declared it a World Heritage Site.

The 2004 tsunami that hit the coast here particularly hard did not damage the Shore temple but did carry off an enormous amount of sand. In the process it has uncovered the foundations of another huge temple, lying a few hundred metres to the south of the Shore temple, apparently also dating from the Pallava era. This has led to renewed speculation about the presence of yet more temples, the so-called "Seven Pagodas" reported by early European travellers to this coast. The huge waves also uncovered a long wall running north of the Shore temple, so there is evidently much still to be discovered about the site.

The other wonders of Mamallapuram are the *mandapams*, caves scooped from the hillsides and ornamented with pillars and great sculptured panels that are an integral part of the excavation, and the *rathams*, monolithic rock-cut shrines that have inspired generations of South Indian temple-builders. In the **Krisna mandapam**, the serenity of a pastoral scene is ensured by Krisna protecting all God's creatures from a storm's fury with his massive umbrella, the Govardhana mountain. In the **Varaha mandapam**, Visnu in his incarnation as Varaha the boar bursts from the ocean clutching the rescued Earth Goddess. And in the **Mahisasuramardini mandapam**, the goddess Durga, astride a lion, battles the powerful buffalo-headed demon, Mahisasura.

The five *rathams*, named after the Pandava brothers, the heroes of the Mahabharata, and their wife Draupadi, are part of an amphitheatre of art. Each temple is incomplete, yet each remains an architectural gem. Also in this arena are a magnificent elephant and an exquisite Nandi, the sacred bull.

Map on page 138

There are four other *rathams*, the **Trimurti cave**, and the **Adivaraha temple**, where worship still continues, and scores of individual pieces of sculpture, of *yalis*, monkeys and other mythical and living creatures. There is also a smaller open-air museum of scattered sculptural treasures from around the site. In tribute to the skills of the ancient sculptors, a **college of sculpture** is run in the township, not only granting degrees but turning out some excellent work.

Southwest to Kanchi

Leaving Chennai from **St Thomas' Mount**, you go past the airport at **Tirusulam** and then the tree-shaded campus of the Chennai Christian College at **Tambaram**. Beyond Tirusulam are several ancient villages: Tirunirmalai, Kunratur and Pallavaram – all, like Tirusulam, with 11th- and 12th-century shrines. **Pallavaram** is the site of several prehistoric finds and antiquities. **Vandalur zoo** is about one-thirds of the way to Kanchipuram. This, Chennai's zoo, was at least designed with some consideration of the animals' needs. Keeping the animals and birds in large enclosures as close to natural settings as possible means that the visitor has to walk quite a distance to see different species. However, the concept of zoos in general is controversial and Indian zoos in particular are depressing places (for more information see www.petaindia. com/zoos.html and www.aapn.org/zoopage4.html).

Kanchipuram

Just 60 km (37 miles) southwest of Chennai and northwest of Mamallapuram is Kanchipuram, one of the seven most sacred cities of the Hindus and one of the oldest towns in South India. But before "Kanchi" is **Thirukkalukundram**, halfway house on the road from Mamallapuram. Here, atop the 160-metre (525-ft) high Vedagiri hill, is a sculpture-rich Siva temple. The view from the hilltop is spectacular, but many pilgrims make the steep climb to the top to see the two kites that

BELOW: bas relief of the Descent of the Ganges, Mamallapuram.

come every noon to feed on the consecrated food spread for them by the temple priests.

Kanchipuram ❸, the "golden town of a thousand temples", has about 125 officially-recognised shrines, all of them centuries old. Dating back to the early Jain kingdoms, Kanchipuram was successively capital of the Pallavas, the Cholas and the Rajas of Vijayanagara. The height of Kanchi's glory was as the capital of the far-flung empire of the Pallavas from the 6th to the 8th century, when Mamallapuram and Mylapore were its great ports. All that is left of that glorious era are its magnificent temples. The highlight here is a 1,000-year-old mango tree which occasionally still bears fruit. The **Ekambaresvara temple**, a fairly new temple dating from the 16th century, is the largest of the Siva temples and sprawls over 8 hectares (20 acres) and more. It has a magnificent 1,000-pillared hall and a towering *gopuram*, at almost 60 metres (200 ft) one of the tallest in South India.

The **Kailasanatha temple**, which is over 1,000 years old, is a Pallava creation dedicated to Lord Siva. The narrow cells linking its courtyards have paintings and sculptures dating back to the 7th and 8th centuries, narrating the story of Siva.

The **Kamaksi temple** is dedicated to Parvati, "the goddess with the eyes of love", who playfully blindfolded her consort Siva and had to do long penance for her mischievousness. Parvati is said to have been eventually forgiven by the god at the spot where the temple now stands.

A perfect specimen of Pallava temple-building is the **Vaikuntha Perumal temple** dating back to the 8th century. A unique frieze narrates the history of the Pallavas and the battles they fought against the Chalukyas. Of note here are three sanctums, one atop the other.

A relatively recent temple is the **Varadarajasvami temple**, with beautiful pavilions in its courtyard, a splendid 100-pillar hall that is a work of art and a 31-metre (100-ft) tall seven-storey *gopuram*

Map on page 138

of rare beauty. Some of the most beautiful sculpture in all Kanchipuram is to be found in this temple.

Kanchi's other claim to fame is its production of silk *saris*, renowned for more than four centuries. Vibrantly contrasting colours, borders woven in gold thread, with traditional motifs such as peacocks, parrots, mangoes and leaves, made out of silk that is woven to last, make these the richest *saris* in India and certainly the most sought after. The *saris* are priced according to their weight, taking into consideration the substance of the silk and the extent of the gold thread.

A unique system of weavers' co-operatives makes and sells Kanchi *saris*. Shops are on the main street, and shopkeepers are as pleased as the weavers in the bylanes are to display their range and show the art and skills that have been handed down over the generations. The cooperative showrooms sell silk and cotton *saris*, as well as silk by the metre, stoles and scarves.

Beyond Kanchi, to the east, is **Vellore**, noted for its Christian Medical College but most of all for its spectacular fort. It was first built by the rulers of Chandragiri (now in Andhra Pradesh) before being taken over by Vijayanagara in 1604. The well-preserved battlements are protected by a wide moat.

The Coromandel Coast

South of Mamallapuram is **Sadras** ❹, with the ruins of the early 18th-century Dutch fort, and its lovely, almost deserted beach inviting sunbathers. As in Mamallapuram, swimming is reasonably safe except during the monsoon.

Inland and westwards, just to the west of National Highway 45, is **Vedanthangal** ❺, one of the best bird sanctuaries in South India. From October to March, but especially in December and January, just after the rain, the trees in the 30-hectare (74-acre) wetland are covered with birds and their nests. Over 100,000 migratory birds descend on Vedanthangal every year.

EFT: entrance ɔ the Krisna ⁄landapam, ⁄lamallapuram. **ELOW:** on the ʼain.

Further south and again west of NH-45 is 700-year-old **Gingee fort** ❻, one of the most magnificent military sites in the South with its battlements stretching over three hills. A Vijayanagara fort that the Marathas, the Mughals, Arcot and the French added to over the battle-scarred years, Gingee has within its walls several richly carved temples, a palace and a harem, a mosque, an audience hall, a gymnasium and granaries. It had an interesting system of plumbing and water storage, the remnants of which can still be seen. Towering over all of them is Rajagiri, a steep hill 150 metres (500 ft) high, "which nature hath made secure and art impregnable".

Doubling back to Tindivnam junction on NH-45, the journey east to Cuddalore begins. Just before you reach the coast, you can pause to go back 20 million years in time into the Miocene Age. The small fossil park at **Thiruvakkarai** exhibits huge logs that ring like metal when struck by a hammer and chips of wood that sink when placed in water. The slopes of the nearby ravine are covered with similar logs, relics of that age when the now almost bare Eastern Ghats were a magnificent mountain range covered with majestic trees. In the neighbourhood are several prehistoric burial sites. Pondicherry and Auroville, described elsewhere *(see pages 176–81)*, are close by.

Another lovely beach is the one located at Tegnapatnam, **Cuddalore** ❼, once watched over by Fort St David. As Governor of the fort, Elihu Yale named it as much after the young son he buried in Chennai as after the patron saint of his native Wales. Little remains of this major fort whose existence gave the British the foothold they needed to wrest Chennai from the French in the 18th century and establish the Indian Empire. Clive learned the art of war here and his old house is now the Collectorate. Fort St David's walls have bungalows built on them, by the 200-year-old Chennai commercial house, E.I.D. Parry (India) Ltd.

Map on page 138

Parry's own buildings in Cuddalore town date back to the early 18th century when they housed the East India Company's Deputy Governors in the **Factory House**. Next door is Christ Church, consecrated in 1767 and to all intents and purposes a "Company church"; here lies Thomas Parry, one of the founders of modern Indian commerce. Not far from Cuddalore inland is **Nellikkuppam**, the site of Parry's sugar mill, one of the oldest in the country; its club and staff quarters give visitors an idea of what a British "Company town" was like. If you are interested you can ask at E.I.D. Parry (India) Ltd in Chennai (www.eidparry.com, *see page 132*) for a tour of their facilities in Cuddalore and its environs.

Parry's were also once in **Portonovo** (now Parangipettai), further south. Established in 1575 by the Portuguese and occupied by the Dutch until 1781, when the British took control and turned it into a trading post, it was once one of Portugal's finest harbours in the east, and vestiges of the fort can still be seen. One of the country's foremost marine biology research stations is located here, the institute affiliated to Annamalai University in the nearby temple and university town of Chidambaram.

Portonovo offers boating in its bay and backwaters, but this is more enjoyable and better organised in adjacent **Pichavaram** ❽. The backwaters here are fringed by 121 hectares (300 acres) of the finest mangrove forests in the country and provide hundreds of sheltered boating trails, the tree canopy overhead offering much to excite the birdwatcher as well.

Chola country

From here on to Point Calimere (Kodikkarai), almost the entire hinterland is the heart of the Chola country: here are some of the finest temples in India, almost every village boasting a magnificent shrine. The temples of Chidambaram, Thanjavur and the rest of Cholanadu are described in detail elsewhere *(see pages 147–55)*. On the coast, however, is the

LEFT: Rajgiri from Gingee Fort.
BELOW: a busy street in Vellore.

splendid temple at **Tirumullaivasal** – an appetiser for the magnificence that lies in the hinterland beyond.

Now the traveller is in the rice bowl of Tamil Nadu, the delta of the sacred river Kaveri. In this land of sparkling green fields of paddy and groves of coconut and mango is **Poompuhar** on the coast, the once great port of the Cholas known as Kaveripumpattinam, "the Flower of the Kaveri". It was from here that South Indian culture went across the seas, and it was here too that the Greeks and Romans first called, making it an international emporium. There are a few archaeological excavations and a museum telling in bas-relief the story of the town.

Tranquebar

Another such town is Tarangambadi, "the Village of the Dancing Waves". More popularly known as **Tranquebar** ❾, it was a Danish settlement that made a considerable contribution to Indian printing and education. The ramparts of Dansborg Fort, built by Ove Gedde around 1620, are crumbling but still fascinating. In the fort is a small museum with artefacts from the period of Danish rule (open Sat–Thur). The deserted Tranquebar Mission premises, church and cemetery are not as well preserved. This was the first Protestant mission to establish a foothold in India, and it was here that the missionary Bartholomeus Ziegenbalg began producing Tamil editions of the New Testament on an early printing press.

Pilgrim centres

Not far from here are three pilgrim towns within easy distance of one another, all demonstrating the religious tolerance that has long prevailed on the Coromandel. In each of these towns are shrines of different religious sects, the best known in each of them visited by people of all faiths. **Karaikkal** ❿, once French and now part of Pondicherry's territory, has many relics of the French age, but the town's chief attraction is the **Sannisvara temple**. The

Map on page 138

temple is a rarity, one of the few in the country dedicated to Sani (Saturn). This fishing port was one of the places badly hit by the 2004 tsunami, as was **Nagapattinam** further south.

At **Nagore**, the place of the Naga trees, five minarets and a golden dome glitter in the sun above the 500-year-old tomb of the Muslim saint Hazrat Mian Sahib. At this shrine Hindus offer their hair in penance and people of all faiths seek miraculous cures from bathing in the shrine's tank, **Pir Kulam**. In the huge church of **Velankanni** ⓫, dedicated to Mary, with its towering steeple visible for miles around, people of all religions light tall candles and beseech the Virgin Mary to intercede for them. Hindus, Muslims and Christians all walk this short stretch of Cholamandal every year, to consult the divine guardians of these sacred places.

Vedaranyam, just before Point Calimere, is called Daksina Kailasam (the southern Kailasa, Siva's mountain in the Himalayas) and is one of the sacred places of the Hindus. It is also associated with the story of Rama, as one of the places where he stopped on his return from Lanka. The Archaeological Department tends a mound near here where the footprints preserved in the rock are said to be those of the hero of the *Ramayana*. Saltpans stretch all around the temple and, many years ago, Congress volunteers marched here defying the British salt regulations. The march, duplicating Gandhi's Dandi March which began India's historic Satyagraha campaign, is commemorated here and draws its own share of pilgrims.

A bit further on is the sanctuary of **Point Calimere** ⓬ (now Kodakkarai). In the last quarter of the year, migratory bird life finds a haven in the 50,000 acres of salty marshland which is now a wildlife and bird sanctuary (open all year). The highlight is the spectacle of 30,000 to 50,000 flamingoes suddenly swooping down on the swamp, turning it into a black-streaked white and blushing pink sea, before departing again as suddenly. ❑

LEFT: Karaikkal tank.
BELOW: a village shrine.

Map on page 138

THE KAVERI DELTA

This is the Tamil heartland; the fertile delta is home to some of the most sacred sites in India, from the Nataraja temple in Chidambaram to the Brihadesvara temple of Thanjavur

The river Kaveri starts as little more than a trickle among the hills of the upper reaches of Karnataka. It meanders slowly down to the plains, gaining in width and strength, and cuts across several districts of Tamil Nadu before debouching into the Bay of Bengal. It is a lifeline: the Tamils, who developed a culture of their own over 2,000 years ago, recognised the role played by the river in their economic life, and they worshipped it as a goddess, celebrating it in song and story. All along the banks of the river there are holy towns and hamlets, and innumerable temples. However, the river really comes into its own as it creates a vast delta right in the middle of the Tamil Nadu coast.

It is difficult to demarcate the precise area of the delta, but for practical purposes it lies between Chidambaram, near the coast where the river enters the sea, and Tiruchchirappalli, 200 km (125 miles) inland south. This is rice country: paddy fields, with almost every few kilometres a temple tower rising out of the green expanse. Most of these temples were built by the pious Cholas. The visitor can reach Chidambaram by road or rail from Chennai in six to seven hours. It is an even shorter journey from Pondicherry, especially by road.

Chidambaram

The best place to start this temple tour is **Chidambaram ⓭**, where the celebrated **Nataraja temple** – the temple of the Dancing Siva – is situated.

Chidambaram too has a story about its origins. The god Siva performed his cosmic dance after humbling several conceited *risis* (sages) who believed they had acquired extraordinary powers through their rigorous austerities. Other sages, as well as the gods and goddesses, begged to see the dance, and Siva agreed to dance for them in the forest of Thillai (another name for Chidambaram). The situation acquired an additional piquancy when the guardian of the forest, Kalika Devi (in reality Sakti, the consort of Siva), challenged him to a dance contest. By performing movements which she as a modest woman could not, Siva defeated her. He concluded his performance with the dance of bliss. In response to the *rishis'* request, Siva dances the cosmic dance for all time to come in Chidambaram, as depicted in the beautiful bronze image in the temple.

The dance has many mystic interpretations: as a famous scholar said, it is a symbol of god's rhythmic play as the source of all movement within the cosmos; it

LEFT: The Nataraja temple, Chidambaram. **RIGHT:** a woman draws a *rangoli* at Kumbakonam.

releases the souls of men from the snare of illusion; and that it is actually within the heart of the individual.

The iconography of the figure of the dancing Siva exemplifies these concepts. Nataraja holds a *damaru* (drum) in his hand: with the beat of this drum, he brings all creation into being. The deer he holds in the other hand stands for the nimble and leaping mind of the individual. The tiger skin he wears is the skin of egotism which he has killed. The river Ganga whom he has trapped in his matted locks represents wisdom, which is cool and refreshing. He stands on the demon of illusion *(maya)* on one foot, while the other is raised to represent a state of transcendental bliss. Other symbols stand for the concept that the ego or self must be destroyed if humans are to have control over themselves.

The Nataraja concept must have exercised the imagination of artists down the centuries until it found its finest interpretation in the hands of the Chola craftworkers, who repeated it untiringly in bronze and stone. The French sculptor Auguste Rodin considered it the most perfect expression of movement, while Einstein said that all his thoughts on the structure of the world and its movements found lucid expression in the image of Lord Nataraja.

Much of the temple as seen today was built by the Chola emperors. Massive *gopurams* soar over great entrances. There are several shrines in the temple complex, including one for the god Visnu. The sanctum sanctorum enshrines the god in his dance pose. Adjacent to it is the sanctum of the goddess, whose name here is Sivakamasundari, "the beautiful woman who evoked the love of Siva". An unusual shrine is one without an image in it; this is known as the secret of Chidambaram – the implication being that god is to be found everywhere, and especially in the heart.

The roof of the temple is gold-plated. As befits a temple dedicated to the god of dance, poses now adopted by the classical

Map on page 138

Bharata-natyam style are sculpted around the shrines and on the gateways. Scholars consider these to be in their entirety a veritable encyclopaedia of *Bharata-natyam*.

Chidambaram is a somewhat cluttered town, completely dominated by the temple; rice fields outside the town take away a little from its drabness. Visitors and pilgrims are the principal contributors to the local economy. Besides the temple, the town's other claim to glory is the modern Annamalai University, located in the eastern part of Chidambaram. The university, founded over 50 years ago by a philanthropist, conducts courses in arts and sciences, as well as in technology, medical sciences and agriculture.

The quickest way to travel from here to Thanjavur (Tanjore) and Tiruchchirappalli (Trichy) is by road, and there are frequent bus services in every direction. There are several small roadside temples dedicated to a village deity who protects its borders. The railway takes longer but it is a more comfortable and an equally scenic journey.

Kumbakonam

The road from Chidambaram to Thanjavur passes through villages and small towns, all of which have temples, but the one stop that should be made is **Darasuram**, just outside the bustling town of Kumbakonam.

Darasuram has a magnificent Siva temple, the **Airavatesvara temple** built by the Chola king Raja Raja II in the 12th century. Because of neglect over the centuries, much of the temple has crumbled, but what remains reveals a gem of Chola architecture and sculpture. The main shrine with a 26-metre (85-ft) tall *vimana* (superstructure) and the shrine of the goddess are in a fair state of preservation. The entrance hall is shaped like a chariot, and the steps leading up to it give a musical ring when struck. The exuberance of the sculptures makes one wonder what the temple must have been like in its heyday. Sculptures and remnants of paintings create a whole world of dancers and acrobats, and depict a variety of scenes from everyday life. It was known as "the temple of perpetual entertainment".

Kumbakonam ⓮ has a large number of temples, some of them quite imposing in appearance, but they are of religious rather than of significant artistic importance. Before leaving the area, however, the visitor is well advised to make the short trip to **Svamimalai**. There is an ancient and sacred temple on a small hill here, but the real attraction of Svamimalai is that it is one of the places where bronzes are still made by traditionally-trained artisans. These artists aim for the heights of excellence achieved by their famous Chola ancestors, following the same rules, pouring the molten metal into carefully crafted moulds and giving the finishing touches by hand.

Thanjavur

As the road winds past small villages, paddy fields and temple towers in the distance, you reach **Thanjavur** ⓯ in just over an hour's time. Even at a distance the magnificent tower over the sanctum of the **Brihadesvara temple** can be seen.

LEFT: the temple tank at Chidambaram. **RIGHT:** a flower seller, Kumbakonam.

Tanjore Paintings

Icons for domestic worship are a little different to those used in temples. Throughout South India houses are adorned to welcome the gods. The front is swept and cleaned, and the women of the house make intricate *kolam* designs on the floor with white rice paste, chalk and flowers. The main door lintel is often decorated with mango leaves and colourful flowers. Within the house a special nook is set aside specifically for the deities of the family, who are worshipped every day with flowers, incense and oil lamps. The deities are represented by sculptures either in metal (bronze or silver), wood or clay, or painted images; today, calendar pictures and postcards are frequently added. The genre known as Tanjore paintings grew out of this demand for household images.

"Tanjore painting" is a generic term for many styles; there are paintings from Karnataka, from Sholapur in Maharashtra, wrought on wood, cloth, or on glass after it was introduced in the 18th century. Today it is mainly practised in the districts of Trichy, Kumbakonam, Pudukottai and several others in Tamil Nadu. Traditional artists skilled in sculpture or painting were commissioned to make the images to the exact size, specifications and budget of the customer.

In some styles the artist stretched and fixed a cloth over a plank of wood. The design, usually consisting of the figure of the main deity, consorts and minor figures on either side, was then traced onto the cloth. As in sculptures, the deity was shown standing, sitting or lying, on a lotus or throne or on his animal mount *(vahana)*. The figures were framed by a flat background of colour, often a brilliant red, around which decorations of mango leaves, flowers and (later) draped curtains were added. The drawing was finally embellished with relief work with a paste of glue and chalk to highlight jewellery: crowns, necklaces, garlands, belts, bracelets and anklets, and sometimes the border designs as well. Onto this the artist pressed beaten gold leaf, often punched with fine designs. In the Thanjavur area uncut diamonds, rubies and emeralds were added, or, if the customer's purse did not permit this extravagance, semi-precious or artificially coloured stones.

The colour palette of Tanjore paintings is derived from pigments with a predominance of red, blue, black and white. Each colour had its codified symbolism, as seen in the Kathakali dance makeup where every character is portrayed in a specific colour. Paintings on glass were less expensive, and portrayed patrons as well as the deities. The subject matter varied greatly depending on the period when they were first created. Court scenes, amorous couples, top hats and dancing shoes, sofas and flower vases began to feature in later paintings for the first time.

Tanjore painting was initially encouraged and subsidised by the Maratha ruler of Thanjavur, Serfoji. Some varieties are made of mica, or ivory and glass. An interesting feature is that Krisna, the god usually depicted as blue or black-skinned, is always pale coloured on the precious paintings. Since the colours must symbolise character qualities, the divine is shown as pure white. The most popular subject is "Balakrisna", depicted as a child or playing with the *gopis*. ❑

LEFT: musicians playing for a dancer, Thanjavur, 1850.

Map on page 138

Unlike other temples in the South, the entrance *gopurams* of this temple (aptly called the Big Temple) are dwarfed by the *vimana* over the sanctum. The *gopurams* are over 27 metres (90 ft) high, and are exquisitely sculpted. They lead to a vast courtyard in which the main temple stands, guarded by two enormous *dvarapalakas* (sentries) carved out of single stones, with disarming smiles in spite of their fearsome teeth. Separated by a corridor and facing the sanctum is a Nandi (bull), Siva's favourite vehicle.

Inside the sanctum stands a *lingam* (phallus), symbol of the god Siva, which is reputed to be the largest in the country. The corridors around the sanctum in which devotees circumambulate, going from left to right, have many sculptures; some wonderful Chola frescoes have also been discovered here.

The *vimana* over the sanctum is a pyramidal structure, soaring 65 metres (216 ft) above a platform nearly 30.5 metres sq (100 ft sq). A beautifully carved octagonal cupola with a glittering finial called a *kalasa* 3.8 metres (12.5 ft) tall, crowns the *vimana*. The cupola itself, carved out of a single stone, is gigantic.

The sides of the *vimana* are covered with beautiful sculptures, and numerous niches, small pillars and balcony windows frame many of the carvings. The *vimana*, a slender pyramid in shape, has been so accurately constructed that its shadow never falls on its base. The total effect is one of magnificence. An eminent scholar considered it "unquestionably the finest single creation of the Dravidian craftsman". A World Heritage site, the size of the compound is such – 150 x 75 metres (500 x 250 ft) – that even on busy days the atmosphere in the temple complex is one of serenity.

Right around the corridors are as many as 250 *lingams*. There are also some subsidiary shrines, of which the beautiful **Subramanya temple** deserves special mention. The Big Temple was built by the great Chola emperor Rajaraja I, towards the end of the 10th century. The Subramanya temple was a later addition and was probably built by one of the Nayak kings of Madurai. This is a small and exquisite temple, full of sculptural ornamentation.

From the temple, the next logical stop is the **Palace** (open daily 9am–6pm, entrance charge) to the northeast. Remnants of the fort that surrounded the palace can still be seen, and a 58-metre (190-ft) high lookout remains in good shape. Members of the former royal family of Thanjavur continue to occupy some apartments in the inner recesses, but for all practical purposes the palace is now used mainly as an art gallery and to house the Saraswathi Mahal Library. The Sangita Mahal is a music hall with great acoustics.

The **Art Gallery** (open daily 9am–1pm, 3–6pm) was set up almost accidentally around 1951. The story goes that a beautiful statue of Brahma was lying uncared for in a village, but when someone tried to remove it and take it away, the villagers went up in arms. An imaginative Collector of Thanjavur (the administrative head of the district) heard about this, went to the village, and persuaded the villagers to let

RIGHT: the Brihadesvara temple, Thanjavur.

him take it away to Thanjavur to be displayed in a good public location. It was set up at the entrance to the present art gallery. The Collector also began to retrieve sculptures from decaying temples and abandoned locations, and soon he had an art gallery on his hands. Over the years the collection grew, and a separate collection of bronzes was added to the gallery. As Brahma is the Creator in the Trinity, it is apt that he should have been responsible for the creation of the art gallery. Today the gallery houses some of the most beautiful sculptures of the Chola period, mainly from the 9th to the 14th century, and a magnificent collection of Chola bronzes, including some unique representations of Siva as Nataraja.

The sculptures include freestanding pieces (many of them from the temple in Darasuram mentioned earlier) as well as groupings. One of the most beautiful of the ensembles shows Siva as a handsome mendicant, making the chaste wives of several *rishis* fall in love with him. The *rishis'* wives had become arrogant because their husbands were noted for their penance and austerities, and Siva decided to chasten them. It is extraordinary how the sculptor has managed to depict so many delicate nuances of love and desire on the faces of the women.

A recent addition to the art gallery is the **Rajaraja museum** (open daily 9am–6pm) which houses Chola artifacts, many excavated from the site of the palace of Rajendra Chola at Gangaikondacholapuram. These exhibits include coins, terracotta objects, carved conch shells and metal vessels and measures.

One of the greatest collections in India is in the **Saraswathi Mahal Library** (open to researchers Thur–Tues 10am–1pm, 1.30–5.30pm), housed in another part of the palace. The Maratha rulers of Thanjavur in the 17th and 18th centuries were enlightened monarchs who patronised art and culture. The greatest of them, King Serfoji, started the Library. An engaging and infinitely curious intellectual,

BELOW: the Brihadesvara entrance.

Map on page 138

he collected not only manuscripts and illuminations but also books in many European languages. There are over 40,000 items in the collection, and they include rare books on the arts and sciences, many of them written on palm leaves. Serfoji's advisor and confidant was a missionary named Schwarz, and the church he built for the priest in 1779 to the east of the palace is still in use.

The Musical Trinity

Thanjavur is a small town, easy to get around. January is a good month for a visit, as the visitor can also take in the annual music festival in **Tiruvayaru** ⓰, 11 km (7 miles) away, in honour of the great singer-saint and composer Tyagaraja.

The musical connection is continued 55 km (35 miles) to the east at the temple town of **Tiruvarur** ⓱. The town was the birthplace of three of the greatest South Indian composers, known collectively as the "Trinity" – Syama Sastri (1762–1827), Tyagaraja (1767–1847) and Muttusvami Diksitar (1776–1835) – whose compositions still form the basic repertory of Karnatak music. The Cholas also left their mark here, with their great temple dedicated to Somaskanda (also known as Tyagaraja, an aspect of Siva). The large temple enclosure is bordered by a huge tank on the west side, and the 12th-century *gopurams* are wonderfully sculpted.

Gangaikondacholapuram

Before going on to Tiruchchirappalli, it is well worth taking a detour to **Gangaikondacholapuram** ⓲, about 64 km (40 miles) from Thanjavur. This elaborate name means "the City of the King Who Conquered the Ganga" (Ganges), and commemorates the triumph of Rajaraja's son Rajendra. He invaded the north and conquered many territories, reaching the Ganges in the process. On his return he built a city, and a **Brihadesvara temple** which is almost the equal of the eponymous temple in Thanjavur. Some even assert that the sculptures in this temple are superior. This small village is all that remains of a grand 11th-century city, but the temple is a remarkable monument. Modelled on the Thanjavur temple, it too has a large enclosure, at the centre of which is a shrine containing a huge Siva *lingam*. Close by is a small museum with finds from local excavations (open daily).

Tiruchirappalli

Tiruchirappalli ⓳ ("Trichy") is about an hour away from Thanjavur, by road or rail. It has an airport from which one can fly to and from Chennai and Madurai, and some travellers fly to Trichy and tour from there. Trichy is another historical town, the capital of the Chola rulers for a period. Approaching by road, rail or air, the first thing you see is the **Rock Fort**, 90 metres (300 ft) high, which dominates the landscape. At its summit, alongside a rock which looks from certain angles like a bull with a raised head, is a Ganesa temple, a popular place of worship in spite of the steep climb involved. There is also a 100-pillar *mandapam* which was used for music concerts and religious discourses. The top of the rock affords a fine view.

RIGHT: bathing in the temple tank, Srirangam.

Trichy is a busy industrial, commercial and educational centre, a little confusing being long and meandering. However, the British Cantonment of the city is a pleasant area with a few colonial monuments, in particular the Church of St John. Also here is the **Government Museum** (open Sat–Thur, closed second Sat in the month, 9.30am–5pm, entrance charge), with good examples of local sculpture.

The main attraction of Trichy is actually across the Kaveri river on the island of **Srirangam**, 10 km (6 miles) away. Srirangam is a temple-town sacred to the god Visnu. He is depicted in the sanctum as **Ranganatha**, in a reclining posture on his five-hooded serpent, Adisesa. The temple is practically a town in itself, with several residential streets within its 1.6 sq km (1 sq mile) compound, not to mention a number of shopping streets. Srirangam is one of the holiest temples for devotees of Visnu, and its annual winter festival (December to January) attracts thousands. It is a rather confusing complex since it was built over the centuries. Surrounded by crumbling granite walls, with 21 ornamental towers, most parts of the temple are open to non-Hindus. The main charm of Srirangam is that it is a living temple – much like Madurai's Minaksi temple *(see page 157)*.

The two main features of the temple are the shrine dedicated to Krisna, the **Venugopala temple**, and the equestrian statues. The carvings of *gopis* (female cowherds who loved the god Krisna) in the Venugopala temple are remarkable. The *gopis'* faces expressively depict the many aspects of love, and their figures are rendered with unusual sensuousness. The equestrian statues, made during the Nayak rule in Madurai, are carved on monolithic pillars, and are so vibrantly realistic that they seem ready to take off any minute. On the way back to Trichy, take a look at the **Siva temple** of Jambukesvaram in **Tiruvanaikkaval**. This is a temple which is not open to non-Hindus; they may, however, walk into the compound where some interesting sculptures of animals

Map on page 138

dating back to the 16th century have been carved on walls and pillars.

Pudukkottai

Pudukkottai ⓴, 50 km (30 miles) from Trichy, is infrequently visited, but it has some attractions to offer. It was a princely state for 30 years until 1948, and developed its own courtly traditions. The Rajas were great patrons of the arts, and music and dance flourished in the tiny state. The city itself has few sights. The palace is a grand building but it is now used for government offices. Aside from the **Gokarnesvara temple**, the principal reason for visiting Pudukottai is the nearby **Government Museum** (open Sat–Thur, closed second Sat in the month, 9.30am–5pm, entrance charge). It has some excellent examples of local bronze casting.

The main sights lie outside the town of Pudukkottai at varying distances. A few kilometres before Pudukkottai on the way from Trichy is **Narthamalai** ㉑, about 1.5 km (1 mile) off on the right side of the road. Here on the scarp of a hill stands the **Vijayalaya Chelesvaram temple**, one of the earliest Chola temples built by Vijayalaya, the first Chola ruler of the period. A small temple, it nevertheless includes all the facets of the Chola style of temple architecture that came to full bloom in Thanjavur and elsewhere. It also marks the transition from the earlier Pallava style to the Chola style.

Near to Narthamalai is a Jain cave in **Sittannavasel**, scooped out of the top of a hill, and decorated with frescoes, in the style of those found in Ajanta and Ellora. Despite their age, it is still possible to see how beautiful the colours of these flowers, birds, fishes and animals must have been.

Within a distance of about 30 km (18 miles) from Pudukkottai, there are a number of small villages, such as **Kudimiyamalai**, **Kunnadarkoil** and **Kodumbalur**, all of which have small but remarkable temples constructed by the Pallava and Chola rulers, and filled with exquisite sculptures. ❑

LEFT: rooftops near the Srirangam temple.
BELOW: the *gopurams* of Srirangam.

Map on page 136

MADURAI AND THE SOUTH

The temple city of Madurai with its brightly painted gopurams is one of world's greatest sights, while to the south lie the mansions of Chettinad and India's "lands end" at Kanniyakumari

City of Sweetness, Temple City, City of Festivals – these are among the better known epithets of **Madurai** ㉒, an ancient and fabled city with a history that goes back to the pre-Christian era. Its origin is believed to be sacred: an early Pandya king, hearing reports of celestial beings coming down to earth to bathe in a certain tank and worship Siva, caused a temple to be built there in which a *lingam* was installed. A city came up around the temple. When it was to be named, Lord Siva appeared and blessed the people. Drops of nectar fell from the coils of his hair onto the city; from this it derived its named Madhurapuri, City of Nectar.

Madurai was the capital of the Pandya kingdom until the 10th century. It was a commercial centre and business entrepot, trading with many countries including China, Greece and Rome. Megasthenes, writing in the 3rd century BC, bears testimony to Madurai's grandeur and prosperity; so does Marco Polo, 15 centuries later. Madurai flourished under the Pandyan kings until the Cholas overcame them in the 10th century. The Pandyans regained power in the 13th century, only to lose their kingdom to the armies of Allauddin Khilji, then Sultan in Delhi. The Muslim rule was in turn ended by the Vijayanagara emperors. The new rulers left their far-flung territory in the charge of governors, called the Nayaks, who in time became the de facto rulers. It was during their reign that the magnificent temple and other buildings were constructed. The Nayak rule lasted until the middle of the 18th century, when the British gradually took over.

Through its vicissitudes Madurai has remained a great city, its temple a magnet for pilgrims from all over India. The tradition of literary Tamil in Madurai dates from pre-Christian times, with successive academies (Tamil *sangams*) serving as the nerve centre of Tamil culture. The Madurai temple, in a sense, symbolises all that being a Tamil means. Even today, when the city has a population of over a million, the temple's presence can be felt everywhere in Madurai.

The Minaksi temple

Myth and legend take concrete form in the city. The **Minaksi Sundaresvara temple** (commonly known as the Minaksi temple; inner temple open 5am–12.30pm, 4–9.30pm) in the heart of Madurai is probably the biggest temple in the country, both in area and in the number of structures within a single compound. The area of the temple, an approximate square about 245 metres (800 ft) by 228 metres

LEFT: a Minaksi temple *gopuram*. **RIGHT:** a devotee at the Minaksi temple.

(750 ft), contains a multitude of shrines, halls and colonnades. It is believed there are 33 million sculptures in the temple. While this figure might be an exaggeration, there are a sufficient number to keep the visitor occupied for days.

The primary deity in the temple is not Siva, but his consort Minaksi. Though the temple was originally established around the *lingam* that Indra, the king of gods, is said to have found in this area, it was consecrated to Minaksi, daughter of a Pandyan king, who was wooed and won by Siva. (Minaksi and Sundaresvara are among the names by which Sakti and Siva are known.)

At first glance, the outstanding features of the temple are the four towers at the four points of the compass, soaring between 43–49 metres (140–160 ft). There are other towers inside the temple complex also, but the four corner *gopurams* are the most striking. These are essentially entryways into the temple; more precisely, they surmount the huge entrances which are about 18 metres (60 ft) high. Each *gopuram* is adorned with numerous sculptures of gods and goddesses, people, animals and birds. The tallest of the towers, the southern one, can be climbed for a small fee. The visitor will encounter both grimy steps and bats, but will be rewarded with a spectacular view.

The towers are periodically renovated, with new sculptures replacing old, damaged ones, and then everything is gaily – or garishly – painted, as has always been the custom here. When newly painted the colours are particularly bright and it is interesting to consider that this would have been how Greek and Roman temples, as well as many Western cathedrals, would have initially appeared. Over the years, wind and rain soften the new sculptures so they blend in well with the original works. It should also be remembered that, without binoculars, these sculptures are seen from a distance of at least 20 metres (60 ft).

However, the sculptures inside the temple are, for the most part, at eye level. It is

Map on page 136

customary to enter a temple by its eastern entrance, but in the Minaksi temple the eastern entrance with its magnificent tower is permanently closed, though it is the oldest. Some centuries ago, a temple servant committed suicide by flinging himself from the top of the *gopuram*. Since then, visitors enter the temple by an adjacent gateway which has no tower over it. This leads to the **Asta Sakti mandapam**, a hall with sculptured pillars which represent the various aspects of the goddess Sakti, as well as scenes from some of the miracles – there are 64 of them in all – that Siva performed in Madurai. Shops selling the paraphernalia that devotees need for worship flank the hall. Next to this hall is the **Minaksi Nayakkar mandapam**, also known as the **Yali mandapam** because on each of its 110 pillars is a carved *yali*, a mythical animal somewhat akin to a griffin. This hall has a votive lamp-holder with 1,008 lamps, which are lit on festive occasions and present a spectacular sight.

LEFT: religious instruction in the Minaksi temple.
BELOW: a pillared arcade by the temple tank.

The **Chitra gopuram**, adjacent to the Yali *mandapam*, is the tallest tower within the temple. It has seven storeys covered with sculptures, and leads into a passage which has a sculpture of Siva as a mendicant. Next is the **Potramaraikulam** (Tank of the Golden Lotuses) and the magnificent colonnade which surrounds this reservoir. The colonnade has an assortment of sculptures and paintings all around, most of them depicting Tamil poets and poetry, and the various aspects of the temple. From the colonnade, the steps lead down to the tank in which the god Indra is believed to have bathed. An important part of attending the temple for devotees is to take a dip in its holy waters.

Passing by the **Rani Mangammal mandapam**, and the **Unjal mandapam** (so called because it has an *unjal* or swing on which golden images of Siva and Minaksi are placed every Friday and rocked to the chanting of hymns by the priests), the visitor comes to the **Kilikkundu mandapam** (Parrot-cage

Hall) which has not only caged green parrots, Minaksi's sacred bird, but another set of huge monolithic pillars, each depicting a character from mythology and the epics. On the western side of this hall a three-storey tower leads to the shrine of the goddess; non-Hindus are not admitted in here. While the sanctum houses the image of Minaksi, the shrine comprises two concentric corridors and several halls and galleries.

A tower north of the Parrot-cage *mandapam* leads to the shrine of **Sundaresvara**. The first thing the visitor encounters here is a huge monolithic figure of the elephant-headed god Ganesha, which is supposed to have been unearthed when the Mariamman Teppakulam was being excavated. The most important part of the shrine is the **Kambattadi mandapam** around the flagstaff in front of the sanctum. It is difficult not to indulge in superlatives when describing any part of the Madurai temple, but the temptation becomes acute when contemplating the magnificence of the monolithic sculptured pillars in this hall. The most beautiful of them all depicts the god Visnu giving away his sister Minaksi in marriage to Sundaresvara. Other spectacular sculptures are those of Siva in an acrobatic dance pose and Parvati in the aspect of Kali. Beyond this *mandapam* is a three-storey tower marking the entrance to the sanctum of Sundaresvara. Non-Hindus are not allowed to enter the inner sanctum.

The **Ayirakkal mandapam** – the 1,000-pillar hall – which lies to the east of the sanctum is one of the great glories of the temple. There are actually 985 pillars, and they are a riot of sculptures, depicting gods and goddesses as well as human beings. The hall now serves as an **Art Museum** (open daily 6am–8pm, entrance charge) which exhibits bronzes and other artifacts, as well as paintings and photographs which outline Tamil culture and architecture, and selected episodes from mythology.

BELOW: the Tirumalai Nayak Palace.

Map on page 136

The Minaksi temple is no museum; it is a vital, living temple. Devotees worship at its many shrines several times a day. There is a festive atmosphere all the time: in fact, there is a major festival at least once a month, the most important among them being the **Chitra festival** (April to May) to celebrate the wedding of Minaksi and Sundaresvara. This festival draws over 100,000 devotees from different parts of India. The temple is also a living entity in the sense that people live out their lives in its premises: weddings take place, classes are held, people eat and sleep there and run the numerous shops it houses.

Across the east gate is another architectural gem, the **Pudu mandapam** (New Hall). It is a large rectangular hall, supported by 124 sculpted pillars, each over 6 metres (20 ft) high. The pillars are most intricately carved, and no two are alike. During the Chitra festival, the images of Minaksi and Sundaresvara are kept here for a while. Unfortunately, except during the festival, the Pudu *mandapam* is cluttered with all sorts of shops, and it is sometimes difficult to view the sculptures, except those on the outside. An unfinished tower east of the Pudu *mandapam*, huge in conception – its base measures 64 by 36 metres (210 by 120 ft) – is yet another legacy of Nayak construction.

There are several other temples in Madurai which are worth seeing. The **Kudal Alagar**, a Visnu temple, may be as ancient as the Minaksi temple, and it has beautifully carved stone lattice windows.

The visitor should also make a special effort to see another Visnu temple, the **Kallalagar temple** in **Alagarkovil** ㉓, about 20 km (12 miles) to the northwest of Madurai. It is located on a hill in the forest, and has some splendid sculptures depicting the various incarnations of Visnu. It is also the place from which Visnu is supposed to have travelled to Madurai, crossing the river Vaigai on his way to the temple to give his sister Minaksi away in marriage to Sundaresvara.

Tirumalai Nayak Palace

The splendour of the Nayak rule in Madurai is evident in the remains of the **palace of Tirumalai Nayak** (open daily 9am–1pm, 2–5pm, entrance charge), the most famous king of the Nayak dynasty. The palace originally occupied an area of nearly 300 metres (1,000 ft) by 213 metres (700 ft), and consisted of many splendid apartments and galleries, as well as gardens, tanks and fountains. Much of it is gone now, but for the great audience hall, a three-sided pavilion about 67 metres (220 ft) by 33 metres (110 ft); the courtyard, supported by pillars 18 metres (60 ft) high and 3.6 metres (12 ft) in circumference; and a dome over 18 metres (60 ft) high, unsupported by girders or rafters. These indicate the magnificence of the palace as it must have been. Some of the original apartments still remain, and a museum has been set up in one of the halls. *Son et lumière* shows which vividly portray the Nayak period in Madurai's history are held every day (6.45–7.30pm).

IGHT: the alace's pectacular terior.

Yet another Nayak legacy is the **Mariamman Teppakulam**, one of the biggest and most beautiful tanks in the country. The tank is at Vandiyur, in the eastern part of the city. The great Ganesha in the Minaksi temple was found here when the earth was being dug up for use in the construction of the palace and the temple. Rather than leave a big hole in the ground, Thirumalai Nayak converted it into a tank, and set up an engineering system by which it was fed from the waters of the river Vaigai, north of the city. Unfortunately, the tank now remains dry for much of the year due to the absence of the monsoons, but water is usually let in for the float festival, a colourful occasion when a decorated and illuminated float goes around in the gentle waters of the tank. There is a many-tiered pavilion in the middle of the tank which is accessible by boat.

Today, Madurai is a bustling and populous industrial and commercial city. It has large textile mills, automobile ancillary works, and a variety of small-scale industries. Traditionally it was a town of weavers, who still continue to produce rich textiles in both silk and cotton.

Mahatma Gandhi Memorial

Before leaving Madurai there is one more recommended stop visitors could make. This is the **Mahatma Gandhi Memorial**, in the Tumkum Palace in Tallakulam, in the northeast part of the city. The Memorial offers an overview of the Mahatma's life through paintings and a variety of memorabilia. Some of his possessions are preserved here, but the most interesting exhibit is a model of the hut in which Gandhiji lived in Sevagram. It displays his minimal personal belongings, a replica of his bed, and other furniture. The campus is also the location of Madurai's **Government Museum** (open Sat–Thur, closed second Sat in the month, 9.30am–5pm).

The Tumkum Palace was built in the late 17th century by a great queen of the Nayak dynasty, Rani Mangamma. It is a

Map on page 136

relatively simple structure set on two levels, with a cupola on top, but it has great dignity. An air of peace surrounds the palace, set in the middle of a well-kept garden. In the period of British rule it was known as Tumkum Bungalow, and was occupied by successive Collectors of Madras (Chennai).

Chettinad

A two-hour journey east of Madurai or south of Tiruchchirappalli leads into the heart of **Chettinad**, the land of the Chettiars. The 78 villages left of the original 96 remain a fascinating study for those interested in architecture and artisanship, faith and culture, banking and investment, antiques and jewellery, comfort and cuisine.

An ancient merchant community, the Chettiars were renowned in the 19th century as the bankers of South India. Their financial reputation and their wealth were both earned in India and overseas, in Burma, Sri Lanka, Malaysia, Indo-China and Singapore. The riches earned abroad were always brought back to the ancestral villages from which the Chettiars hailed – and there, in the parched wilderness of scrub, they built mansions the like of which are rarely found in South India. They also made Chettiar hospitality and philanthropy known all over the country.

To the newcomer travelling from village to village, the block-long mansions emerge almost like gigantic mirages from the swirling dust. A greater surprise awaits inside. Pillars of teak or satinwood or gleaming black granite are to be found by the score in every house, as well as intricately carved doors of solid teak. Marble from Italy appears to have been favoured for much of the flooring. The walls are gleaming white, and a secret process in the finish makes them velvet-smooth to the touch. Traditionally, lime, egg white, powdered shells and an astringent fruit called myrobalan are mixed to a paste which dries to produce the finish. The

LEFT: testing the waters at the Minaksi temple.
BELOW: a bullock cart on the road near Nagercoil.

quality of the wood carving, especially on the doors, is fine. As final touches, the deserted mansions are hung with chandeliers, fittings and paintings worthy of a palace. Some of the finest mansions can be found in **Karaikkudi** ㉔, the largest village in the region, and nearby **Kanadukathan** ㉕.

For nearly a century before Independence, each house was filled with kitchenware of brass and stainless steel, with cupboards, mattresses and pillows and anything else an establishment might need in quantities fit for an army. The strongest safes in the house would keep silverware and traditional jewellery of gold and diamonds, rubies, emeralds and pearls, every bit fit for royalty.

But all that was in the years from the late 19th century until Independence. The winds of change that first stirred in India also brought independence to the countries where the Chettiars had made their fortunes. The new nationalism brought in its wake a Chettiar exodus; they had to return home to an uncertain future with only their material possessions to fall back upon.

The Chettiars, however, are traditionally hardy and resourceful, and forsook banking and financing – their previous means of earning a living – to become successful professionals and industrialists. But the wealth required to maintain the homes no longer exists. Today almost every Chettiar village is deserted, large numbers of its splendid houses have been pulled down, most of the rest becoming ghostly homes, maintained at a fraction of the standards that once prevailed. To make survival possible, many Chettiar families have had to sell off family possessions in bits and pieces, and today around 90,000 members of the community live outside the ancestral stronghold. The antique shops in the bylanes of Karaikkudi still have a few treasures from those houses. Antique dealers were attracted in droves. Most of the treasures have long been auctioned off, though a

Map on page 136

few pieces of the fine furniture in seasoned Burma teak can still be found.

To go through these decaying mansions is to marvel at the wealth that went into them and the achievement of the untrained local artisans who built them. If you were lucky enough to attend a Chettiar wedding – now reduced to just a day from the week-long celebration it used to be – you would wonder what the hospitality, constrained by circumstances now, would have been in the past before Chettiar fortunes fell low. The legacy of Chettinad culture survives best in the cuisine, which is popular far outside the former princely state of Pudukkatai, with its taste for unusual spices and peppery meat, with dried fruits added.

LEFT: basalt columns on the coast.
BELOW: the pillared corridor at the Ramesvaram temple.

Palk Bay

Around the corner from Point Calimere, the Palk Bay begins to curve inwards. Along this coast, bathed by calmer seas than on the Coromandel, are the ports from which migrant labour went from India to Sri Lanka: Athirampattinam, Tondi and **Devipattinam** ㉖. The last-named is also associated with the legends surrounding Lord Rama. By Devipattinam's temple there are nine stone pillars in the sea where Rama is said to have worshipped the nine planets. Where the bay curves out and opens onto Palk Strait is **Mandapam**, a major marine research centre.

Ramesvaram

Across the bridge from Mandapam is the sacred island **Ramesvaram** ㉗, one of the holiest places of the Hindus. Several places on the island are associated with the epic hero, Lord Rama. It is believed that the two *lingams* in the sanctum of the magnificently sculpted **Ramanatasvami temple** were installed on this spot by Rama himself. The temple, it is said, took 350 years to complete; its crowning glory is a magnificent 1,220-metre (4,000-ft) long pillared corridor that surrounds the main quadrangle.

The **Kotandrasvami temple** at **Danushkodi** on the island, with its bronzes of the victors of the *Ramayana*, and **Gandamadanam hill**, where Rama's footprint is enshrined at the site of Hanuman's leap to Lanka, are other places pilgrims visit in Ramesvaram. More secular attractions are to be found on some of southeastern India's finest beaches.

Ramesvaram is connected to the mainland by road and rail. Looking over the road bridge, travellers will see huge boulders in the sea: these are in fact an extension of Adam's Bridge, the mythical land link between India and Sri Lanka. A ferry service once served as the link between Ramesvaram and Talaimannar on Sri Lanka, but now it awaits more propitious times for its revival.

Back on the mainland south of Mandapam lies the Fisheries Coast. Here fishing villages vie with one another to build a bigger church with a taller steeple, often with spectacular results. These villages once sent out the divers who made the Gulf of Mannar renowned even in Roman times for its pearl fisheries.

Part of the gulf is now protected as the **Mannar Marine Park**, centred around 21 uninhabited coral islands. The waters here are one of the last refuges of the endangered dugong, and, although access is restricted, the ecosystem is under threat from both illegal sand extraction and plans to dredge a channel for commercial shipping through the straits.

Tuticorin

Today ports like Kilakkarai and Sethukarai are almost deserted, but the fortunes of **Tuticorin** ㉘, the Tutukudi of the Tamils, have revived. Its new port is one of the most modern in India, and has helped develop an industrial hinterland. Once every few years, Tuticorin organises a small pearl fishery, and although the yields are poor it helps to keep a diving tradition alive.

South of Tuticorin is the shore temple of **Tiruchendur** ㉙, perched on a rocky

BELOW: Vivekananda's rock at Kanniyakumari.

Map on page 136

ledge that falls sheer to the ocean. One of the six abodes of Lord Murugan, the temple is more than 1,000 years old. Few temples elsewhere in India are more scenically located, and even fewer more beautifully built. Near Tiruchendur there are also other well-known temple towns in the area, such as Alvar Tirunagiri and Sri Vaikundam.

Kanniyakumari

Beyond these lies **Kanniyakumari** ㉚ (Cape Comorin), India's southernmost point, where three seas meet, and sacred to the virgin goddess Kumari. It is an important Hindu pilgrimage site; after bathing in the Ganges at Varanasi it is said you should bathe in the sea at Kanniyakumari and worship the goddess to complete the pilgrimage and attain salvation. Her temple is a magnificently sculpted structure and the image of the goddess in its sanctum (closed to non-Hindus) is famous for its diamond nose ring.

The **Gandhi Mandapam**, built in Kalinga style, commemorates the immersion of the ashes of Mahatma Gandhi, the Father of the Nation, in the waters by the temple. In the large hall is a statue of the Mahatma and above his head is an opening in the roof through which every 2 October, his birthday, sunlight streams to light up his brow, symbolising the light of freedom. The other memorial, dedicated to **Svami Vivekananda** (open Wed–Mon 7–11am, 2–5pm, entrance charge), is built on the rock 200 metres (650 ft) from shore where he meditated in 1892 before taking the message of Vedanta, his version of Hindu philosophy, to the West. The memorial can be reached by ferry.

The church of Our Lady of Joy, which Francis Xavier founded in the 1540s, the beaches with their celebrated sands and rocks in seven colours, the rising and setting of the sun, and of the moon on full moon nights, are further attractions of the pilgrimage town.

Further up the coast is the temple in **Suchindram** ㉛ with some of the finest specimens of temple art and sculpture in the country. The *devadasis* no longer dance for the gods, but the music to which they performed finds echoes in the "musical pillars" that have been sculpted in the north corridor out of single blocks of granite. When tapped, musical sounds can be heard, each pillar producing a different note.

Padmanabhapuram

Nagercoil, with its temples and churches, and the inviting beach at **Colachel**, overlooked by a Circular Fort, are breaks on the way to the palace at **Padmanabhapuram** ㉜ (open Tues–Sun 9am–1pm, 2–4.30pm, entrance charge; *see also page 192*), Tamil Nadu's legacy from Kerala. The splendid fort and palace set out around four courtyards were once the seat of the Maharajas of Travancore, before the capital moved to Thiruvananthapuram in 1790. The museum in the palace has a fine collection of murals, stone sculpture and beautiful wood carving. The lush tropical vegetation is a contrast to the disciplined fields and groves of the Kaveri delta and the aridity of the rest of the coast. ❑

RIGHT: Padmanabhapuram.

Map on page 170

THE HILL STATIONS

High in the Nilgiri Hills are the cool summer retreats of the British, set in lush, beautiful countryside and surrounded by wonderful views

The resorts of Tamil Nadu are all in the hills, a hangover from the days of the Raj when the British took to the plateaux and hilltops to escape the heat of the plains. These days the hill stations are even more crowded during the "season", from late-March to mid-June. At other times of the year, if the visitor is willing to cope with drizzle and showers, bright moments of sun that vanish into various shades of dull grey mornings and bundled-up evenings, the hill resorts are ideal.

Tiruvannamalai

Southwest of Chennai is the **Vedanthangal** sanctuary *(see page 141)* and 100 km (63 miles) to the west is the sacred Arunachala Hill of **Tiruvannamalai** ❸❸. The **Arunachalesvara temple** is one of the most sacred and largest shrines in India which attracts a huge number of pilgrims. Sprawling 10 hectares (25 acres) and more over the hillside, it is entered through a giant gateway over which towers a 66-metre (200-ft) high, 11-storey *gopuram*. Within the regularly laid-out temple compound – much of it built by the Vijayanagara rulers – are a number of shrines, including those to Subramanyam and Ganapati (both sons of Siva and Parvati), and a monumental Nandi. However, the central sanctum sanctorum (which dates back to the Cholas) is dedicated to Siva in the form of a *lingam*. During the temple's festival in November–December, the sacred beacon lit on the hilltop can be seen for miles around.

Some way west of Tiruvannamalai are the waterfalls at **Hogenakkal** ❸❹. The waters of the falls are said to have medicinal properties. A massage with mineral oils, available from scores of local masseurs, is an invigorating part of the bathing ritual. Another exhilarating experience is boating in frail coracles made of hide on the "rapids" at the foot of the falls.

LEFT: the train makes its way up to Ooty. **RIGHT:** A garlanded Nandi at Tiruvannamalai.

Salem and Coimbatore

Southeast of Hogenakkal is the commercial centre of **Salem** ❸❺. Well known in India for its steel industry, this is a modern, busy junction that serves as a good place to reach the hills just beyond the city. If you need to kill time here, there is a small **Government Museum** (open Sat–Thur, closed second Sat in the month) on Navalar Road with some local archaeological and anthropological exhibits.

Up the winding roads to the northeast of Salem is **Yercaud** ❸❻ in the Shevaroy Hills. Set in coffee and orange country, the sleepy old school town is still much quieter than some of the better-known hill stations, and the visitor has a choice of wandering through tree-shaded estates,

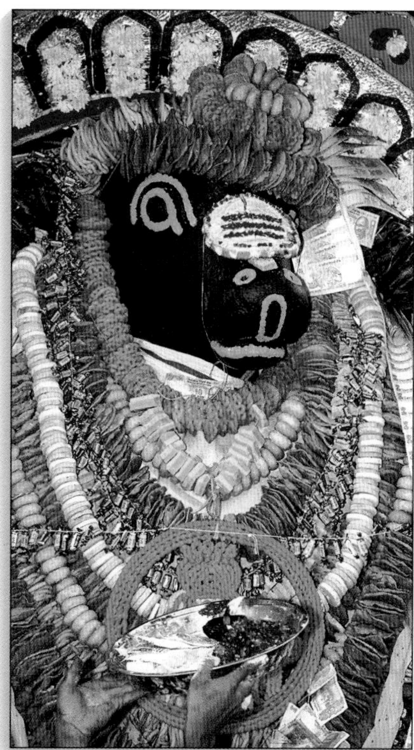

trekking along mountain trails or strolling around the lake. Several local apiaries supply delightful fresh honey.

Bhavani Sagar 37, the lake to the southwest of Salem, has the longest multi-purpose dam in the world, 8 km (5 miles) across. It is also the halfway house between Salem and the industrial centre of Coimbatore, from where begins the climb into the Nilgiris, the Blue Hills. **Coimbatore** 38, the centre of black-soil cotton country, is known as the Manchester of South India for its concentration of textile mills. Aside from the well-decorated Siva temple at **Perur** (6 km/4 miles from the centre), the attractions in the city include the **botanical gardens** on the outskirts and the nearby **Gass Forest Museum** (open Mon–Fri 9am–1pm, 3–5.30pm) which concentrates on local flora. The Government Museum on Mettapalayam Road (open Sat–Thur, closed second Sat in the month, 9.30am–5pm) has a small collection concentrating on local social and natural history.

Northwest of Coimbatore are the Nilgiris. The climb into the hills begins at **Mettupalayam** 39 and offers wonderful views from the switchbacks.

Coonoor and Ooty

A more exciting way of getting up to Ooty, or Udagamandalam, as it is now called, is on a tiny metre-gauge train with takes you up in a series of switchbacks. Starting from Mettupalayam, a steam train runs on a rack up to Coonoor at 1,650 metres (5,500 ft), before switching engines for the run up to Ooty at 2,250 metres (7,500 ft). At times the train seems to be clinging to the edge of the mountain, at others it chugs comfortably through the middle of small hill villages, proceeding all the while at walking pace.

Coonoor 40, surrounded on all sides by hills and slopes of tea, is a small, quiet town of old colonial houses. Sim's Park is a pleasant botanical garden and there is a nearby lake to walk around. A popular excursion is to **Catherine Falls** some 11

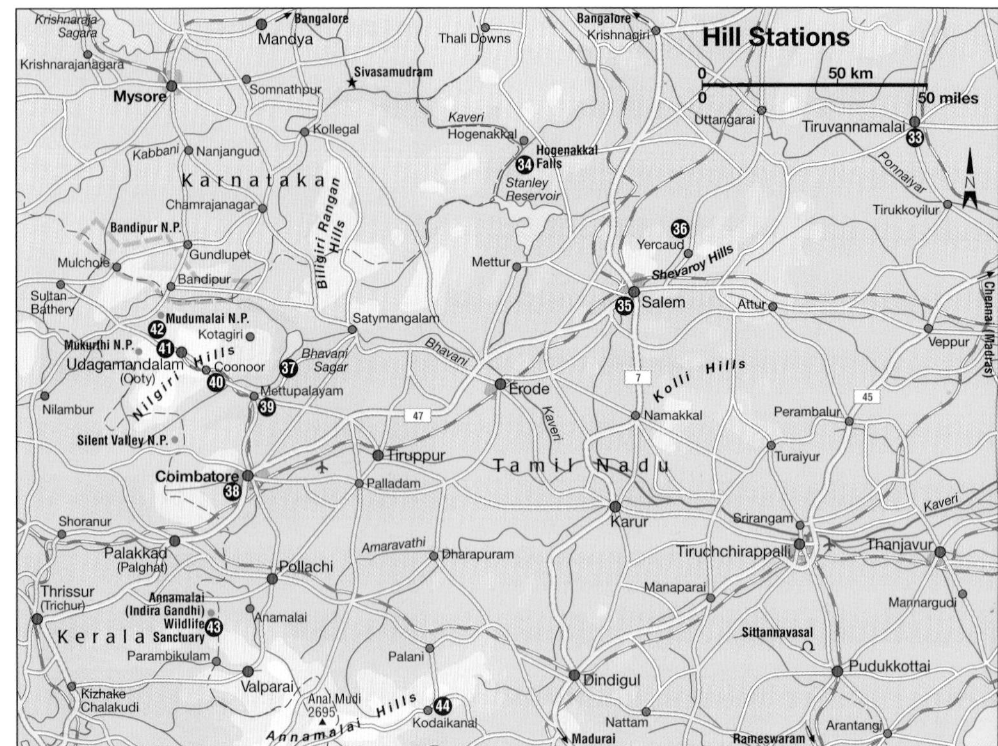

Map on page 170

km (7 miles) away at a vantage point known as **Dolphin's Nose**, while more fine views can be had from **Lamb's Rock** (7 km/4½ miles). Coonoor is also a research centre, with several experimental fruit farms and the Pasteur Institute. Tea auctions are held here and in the nearby cantonment town of **Wellington**. It is the home base of the Chennai Regiment, the oldest unit in the Indian Army, and houses the Staff College of the defence forces. They have a small museum here (open daily summer 8.30am–1.30pm, 3–5pm, winter 8.30am–1.45pm, 3.30–5.30pm).

Udagamandalam ㊶ is the best known of the Tamil hill stations. Now quite built up and very crowded in high season, it has lost some of its charm, but there is still plenty to see and off the beaten track there are some nice, quiet corners. The **botanical gardens** (open daily 8am–6pm, entrance charge) are a blaze of colours during the annual flower show in May, and a delightful excursion during the rest of the year. The town's main junction is called Charing Cross – remember, the locations were named by the British – and close by are a number of colonial buildings, of which the most important is St Stephen's church, built in 1831. Beyond the church is Ooty club, where snooker is said to have been invented.

The large **lake** at the other end of town has rowing boats for hire. Other activities in the area include horse riding and walking. Numerous peaks and waterfalls await exploration: Dodabetta is the highest peak in the area at 2,637 metres (8,605 ft). Ooty is also tea country, and a visit to a tea estate is easy to arrange; contact the headquarters of the United Planters' Association of South India (UPASI) in Coonoor.

The original inhabitants of the Nilgiris were Adivasi peoples, including the Kotas and Todas. They were initially dispossessed of their land by the British, a process continued by successive Indian governments, and, although they have now been given some land back, they continue to face the erosion of their traditional ways of life, many of which have now died out.

BELOW: the Nilgiri landscape.

Mudumalai

To the east of Ooty, located at 1,950 metres (6,500 ft), is **Kotagiri**, which was the first hill station in the Nilgris. Nearby are **Kunda** and **Pykara** alongside hydroelectric projects, and to the north of Ooty is **Mudumalai** ❹❷ (open all year, 6–9am, 4–6pm). This is Tamil Nadu's biggest wildlife sanctuary, and forms an important wildlife corridor as it is contiguous with Karnataka's Bandipur and Kerala's Waynad.

Mudumalai has a wealth of wildlife; deer, wild boar, monkeys and birdlife. Occasionally an elephant herd may be seen and, with some luck, a tiger, a leopard, packs of wild dogs or any of a variety of resident reptiles. The pride of Mudumalai is its gaur, the Indian bison, nearly decimated by disease in the past but now seen again in numbers.

Back in the plains, heading south of Coimbatore, you reach the lower slopes of the Annamalai Hills, from where a climb takes you to **Top Slip**, the main camp of the **Indira Gandhi Wildlife Sanctuary** ❹❸ (open all year, 6.30am–6.30pm). Here are some of the thickest rainforests in South India and it is difficult terrain to get around in; knowledgeable guides can take you deep into the forest.

East of **Pollachi** is **Palani**, a major pilgrim centre beside the huge Vyapuri tank and main base for the journey into the tea hills and wildlife sanctuaries of the Annamalais. It is the most renowned of the six abodes of Murugan, the son of Siva. Its annual festival in January–February brings thousands from Tamil Nadu; they trek all the way to Palani and then climb the 659 steps to the 135-metre (450-ft) high peak to worship at the temple at the summit.

Kodaikanal

South of Palani and not far from it, in fact on the southern crest of the Upper Palani Plateau, at an elevation of 2,100 metres (7,000 ft), is the other famed hill station of Tamil Nadu, **Kodaikanal** ❹❹. Smaller than Ooty and less congested, Kodaikanal owes its development to American

Map on page 170

missionaries working in Tamil Nadu and northern Sri Lanka. Looking for a rest station and sanatorium, they chose "Kodi" in the 1840s, but it was only after the British Governor Sir Charles Trevelyan's visit in 1860 that the site began to develop as a hill station.

Kodi's pride is its star-shaped lake, which offers boating and a 4.8-km (3-mile) promenade. Beside the lake is Bryant Park. It is at its best during the fruit and flower show in May. An even better flower show is laid on by nature when the Kurinji blooms once in 12 years, carpeting the hillside with pale blue; the next bloom is due in 2006. The church at the end of the bazaar marks the start of Coaker's Walk, named after the military engineer who laid it out; the views from the path are superb. The three 120-metre (400-ft) high **Pillar rocks**, 7 km (4½ miles) away, are another popular excursion with similarly spectacular views.

South from Kodi, there are a few delightful places in the foothills of the Western Ghats. About 300 metres (1,000 ft) above sea level is the quiet town of **Kuttalam** ㊺. Set amidst low hills and forests, Kuttalam is renowned for its five waterfalls and fine climate. June to October is when the Cittar river cascades down the rocks and the waterfalls are at their best. Bathing in the mineral-rich water is a great restorative.

In another forest setting a little southwest are **Papanasam falls** and its temple whose deity absolves all sin. Together they make Papanasam an important pilgrim centre. Just east of here is the **Mundanthurai** sanctuary, sited on the slopes (600 metres/2,000 ft) of the Papanasam hills and now a Project Tiger reserve. To the east, near Tirunelveli, is the **Kalakad** sanctuary, now administered as part of Mundanthurai. Deer and four monkey species – Nilgiri and common langurs, bonnet and lion-tailed macaques – are found here.

From Kalakad to the temples of **Tirunelveli** ㊻ and the churches of **Palayamkottai** ㊼ down on the plains it is only 32 km (20 miles). ❑

LEFT: Nilgiri tea pickers.
BELOW: Nilgiri view: the Blue Mountains.

PONDICHERRY

Map on page 136

Part of France until Independence and still retaining a faint Gallic flavour, Pondicherry is unlike anywhere else in India, especially as it is now home to Auroville, the "City of Dawn"

The former capital of the French territories in India was **Pondicherry** ❹❽. Its history was one of constant conflict, first with the Dutch, then with the British, who attacked the French in India whenever there were hostilities between England and France in Europe. They occupied Pondicherry several times, and during one such period, from 1761 to 1765, they razed the town to the ground, leaving unscathed just a few places of worship. It was only from 1816 that Pondicherry enjoyed a period of stability and peace. The city which we now see came up gradually, literally on the ashes of the old one. Today it is the administrative capital of a Union Territory which also includes former French enclaves elsewhere in the South – Mahé in Kerala, Yanam in Andhra and Karaikkal, also in Tamil Nadu.

Pondicherry lies within an oval boulevard which girdles the entire town. Within the oval, streets are laid out running east to west, and these are bisected by streets that run from north to south. The layout of the town is thus (except for the later additions) a series of squares and rectangles, which makes it easy for visitors to find their way around. The French reserved the seafront for their homes and offices, and laid out five streets parallel to the beach on which they built fine mansions. This was known as the *Ville Blanche* or White Town, and demarcated by a canal from the *Ville Noir* or Black Town. In the course of time the canal dried up, and now unfortunately serves as a dumping ground for garbage.

Pondicherry is located on the east coast of South India, 160 km (100 miles) south of Chennai. It is routine for guidebooks to describe Pondicherry as "a sleepy French provincial city", an impression based almost entirely on recollections of the seafront, which looks vaguely Mediterranean, and of the former White Town where the streets tend to be quiet and clean, and high-walled compounds protect gracious old buildings set among shady trees. Pondicherry today is a bustling town with a population close to 736,000. Over the years the French influence has declined, but enough remains to mark out Pondicherry as different. The French have an active cultural presence. Their language is still spoken extensively among older residents and French citizens of Indian origin. A number of streets still bear their original French names, commemorating famous generals: Rue Suffren, Rue Law de Lauriston, Rue Mahe de la Bourdonnais, for example. Bastille Day is still celebrated with some of the fervour one would see in France.

PRECEDING PAGES: a devotee is watched by a palm squirrel at the Aurobindo Samadhi.
LEFT: Pondicherry's mix: Jewish symbols on an art deco facade.

The quickest way to get to Pondicherry is by bus from Chennai. There are several buses a day, some air-conditioned, the roads are reasonably good, and the travelling time is about four hours. There are several daily railway connections with Chennai via the broad gauge junction at Villupuram, but the journey takes a bit longer. Pondicherry also has bus connections with a number of other towns in Tamil Nadu. The weather is hot and humid for most of the year, but pretty equable from November to March. Warm clothing is rarely required.

It is fortunate that quite a few of the sights in Pondicherry are in the old White Town or nearby. The visitor cannot do better than to start with the **Raj Nivas**, the residence of the Lieutenant Governor of Pondicherry, even if one can do little more than peer at it from the outside. It is a handsome 200-year-old building which was once the residence of the redoubtable Marquis Joseph-François Dupleix, a great governor and builder of Pondicherry. It represents the best of the period's French and Indian style of architecture, a fusion not in the least jarring. The furniture is French in style with carved Indian motifs (a kind still to be seen in many old houses in Pondicherry). There are several stone sculptures in the garden, the most prominent of which is a representation of the god Visnu in his incarnation as a boar.

The Raj Nivas faces **Government Park**. This is the old **French Place**, renovated and somewhat Indianised. It is a pleasant site, with well laid-out paths and lawns. A number of sculptures, most of them brought back from Gingee after a long-forgotten war, add to the attractions of the park. The park also boasts a few fountains, one of them dating back to the time of Napoleon III, and a mysterious monument at its centre about which different tales are told. Several government offices, the Pondicherry Legislative Assembly, the Tourism Department, and the Romain Rolland Library are located on the streets around the park.

ELOW: the acade of the rench colonial acred Heart hurch.

The library and museum

The **Romain Rolland Library** (open Tues–Sun 7.30am–8.30pm) is well worth a look. Founded in 1827, it is one of the oldest public libraries in India, and with over 315,000 volumes on its shelves, it has a superb collection of French and English books, many of them on Indian topics and many of them rare.

The **Pondicherry Museum** is located on Saint Louis Street (open Tues–Sun 10am–5pm). The museum has an outstanding collection of artefacts, especially relating to all aspects of the French Indian past. It has attempted with some success to recreate a French ambience in one section where the rooms are furnished in French style, and decorated with paintings, marbles, mirrors and clocks. The atmosphere is very much that of an elegant French home of the early 19th century. A display of antique armaments and weapons makes for another interesting section. The museum also houses rare bronze and stone sculptures from the Pallava and Chola periods in Indian history, and Roman artifacts excavated in nearby Arikamedu. Its prize exhibit is the bed that Dupleix slept on when he was Governor of Pondicherry.

From the Government Park, a short distance eastward is the beach, dominated by a 4-metre (13-ft) statue of Mahatma Gandhi in his familiar walking pose, stick in hand. Tall sculpted stone pillars, probably again from Gingee, encircle the statue. Slightly to the north of the Gandhi statue is the Memorial raised by the French in honour of the soldiers from French India who died in World War I. This is a poignant piece of art, the centrepiece of which is a soldier with his head bent in reverence. Moving scenes are engraved on the back of the monument, which is a large rectangular slab. It is surrounded by beautifully maintained lawns and hedges.

The beach in this part of Pondicherry is narrow, but pleasant and clean. For about 6 km (4 miles) south, this is a very good place to swim. The boulevard in front of

BELOW: a cycle rickshaw makes its way through Pondicherry's streets.

Map on page 136

the beach here, known as **Goubert Salai**, is wide and well maintained and provides a promenade for jogging, walking or simply sitting, both morning and evening.

Going south along the boulevard, the visitor soon reaches the **lighthouse** and the new **pier**. At this point, where the coast begins to curve, a magnificent statue of Dupleix, which originally stood on the pedestal now occupied by the statue of Gandhi, has been re-erected. Set in the middle of a small and beautifully manicured children's park, the statue dominates this part of the beach as much as the Gandhi statue does the northern end.

The Botanical Gardens

Before turning back into the city the visitor can follow the boulevard, which now becomes the South Boulevard, all the way to the Botanical Gardens. The major attraction on this road is the **Church of the Sacred Heart of Jesus**. Gothic in style and serene in atmosphere, it has some noteworthy features: three large stained-glass panels that tell the life of Jesus, and many handsome arches that span the nave. Further along the boulevard on the southern side is the **cemetery**. Those interested in monuments will find several interesting tombs with marble decorations from Europe. The **Botanical Gardens** mark the end of the South Boulevard and the beginning of West Boulevard. Set up in 1826, it has grown over the decades to become one of the best botanical gardens in the South, with unusual and exotic plants from all over the country and abroad. An interesting little aquarium is an adjunct to the Gardens.

Getting back to the beach-front area again, the visitor comes upon a statue of Joan of Arc on Rue Dumas, set as usual in a garden (which, however, is not as well maintained as it should be). A universal symbol of resistance, the Maid of Orleans is shown in an appropriately heroic pose. A short distance away is the church of **Notre Dame des Anges**, a striking structure with twin square towers. Built around 1865, the church boasts a rare oil painting of Our Lady of the Assumption, another gift from Napoleon III.

The Institute of Indology

On Saint Louis Street is the **French Institute of Pondicherry** (open Mon–Fri 8.30am–5.30pm, www.ifpindia.org). Established in the mid-1950s by an eminent French Indologist, Dr Jean Filliozat, the Institute has expanded its scope to include various scientific disciplines. It is now an internationally renowned research organisation and provides an abiding link between France and India, since it works in cooperation with several French universities and research organisations.

The French Government maintains the **Alliance Française** (www.afindia.org), located at 58 Suffren Street, which promotes French culture and the teaching of the French language. It has a well-equipped library of French books and periodicals, and organises shows of French cinema, music, theatre and art.

One of the most eminent Indians in the history of Pondicherry was Ananda Ranga Pillai. He was Dupleix's trusted confidant and trade agent, and he enjoyed unlimited

RIGHT: inside the Sacred Heart church.

powers and prestige during his lifetime. His more important claim to fame lies in his diary, covering the period 1736–60. It is a storehouse of information not only about the French rule in India, but also about the social customs and manners of the period. His house, on Rue Rangapoulle, has been converted into a **museum** (apply in advance for permission to visit). Architecturally, it is a fusion of the French and Indian styles – a graceful building, lavishly furnished and decorated. It gives the visitor an understanding of how an 18th-century Indian nobleman lived in Pondicherry.

The Indian side of Pondicherry's culture is more on display at the **Bharatiyar Memorial Museum and Research Centre** at 20 Easwaram Dharmaraja Koil Street (open Tues–Sat 9am–12.30pm, 2–5.45 pm, Sun 9am–12.30pm). The museum contains manuscripts, letters and photographs of the Tamil poet and freedom fighter.

The visitor moves on to what might be called the traditional part of Pondicherry. Rue Rangapoulle branches off Jawaharlal Nehru Street, the main shopping centre of the city. The stretch from the canal to West Boulevard is filled with shopping areas, restaurants, teashops and bars.

Auroville

The last stop for the visitor is **Aurobindo Ashram**, the best-known landmark of Pondicherry, the presence of which is felt in every part of the town. Sri Aurobindo, after whom it is named, was an accomplished scholar in English and several European and Indian languages. After a stint of teaching, he plunged into the freedom movement with great fervour, but was eventually disillusioned about obtaining any immediate results. He was imprisoned by the British three times but never convicted. His mind gradually moved towards the spiritual, and during his last period of imprisonment he began to practise yoga intensely. In 1910 he retired from politics and found political asylum in Pondicherry, where he continued his

BELOW: an old French barracks.

Map on page 136

spiritual discipline of yoga, in search of a complete realisation that would unite spirit and matter. A few disciples joined him in this quest, but it was not until the Mother, born Mira Alfassa in Paris, joined him, that the Ashram began to be organised. Sri Aurobindo soon retired into the exclusive practice of yoga, leaving it to the Mother to guide the disciples and the way of life of the Ashram. Sri Aurobindo died in 1950, and the Mother in 1973. Their **Samadhi** in the main **Ashram** (open 8am–noon, 4–6pm) is the focal point of all disciples and followers. (The main Ashram buildings are in the block bounded by Rue de la Marine and Rue Giles.) The tomb has two chambers, one above the other, in which lie the remains of Sri Aurobindo and the Mother.

The Ashram, in addition to practising its primarily spiritual vocation, also provides scope for concrete practical activity for its followers who come from all over the world. These include all spheres of enterprise, from construction and farming to shoe-making and laundering. It has a large library and an active publishing programme. The visitor is advised to go to the Reception Centre in the main building to obtain the guide to the Ashram. Those who stay in one of the Ashram guesthouses are issued special passes which enable them to visit Ashram installations that are out of bounds to others.

Auroville, the City of Dawn, reflects the aspirations that Aurobindo and the Mother had for mankind. It is intended to be a future-oriented international city where all persons of goodwill can come and live together in peace and develop all aspects of life, "obeying only one authority – that of the Supreme Truth". Auroville is a voluntary commune, 10 km (6 miles) northwest of Pondicherry. Though it is eventually expected to be an integrated city for a population of 50,000, construction in Auroville has not been following a logical pattern. It does indeed look like a city of the future with its near-surrealistic architecture, the result of diverse experiments in building materials, techniques and styles.

Auroville has as its core the **Matrimandir** (open daily 4–5pm), built in the form of a large sphere. It is the spiritual centre of the city, intended for meditation on the divine consciousness. Its universality is symbolised by an urn in its amphitheatre which contains earth from 124 countries and all the states of India. **Bharat Nivas** is a centre for Indian culture, arts, products and cuisine. Auroville, built on arid land, has cultivated a considerable portion, and has constructed small dams, wells and other sources of water supply, and planted many trees. It produces nearly half the food supply for its residents. The institutions and structures in Auroville are spread out and it would be quite difficult to look around without a car. Upon arrival in Auroville, the visitor should go to the Information Centre (open 8am–noon and 2–6pm) at **Promesse** for guidance. The Boutique d'Auroville also sells handicrafts, souvenirs and a range of incense and natural perfume oils. There is also a good vegetarian café next door. ❑

IGHT: ondicherry's *endarmerie.*

KERALA

Lush, green Kerala varies from tea estates and forests in the Western Ghats, to palm-fringed lagoons and beaches

Just over 39,000 sq km (15,000 sq miles) in area, Kerala is a long (576 km/360 miles) and narrow (averaging 48 km/30 miles, and not broader than 120 km/75 miles) strip along the southwestern tip of India. The narrow ribbon of palm-fringed beaches gives way inland to the highlands of the Western Ghats, rising to 1,525 metres (5,000 ft) at their highest point in the state. No less than a quarter of the area is covered by forests, with more than 600 identified varieties of trees. With an annual rainfall exceeding 2.54 metres (100 inches) in several districts, it is green and lush throughout the year. Paddy fields and coconut palms cover the plains, while up in the hills there are plantations of arecanut, cardamom, rubber, pepper, tea and coffee.

Today, with 31.8 million people, Kerala is not only one of the most densely populated of all Indian states, but also the most successful in terms of family planning and literacy. The official language is Malayalam. The people of Kerala have traditionally been distinguished for their ingenuity and daring. The Malayali diaspora has taken its people to virtually every inhabited continent of the world, but their link with their beautiful home state invariably remains strong.

Whilst the majority of Kerala's population is Hindu, one third is Christian – Syrian Christians, converted in the early years of the last millennium, and Roman Catholics, converted in the 16th century. There is also a sizeable population of Muslims of Arab descent and converts. There was once also a thriving Jewish population in Kochi, but this has dwindled since the establishment of the state of Israel. All of these communities generally co-existed harmoniously; paradoxically, though Keralites are religious, they pride themselves on their rationalist tradition and have more than once elected Communist governments.

Kerala is rich both in the bounty of nature and in the creations of man: beautiful beaches and rivers, hills and forest sanctuaries, forts and palaces, monuments and memorials, shrines and festivals, and a fascinating heritage of art and culture.

PRECEDING PAGES: Kerala's idyllic backwaters.
LEFT: trainees in *Kalaripayattu*, Kerala's martial art.

Maps:
Area 196
City 188

THIRUVANANTHAPURAM

Kerala's state capital is immediately attractive, with an impressive temple, delightful museum and a nearby beach and royal palace

Once, long, long ago, the sage Parasurama hurled his battle-axe into the sea and renounced all war. The waters parted and the receding sea threw up a lovely tropical paradise in the furthest southwestern reaches of India.

It was to this land of spices, timber and ivory that the biremes of King Solomon and the faith of St Thomas came, and the Arabs, the Jews and the Chinese, the Greeks and the Romans, and – following Vasco da Gama's route – the Portuguese, the Danes, the Dutch, the French and the English. What they found was one of the world's most hospitable regions.

Judaism, Christianity and Islam first arrived in India in Kerala and found a haven, long before they went westwards. The visible symbols of the contributions made to Kerala by the great religions of the world are their shrines found everywhere, their festivals celebrated by all, and the peace in which people of all faiths have lived for 2,000 years.

The main entry point into Kerala is Trivandrum, or what is called **Thiruvananthapuram** ❶ today: the abode of the sacred snake Ananda on which Lord Visnu, the Preserver, reclines. It is also one of the loveliest capital cities in the country, small, green and clean. Thiruvananthapuram is also developing as a science research centre and there are several research laboratories here. Many of them welcome visitors – with prior permission, of course. Visiting the Space Research Centre, however, is likely to be more difficult.

The Fort

The oldest part of the city is that delineated by the old laterite wall of the **Fort** (only parts of the walls now remain) to the southwest of the railway station. This was the core of royal Thiruvananthapuram, containing the city's main temple and the royal palace. At the centre of the fort is a large tank, away from which there are roads lined with traditional shops.

The **Sri Anandapadmanabhasvami temple** Ⓐ dominates Thiruvananthapuram. This ancient Visnu temple with a seven-storey *gopuram* is a splendid example of Dravidian temple architecture in the Tamil style, to which the barest embellishment of the purely Keralan variety has been added. Keralan influence is more obvious in the other gates leading into the courtyard. Exquisite stone carvings and pavilions with beautifully sculpted pillars – the Kulasekhara Mandapam and the temple corridor are eye-catching – abound in this temple which overlooks a tranquil tank, the **Padama Tirtham**. The image of Lord Padmanabha reclining on Anantha

LEFT: women at the *Pongol* festival.
RIGHT: a lemon seller in the market.

is viewed through three doors opening onto the sanctum.

Legend has it that the temple was first built to house an idol found in a nearby forest. Over the years the temple grew, till in the 18th century the princely state of Travancore, the southernmost part of Kerala, was dedicated to its deity. Since then, the rights and the possessions of its rulers belonged to the deity, and the Maharajas of Travancore were considered only the regents of the deity. They rebuilt the present temple in 1773. It is open only to Hindus, and only at specific times. All those entering its precincts have to conform to its code of attire. Despite the entry restrictions, the temple is still a fine sight across the tank, and a walk around its square will offer glimpses of both a glorious architecture and a fervent faith.

The Maharajas of Travancore moved their capital to Thiruvananthapuram from Padmanabhapuram *(see page 192)* in 1790 and took up residence alongside the temple on the southern side of its tank. The **Puttan Malika Palace** (open Tues–Sun 8.30am–1pm, 3–5.30pm, entrance charge) was their city residence. You must take off your shoes and go around with a guide (a small tip is appreciated). The attractive wooden-built structure – very cool in the summer heat – is set in quiet gardens and contains a number of royal possessions, including an ivory cradle, Svati Tirunal's ivory throne and a large collection of weapons. However, it is the building itself that is most impressive, with beautifully carved ceilings and the two delightful end rooms on the upper storey. The one nearest the temple was Svati Tirunal's composing room whilst at the other end is the "Dancing Hall", linked by a corridor decorated on the outside by 122 horses carved in teak.

Across M.G. Road, away from the fort, near the stand from where you catch the bus to Kovalam, is **East Fort**. This is the traditional shopping district of Chalai Bazaar, and this is where the city's main fruit and vegetable market can be found, along with small shops selling just about

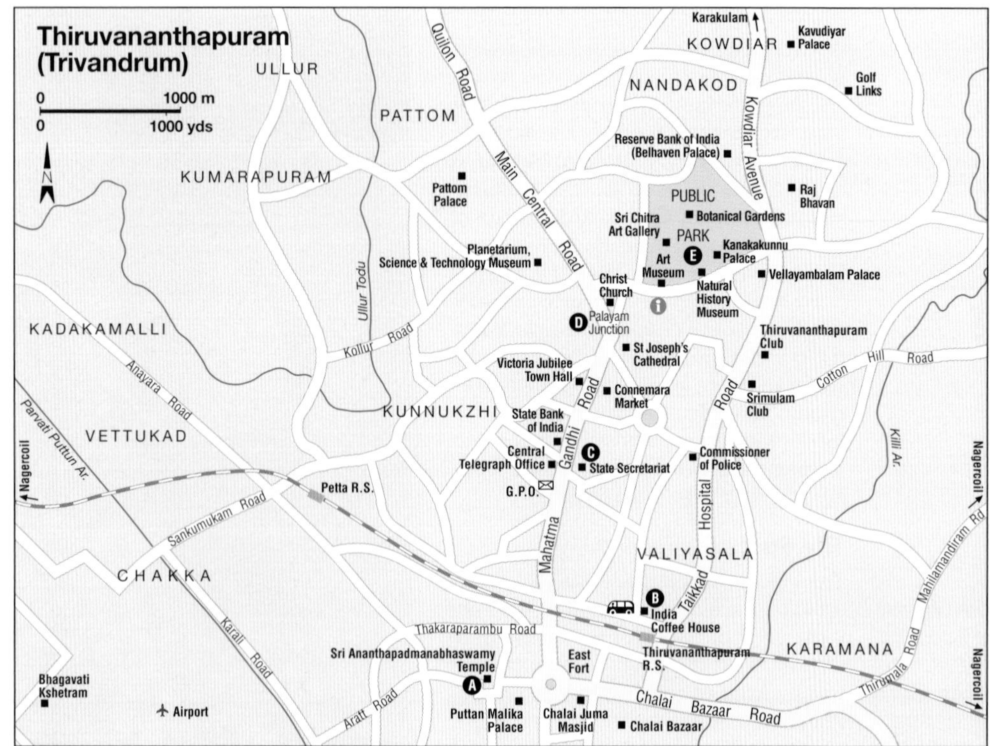

Map on page 188

anything huddled together down narrow roads. Temporary fairs and exhibitions are often held on the piece of open ground beside the bus stand.

The Secretariat

The modern city lies to the north of the railway. Opposite the railway station, by the main bus stand, is Laurie Baker's spiral building for the **Indian Coffee House** **B**, a good place to stop for a snack or light meal. Laurie Baker is a British architect, who made Kerala his home and propagated a low-cost style of architecture that blended the traditional with the modern.

Running north from Thampanoor Junction is Aristo Road, one of the city's main thoroughfares. Though there is little of tourist interest on the road itself, the narrow streets between here and M.G. Road are delightful and fun to explore. Taking Press Club Road will bring you up to the back of the **State Secretariat** **C**, built in 1939, at Statue Junction. Across from the Secretariat are some excellent cheap "meals" places.

BELOW: the Sri Anandapadmanabhasvami temple.

South of here, on M.G. Road, are some good bookshops, whike to the north, past Spencer Junction where there is a useful supermarket, is the impressive **Victoria Jubilee Town Hall**. M.G. Road continues up to **Palayam Junction** **D** where the city's two main places of Christian worship can be found: the neo-Gothic Catholic **St Joseph's Cathedral**, and the equally imposing Anglican **Christ Church** built in 1859. Beyond these are many of the Indo-Saracenic buildings of the university.

The Public Park

M.G. Road ends at Museum Road, lining which is Thiruvananthapuram's beautifully laid-out **Botanical Gardens** **E**. Here is the city's museum, consisting of: the **Art Museum** (previously the Napier Museum), the **Sri Chitra Art Gallery**, the **Paniker Gallery** and the **Museum of Natural History** (all are open Tues, Thur–Sun 10am–4.30pm, Wed 1–4.30pm, entrance charge). A combined ticket for the museums is available from the booth near the entrance for the city zoo.

The sprawling gardens with their wealth of plant life are far more attractive than the depressing zoo with its poorly caged animals. A better view of local natural history can be found in the Museum of Natural History which, as well as various pickled snakes, marine specimens washed up on the city's beaches and unfortunate stuffed birds and animals which fell foul of colonial hunters, has informative displays of local costume and an excellent model of a *tharavad*, the traditional home of a Nair community joint family.

Art Galleries

The highlight of the museum complex is the Art Museum (Napier Museum), housed in an extraordinary Indo-Saracenic building designed by Robert Fellowes Chisolm for Lord Napier in 1880; its many gables and sloped roofs fuse the traditional architecture of Kerala with a British Colonial style. It has a superb collection which includes jewellery, ivorywork, Chola bronzes and Keralan woodcarvings.

The Sri Chitra Art Gallery has several good Chinese and Japanese paintings, a series of Tibetan thankas (religious paintings), and a surprising number of works by Nicholas and Svetoslav Roerich who painted mystical scenes of the Himalayas. The bulk of the collection, however, is the work of Raja Ravi Varma (1848–1906), a member of the Travancore royal family and considered one of India's finest painters. His rather academic paintings are based for the most part on Hindu themes and they can still be seen in reproduction all over India; they are a little syrupy for modern tastes.

Also in the grounds is a gallery given over to a collection of works by the 20th-century South Indian artist K.C.S. Paniker (1911–77), some of whose early paintings are quite charming.

To the east of the park are a handful of other sights. One of these is the city's **Observatory**, just beyond which (north and south of Museum Road) are the

Maps: City 188 Area 196

Kanakakunna and **Vellayambalam** palaces, both dating from the early 20th century and set in large grounds. Museum Road is also the location for a number of offices, including those of Indian Airlines.

Cultural events

Thiruvananthapuram offers the traveller more than sightseeing, however. **Shanmukam beach** by the airport is a pleasant, clean stretch, but not really a bather's beach (for which one has to go further afield). The city does, however, have institutes which teach the famed martial arts of Kerala, *Kalaripayattu* being the best known of them, as well as recitals of the ancient Kerala masked dance-drama, *Kathakali*. Superb masks in brilliant colours, gorgeously ornate costumes that weigh as much as 40 kg (80 lb), the oil-lit atmosphere and storytelling in mime and gesture make this an experience not to be missed in Kerala. The occasional *Mohini Attam* recital, a graceful dance full of seductive lyricism, is perhaps easier to appreciate, but the rich and dignified stylisation of Kathakali makes it an art form that transcends the charms of pure rhythm. At the **Margi Kathakali School**, in East Fort, visitors are allowed to watch Kathakali dance-drama classes and can enquire about future performances.

Thiruvananthapuram – and indeed all of Kerala – offers a variety of handicrafts with its ivory and wood carving, and its delicate lacework, and there are many places offering these and wonderful fabrics. One good place is the government-run SMSM **Handicrafts Emporium**, near the Secretariat, which has a huge variety of goods.

Kovalam

Many visitors to Thiruvananthapuram, however, come in quest of Kerala's beaches, and **Kovalam** ❷, 15 km (9 miles) to the south, is one of the best.

Idyllic Kovalam, a sheltered natural bay with a broad, dazzling white palm-fringed beach, is no longer a secret and is extremely busy during high season. Almost all the

LEFT: the Art Museum.
BELOW: transport for an elephant.

usual facilities are on offer, including yoga, meditation, *ayurvedic* massages and *Kathakali* in the dim flickering light of traditional temple oil lamps. There is ample space for sunbathing, safe bathing (outside of the monsoon) in the placid blue waters of the bay, and plenty of water sports. There are also many hotels that offer every kind of accommodation from basic rooms to sumptuous five-star comfort. The most famous resort is the Leela complex (previously the Kovalam Ashok), designed by Charles Correa and incorporating the Halcyon Castle, one of the summer residences of the Maharajas of Travancore. Round the corner from the bay itself, there are several cottages and guesthouses which supply simple – and cheaper – rooms.

Padmanabhapuram

Until Independence and the reorganisation of the princely states, much of this coastal strip was part of the erstwhile kingdom of Travancore, now southern Kerala. It is not surprising to find in **Padmanabhapuram** ❸ a palace of the Maharajas of Travancore *(see also page 167)*. Padmanabhapuram, 55 km (34 miles) from Thiruvananthapuram and actually across the border in present-day Tamil Nadu, was once the capital of Travancore; now it is a village in decline, with only its preserved 17th-century palace and museum of interest. Window panes of mica cast a magical light into the carved rooms cooled with natural air conditioning using inner courtyards. An imposing royal bed, a single granite slab, is placed atop a gleaming black floor made from egg whites and burnt coconut shell.

Puvar, the ancient Ophir with which King Solomon traded, is now a fishing village with few relics remaining; **Colachel** has a Danish fort, a great beach and **Suchindram**, a magnificent temple. Nearer Thiruvananthapuram is the **Neyyar Dam** ❹. The Shivananda Yoga Vedanta Ashram here holds year-round classes and is a recommended place for anyone with an interest in yoga. The Neyyar reservoir is set in a wildlife sanctuary where elephants, wild

LEFT: Kovalam beach.
BELOW: fishermen bring in the catch, Kovalam.

Map on page 196

dogs, wild bears, monkeys and a rich variety of birds can be spotted. A crocodile hatchery and a deer park have also been opened by the side of the reservoir.

Another sanctuary further on, just 10 km (6 miles) short of Ponmudi, is the **Peppara Wildlife Sanctuary** in the Cardamom Hills. This too is elephant country, and rich in birdlife as well. **Ponmudi** ❺, the "golden crown" of the Golden Valley, is Thiruvananthapuram's own hill station. About 60 km (35 miles) northeast of Thiruvananthapuram, and located at 1,066 metres (3,500 ft) in the Cardamom Hills by the Tamil Nadu border, Ponmudi is unspoilt, refreshingly cool and mist-shrouded almost all year round. It is surrounded by tea estates and hill ranges covered with forests. A visit to Ponmudi offers treks in the forests, visits to tea estates, and discovering the flora and fauna of the hills.

Varkala

Three interesting sites lie to the north of Thiruvananthapuram. **Anjengo** ❻, about 25 km (15 miles) out of the city, was the East India Company's first settlement on this coast, established in 1684. **Aruvikkara** ❼, just outside Thiruvananthapuram, and **Varkala** ❽ are both major pilgrimage centres 55 km (34 miles) north of the city.

The English cemetery and other relics of the past in Anjengo will interest the historian. Aruvikkara is a picnic spot but is better known as a pilgrim centre. Varkala, known to travellers for its beautiful beach, is one of Kerala's major Hindu pilgrim centres. The Janardana temple here is believed to be over 2,000 years old. Its bell is said to be from a 17th-century Dutch sailing ship, whose captain gave it to the temple when his prayers were answered. The mineral springs here are much sought after for their curative properties.

In an eastern suburb of Varkala is **Sivagiri Hill**, where Sri Narayana Guru, the philosopher-saint, established an *ashram*. The *ashram* and the great social reformer's *samadhi* (sanctified tomb) attract many pilgrims. ❑

BELOW: Varkala.

Map on page 196

THE BACKWATERS AND KOCHI

The vast complex of beautiful lagoons and canals that lies along the Keralan coast leads up to the state's largest city, the historic and lively port of Kochi

A special delight Kerala offers is the trip on a slow boat through its forests and its palm-shaded backwaters and canals, enjoying magnificent scenery all along the waterways and stopping to admire what history and religion have left in many towns and villages along the way. Motor-powered launches provide regular passenger services for locals and tourists alike, but the same experience in a covered country boat is also pleasurable and authentic. The design of these boats goes back to the Chinese influence on this coast.

It is possible to make a backwater journey from Thiruvananthapuram to Kodungallur, a distance of approximately 250 km (155 miles), or from Thiruvananthapuram to Kottayam, 175 km (110 miles). But both journeys really start from the ancient town of Kollam (formerly Quilon), 70 km (44 miles) to the north of Thiruvananthapuram. The 150 km (90 miles) to Kottayam from Thiruvananthapuram can also be covered by road or rail; however, many tourists opt to take the boat between Kollam and Alappuzha (previously Alleppey), taking the train or bus before and after these two towns. Two companies run the cruises: the state Water Transport Department boats are usually slower than those of Alleppey Tourism (the trip lasts up to eight hours depending on the route).

Kollam

Once a major international entrepôt known to the Phoenicians and the Arabs, the Romans and the Greeks, the Chinese and the Persians, **Kollam** ❾ is still a major commercial centre in Kerala. Together with two other important trading centres, Alappuzha and Kottayam, it forms a triangle that is not only commercially affluent but also set in lovely natural surroundings.

Beautifully situated in the midst of coconut groves on the southern banks of the vast **Astamudi Lake**, the "Lake with Eight Creeks", with its shore-level promontories of red laterite and china clay, Kollam is a picturesque town, and commercial activity seems a world away. Cashew is its main business now, but medieval sailors from east and west came to Kollam in search of spices, timber, fauna, ivory and textiles. The Chinese established a trading settlement here as far back as AD 9. They also exchanged envoys during the time of Kublai Khan, and left behind a heritage of fishing nets fixed to poles, cargo boats covered with thatch, and many shards of exquisite chinaware that have been excavated in and around Kollam.

LEFT: the backwaters.
RIGHT: a shop keeper in Kochi.

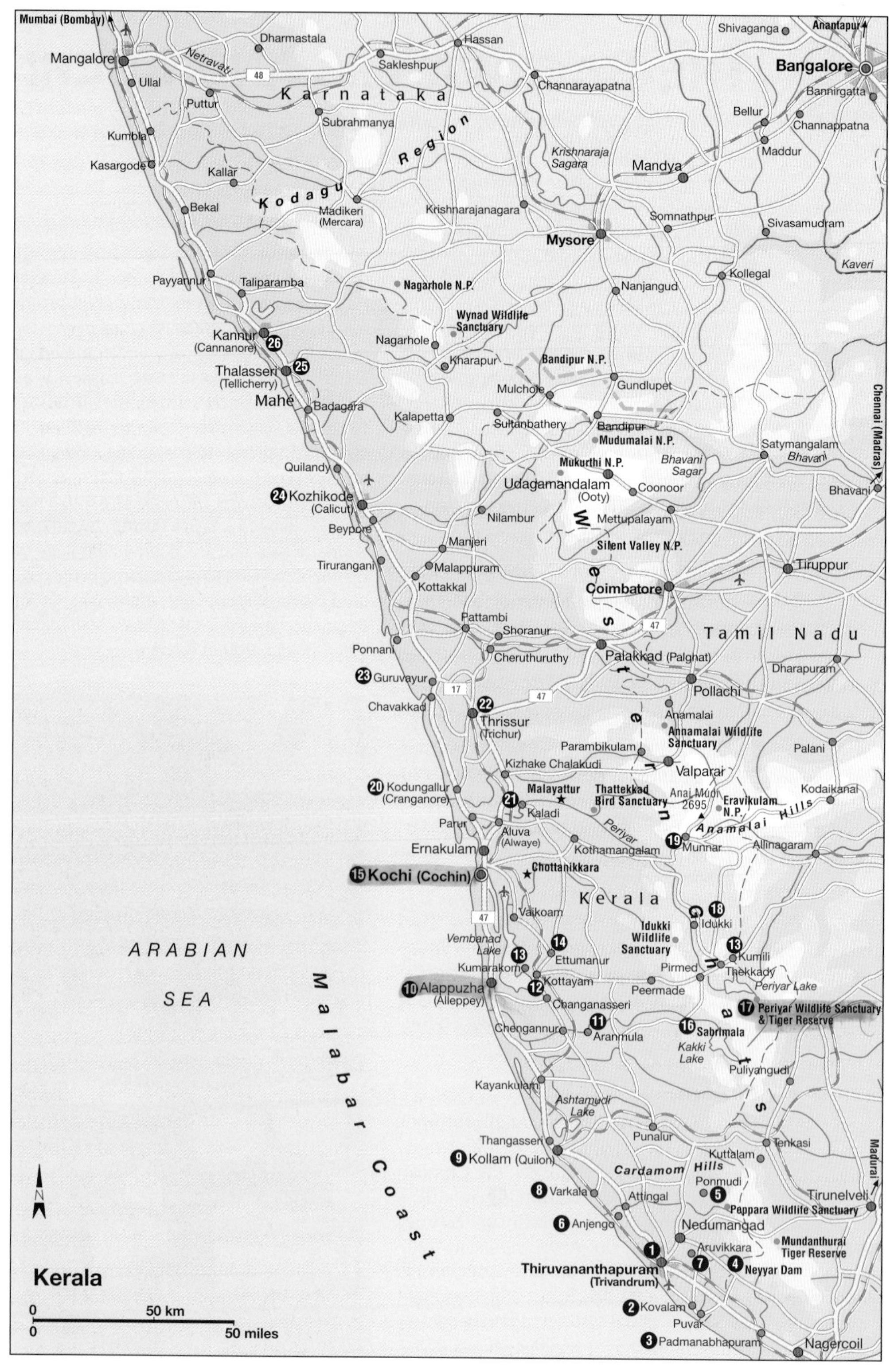
Kerala
Mumbai (Bombay)
Mangalore
Ullal
Dharmastala
Netravati
Hassan
Sakleshpur
Shivaganga
Anantapur
Bangalore
Bannirgatta
Channarayapatna
Karnataka
Puttur
Subrahmanya
Kumbla
Kasargode
Kallar
Kodagu Region
Madikeri
(Mercara)
Bekal
Krishnaraja Sagara
Mandya
Bellur
Channappatna
Maddur
Krishnarajanagara
Somnathpur
Sivasamudram
Mysore
Kaveri
Kollegal
Payyannur
Taliparamba
Nagarhole N.P.
Nanjangud
Wynad Wildlife Sanctuary
Kannur
(Cannanore)
Nagarhole
Kharapur
Bandipur N.P.
Thalasseri
(Tellicherry)
Mahé
Badagara
Mulchole
Gundlupet
Kalapetta
Sultanbathery
Bandipur
Mudumalai N.P.
Chennai (Madras)
Satymangalam
Bhavani
Quilandy
Mukurthi N.P.
Bhavani Sagar
Udagamandalam
(Ooty)
Coonoor
Kozhikode
(Calicut)
Beypore
Nilambur
Mettupalayam
Manjeri
Silent Valley N.P.
Tirurangani
Malappuram
Tiruppur
Kottakkal
Coimbatore
Western Ghats
Pattambi
Shoranur
Tamil Nadu
Ponnani
Cheruthuruthy
Palakkad (Palghat)
Dharapuram
Guruvayur
Pollachi
Chavakkad
Thrissur
(Trichur)
Anamalai
Annamalai Wildlife Sanctuary
Parambikulam
Palani
Kizhake Chalakudi
Valparai
Kodungallur
(Cranganore)
Malayattur
Thattekkad Bird Sanctuary
Anaj Mudi 2695
Eravikulam N.P.
Kodaikanal
Kaladi
Anamalai Hills
Parur
Aluva
(Alwaye)
Periyar
Munnar
Allinagaram
Ernakulam
Kothamangalam
Kochi (Cochin)
Chottanikkara
Kerala
Vaikoam
Idukki
Idukki Wildlife Sanctuary
Vembanad Lake
Ettumanur
Kumili
ARABIAN SEA
Kumarakom
Pirmed
Thekkady
Periyar Lake
Alappuzha
(Alleppey)
Kottayam
Peermade
Changanasseri
Periyar Wildlife Sanctuary & Tiger Reserve
Chengannur
Aranmula
Sabrimala
Kakki Lake
Malabar Coast
Puliyangudi
Kayankulam
Ashtamudi Lake
Thangasseri
Punalur
Tenkasi
Kollam (Quilon)
Kuttalam
Madurai
Cardamom Hills
Ponmudi
Varkala
Attingal
Peppara Wildlife Sanctuary
Tirunelveli
Anjengo
Nedumangad
Mundanthurai Tiger Reserve
Aruvikkara
Thiruvananthapuram
(Trivandrum)
Neyyar Dam
Kovalam
Puvar
Padmanabhapuram
Nagercoil
N
0
50 km
0
50 miles

Map on page 196

Three places to visit are **Chinnakkada**, the busy bazaar that is the heart of Kollam, the **Thirumullavaram beach** and the park and beach at **Kochupilamudu**. The town gave its name to the present Malayalam era in AD 825 and through that is central to Kerala's history. So is the Roman Catholic cathedral, the history of which goes back to the creation of the first Roman Catholic See in India, when Friar Jordanus was consecrated Bishop in 1530.

About 3 km (2 miles) north of Kollam is the historic town of **Thangasseri** where you can picnic among the relics of its European past or walk on the beach in the shadow of the old lighthouse, one of the earliest built in British times. The old Portuguese, Dutch and English cemeteries have many tales to tell; the remains of the Portuguese and Dutch fortifications are memorials to a colonial past; and the old British Residency is now a lovely government guest house on the shores of Ashtamudi Lake.

Alappuzha

North of Kollam, 85 km (53 miles) away, is **Alappuzha** ❿ (formerly Alleppey), the "Venice of the East", situated on Vembanad Lake, the longest lake in India. A maze of canals and a network of bridges give this busy commercial town its descriptive sobriquet. Alappuzha is known for its coir, the retted fibre of the coconut husk, and for black pepper. Coir yarn, coir mats and matting, and a wealth of other coir products are manufactured in Alappuzha and are good buys.

August to September is the season of *Onam*, the harvest festival of Kerala. This is one of the best times to visit the backwaters. The colourful water carnivals, graceful dances, the ornate and bright-hued floor decorations (*kolam* and *rangoli*) using coloured powder or, more beautifully, flowers, and the festive spirit, make Kerala a lively place at this time of the year. But what sets the backwaters region apart are the *Vallam Kallis*, the boat races.

The Nehru Trophy Boat Race Day, held at Alappuzha on the second Saturday of August every year, sees one of the most colourful events in Kerala. There are races for a variety of boats, but the biggest race of the day is the one for the *chundan vallams*, the giant snake boats. Each boat is over 30 metres (100 ft) long, with raised snake-like prows, and is gaily decorated. With crews of more than 100 men rowing in perfect rhythm to traditional boat songs, the race is an unforgettable drama for the thousands who line the banks to cheer themselves hoarse. There is nothing like it anywhere else in India – except at other boat-race centres on the backwater. It is no wonder that the Sports Authority of India has set up its Kayaking and Canoeing Centre here to train young rowers.

About 50 km (30 miles) southeast of Alappuzha, near the town of Chengannur, is **Aranmula** ⓫, where the second of the most famous boat races is held. Aranmula, on the banks of the placid river Pamba, is a pilgrim centre where the temple is dedicated to Lord Parthasarathi – Lord Krisna in the role of charioteer to Arjuna – and its boat race is part of the temple ritual. The

RIGHT: a *kettuvallam* (traditional rice boat).

annual commemoration of the deity's installation is celebrated on the last day of the week-long Onam festival. It is on this auspicious day (in August–September, though the day changes from year to year according to the Malayalam calendar) that the snake boats race against each other on the river Pamba, thousands of singers churning up the calm waters of the river with their short oars in time to the chanted beat.

Other boat races are held in Kottayam, but almost every backwater in this part of Kerala celebrates *Onam* by taking to the water. The Kochi and Kottayam races are of recent origin and are more in the nature of sport than of religious ritual. But at Payipad, 3 km (2 miles) from Haripad, where there is a famous temple of Lord Subramaniya, the races are associated with the temple festival. The three-day festival starts on *Onam* day, and on the first two days snake-boat processions are held on the Acharkovil river. The third day is race day, the climax of the festival.

Kottayam

Approximately 25 km (15 miles) as the crow flies from Alappuzha is the prosperous town of **Kottayam** ⓬, the first in India to claim 100 percent literacy. A major commercial centre of Kerala, Kottayam lies in the foothills of the Western Ghats, beautiful backwaters to its west and scenic, fertile mountains to its east. A major centre for the trade in rubber, tea, coffee, pepper, cardamom (Kerala is the original home of cardamom), and other produce from the plantations in the Ghats, Kottayam's prosperity is echoed in the city's facilities.

A major educational and Malayalam publishing centre, Kottayam is a city of handsomely built schools, commercial complexes and civic facilities. It also has the most successful writers' co-operative in India, and its publishing activity is phenomenal. But, as Kerala's largest Christian centre, Kottayam has a strong spiritual side to it too. There are several sects and divisions of the Syrian Christian faith –

BELOW: backwater boats at Alappuzha.

Maps: Area 196 City 200

for complex historical reasons – and many of them have their episcopal seats here.

The best-known churches are the **Valiapalli** and **Cheriapalli**, both with colourful frescoes enriching their dim interiors. In the 16th-century Valiapalli, there are Pahlavi inscriptions and a stone cross said to have been carved by St Thomas. This cross, it is believed, came from the first church Thomas founded in Kerala, in Kodungallur.

Ten kilometres (6 miles) to the west of Kottayam is **Kumarakom** ⓭ on the eastern shore of the Vembanad Lake. The islands on the lake across from Kumarakom are home to a large variety of migratory birds. The birds can be watched from the comfort of Baker's Bungalow or other vantage points on the lake's shore. The mansion is now part of the Taj hotel chain, and they have done well to preserve much of its yesteryear charm. The *punkahs* still hang from the ceiling, but no one manually operates those cloth-on-wood-frame fans any more. They remain, like much else in Baker's Bungalow, symbols of another age.

Another 10 km (6 miles) north of Kottayam is **Ettumanur** ⓮, famous for its Siva temple. Beautiful murals on the inner and outer walls and some superb sculpture in the temple are the special features of this ancient shrine. Non-Hindus are prohibited from entering.

Northwest of Ettumanur, about 25 km (15 miles) along the road to Kochi, is **Vaikom**, where there is another famous Siva temple. Here, too, non-Hindus are not allowed to go beyond the temple gates. About 40 km (25 miles) beyond Vaikom is the large joint city of Kochi-Ernakulam, one of Kerala's most attractive tourist destinations in its own right.

Kochi-Ernakulam

Cosmopolitan **Kochi** ⓯ (formerly Cochin), the commercial capital of Kerala, glories in the title of "Queen of the Arabian Sea". A city of peninsulas and islands with a mainland centre, Kochi has a magnificent natural harbour, almost in the middle of the city separating it from Ernakulam, created by the underwater Malabar mud banks that ensure calm waters.

Cruising around the islands through the backwaters extending to the south and the east from the sea and skirting the harbour is one of the many delights Kochi has to offer. Motor launches from jetties on mainland Ernakulam will take you to Fort Cochin and Old Cochin on the southern peninsula, as well as around the islands.

Old Cochin

Old Cochin is the peninsula comprising Fort Cochin and ancient Mattancherri. Its history predates its Western conquerors. Some of the most interesting buildings in India are to be found here – old Portuguese, Dutch and British architecture, preserved as a striking contrast to styles found in the rest of Kerala.

What is most distinctive about Old Cochin, especially viewed from the sea, is its skyline. Giant contraptions that seem to be from another world dominate the coast all around the Fort: these are the Chinese fishing nets, unique to this part of Kerala and living symbols of a

RIGHT: Chinese fishing nets in Kochi.

centuries-old Chinese influence on this coast. The palm-woven, broad-brimmed conical hats the fishermen wear are yet another reminder that the Chinese had a thriving settlement in this part of India. So are the roofs of many buildings in Kerala which turn up slightly at the corners, *china* firecrackers that explode with a thunderous noise, and clay jars distinctly in the Chinese style. However, it is the giant Chinese fishing nets, similar to those used in Southeast Asia, that attract every visitor, especially those with cameras.

These fishing nets are as effective as they are dramatic. Ingeniously constructed, these giant cantilevered fish traps comprise coconut trunk platforms on elephantine teak-log legs stuck solid in the beach, and supporting teakwood frameworks and extended poles from which hang giant nylon nets. The net, tied to four poles that link it to pulleys and counterweights, is lowered into the water by ingenious use of the counter-balancing rocks and then hauled out of it 15 minutes later by a team of four manning each platform. By pulling on the rope with the counterweights, the team raises the net to platform level; then one of the team members climbs up one of the poles from which the net hangs and skilfully scoops the catch into a basket, and back goes the net into the water again.

Except during the May–August monsoon season, the nets are worked throughout the year. When in use they seem a throwback to another technological era and of limited effectiveness in this day. But as a way of life, as traditional symbols of a historic past and as a sight that rivets the attention of any visitor to Kochi, they are permanent features of the Kerala scene that few would wish to vanish.

Behind the Chinese fishing nets are garden houses, stately office buildings and tree-lined lanes of another age. The occasional multistorey building has made some inroads into the 18th- and 19th-century street facades, but generally Fort Cochin has looked much the same for decades.

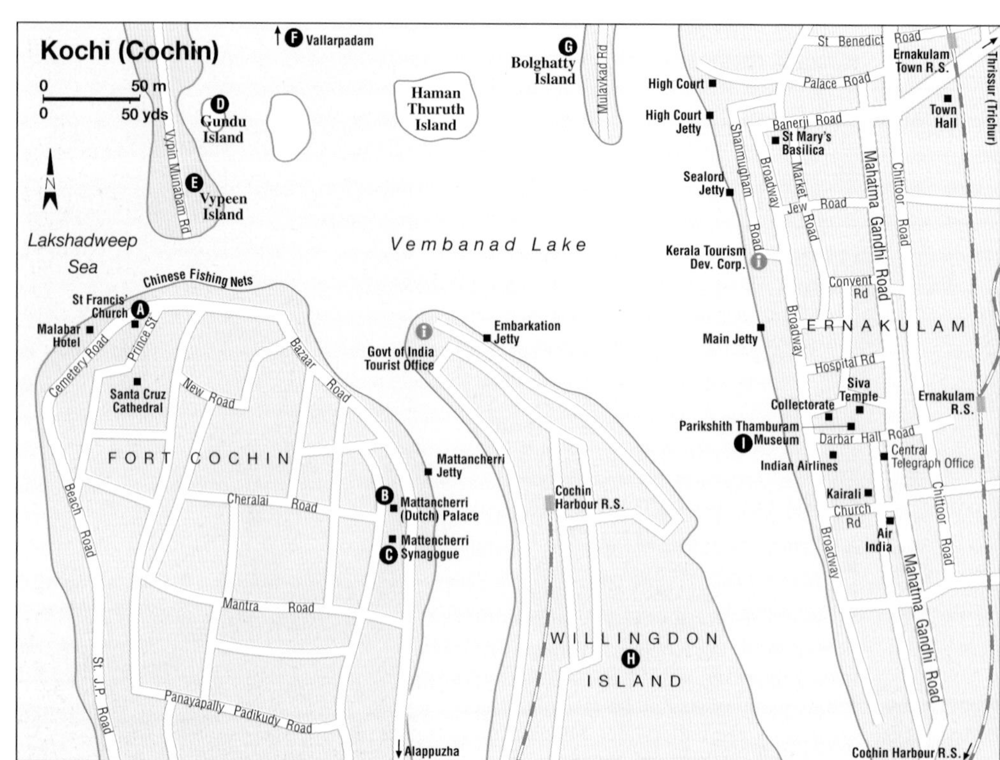

Map on page 200

Vasco da Gama's church

St Francis's Ⓐ of Kochi (open Mon–Sat 7am–6pm) is the oldest European church in India, its change from Catholic chapel to Protestant shrine a reflection of Kochi's history. On Christmas Day, 1500, just two years after Vasco da Gama had landed near Kozhikode, the Portuguese were granted the right to trade on the Kochi coast. Three years later, Alphonso de Albuquerque built a stockade of coconut trunks lashed together with coir ropes on the site of today's Fort. There, in Fort St Emmanuel, five Franciscan friars built the chapel of St Bartholomew. After Admiral Almeida negotiated a more permanent settlement here in 1506, stone-and-mortar buildings were constructed, including the church of St Anthony, consecrated in 1516 on the site of the earlier chapel.

Vasco da Gama, who had returned to the east as the Governor of the Indies in 1524, died on Christmas Eve that same year during a visit to Kochi. He was buried in St Anthony's Church, and the original rails and tombstone still mark the spot where the great navigator was buried. His remains were taken to Lisbon in 1538, but the man who discovered the route to the Indies in 1497 has not been forgotten.

It was in 1663 that St Anthony's passed into Dutch hands and became a Lutheran church, remaining so long after Kochi came under British control in 1795. In the middle of the 19th century it became an Anglican church and acquired its present name, St Francis's. The church has several antiquities, including a wealth of records. Some of its prized possessions are a palm-leaf title deed which the local Raja gave the Portuguese in 1503, the *Doop Boek* – a Dutch baptismal register dating to the days the church became Protestant – and stately *punkahs*, those ancient cloth-on-wood-frame fans that had to be manually pulled.

Not far from St Francis's Church is **Santa Cruz Cathedral** (open Mon–Sat 9am–1pm, 3–5pm), a Roman Catholic church of a later age. The paintings in the cathedral are particularly beautiful.

BELOW: Santa Cruz Cathedral.

Mattancherri Palace

Around the corner from the church and the battlements, and facing Willingdon Island to the west, is the Mattancherri jetty. Beside it, more of Kochi's fascinating 16th-century history is revealed: the **Mattancherri palace** Ⓑ (open Sat–Thur 10am–5pm, entrance charge) was built by the Portuguese in 1555 and then given to the Raja of Kochi. Built in an amalgam of Portuguese Colonial and Keralan styles, it was extensively renovated in Burgher Bungalow style by the Dutch in 1663, as a token of their regard for Kochi royalty; it henceforth became known as the Dutch Palace.

The Rajas of Kochi were crowned in the palace's *darbar* hall; today it is their portrait gallery. In these ancient rooms are 17th-century murals on the walls that relate in vibrant colour the story of the epic *Ramayana*. The murals of Kerala are of a unique style which is known as "Fresco-Seco". They are painted with vegetable- and mineral-based colours, and then coated with pine resin. Various shades of ochre red, white, yellow and green are the predominant colours. Palanquins, coronation robes, furniture, weapons and the woodwork in the palace are other items that can be seen during a tour of the building.

The same compound houses two temples used by the Kochi royalty for worship, the **Bhagavati temple**, and the circular, stupa-like **Krisna temple** reflecting the Buddhist influence that existed here until the 8th century. Sharing a wall with the latter is one of the most interesting parts of Kochi, the **Mattancherri Synagogue** Ⓒ and **Jew Town**.

Legend dates Jewish trade with Kerala from the times of Solomon and Nebuchadnezzar. The stories of Saint Thomas record that Jews followed the same trade winds from West Asia and settled here long before his arrival. Certainly there would have been Jewish settlements after the Roman destruction of the Second Temple in Jerusalem in AD 70, and records of AD 370 speak of over 10,000 Jews living in and around Musiris, the Kodungallur of today.

There are not many of these Asian Jews (locally called the "Black Jews") left, and most of their synagogues are now closed: the two in Ernakulam, mainland Kochi, one in Parur, two synagogues in Mattancherri, one in Chennamangalam and another in Mala are now all shut. One of the two synagogues in Ernakulam was the biggest in Kerala and claimed to have the oldest copy of the Old Testament in the world, which was stored in a gold-plated box. These synagogues were built when the Black Jews fled Portuguese persecution in Cranganore and sought the protection of the Rajas of Kochi in the mid-16th century.

It was to Kerala's shores that the Sephardic or "White Jews" also came in the early 16th century when the Inquisition drove them from Spain and Portugal. They were joined by Ashkenazy Jews from Central Europe and together, for social and cultural reasons, they formed settlements separate from the Black Jews in Kerala. That separation continued even

LEFT: Mattancherri Synagogue.

Map on page 200

when they fled Portuguese persecution in Cranganore and settled in Kochi, establishing what is called Jew Town.

There are very few Jews in Jew Town and Fort Cochin today (most have migrated to Israel), but the district retains the ambience of the "town" they founded, a street or two of picture-postcard houses, in 17th-century Dutch and traditional Keralan styles. Here, the **Pardesi synagogue** (open Sun–Fri 10am–noon, 3–5pm, entrance charge) is the best maintained synagogue in India, built in 1568, rebuilt in 1664, two years after the Portuguese depredation, and restored 100 years later.

Exquisite, hand-painted Chinese tiles, no two of which are alike, pave the floor, and the gleaming embellishments in the synagogue make it one of the most striking places of Jewish worship anywhere. Its treasures include ancient scrolls of Mosaic law in the tabernacle, golden crowns given by the Maharajas of Travancore and Kochi, silver lamps presented by the first British Resident to the court of Kochi, and the copper plate grant from the Rajas that enabled the Jews to call Kerala their home. A congregation still just about gathers here, for wherever 10 adult male Jews assemble services can be conducted. The Sabbath is still celebrated, as are Purim and Passover and all the other Jewish festivals. Such celebrations are what made Jew Town and its synagogue a living symbol of the tolerance with which the Malabar coast received all religions, but in this particular case it seems inevitable that the Jews of Kochi will soon be only a memory.

Not very far from the Mattancherri synagogue is the "leaning" **Coonen Cross**. Tying themselves to this cross, the Thomas Christians revolted against the Latinisation of their Church by the Portuguese in 1653. They took the Oath of the Coonen Cross, vowing to resist the Roman Church and to remain true to the patriarchy of Antioch and the Syriac rites they had practised long before the Western world had heard of Christianity.

BELOW: a Mattancherri Palace mural of Krisna.

Kochi has several well-organised museums and theatres. One of the most interesting is the **Museum of Kerala History and its Makers** (open Tues–Sun 10am–noon, 2–4pm, entrance charge) in Edappally, on the road to Alwaye. Starting with Neolithic man, the Museum narrates the story of Kerala – from St Thomas, Vasco da Gama, to the Rajas and the scholars.

The islands

Factories producing coir goods and frozen shrimp are found on all these islands in the backwaters that are part of the huge Vembanad lagoon. **Gundu Island** **D**, the tiniest of the islands in the lagoon, nestles in a small bay that dents the biggest island of them all, Vypeen. It has a model coir cooperative, the only building on its five acres. You can watch the coconut fibre being woven on looms into beautiful mats and fashioned into other household articles.

At Narakkal, on **Vypeen** **E**, is the **Veliyatta Parambil temple**, where trial by ordeal, using molten metal, was practised until 200 years ago. There is also a Siva temple nearby that celebrates Sivaratri handsomely. At the other end of the island, **Pallipuram**, almost overlooking Kodungallur, is a Portuguese fort. Together with the one in Kodungallur, the fort ensured that no unwanted vessels sailed up the narrows here.

Vallarpadam **F**, a large island to the northeast of Gundu, is home to an ancient church dedicated to St Mary. The miracles she is believed to have performed over the years bring the faithful in their numbers on an annual pilgrimage to this old shrine. To the east of Vallarpadam is beautiful **Bolghatty** **G**, with a Dutch palace at its southern tip, built in 1744 in the Dutch-Kerala style. Until 1947 it was the residence of the British Resident to the court of Kochi. The situation of the palace is enchanting, but it was converted into a hotel is now very run-down.

South of Bolghatty, and across the main channel leading into Kochi harbour, is the most commercially important part of

BELOW: a Kochi spice warehouse.

Map on page 200

Kochi, **Willingdon Island** Ⓗ. This is a man-made island, created in the early 20th century with sand dredged from the harbour. It serves as the headquarters of India's Southern Naval Command. One of the major Indian seaports, it also houses the airport, railway terminus and several government offices. The naval airstrip was previously also used as Kochi's civilian airport but a new international terminal has been built 36 km (22 miles) north of the city.

Kochi also has beaches, but they are not the best in Kerala. What they do have is atmosphere, the air of a more leisurely and gracious age. Nowhere is this more evident than in the **Malabar Hotel** on Willingdon Island. An old-world hotel of the 1930s, the Malabar (now run by the Taj group) still remains, for all its modernisation and new block, a very pleasant place for a drink or dinner overlooking the harbour.

Ernakulam

Across the harbour is the busy and expanding city of Ernakulam, a modern commercial centre. There are relatively few tourist sights here, but it is the location of the main railway station and M.G. Road is good for shopping. It also has a number of good hotels and can make a convenient, and cheaper, alternative base to Old Kochi. The **Siva Temple**, whose shrine can sometimes be seen appearing above the rooftops, is an important focal point for local Hindus, although non-Hindu visitors are not allowed in.

Close to the temple, which is just off M.G. Road, is **Darbar Hall** Ⓘ, on Darbar Hall Road. This impressive 19th-century building used to hold the Pariksith Thamburam Museum, but its exhibits have now been moved to the Hill Palace (see below). The building has been taken over by the **Kerala Lalit Kala Akademi** (Kerala Academy of Art), which uses it to hold temporary exhibitions of contemporary art. The cool and airy colonial building is set in large grounds that provide a respite from the busy M.G. Road nearby.

The **Hill Palace Museum** (open Tues–Sun 9am–5pm) is in Tripunithura, about 10 km (6 miles) southeast of Ernakulam. This building was the seat of the former ruling family of Kochi, and has now been converted into a museum. There is a fine collection of 19th-century paintings, copies of ancient murals and sculpture, and memorabilia of the Kochi royal family on display.

There are several palaces here, including the Hill Palace, now a museum (see above). The Sri Purnathrayeesa temple also draws crowds. About 7 km (4 miles) east of Tripunithura is **Chottanikkara**, famed for its Bhagavati temple, and about 6 km (3 miles) south is **Mulanthuruthi**, a major centre of the Jacobite Syrian Christians. Their 700-year-old church has several beautiful frescoes that date back to its foundation.

Kathakali performances

Kathakali (*katha*-story, *kali*-play), the 400-year-old dance-drama form that once used to bring Hindu mythology alive in Kerala's Hindu temples, is now staged for tourists in Kochi's art centres and auditoria *(see page 345)*. ❑

RIGHT: Kerala has a strong Communist tradition.

Map on page 196

THE WESTERN GHATS

High up in the spine of mountains that rises just inland are tea estates, pilgrimage sites and one of the finest wildlife parks in India

East of Kottayam lies plantation country: rolling estates of tea and coffee, rubber, cardamom and pepper, interspersed with forests and game reserves. The Western Ghats north of the Periyar river are the High Ranges, locally called the Annamalais – the Elephant Hills – with Anaimudi, at a little short of 3,000 metres (10,000 ft) the highest peak in the South. Below the Periyar are the Cardamom Hills, not so high but thickly forested and developed only in their southernmost reaches.

Ponmudi

Ponmudi in the southern Cardamom Hills is the only hill station of note near Thiruvananthapuram and has already been mentioned *(see page 193)*. The High Range, however, is altogether more interesting; it offers not just a day's excursion in the country, but a whole holiday out in the open. At one time, travellers had to rough it out in this country, but now "mod cons" are easily available. It is still not the easiest of country stretches to travel in, but offers visitors an enjoyable experience.

The road that goes east from Kottayam to the Periyar Wildlife Sanctuary, about 120 km (75 miles) away, is a driving experience in itself. The road winds up the mountains, climbing through a carpet of tea bushes, estates of tall rubber trees and gardens of coffee, cardamom and pepper. A good place to rest during the drive is the pretty little hill town of **Peermade**, about 75 km (47 miles) out of Kottayam. The club here is something out of a picture postcard, a splash of colour surrounded by a carpet of tea-green, and set amidst rolling hills of all shades of dark green, misty purple and smoky blue. Now you are in the High Range and travelling at heights that average 2,100 metres (7,000 ft) and more, about the height of the tallest peak in the Cardamom Hills.

LEFT: tea pickers at work near Munnar. **RIGHT:** casting a net in the Ghats.

Sabrimala

Just south of Peermade is **Sabrimala** ⓰, the abode of Lord Aiyappa, but it has to be approached from a road going south from Kottayam and curving up to the Pamba river. A 5-km (3-mile) trek from the river through thick forest brings you to the hill temple in the wilderness to which the faithful come from all parts of South India. During the main festival season in December–January, the four-hour trek often takes longer because of the throngs of people on the path. Pilgrims, most of them men (only prepubescent girls and postmenopausal women may take part in the pilgrimage), take strict vows that restrict them to a life of austerity. During the days leading up to the Sabrimala festival, a

common sight in South Indian cities is the large number of men wearing black or saffron and sporting the beards that proclaim the vows they have taken of self-denial.

In the last 20 or so years the number of pilgrims has increased dramatically from around 10,000 to between 150–200,000 people. The timing of the pilgrimage coincides with South Indian holiday of Pongol, the most important day being 14 January. This is Sankramam, or the beginning of the Hindu New Year in the South. The preparations by the devotees will have started long before, sometime around 15 November. Then, or even earlier, the potential pilgrim takes the vow of abstinence at a local temple and starts wearing the holy beads of a pilgrim. Traditionally the period of penance lasts 41 days, during which they dress in black, eat vegetarian food and abstain from sex. Each evening the Aiyappans (for the period of the worship the devotees assume the name of the god) gather at each other's houses in turn to chant the name of Aiyappa and sing devotional songs. After singing, the devotees may dance frenetically.

The pilgrimage itself takes a week. Each Aiyappan takes a bag with two compartments, which is worn on the head. In one half is a coconut filled with *ghi*, an offering to the god, in the other is rice, a sugar ball and a stick of camphor. There are two routes up to the shrine. The longest, and most holy because it was the one taken by Aiyappa himself, starts at Erumeli and is about 72 km (45 miles). The alternative, and much shorter, route is the one taken by the majority of pilgrims. This starts at Chalakayam and has a road up which vehicles can travel. As the Aiyappans trek towards the temple they chant the name of the god, *Svamiye Saranam Aiyappa*. On reaching the temple the devotee is confronted by 18 steps, and the coconut from the bag is smashed on one of the steps. It is said the pilgrim should return each year for 18 years, smashing a coconut on each step in turn.

The road continuing east from Peermade takes the visitor to a place away from the temple in the wilderness and the sanctity that surrounds it. But in the forests and meadowed hills around the artificial Periyar Lake is an attraction of another kind. Here, in a large area of nearly 800 sq metres (8,608 sq ft), at heights ranging from 900–1,950 metres (3,000–6,500 ft), is one of India's most sucessful wildlife sanctuaries and tiger reserves.

Thekkady

The road from Peermade joins the road from Madurai in Tamil Nadu at Kumili, and snakes through the eastern reaches of the park to reach **Thekkady**, overlooking the lake. This is the base camp for the **Periyar Wildlife Sanctuary and Tiger Reserve** ⑰. Accommodation ranges from deluxe comfort to dormitories, but if you have the choice, try the Government-run **Lake Palace** (www.ktdc.com); this erstwhile palatial watch-hut of the Maharajas of Travancore offers a serenity that cannot be matched by the other more crowded Thekkady lodgings.

Treetop lookouts for those who want to catch a glimpse of animals by night – or

LEFT: elephants love a good scrub.

Map on page 196

even during the day – are few and far between in the reserve, but offer good watching, especially if a Forest Ranger is on hand. The more conventional method is to take a couple of hours in the morning and a couple more in the evening in one of the many launches that slowly circle the lake. However, the wildlife watching from these is less good as the crowds on board tend to be quite noisy.

Forest rangers help you spot distant animals, but in this finest of elephant sanctuaries in India, you do not need much help to spot the herds of elephants. Herds of 20 to 30, sometimes more, are often spotted slowly meandering up and down the hillside, playing in the water or swimming across small necks in the lake to cross over to the other side. Often a ranger will take a boat close to a herd in the water. Spotted deer and sambar, gaur and a variety of waterbirds are easy to spot, but you need luck to see a bear, leopard or tiger, or birds of rare species. Nevertheless, the experience can be quite wonderful.

Day-long excursions from Thekkady include Crusoe Island (19 km/12 miles), Manakavala (10 km/6 miles), Mullakudy (129 km/80 miles), the Periyar Dam (15 km/9 miles) and Thannikudy (38 km/24 miles). Back at Kumili, the twisting mountain road heads north for the highest ranges and the biggest plantations.

Idukki

Munnar is the road's eventual destination, only about 70 km (44 miles) away, though the twisting road makes it seem miles further. But there is one stop to make before that in this rugged terrain, and that is **Idukki** ⓲. Idukki means "narrow gorge", and that is exactly what the Periyar river gushes through to the west of the Kumili-Munnar road.

On either side of the river, creating the gorge, are **Kuravan** and **Kurathi**, hills which, according to folklore, are Adivasi lovers who were turned into granite rocks because of a curse. Bridging the gorge is the magnificent Idukki arch dam, set

BELOW: tea bushes and mountain peaks.

against densely wooded hills and valleys traversed by hundreds of rushing streams. The dam is surrounded by wilderness, gardens, and the **Idukki wildlife sanctuary**. The flora and fauna in the sanctuary are similar to those in the Periyar sanctuary and it sees fewer visitors, but there are fewer facilities for animal watching. Carmelia Haven at Vandanmedu near Periyar, is set in beautiful surroundings and has an excellent restaurant.

Munnar

Heading towards **Munnar** ⓳, the road winds its way through Devikolam, the nearest settlement of any sort, and then you are in the company town, surrounded by plantations. British companies owned most of the large plantations in Munnar, with the exception of one Indian, Kannan Devan, who owned plantations even during the heydays of the Raj. The most important planter in the High Range today is Tata Tea, which oversees almost every public facility in the vicinity.

Munnar is situated at the confluence of three rivers, at a height of about 1,800 metres (6,000 ft). It is the highest town in Kerala and lies at the heart of tea country. It has some of the biggest tea estates in Kerala and on either side of the High Range. Beyond lies Anaimudi (the highest peak in the Western Ghats at 2,695 metres/9,000 ft) and the rich tropical forest of the Annamalai Sanctuary in Tamil Nadu, and the **Eravikulam National Park** (closed during the monsoon) in Kerala. Access to the Park is controlled by the warden of the Kerala Wildlife Department in Devikulam. Visitors are limited to a small section of the sanctuary to protect the rare flora and fauna of the region.

Map on page 196

The Nilgiri tahr in Eravikulam is one of the rarest mountain goats in the world. Until a few years ago the species was fighting a losing battle for survival; now herds of 30 and more can be seen at a time. In the park, and around the estates in the Annamalais, elephants move across the border; Nilgiri langurs, lion-tailed macaques and other monkeys abound; sambars are often seen; and wild dogs regularly trace the path of their prey.

A further excursion from Munnar is to the east, up to **Mattupatty Lake** and the viewpoint at **Top Station** (actually just inside neighbouring Tamil Nadu). As you leave Munnar you might like to stop off at the Kerala Forest Development Corporation's **Orchidarium**, where there is a beautiful display of plants and flowers for sale.

The road on to Mattupatty winds up and up through beautiful landscape, dotted with tea estates, plantations and woods, all the while ringed by the mountains. The large Mattupatty Dam has created a large lake that extends back into the hills. You can hire boats to explore the waters further. About halfway along the lake you come to Echopoint (easily spotted by the hawkers that congregate here). Shouting out over the water, your words are bounced back from the opposite shore. On again, and much higher up, you reach Top Station, marked by a few tea stalls and basic eateries. The views from here are breathtaking, though they are sometimes obscured by mist. ❑

LEFT: orderly tea bushes.

Tea and Coffee

Today India is the largest producer of tea in the world. Assam and Darjeeling lead the way, but much is grown in the Nilgiris. The earliest tea plantations in South India were developed in the Nilgiri hills between 1859 and 1869. Unlike in Assam, tea in South India tends to grow on hill slopes; it is believed that the higher the elevation, the better the flavour. Tea plantations stretch all the way from the Nilgiri hills to the southern parts of Kerala. (For a full history of tea planting in India turn to Roy Moxham's book *Tea: Addiction, Exploitation and Empire.*)

Tea is an agro-industry, processing its raw materials, namely the green leaf, in factories situated on or near the plantations. The manufacturing process consists of curing the green leaf, rolling and fermenting it, and drying and grading. This is the orthodox way of manufacturing the leaf and the dust, though many innovations in the process have been introduced. Production in tea has soared since Independence, and the international price has declined in turn. Much tea grown in India, however, is consumed within the country.

In Nilgiris the CTC method – crushing, tearing, curling – produces a darker, stronger brew using a machine invented in 1930 in Assam. Contact the United Planters Association of Southern India (UPASI), Glenview, Coonoor if you wish to visit tea or coffee plantations here. The coffee from this area is also excellent, prepared with roasted and ground beans, which are filtered and then served with hot milk.

Coffee made its advent in India in the 17th century, nearly 200 years before tea, and that too under Indian auspices. An Arabian saint, Hazarat Shahi Janab Allah Mogatabi, popularly known as Baba Budan, sowed seven coffee seeds he had brought from a pilgrimage to the holy places of Islam. The seeds were sown in the hills in Karnataka, which still bear his name. Karnataka continues to be the largest producer of coffee, followed by Kerala and Tamil Nadu. The two major varieties grown are the Arabica and the Robusta. The fruit crop gathered is pulped in the pulper house, and the separated coffee seeds are dried and sent to the curing works. The process is simple, compared to the complex processing of tea. Multinational companies have set up factories to manufacture instant coffee, an increasingly popular drink, the appearance of which is greatly bemoaned by fans of real South Indian coffee.

The legacy the British planters left behind is still very much in evidence. The plantations remain a significant part of the Indian national wealth. With their neatly laid out rows of tea on the slopes, the winding roads and the colonial bungalows, they are one of the few worthwhile legacies of British rule.

Coffee country is also beautiful. In the coffee blossom season, the stretches are decked with a mass of white flowers, wafting a heady fragrance for miles around. When they turn into green berries and then into red fruits, it is yet another cropping season for coffee. Among the amenities the plantation country affords is ample opportunity for outdoor activities such as trekking and wildlife watching. A number of sanctuaries in the South, including Mudumalai and Thekkady, are located near the plantations. ❑

RIGHT: picking coffee beans.

NORTHERN KERALA

This region is little-visited compared to the rest of the state, but it is home to Kerala's most important temples, beautiful beaches and undisturbed tropical rainforest

Heading northeast from Ernakulam, the National Highway heads northeast to **Aluva** (Alwaye), a major junction and industrial town on the Periyar river. The *Sivaratri* festival on the banks is a colourful celebration in which the devotees pay homage to the Siva *lingam* on the sandbank. The Union Christian College here is the first college to have been started by Indian Christians, not foreign missionaries. And the tourist guesthouse, beautifully situated on the riverbank, is a splendid old palace.

Parur and Kodungallur

Continuing northeast from Alwaye, you come to **Parur**, one of the towns of Thomas and what was also a major Jewish settlement. From here you can then continue on to an interesting, but now little-remembered, historical location at the furthest extremity of the Vembanad Lake. This is **Kodungallur** ⓴, once known as Muziris to the Greeks and Cranganore to the Europeans. It was also known as Mahodyapuram to the Cheraman Perumals who ruled from here.

The **Cheraman Mosque**, although it now has a modern appearance, is believed to be the oldest in India. It is said to have been founded by the Islamic missionary Malik ibn Dinar in 629. The present appearance dates from 2001 when it underwent a thorough restoration. The tombs of Malik ibn Dinar and his wife behind the main prayer hall are ecumenical, attended by both Muslim and Hindu women.

It was not only the Muslims who are first thought to have set foot in India on this spot. Kodungallur is also said to have been where the Apostle Thomas landed (in, allegedly, AD 52). Close by, at **Azhikod**, the large church is said to hold the grizzly relic of St Thomas's forearm. The town was also one of the first places settled by Jews fleeing persecution.

There are, however, also very important Hindu shrines here. The **Tiruvanchikulam Temple** close to the mosque is a splendid Siva shrine, a fine example of traditional Keralan temple architecture, while the most lively and popular shrine in Kodungallur is undoubtedly the **Bhagavati Temple**, dedicated to the goddess, which sits in a large compound at the centre of the town. The Bhavani Festival in March–April sees many visitors. Both temples do not allow access to non-Hindus and visitors may wish to keep their distance at festival time.

From Aluva, the northeast branch of the road runs to **Kaladi** ㉑, on the banks of the Alwaye river. This is the birthplace of the great 8th-century Advaita philosopher

LEFT: a dancer at the Thrissur temple.
RIGHT: a toddy tapper.

and religious reformer of India, Sri Shankaracharya, and is a major pilgrim centre. One of the two temples here contains an image of Sri Adi Shankaracharya as Daksinamurti, and the other an image of the Sringeri Muth's tutelar deity, Saradamba. Near the **Saradamba temple** is another temple, with an image of Lord Krisna believed to have been installed by Shankaracharya himself.

On the road to the temples is the **Sri Adi Sankara Kirthi Sthamba Mandapam**, a 46-metre (150-ft), nine-tier octagonal tower, commemorating Sri Shankaracharya's life and his work in words, symbols and pictures.

Into the hills

A few miles beyond Kaladi, at the top of a 610-metre (2,000-ft) hill, is a shrine dedicated to St Thomas. The footprints in the rock at **Malayattur** are said to be his. The help of St Thomas, who is believed to have meditated here and built a shrine, is invoked every year by thousands of pilgrims. The Malayattur Perumal festival in March–April is one of the biggest Christian festivals in South India.

A little to the south, near **Perumbavur**, is a rock-cut temple, Jain in character but Hindu in ritual. From the **Kallil temple**, 120 steps lead to a statue of Mahavira cut out of the rock. To the west, near Kothamangalam on the Ernakulam–Munnar road, is the **Thattekkad Bird Sanctuary**. The only bird sanctuary in Kerala, it covers the Periyar river and teak plantations, a perfect setting for a wealth of birdlife including hornbills, rollers, parrots, water birds and migratory species.

Thrissur

Thrissur ㉒ (formerly Trichur), 53 km (33 miles) from Aluva on the national highway, has a good claim to be the cultural capital of Kerala. Three state academies – the Kerala Sahitya Akademi (literature), the Sangeet Natak Akademi (music and drama) and the Lalit Kala Akademi (visual arts) – have their headquarters here, the School of

BELOW: rainforest in the hills.

Map on page 196

Drama run by the University of Kozhikode is also based in Thrissur, and the Kalamandalam Art Academy is nearby.

The name Thrissur is an anglicised version of the Malayalam Trissivaperur, meaning the "Town with the name of Lord Siva". It is built around an elevated area, called the "round", in the centre of which is the **Vadakkunnathan temple** (closed to non-Hindus except during *Puram*; *see below*), a typical example of Keralan architecture with exquisite wood carvings, containing the shrines of Paramasiva, Parvati, Sankaranarayana, Rama and Krisna. Legend has it that the temple was founded by the sage Parasurama, who carved Kerala out from the sea.

The Thrissur temple celebrates its famous *Puram* festival every year in April. A spectacular affair, it involves a procession of 30–40 caparisoned elephants, amid the fanfare of the *panchavadya*.

The city's **Archaeological Museum** (open Tues–Sun 10am–5pm) has recently been moved from the town centre to the Kollengode Palace, a 19th-century building about 2km (1 mile) from the city centre. It has an excellent collection of Megalithic finds from the surrounding area, some fine bronzes and interesting wooden models of different Keralan temples.

All those interested in the performing arts should visit **Kalamandalam**, about 30 km (18 miles) from Thrissur on the Thrissur–Shoranur highway. This academy was founded by Kerala's renowned poet, the late Vallathol Narayana Menon, in Cheruthuruthi on the banks of the river Bharathapuzha and provides training in the dance forms *Mohiniattam*, *Kathakali* and *ottan tullal*.

Guruvayur

North of Thrissur, about 30 km (18 miles) away, lies **Guruvayur** ㉓ with its famous Sri Krisna temple, considered the most sacred Hindu religious centre of Kerala. Though the origin of the temple is shrouded in mystery, there is no doubt that it existed from the 16th century at least. Legend says that the consecration of the image was done by Guru, the preceptor of the *devas* (gods), and Vayu, the god of the winds, and so the place came to be known as Guruvayur. Lord Krisna, who is the deity installed in the temple, is also known as Guruvayurappa.

There are regular *pujas* before dawn and at twilight, which attract thousands of devotees (non-Hindus are not permitted within the temple). A large number of Hindu weddings are solemnised here. The devotees give large donations in cash and kind, including grain, vegetables and *ghi*. The temple has a big elephant yard to stable the many elephants presented by the devout. The annual **Ulsavom** or temple festival at Guruvayur is spread over 10 days in February–March, starting off with an elephant race. There is also a colourful elephant procession and a performance of *Krisnattam*, the precursor of *Kathakali*. There is music festival here in November– December.

Palakkad (formerly Palghat), at the base of the Western Ghats, is a busy trading town set in a break in the hills, 79 km (49 miles) from Thrissur. It is the capital

RIGHT: a temple elephant.

Spices

The Phoenicians and the Greeks sailed to the shores of India to gather spices. Indian pepper and cardamom were highly valued, and trade was mainly with the western coast of South India, specifically Kerala. Musiris (now Kodungalloor) and Ophir (present day Beypore) were ports of call even from the days of Solomon. Pepper was called black gold and highly valued – as much as the yellow metal and precious stones for which they were bartered.

Cardamom was also another highly prized item. Today it is a popular seasoning ingredient for Indian curry dishes; cardamom seeds produce a camphor-like aromatic flavour. The small green fruit grows abundantly in the forests of the Cardamom Hills.

Intrepid Arab sailors were regular visitors to the "Malaibar" coast to buy spices long before the advent of Islam, and the beaches of Kerala were busy entrepôts for the spice trade. The trade continued through the centuries and exists even today, though the modes of trade have changed.

Though pride of place goes to pepper and cardamom, other spices such as dried ginger, garlic and turmeric are also in considerable demand. Then comes what are called minor spices – dry chillies, coriander, cumin and fenugreek.

India produces approximately 80 percent of the world's cardamom, and of this, 60 percent is grown in Kerala. Similarly, pepper has been the largest foreign exchange earner among India's cash crops, although the trade is now facing hard times and is under threat from cheaper spices grown in Vietnam. Both cardamom and pepper are commodities with widely fluctuating prices which stimulate the gambler's instinct among the operators on the commodities exchange, though the actual grower of the spices gets little of the benefit from a steep price rise.

Along with spices, another important product is the cashew. The cashew has an interesting history in India. It was introduced by the Portuguese and is considered by some to be one of the few lasting benefits of the Portuguese incursion into India. It is not only grown widely in Goa but also in Kerala where it is a valued cash crop which earns foreign exchange. The cashew workers of Kerala, mainly in Kollam, are among the most skilled in the world. Cashew nuts are an important ingredient in South Indian vegetarian recipes as well as in some meat dishes.

India produces about two million tons of spices each year, including around 40 percent of the world's black pepper. Besides pepper, India exports two varieties of cardamom, chillies (which are a transplant from the New World brought by the Portuguese), ginger, coriander, turmeric, cumin, celery, fennel and fenugreek.

Along the shore and on the tropical hills beyond, spices grow in profusion. The turmeric plant, with shining leaves obscuring its yellow flower spikes, and shoots of ginger are rampant. The nutmeg trees were originally brought from the Moluccas. Cardamom shrubs tower over your head, pepper vines tangle around the jungle trees, black and green peppercorns make a kaleidoscope of spiced colour against stacks of cinnamon bark peeled into curled quills. ❑

LEFT: a pepper vine.

Map on page 196

town of the district which is considered one of Kerala's rice bowls. It has a well-preserved fort built by Hyder Ali, Sultan of Mysore, which is maintained by the Archaeological Survey of India. Fourteen kilometres (9 miles) from Palakkad is the **Malampuzha dam** complex. The dam has been built across the Bharatapuzha river, near the foothills of the Western Ghats. The huge lake has an attractive terraced garden with statues created by Keralan sculptor Kanai Kunhiraman.

Silent Valley

North from Palakkad on the Coimbatore–Kannur National Highway, you finally reach **Attappadi**, a centre of the Irular, Mudugar and Kurumbar peoples. Another 12 km (7 miles) is **Silent Valley**, one of the few tropical evergreen rainforests left in the country. Elephants, tigers, wild dog, flying squirrels and lion-tail macaques are found in this valley, in addition to a wealth of plant life. Entry into the area is strictly regulated by permits issued by the Forest Department.

At Mannarghat you rejoin the National Highway on the way to **Nilambur** about 60 km (37 miles) away, passing through extensive rubber plantations. Nilambur serves as the headquarters of an important forest division in Kerala. Here there are fine teak plantations, almost a century old, and the quiet and restful **Nellikuthu**.

From Nilambur you can go on to Kozhikode through Moplah country to **Malappuram**, the district headquarters. The ancient mosque here has a colourful annual *nercha* (festival). On the parallel road, which is the main highway, is the Kozhikode University at **Chelari** south-east, and the pleasant town of Mamburam on the banks of a small river. Further on is Feroke, which has a tile industry on the banks of the river Chaliyar. Kozhikode is 12 km (7 miles) beyond.

Kozhikhode

Kozhikode ㉔ (formerly Calicut) was once the dominant port of the Malabar coast, and known to the Phoenicians and the Greeks for its export of spices and cloth. This town gave to the English language the word *calico*, after a type of cotton material. The first colonial adventurer from the West, Vasco da Gama, landed near **Kappad**, 14 km (8 miles) north of Kozhikode. The Zamorin Raja welcomed him and allowed him the same trading rights as many other foreigners, but Portuguese ambitions made conflict inevitable. The Zamorin's navy, composed of Moplah Muslim seamen, put up a stiff resistance under his able admirals, the Kunhali Marakkars. The Portuguese were succeeded by the Dutch and later by the British, with a short French presence in between.

Kozhikode is a busy city and is still an important trading centre. There is the interesting **Pazhassi Raja museum** (open Tues–Sun 10am–1pm, 2–4.30pm) managed by the State Archaeological department and also the connected **Krishna Menon Museum** and **Art Gallery** (open Thur–Sat 10am–5pm, Wed 1–5pm; the Art Gallery is currently closed for refurbishment). Krishna Menon was a prominent Keralan politician and India's first representative to the United Nations.

RIGHT: Silent Valley.

In the Kuttichira district are two early and important sites, the **Misqalpalli** and **Machantipalli** mosques. The former dates back to the 14th century, while the lands for the Machantipalli mosque were granted in the 13th century. Both are fascinating in their adherence to local traditional forms of architecture, with stepped roofs and delicate woodcarving.

Islam in Kerala

It is thought that Islam came to Kerala in the 7th century AD through interaction with Arabs who had been trading for centuries with what they called Malabar. It is still believed by many that Cheraman Perumal was attracted to the tenets of Islam and sailed to Jeddah to meet the Prophet. He was converted to Islam, called himself Tajuddin and married the sister of a great sailor and teacher by the name of Malik ibn Dinar. As well as the mosque at Kodungallur, Malik ibn Dinar is said to have established nine other mosques which are still extant. Among them are the ones at **Chaliyam**, near Beypore, **Kollam**, Madayi near Kannur and Ezhimalai on the way to **Kasargode** – all coastal towns, testifying to the close connection between maritime trade and the advent of Islam.

Waynad

Fifty-five kilometres (34 miles) east of Kozhikode is the **Waynad plateau**, 610 metres (2,000 ft) high. Waynad is known for its plantations of coffee, cardamom, pepper and rubber. **Lakidi** en route is a quiet place of great beauty with hill streams and the scenic **Pukote Lake**. Of great importance is the **Waynad Wildlife Sanctuary**, which is joined to the Mudumalai and Bandipur sanctuaries in Tamil Nadu and Karnataka respectively. It protects a large area of Kerala's densely forested hills.

Waynad is a separate district with headquarters at **Kalapetta**. There is a famous Jain temple here (Kalapetta was once the stronghold of the Jains), and natural caves in nearby **Edakkal** with prehistoric carvings. The highway branches off at Chun-

BELOW: the beach at Bekal, seen from the fort.

dale, in one direction leading to Ooty and the other to Mysore. The last town in Waynad, called **Sultanbathery**, has a now very ruined fort built by Tippu Sultan. A parallel highway in Waynad connects Mysore with Thalasseri and Kannur, passing through Manantodu and the extensive Avalam farm and wildlife sanctuary.

Very close to Kozhikode lies the major fishing harbour of **Beypore** at the mouth of the river Chaliyar. Once known to the Arabs and the Greeks, it has a boat-building yard which has been building vessels for Arabs from the Gulf and Kuwait for centuries.

To the north of Kozhikode the highway passes through the suburb of West Hill to **Kappad beach** 15 km (10 miles) away. Said to be where Vasco da Gama landed, and it is now a quiet village with a picturesque seashore. Further north you pass **Quilandy** (nearby **Kollam** is a more likely spot for Vasco da Gama's first landing), where there are families who can trace their descent from Arab settlers, and **Badagara**, an important trading centre. Just off Badagara is **Lokanar Kavu**, the home of the Kurups who were heroes of *Vadakka Pattu*, the Northern Ballads. They are exponents of the martial art of *kalari payattu* which ues sticks and staves and thin steel swords known as *urumi*. Northward from Badagar you reach **Mahé**, formerly a French enclave and now administrately part of Pondicherry. It still maintains a French air and it retains a number of colonial buildings, including the baroque church of St Therese and the former residency.

Thalasseri and Kannur

About 3 miles (5 km) further north lies **Thalasseri** ㉕ (formerly Tellicherry). The fort here was built by the East India Company in the early 18th century overlooking the Arabian Sea. The small **State Arts Museum** here has excellent bronzes and wood carvings. There is also a small Armenian church, and a mosque founded by Haider Ali. Thanks to the pioneering effort of Kilari Kunhikannan Gurukkal, Thalasseri has a Circus Academy and Gymnasium built near the beach. Most Indian circuses are now full of gymnasts trained in the Thalasseri academy.

Northwards, 29 km (18 miles) away, lies **Kannur** ㉖ (formerly Cannanore), once the capital of the Kolathiri Rajas and also the seat of the Arakkal Rajas, the only Muslim ruling family in Kerala. **St Angelo's fort**, built by the Portuguese in the 16th century, overlooks the interesting Muslim town. About 50 km (30 miles) north is **Ezhimala** on a high promontory overlooking the sea and a beautiful beach. On the way is **Taliparamba**, where there is a snake farm.

About 100 km (63 miles) north of Kannur on the National Highway lies the fishing centre of **Kasargode**. The Muslims of the town are considered expert seamen, with a reputation for intrepidity and adventure. The beach here stretches as far as **Bekal fort** (open 8am–5pm, entrance charge), some 10 km (6 miles) from Kasargode, which is well worth a visit. Situated on a jutting beachhead high above the shore, at a strategic curve on the coast, this huge fort, built of red laterite by a Kannada chief, served as a vantage point to look out for naval marauders. ❑

RIGHT: buffalo racing.

THE LAKSHADWEEP ISLANDS

A chain of coral islands, of which only a handful are inhabited, surrounded by crystal-clear seas and fringed by white sand beaches and coconut palms

Thirty-six tiny islands with a total land area of only about 3 hectares (8 acres) constitute the archipelago of Lakshadweep, the smallest of the States and Union Territories of India. However, the geographical area including the lagoons adds up to approximately 419 hectares (1,035 acres), and the territorial waters to almost 2,023 hectares (5,000 acres). Lakshadweep means one lakh – one hundred thousand – islands and originally referred to the island chain including the Maldives and Minicoy.

Until 1956, the islands formed part of the state of Madras, and were known until 1973 as the Laccadive, Minicoy and Amindivi Islands. Only ten of the islands are inhabited. They are, in descending order of size, Minicoy, Andrott, Kavaratti, Kadmat, Agatti, Kalpeni, Amini, Kiltan, Chetlat and Bitra. However, entry to many of the islands is restricted to protect the fragile ecosystem which consists of lagoons and land which is barely 2 metres (6 ft) above sea level. International tourists are permitted to stay only at Bangaram and Kadmat, both of which were originally uninhabited; Indian nationals, however, can stop over at Agatti, Kalpeni, Minicoy and the capital, Kavaratti.

India's coral islands

The islands are located between 8° and 12°N and are about 322 km (200 miles) away from the Keralan coast on the Indian mainland. The Lakshadweep cluster is India's only coral islands. The archipaelago has 12 atolls, three reefs and five submerged banks. Almost all the atolls have a northeast-southwest orientation with magnificent lagoons in between, opening out to the sea through one or more channels. The climate is tropical throughout the year, with a maximum temperature ranging from 35° to 38°C (95° to 100° F) and minimum from 17° to 18°C (62° to 64° F). The monsoon arrives in May and it rains till the end of September. During this period, the islands are harder to reach and transit between islands may have to be by helicopter as the sea can become extremely rough.

Lakshadweep's chief attraction lies in its unspoilt and virtually unpopulated sandy beaches, its verdant coconut groves and its crystal-clear lagoons which range in colour from pale aquamarine to dark lapis lazuli. These lagoons are shallow, calm and safe for swimming. They abound in a variety of brilliantly coloured tropical fish. For the more adventurous, it is possible to go snorkelling or to hire scuba equipment to investigate the enchanting coral reefs.

PRECEDING PAGES: Lakshadweep's coral reefs teem with coloured fish

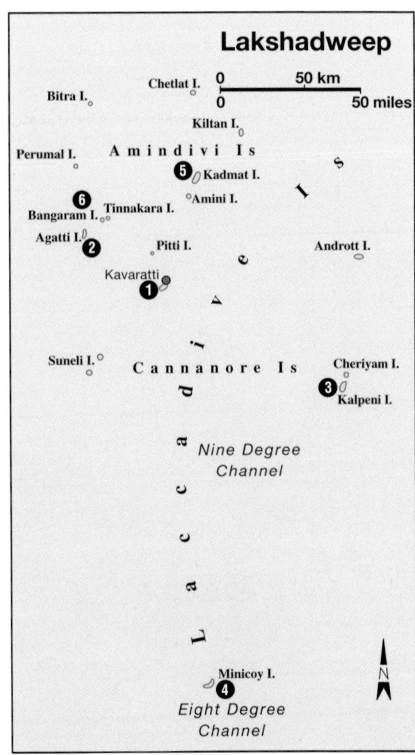

The sea life on the reefs and within the lagoons is impressive. As well as a huge variety of corals, there are over 1,000 species of fish, including butterflyfish, clownfish, wrasses, parrotfish, goatfish and lionfish. Among the more spectacular sights are the turtles, harmless sharks and manta rays, and visitors may also encounter dolphins in the lagoons.

Access to the islands is controlled and limited by the Indian Government, and foreign tourists must book through one of two tour operators. For Bangaram Island Resort, contact CGH Earth (previously the Casino Group), tel: 00 91 484 266 8221, www.cghearth.com; for Kadmat, contact Lacadives, tel: 00 91 484 311 9494, www.lacadives.com. Both operators offer diving packages for experts as well as beginners. If you are planning on diving you will need a certificate of health from your doctor. In addition, it may, at times, be possible for foreign tourists to stay at the small resort complex close to the airport on Agatti.

Boats and planes

The only accommodation available on the islands is sparsely furnished tourist huts, though the bungalows on Agatti are more comfortable. If the visitor is stopping off at a number of islands it might be best to stay on board ship. The *M.V. Tippu Sultan* which the administration has chartered from the Shipping Corporation of India (*see* www.lakshadweep.nic.in for details of tours and latest schedules) provides accommodation for its passengers. Aboard the vessel are 6 four-berth cabins, 2 two-berth cabins and economy-class dormitory accommodation for up to 16 people.

For those visitors wishing to explore the islands from Kochi, the journey by ship to the closest island, Kalpeni, takes 15 hours. Travellers are then taken to Kalpeni on the first day, Minicoy on the second and Kavaratti on the third, and the ship returns to Kochi on the fifth day. Indian Airlines also operates regular flights to Agatti, the closest inhabited island to Bangaram.

BELOW: the boat from Agatti enters the Bangaram lagoon.

The islanders

The population of Lakshadweep is relatively high, just over 60,000 in 2001. Most of the islanders are of Keralan descent – originally Hindu, as the prevalent systems of caste and of matrilineal inheritance bear out. The language spoken on all the islands except Minicoy is a dialect of Malayalam. Mahl is normally spoken in Minicoy, which is close to and has historical links with the Maldive group of islands. Ninety-six percent of the population is Muslim, Islam having been brought to the islands by Hazrat Ubaidullah in the 7th century.

Coconut cultivation, fishing and a small amount of tourism are the chief occupations of the inhabitants. There is virtually no industry other than producing and processing coir. Coconut shells are also used in making handicrafts and souvenirs. Local transportation on the islands is also limited, and is mainly restricted to the movement of goods, and the ubiquitous bicycle is the usual mode of transport.

The people of the islands are polite and friendly, and the level of education is among the highest in India. There is no reported crime of any kind on the islands and it is common to see even small children wandering around with gold necklaces around their necks without any fear of being robbed.

Kavaratti

Kavaratti ❶ is the administrative capital of Lakshadweep and has a sizeable number of mainlanders, chiefly working for the Government. Ujro Mosque is worth a visit; it has an ornately carved ceiling, said to be made of driftwood. The Aquarium here is also interesting, with its fine collection of colourful fish and coral forms.

Agatti

Set on the edge of a stunning lagoon, **Agatti ❷** is the location of the only airport in the island chain. A 20-seater Indian Airlines plane connects Agatti with Kochi and Goa. Foreign visitors who are heading

Map on page 222

on then have a two-hour boat ride to either Bangaram or Kadmat, both uninhabited and on beautiful clear lagoons. This exciting trip, on what seems to be a very small boat in the swell of the Indian ocean, takes you outside the reef and is likely to be accompanied by dolphins, porpoises and flying fish, as well as large green and hawksbill turtles.

Kalpeni

Kalpeni ❸ is the first island that Indian tourists on package tours are likely to visit. It has a spectacular lagoon and a beautiful bay containing three uninhabited islands, Tilakkam, Pitti and Cheriyam. Kalpeni has been developed for internal tourism and has watersports facilities and tourist huts. Evidence can still be seen of a huge storm that devastated the island in 1847.

LEFT: Lakshadweep schoolgirls. **BELOW:** shallow lagoons and palm-fringed beaches.

Minicoy

Minicoy ❹ is the southernmost island of the archipelago and closest to the Maldives in both geography and culture. The lighthouse built by the British more than a century ago is worth a visit. Tuna fishing and boat-building are important occupations for the inhabitants in Minicoy.

Kadmat and Bangaram

Kadmat ❺ has a beautiful lagoon, ideal for swimming. The tourist huts at Kadmat are in a better condition and provide more amenities than those on the other islands.

Bangaram ❻ is an uninhabited island, developed as an international tourist resort. Those planning for a long stay would be well advised to stay here.

The advent of tourism has brought inevitable change to Lakshadweep and pressures on resources – particularly water – as well as society are likely to intensify. However, it appears that there is a certain degree of sensitivity to these problems on the part of the local authorities and controls are being debated which are aimed at preserving the tranquillity of this beautiful island group. ❑

KARNATAKA

This large and diverse state ranges from the modern city of Bangalore, to the ruins of Hampi, to beautiful early temples

The state of Karnataka, 202,800 sq. km (78,000 sq miles) in area, has a population of 52.8 million. It was formed by amalgamating the princely state of Mysore with the Kannada-speaking communities of the Madras Presidency.

Karnataka has a long coastline stretching from Goa in the north to the Kerala border. It has many beaches, though these are not as well known as those of its neighbours. Inland are the Western Ghats which rise to a subdued 488 metres (1,600 ft) in this state. Both flanks of the Ghats are forested and have large plantations of teak, sandalwood and bamboo. Most of Karnataka lies on the ancient Deccan plateau. Though the state has rivers, waterfalls (the best known being the Jog Falls), game sanctuaries (Bandipur) and a pleasant climate for most of the year, it is its historical legacies – Jain, Hindu and Muslim – that are of particular interest.

Ninety-six kilometres (60 miles) north of Mysore on top of the Hillock of Sravanabelagola is the colossal monolithic statue of Gomateswara, built by the Ganga kings in AD 983. Around the city of Mysore are the great Hoysala temples of Somnathpur, Halebid and Belur, built in the 12th and 13th centuries. In northwest Karnataka at Hampi stand the magnificent ruins of the once great Hindu Vijayanagara kingdom – 14th to 16th century, but destroyed by the Deccan Sultanates after a titanic battle in 1565.

The Muslim Sultans also made a major contribution to the heritage of Karnataka. The Adil Shahi Sultans have left behind in the walled medieval town of Bijapur many beautiful mosques, tombs and palaces built in the Turkish style with simple lines and restrained embellishments. Srirangapatnam, Tippu Sultan's fortress, built on a beautiful island in the Kaveri, bears marks of his struggle and final capitulation to the British at the end of the 18th century. In Bangalore Tippu's father Haider Ali laid out the beautiful Lal Bagh gardens, to this day the city's finest park.

The Hindu Maharajas of Mysore, restored to grace after Tippu's fall, built several palaces in both Mysore and Bangalore and the temple on the hill outside Mysore called the Chamundesvari.

PRECEDING PAGES: Jog Falls.
LEFT: the Gomatesvara statue at Sravanabelagola during the 12-yearly *Mahamastakabhiseka* festival.

Maps:
Area 244
City 232

BANGALORE

An outward-looking city that is home to many hi-tech industries, Bangalore is a pleasant mix of the modern and traditional

Bangalore ❶ is said to be India's most congenial city. Its citizens are contentedly inured to the litany, chanted by all those who come here, which lists the agreeable climate they enjoy, the greenery, the cleanliness, the sense of order, the postcard-pretty streets and the comparatively unhurried pace of life that still manages to co-exist with the accelerating tempo of industrialisation. Other residents disagree and point to the increasing problems of congestion and pollution which the city is being forced to contend with. The beautiful trees that lined the roads are being chopped down to make more room for traffic and the legendary greenery is rapidly being replaced with concrete.

According to a World Bank report, Bangalore is among the fastest growing cities in the world, which might explain why the Bangalorean would rather talk about the present than the past. Under the overlay of Westernisation, however, is a core of tradition not immediately apparent to the outsider or the newcomer who hears English spoken as much as Kannada. The Kannadiga ethos prevails in easy equilibrium with a fluid cultural mix of other religions, languages, manners of dress, customs and lifestyles. The city presents a palette of external influences – from the relics of the once-dominant Raj to the hand-knitted sweaters sold by Tibetan refugees that colour the pavements on Kempe Gowda Road. Through the cosmopolitan hubbub flows the traditional way of life of the native Bangalorean, who still listens to *vina* recitals, whose wife still cooks her sweet *kesari bhath* as her grandmother did, and whose daughter still wears the customary chaplet of *kanakambara* flowers on her hair.

The capital of Karnataka, Bangalore is located in the southeast of the state on the Deccan plateau, at a height of about 1,000 metres (3,000 ft). The vegetation is deciduous and the entire terrain is sprinkled with lakes and ponds, rarely empty even during the peak of summer. The weather is its most alluring feature, with temperatures that range comfortably between 30°C (86°F) and 16°C (61°F). The average annual rainfall, brought by the southwest monsoon from June to August, and the northeast monsoon from October to December, is about 90 cm (40 in) and the area produces an extravagant variety of fruit and vegetables.

Phrases like "Gateway to the South" are bandied about by travel agents, in allusion to Bangalore's proximity to the tourist landmarks of the South. The city has always garnered its fair share of these

LEFT: the traditional, the colonial and the modern in Bangalore. **RIGHT:** the Kempe Gowda Tower, in the Lal Bagh.

labels: Garden City, Pensioner's Paradise, and India's Cheltenham. Current references to it as India's Silicon Valley, in response to all that is happening here in the field of IT, echo Jawaharlal Nehru's description of Bangalore two decades ago as "a picture of the India of the future".

Since the township proper is only about 450 years old, the fact that the area's history predates the colonial presence by several centuries is sometimes overlooked. Its military heritage, for instance, goes back much further than the time when swords, muskets and rockets were manufactured in Tharamandalpet for Hyder Ali, the legendary 18th-century ruler. Battles were fought here in the 9th century – reference to one in the village of Bangaluru is inscribed on a *viragal* (literally, a "hero stone"), found in a temple in Begur village east of the city. Going by the Roman coins found at Yeshwantpur to the north, there was trade too with the West as early as the 1st century AD, probably in spices and textiles.

"The Town of Boiled Beans"

Of the three derivations of Bangalore's name, one has it that a 10th-century ruler, Vira Ballala, lost his way hunting in a forest. Night fell as he wandered around looking for his retinue, going deeper into the woods until, to his relief, he came upon a small hut in which lived an old woman. She offered him shelter and shared with him her modest dinner of *benda kalu*, or boiled beans.

Vira Ballala stayed the night, and before he left he told her (as kings do in such stories) that she could ask him for anything she wanted. All she asked for, however, was a supply of food enough for herself and for any other traveller who might seek refuge. Her request was granted, and this incident became so much a part of local folklore that when a village was set up there, it was called Benda Kaluru (Town of Boiled Beans), a name which was eventually commuted to Bangaluru.

Other stories, not as popular, concern the Vijayanagara chieftain Kempe Gowda

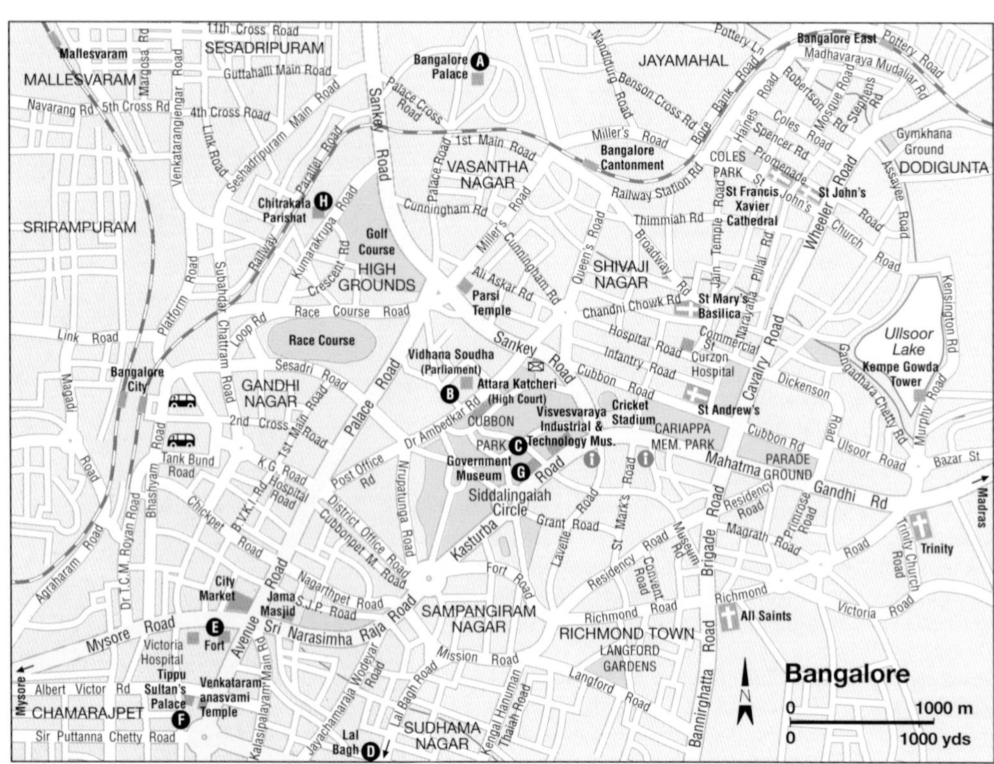

Map on page 232

I, who founded Bangalore. He ruled the township of Yelahanka, on what is now the city's northern outskirts. In 1537, he was looking to expand his overlord Achuta Raya's domain and found this uninhabited tract ideal, with its abundant water and bracing climate. On a day fixed by his astrologer, four carts were harnessed and sent off in four directions, as far as their bullocks could pull them. Kempe Gowda decreed that the points where they stopped would be the outer limits of his new city, and at each of these points he built a watchtower which still stands: in the north on the Bellary Road (in Yelahanka), in the south at Lal Bagh, in the east at Ulsoor Lake and in the west near the Gavi Gangadharesvara temple. (Of course, Bangalore has long since sprawled well beyond these four towers.) Kempe Gowda built a mud fort, first setting fire to the dense forest growth to clear the necessary space. That gave the name its other provenance – Benda Kaduru, the Town of the Burnt Forest.

A third theory is that he named the town after the god Venkata, hence Venkata-uru, which was gradually honed down to Vengaluru and then to its present form.

From Hindu rule to Muslim

Within the walls of Kempe Gowda's fort, various trades and businesses flourished, each defined in its own *pettah*, some of which have still retained their original names – Chickpet, or little town, Hallipet, the cotton market, and Tharagpet, where grain was bought and sold.

The new town's profile was also defined by its founder's religious convictions: a devout Hindu, he built temples, hostelries for travellers and tanks for drinking water, and also awarded land to scholars in acknowledgement of their learning.

After Kempe Gowda, Bangalore was seized by the Sultanate of Bijapur in 1638, from whom it was wrested by the Mughals 50 years later. They leased it to Chikka Devaraya of the Wadiyar dynasty of Mysore, who managed to convince Kasim Khan, the Mughal general, to sell the city to him. This the general did without apparent qualm or foresight, for Rs 500,000.

The 17th century was a period of turmoil, with the British and the French fighting to claim as much of the Carnatic as they could for themselves. The regional rulers too, the Marathas, the Nizam of Hyderabad and the Wadiyars who now owned Bangalore, were all embroiled in strife. This the Wadiyar king could least afford, considering his kingdom was already plagued by internal power struggles and his exchequer depleted. Thus, the time was ripe for an ambitious man like Hyder Ali, a chieftain serving in the Mysore army, to seize power for himself. Hyder Ali deposed the ineffectual Chikka Krishnaraja and made Bangalore his personal fief. From then on, he and his son Tippu Sultan, both accomplished warrior-statesmen, dominated the Carnatic till the end of the 18th century.

With their well-trained armies, Hyder Ali and Tippu Sultan fended off their aggressive neighbours with such ease that even the British found their plans of dominion severely thwarted. Both father

RIGHT: traders outside the mosque.

and son had to fight the British four times, in the Mysore Wars. But in the last Mysore War in 1799, Tippu was killed at Srirangapatnam and finally the Carnatic came under the British. They cannily put the Wadiyar heir back on the throne; as a placatory gesture to his subjects it was well-considered, and politically safe enough since the heir was only a 5-year-old boy.

British influence on Bangalore's development becomes evident only from about 1809 onward. This was when the Cantonment began to be constructed and the first batch of troops moved in from Srirangapatnam to their new barracks at Agram, where the Air Force Hospital is today.

The British city

The British adored Bangalore, its scenery and its weather. Even Winston Churchill, stationed here as a young officer, was moved to effusiveness in his descriptions of an ambience that, to all these homesick empire builders, seemed "a bit of England in an alien land".

The layout of Bangalore's **Cantonment** began in 1809, and it rapidly became much more extensive than a mere encampment for "Lashkars", its original function. It was located to the north of the fort and the old town where the City Market is today. Both were separated by an open stretch of land 2.4 km (1½ miles) wide, the usual strategic practice that included the installation of tollgates to control access to the Cantonment. The Cantonment's centre was the Parade Ground, originally a 3.2-km (2-mile) east-west strip. The Mall that ran along its southern periphery, the South Parade, is now Mahatma Gandhi Road. To the north of the Parade Ground were the sepoys' houses and Infantry Road, while the artillery and cavalry were stationed to the east. The Commissioner's bungalow, to the west, is now the Raj Bhavan, the Governor's residence. Road names were determined either according to troop location and movement (Cavalary Road, Brigade Road), or the establishment of retail enterprise (Commercial Street).

Army families settled in, and the civilians followed. Merchants and moneylenders set up shop. Colonial gregariousness established polo and other horsey pursuits, the event of giddiest social import being the annual Bangalore Hunt.

In 1831 the British seized administrative control of Mysore after an apparent attempt at revolt by the Maharaja. Deciding not to take their hard-won territory for granted, the British not only increased the number of troops at Bangalore, but also established a Commission, making the city their administrative headquarters.

During the remaining half of the century, the series of Commissioners who then came to office were responsible for structures such as the Attara Katcheri that housed the Secretariat, the Central College and the Central Jail. The railway from Chennai that ended at Jalarpet was extended to the city at the instance of Commissioner Bowring.

Many residential areas sprang up called "towns" – Cleveland Town, Fraser Town, Benson Town, painstakingly laid out on the northern and southern sides of the Cantonment, along wide tree-lined

LEFT: the dome of the Vidhana Soudha.

Map on page 232

avenues. Their thoroughfares have names like Wood Street and Hayes Road, both found in what was a nostalgically named Richmond Town. Still visible are many of the bungalows that were built then, between 1880 and 1930, rambling single-storey structures placed neatly in their gardens at the end of driveways, some only symbolic in length, but no less essential for that. Many now sit in the looming shadows of blocks of flats and offices, the inexorable concomitant of city life.

Life in the *pettahs* of the city proper, during the British occupation, was in bustling dissimilarity to the detachment of the Cantonment. It was the archetypical Hindu town where life spilled out of the doorways, strung overhead with rows of mango leaves, and into the streets.

In 1881 Bangalore was restored to the Maharaja, and thereafter his chief administrative officer, called the Dewan, supervised the state. To one such Dewan, Sir Visveswaraya, goes much of the credit for the process of industrialising the state.

Indian maharajas were as much prey to the imperatives of one-upmanship as anyone else, as the **Bangalore Palace** Ⓐ proves. It was built by the Wadiyar king in 1887, in stiff competition with his peers, who were busy reproducing French chateaux, among other genres. The local result was what is apparently a Tudor castle.

Independence

When Mysore joined the Indian Union after Independence, the Maharaja became its Governor and in 1956 Bangalore became the state capital. In 1973, the state's name was changed to Karnataka, a name which (like that of its capital) has different origins, depending on who you ask. It came from either "Karu Nadu", the land of black soil, or "Karnadu", the high country, neither of which appears particularly apt. Nor is the third, though it is certainly a pretty conceit – "Karna-ata", an onomatopoeic amalgam of the sounds of bees, butterflies and birds.

No other state capital has a structure comparable to the **Vidhana Soudha** Ⓑ,

BELOW: an early colonial house.

the Karnataka Secretariat, built in 1956, India's largest legislative-official structure. On the north side of Cubbon Park, its imposing neo-Dravidian lines distinguish it in a city known for its primarily colonial flavour. The traditional Indian inspiration was deliberate: before the building was designed, the then Chief Minister of the State was taking a Russian delegation around the city, whose members could only ask, "Why are all your buildings European? Have you no architecture of your own?"

The building, made mostly of local granite and porphyry, is primarily Dravidian, with a leavening of other ethnic influences, such as the Rajasthani *jharokas* or balconies. Details are conscientious – the pillars with their elaborate bases, the domed ceiling ascending in concentric circles, and the carvings with ornately wrought floral motifs in the temples of Karnataka and Tamil Nadu.

Across from it, housing the High Court, is the elegant, two-storey **Attara Katcheri** or "18 courts", with its fluted Corinthian columns. It was built in 1864; later, the 121 hectares (300 acres) behind it were cultivated into the lush **Cubbon Park** ❸ in the heart of the city.

Further south is another sprawling landscaped park, the **Lal Bagh** ❹ (open sunrise–sunset, entrance charge) – laid out by Hyder Ali in 1740 and improved by Tippu Sultan. Within its 97 hectares (240 acres) is a Glass House inspired by the Crystal Palace in London, the venue of the city's annual flower show.

Forts and palaces

Mud walls may have sufficed when Kempe Gowda built his **fort** ❺ (closed to the public) in 1537, but Hyder Ali, with rapacious neighbours and colonial powers to worry about, rebuilt it in stone and enclosed it in a moat. The walls were embellished with arches in fine Islamic style. Hyder Ali acknowledged other religions (Tippu Sultan's mother was Hindu), which is why you will find a little temple dedicated to Lord

BELOW: flashy modern buildings for Bangalore's hi-tech industries.

Map on page 232

Ganesh still standing within the fort walls, drawing people to prayer.

An excellent example of the aesthetics and dynamics of 18th-century military architecture, the fort has not been well maintained: walls have been knocked down to make way for roads, and parts of the moat were filled in when the Victoria Hospital was built. The eight gates that Kempe Gowda constructed, each named for the different locality it opened to, are no longer usable, except for the one rebuilt in granite by Hyder Ali, called the Delhi Gate. Still, it is a reminder of the other important militaristic influences on the city, apart from the British.

Of the few buildings of historical importance built during the last five centuries, **Tippu's palace** **F** (open daily 8am–6pm, entrance charge) is one. It is Bangalore's foremost example of the Islamic mode, though only serving as an annexe to the main palace that no longer exists. Built mostly out of wood, it has much fastidious carving on the pillars, arches and balconies. It served as another of Tippu's summer retreats, one he was very fond of: he called it Rashk-e-Jannat, "the Envy of Heaven". Much later on, when Bangalore was administered by the British Commission, the palace was used as its office. Now open to the public, it has an air of decline: the murals on the walls and ceilings that portrayed the exploits of father and son are faded, though the garden, laid out in basic Islamic form, is well maintained.

Bangalore's shrines

Next to Tippu's palace is the **Venkataramanasvami temple**, built by the Wadiyars in the Dravidian style. It is around 300 years old, and has been well looked after, with some recent additions being made to its structure, such as the two *gopurams* that were built in the last few years. During the Third Mysore War in 1790, it sustained considerable damage, much of which was restored by the Wadiyars, though some of the lavish stone pillars with the robustly carved lion-brackets remain visibly damaged – gouged and pitted from cannon fire.

Bangalore has many temples of varying antiquity. The newer ones built during the last 50 years are also faithful to the Dravidian style, though the older ones, with their legends and the wealth of associations that attach to them, have a deeper appeal – like the **Bull temple**, built by Kempe Gowda near one of his original watchtowers in Basavangudi, the suburb to the south of the city. It contains a massive, 4.6-m (15-ft) high monolith of Nandi, the bull entrusted with the sacred duty of carrying the god Shiva. Carved from a single boulder, the statue resembles the one on Chamundi Hill in Mysore.

Apparently, the temple was built to placate a rampaging bull that systematically devoured the entire peanut crop in the nearby fields. The original plan was to construct just the monolith, but when it was finished, it suddenly began to grow of its own accord, and ceased only when the temple was hastily erected over it. Whether this unnerved its flesh-and-blood counterpart is not clear, but the bull retired

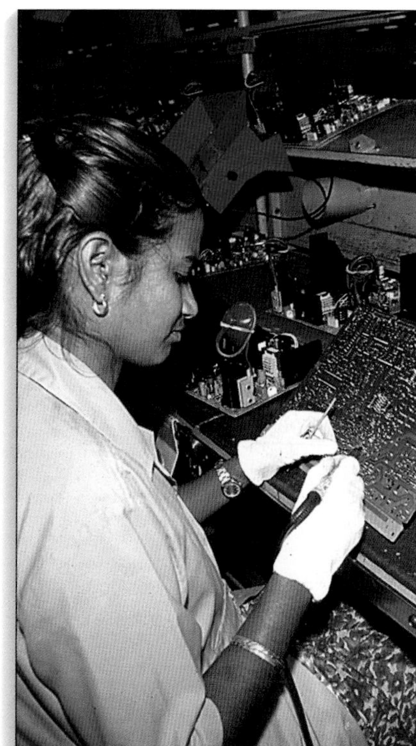

RIGHT: a worker on the assembly line.

from the neighbourhood. Ever since, the local farmers have held a *Kadalekaye Parise*, a fair, outside the temple every year in thanksgiving.

Close by, near the Kempambudi Tank, is the **Gavi Gangadhesvara** shrine, also built by Kempe Gowda. Dedicated to Siva and his consort Parvati, this cave temple contains 33 images, including one of Agni, the god of fire. It incorporates a clever architectural device: Kempe Gowda's architect so planned it that on the festival of Makara Sankranti in the middle of January, the last rays of the evening sun pass through an archway and a window, and between the horns of a Nandi bull, to alight on the image of Siva. Large numbers of pilgrims come every year.

There is a tragic tale about the one other shrine Kempe Gowda built in Koramangala, to the south of where the airport is now. As his fort was being built, its structure kept collapsing, over and over again, despite everything he could do to prevent it. A human sacrifice was proposed as a propitiatory gesture, and though the outraged Kempe Gowda rejected the idea, his daughter-in-law Laksmidevi decided to offer her own life, and did so. The fort was completed, and in the selfless girl's memory this pretty shrine was named.

Every Cantonment layout had at least one church, as integral to the social fabric as the club. Most of Bangalore's churches were built by the British, in either the Gothic or the neoclassical style, with few, if any, of the colonially inspired features that exemplify the architecture of the Raj.

As has been noted, cemeteries in typical Cantonments were not laid out adjacent to the churches, but usually at some distance away. This practice probably had something to do with containing contagion during the many epidemics that besieged the colonial community.

Some of the churches built after Independence are in the older styles, while those whose design references are contemporary do not really make any definitive statement.

BELOW: jacaranda branches frame a colonial church.

Map on page 232

Mosques in the city date back before Hyder Ali's reign, the oldest being the Sangin Jama Masjid off Avenue Road in the city, built by a Mughal officer. The black marble pillars in the Jama Masjid, the oldest mosque in the Cantonment area, just off Commercial Street, were salvaged from Tippu's palace in Srirangapatnam. The most recently built mosque in Bangalore is also its largest, a confection in white marble near the City Market which can hold a congregation of over 5,000 people.

The tomb of the Sufi saint, Tavakkal Mastan, again near the **City Market**, attracts many pilgrims of all faiths, including the members of the annual Karaga procession which stops here. Such compliant secularity might seem unusual anywhere else, but Bangaloreans are comfortable with one another's religions. A healthy percentage of the worshippers at the weekly novenas in St Patrick's, the Infant Jesus and other Catholic churches in the Cantonment are non-Christians.

The Karaga festival is another dramatic local event. It takes place around March or April at the Dharmaraja temple, when the *karaga*, an earthen pot that embodies Shakti, the goddess of primal energy, is taken out in night-time procession by one community of the gardeners' caste called the Thegalas. The honour is not assumed lightly: the chosen one, staff in one hand and sword in the other, must balance the florally-bedecked *karaga* on his head for more than 20 km (12 miles), wearing a saffron *sari* and his wife's conjugal necklace. Drummers and chanting devotees brandishing swords accompany him, and he is under pain of death not to drop his burden. His wife waits at home, a widow for the nonce, till he returns after immersing the pot in the Sampangi Tank.

Years ago, as Tawakkal Mastan rushed out to catch a glimpse of the procession, he tripped and was knocked unconscious, and trampled upon by the crowds. The priests stopped and tended his cuts and bruises with dabs of the sacred red *kumkum* powder, which healed him at once. Awestruck, the saint expressed the wish that the procession should always visit his tomb – which it does, every year.

Museums

The artefacts at the **Government Museum** Ⓖ (open Tues–Sun 10am–5pm, closed every second Sat in the month, entrance charge) on Kasturba Road are definitely worth a look. It is one of the oldest museums in the country and it has finds from the Neolithic era and relics of the 5,000-year-old Mohenjodaro civilisation, in addition to some fine Hoysala, Chalukya and Chola sculptures. The **Venkatappa Art Gallery** nearby (same times as the Museum) has a good display of works by local artists.

The **Chitrakala Parishat** Ⓗ on Kumarakrupa Road (open daily 10am–5pm) has a number of fine paintings in the Mysore gesso technique, still retaining the patina imparted by a finishing rub with jade, and a permanent collection of works by Nicholas Roerich. There are also collections of shadow puppets made from goat and deerskin and brightly painted marionettes, both types still extant in traditional theatre.

RIGHT: the city market.

Two more of Bangalore's museums that might be of interest to the visitor are the **Sasvathi Museum** (open Mon–Sat 10am–4pm) in the Women's College in Jayanagar, and the **Visvesvaraya Industrial and Technological Museum** (open Tues–Sun 10am–6pm, entrance charge) on Kasturba Road. The former has a small but interesting collection of paintings, photographs and domestic artefacts relating the lives of local women; the second has industrial machinery as well as a good transport collection, with a number of interesting working models.

City life

As a result of an influx of migrant workers, dancers and musicians from all over the country perform in the city as frequently as do celebrated Karnatak singers, or the itinerant *Yaksagana* theatre troupe. Karnatak music, like the dance form *Bharata-natyam*, is a classical discipline of the South which has commanded a steadfast following of Bangaloreans. The colourfully vociferous retelling of age-old themes in dialogue, song and dance that is the *Yaksagana prasanga*, or performance, once staged outside temples, is nowadays usually confined to an auditorium stage. Theatres are few and increasing costs also affect Kannada theatre that is otherwise a vital and assured art form in both classical and contemporary idioms.

Theatre performances are not regular, understandably, in the face of the competition from television and the local film industry. Portraits of heroes and heroines in huge billboards loom over movie house entrances on Kempe Gowda Road, and the city's 100-odd cinemas do brisk business, as much in Hindi and English films, Tamil and Malayalam as in Kannada. There are a number of cinemas in Bangalore that show films in English; most of them are located around Brigade Road and M.G. Road.

The popularity of the pub scene has waned considerably in recent years, but some of the old favourites are still worth a visit for the draught beer. The pub scene signifies the gentrification of social drinking; apart from executives and other office workers you will often find couples and sometimes even groups of women, which would be unthinkable in any conventional bar (except perhaps for those in the five-star hotels).

There are a number of excellent restaurants in the city, the best of which specialise in South Indian food. Try the **Coconut Grove** on Church Street for a selection of Keralan, Konkan and Kodagu dishes. Prices are moderate, particularly at those restaurants specialising in the local food. A particular city institution is the vegetarian **Mavalli Tiffin Rooms**, whose mere initials are enough to start the queues forming, as they do outside its door, just down the road from Lalbagh (no. 11), from 6 every morning.

If you are looking for something away from *dosais* and rice, then another Bangalore institution is **Koshy's** on St Mark's Road, which has been going strong since the 1950s. The decidedly period decor and the lengthy, eclectic menu have a charm all of their own.

LEFT: a quiet moment in Koshy's.

Map on page 232

Around the city

Several places within easy reach of the city are good for day or weekend excursions. Among the most popular of these is **Nandi Hills** (60 km/38 miles), a small hill station, yet another retreat for Tippu Sultan. With its excellent natural fortifications, which the Tiger of Mysore improved upon, it made the ideal hideout; the British under Lord Cornwallis tried to dislodge him from it, but were dissuaded after several enormous granite boulders were dropped on their heads.

Nandi Hills was popular with the British subsequently, too, and the commissioner Sir Mark Cubbon built the bungalow named after him at the highest point of the range. The view is magnificent, especially from the part of the battlements called Tippu's Drop, and there are enjoyable rambles to be discovered through the tree-covered hills. There are two Siva temples, both well over a thousand years old, the one at the foot of the hill built by a queen of the Bana dynasty and extended by members of subsequent ruling houses, and the other on top built by the Cholas.

The **Banerghatta National Park** (21 km/13 miles; open Wed–Mon 9am–5pm, entrance charge) is a fenced-in wildlife sanctuary that has a number of lions, gaur, elephants and wild boars. Though few of these will be seen from the brief jeep tour.

Mekedatu (98 km/61 miles) is a beautiful spot, where the Kaveri river surges fiercely through a deeply chiselled gorge a mere five metres wide on top, close enough for a goat to leap over; hence the name – Goat's Leap.

Further afield (200 km/125 miles to the northwest) is **Chitradurga**. Set on a series of granite hills, the fortified site here dates back to the Chalukyas and Hoysalas. The impressive walls are broken by a series of massive gates. Within the fort are a number of interesting temples founded by Hoysala generals, the two of most importance being the **Hidimbesvara** and **Sampige Siddesvara** shrines. ❑

BELOW: Bangalore-style delivery.

Maps:
Area 244
City 246

MYSORE AND THE SOUTH

The regal city of Mysore has one of India's most astonishing palaces, while close by are the temples of Halebid and Belur, and towards the coast the fascinating region of Kodagu

Every year on a certain day in October, as the sun sets on **Mysore** ❷, the florid lines of the Maharaja's palace spring into incandescent relief against the evening sky. Every detail of the building – the fluted pillars, the cupolas, the minarets, the arched canopies, the onion domes and the campanile above them – is etched in light. All around the palace and beyond as well, the silhouettes of the great public buildings start to glitter in unison with millions of tiny bulbs, making the city a metaphor for the triumph of good over evil: this is *Dussera*, the celebration of the slaying of the demon Mahisasura by the goddess Chamundesvari.

So it continues for the next nine days. Each day, prayers are offered to the deities of wealth, power and learning, the nine sacred incarnations of the female principle, Sakti. And each nightfall, should you make your way to the top of nearby Chamundi Hill, you will be dazzled by the city's resplendence. The celebrations reach their peak on the 10th day, *Vijayadasami*, the Day of Victory. This marks the end of the rains, when new ventures can begin: artisans pay homage to the implements of their trade, and businessmen open fresh ledgers for the new financial year ahead.

The day used to have a martial significance as well. It is also known as *Ayudha Puja*, or the worship of weapons, the start of the season of war when rulers set off on new campaigns of acquisition or got on with finishing old ones interrupted by the monsoon.

At the appointed time the procession moves out of the palace, a cavalcade of uniformed soldiers, caparisoned horses and elephants, dancers and floats, accompanied by brass bands thumping out sometimes incongruous but always infectious medleys of Indian and Western tunes. The palace guards and the Mysore Lancers march by in opulent uniform, and the Camel Corps, each rider's dour mount swaying in step. Costumed folk-dancers swirl past in riotous rhythm, and trundling along at intervals in makeshift stateliness are the floats, each bearing its tableau.

In a parade a mile long, the main attraction is undoubtedly the state elephant. Monumental in its golden accoutrements, anklets, bells and chains, with its trunk and body graphically painted, the impressive beast carries a gold howdah, in which is placed the image of the city's patron goddess, Chamundesvari. The Maharaja himself once sat on this howdah, leading the procession, a custom now gone the way of other regal prerogatives. However, for the thousands who have come to see it, some from afar, it remains a spectacle evocative

LEFT: the Darbar Hall, Mysore Palace. **RIGHT:** Mysore Palace lit up for *Dussera*.

Karnataka
0 50 km
0 50 miles
Puné
Sasvad
Puné
Bhiavan
Parenda
Osmanabad
Latur
Udgir
Nagpur
Manjira
Wangi
Barsi
Nilanga
Bhalki
Nizam Sagar
Pochram
Watar
Tuljapur
Krishna
9
Umarga
Maharashtra
Satara
Homnabad
Jogipet
4
Pandharpur
Solapur
Pusesavli
Zahirabad
9
Patan
Sangola
Akalkot
Sargapur
Vita
Zalki
Gulbarga
14
Hyderabad
Nagaj
Bhima
Seram
Charan
Karajagi
13
Almel
Farrukhnagar
Malkapur
Sangli
Miraj
Jevargi
13
Bijapur
Telsang
Yadgir
Badepalli
Kolhapur
Ichalkaranji
Mahabubnagar
Shahpur
Kalvakurti
Phonda
Jamkhandi
Marikal
Basavana Bagevadi
Talikota
Andhra
Ghatprabha
Mudhol
Krishna
Wanparti
Konnur
Bhadwan
Muddebihal
Bagalkot
Raichur
Hatti
Gadwal
Amboli
Yargatti
Badami
16
Aivalli (Aihole)
Mudgal
Belgaum
15
17
Pattadakal
Maski
Srisailam
12
Bail Hongal
Malprabha
Yerdara
Halasi
Mantralayam
Saundatti
Tawargeri
Sidhnur
Tungabhadra
Valpoi
Kittur
Kurnool
Panaji (Panjim)
4A
Dharwad
Gadag
Siruguppa
Adoni
Haliyal
Hubli
Pradesh
Margao
Dandeli
Alur
Goa
Kalghatgi
Tungabhadra
Hospet
11
Hampi
Dhone
Hagari
Magod
Savanur
Bellary
Guntakal
Mundgod
Varada
Karwar
Allagudda
Kudligi
Gudekota
17
Penneru
Hangal
7
Yana
4
13
Gokarna
Rayadrug
Banvasi
Anantapur
Proddatur
Mirjan
Davangere
Honavar
Kargal
Jog Falls
Dharmavaram
Mudigubba
Honnali
Murudeswar
Chitradurga
Penukonda
Bhatkal
Arasalu
Pavagada
Puttaparti
Kadiri
Linganamakki Reservoir
Vanivilasa Sagar
Shimoga
Hiriyur
Bhadravati
Palasamudram
Maravanthe
Hosdurg
Tirthahalli
Hindupur
Sira
Lepakshi
Kundapura
Bhadra Res.
Huliyar
Nandi Hills
Madanapalle
Malpe
Sringeri
4
10
Udupi
Chikmagalur
Halebid
Tiptur
Tumkur
7
Sidlaghatta
Karkal
Karnataka
Devarayanadurga
Mulki
Venur
Belur
6
Shivaganga
4
Kolar
Chennai (Madras)
Dharmastala
Hassan
Hoskote
9
Mangalore
Channarayapatna
Bangalore
Sakleshpur
48
1
Kolar Gold Fields
Ullal
Puttur
5
Sravanabelagola
Bellur
Bannirgatta
Channappatna
Kumbla
Subrahmanya
Krishnaraja Sagara
Banergbatta N.P.
Hosur
Maddur
Region
Kallar
Srirangapatnam
3
Mandya
7
46
Kodagu
8
Brindavan Gardens
Krishnagiri
Bekal
Madikeri (Mercara)
Krishnarajanagara
Sivasamudram
17
Mysore
2
Somnathpur
4
Kaveri
Kollegal
Uttangarai
Payyannur
Nagarhole N.P.
Nanjangud
Stanley Reservoir
Wynad Wildlife Sanctuary
Kannur (Cannanore)
Nagarhole
Bandipur N.P.
Thalasseri
Kharapur
Mulchole
Gundlupet
7
Yercaud
Mettur
Badagara
Sultanbathery
Bandipur
Salem
Udagamandalam (Ooty)
Mudumalai N.P.
Satymangalam
Kozhikode
Erode
Dindigul
Western Ghats
Malabar Coast
N

Map on page 246

of a time when the city was indeed a royal capital, with all the attendant pomp and paraphernalia of a monarchy.

The parade ends at the Banimantap, about 3 km (2 miles) from the palace, in front of the Bani tree worshipped as the embodiment of Sakti. Since homage to Sakti is central to the celebration of *Dussera*, it was the monarchical custom to offer prayers here and then shoot an arrow into the air as a gesture of victory. No longer; the celebration now ends on a more secular note with a torchlight parade by the State Police. The grand finale comes with the fireworks when the sky, like the city beneath it, is drenched with radiance.

The crowds leave, and Mysore goes back to being a sheltered city of quiet beauty with an amicable climate. It lies in a valley 140 km (87 miles) to the southwest of Bangalore. Tree-lined avenues and sumptuous parks make it a contemplative setting for the courtly architecture that houses civic and institutional routine.

Mysore is a place of remembered fragrances – sandalwood, incense and jasmine, the individual aromas of craft, prayer and adornment. To speak of the last is also to summon up associations with silk in all its sensuous, textured variety. Local industry – the government sandalwood and silk factories at the south end of the town, the many homes where *agarbathis*, or incense sticks, are made – sustains these traditional links.

In the streets that lead out from **Statue Square**, where the statues of former kings Krishnaraja and Chamaraja Wadiyar stand under a golden canopy, is a welter of little shops replete with objects in wood, stone and brass, saris and shawls in silk, perfumes and powders, furniture and coffee beans. On Sayyaji Road, the government emporium, **Kaveri**, sells many of the products made by the state's craftworkers.

Mysore, home of the late writer R.K. Narayan, has always fostered a spirit of learning, and academics pursue their studies at establishments as diverse as Manasagangothri, the University of Mysore and the Oriental Research Institute. Its seclusion still appeals to the retired and the elderly, even while industries set up shop, contractors build repetitious residential complexes, ready-to-wear department stores, and video libraries proliferate and traffic increases exponentially.

This is because Mysore, despite its increasing spread, is still very much what history made it. Now a city with a population of over 740,000, it has been the capital of various dynasties from the time it was mentioned as Mahismati in India's great epic, the *Mahabharata*.

Mysore was ruled by the Wadiyar dynasty from 1399 almost uninterruptedly until Independence, except for the 38-year rule of the Muslim Hyder Ali and his son Tippu Sultan in the 18th century. The Wadiyars have in large measure shaped the city's identity. If it seems at first a city only of palaces, there is also the vitality of Mysore's art, music and dance and the crafts of perfumer, florist and wood carver which flourished under their patronage.

The dynasty's founders, Vijaya and Krisna, two brothers of the Yadava family, came to Hadinadu, as Mysore was then called, on a pilgrimage from Gujarat.

RIGHT: a flower seller in Devaraja Market.

According to one story, Vijaya rescued the local king's daughter from the unwelcome attentions of a rival king. Her grateful father gave him the princess in marriage and made him heir to the title of Wadiyar, or ruler.

The Wadiyars were, by and large, responsible rulers, so much held in esteem by their subjects that when Mysore acceded to the Union of India the then Maharaja, Jayachamarajendra Wadiyar, was unanimously favoured as the state's new Governor. The family still live in a portion of the main **Mysore Palace** Ⓐ (open daily 10.30am–5.30pm, entrance charge), cloistered from the eyes of the thousands of tourists who pad by on bare or stockinged feet through the public areas. It is an extravaganza of a structure, embellished with detail on every conceivable surface. To call it overblown would be to deny the ingenuousness of a sensibility that delighted in ornamentation for its own sake.

The palace is basically representative of the Indo-Saracenic school, though the architect Henry Irwin (who designed many public buildings in Chennai) indulged his client's whims with a potpourri of Hindu, Islamic and Moorish styles. Thus the building flaunts arched canopies reminiscent of Rajput palaces and onion domes in the Mughal fashion, surmounted by an unmistakeably European campanile. There is a heady mix of cupolas, minarets, balconies and porches, everything decked out with meticulous carvings of scrolls, flora and fauna, so much so that an early European visitor was heard to mutter, "All curves and carving, there is not an inch of repose on its surface." It is illuminated on Sundays and during Dussera festivities.

Inside is just as grandiloquent: the handsomely proportioned halls and corridors have marble floors and carved mahogany ceilings, stained glass and mosaics. Hunting trophies abound and antique weapons decorate the walls. There are great chandeliers, massive doors wrought in silver, carvings in ivory and other materials, and much elaborate inlay and stucco work.

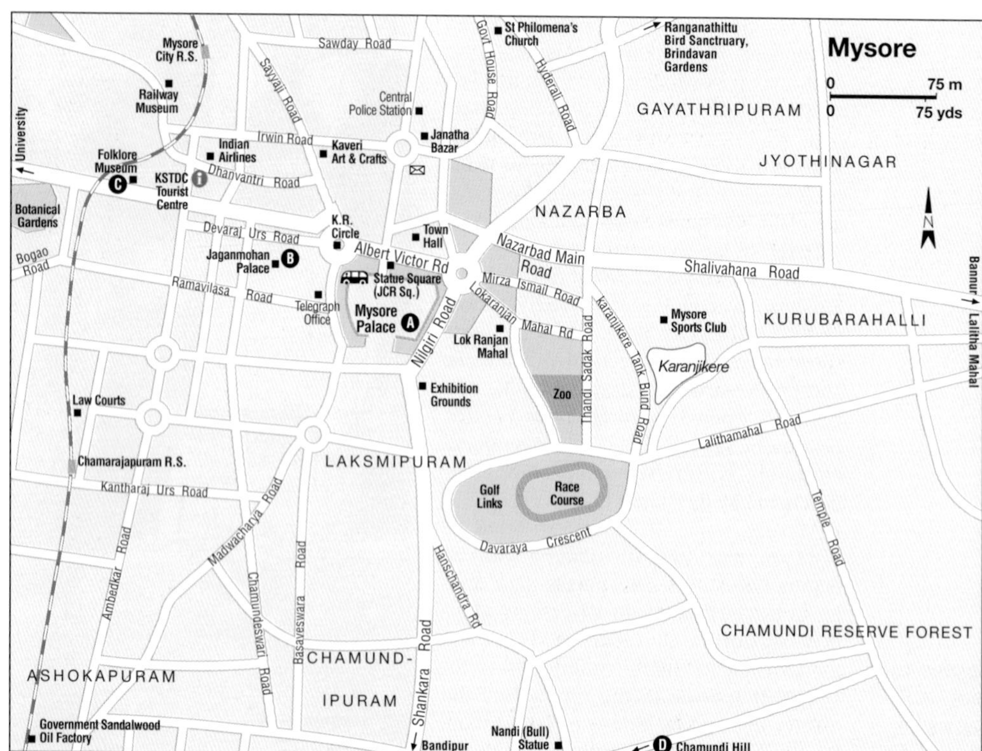

Map on page 246

There is the **Darbar Hall** and the **Kalyana Mandap**, the wedding chamber, with its painstakingly recorded murals of bygone Darbar processions, and the distinctive paintings of Hindu gods and goddesses by Raja Ravi Varma of Travancore. The palace has a throne worthy of its setting. Made of figwood, initially overlaid with ivory and finely wrought with mythological figures, it was subsequently plated with gold and silver and studded with diamonds and precious stones. The throne's gold content is said to weigh about 280 kg (616 lbs), which alone imparts to it a definite curiosity value. The royal elephant throne, as it is called, was apparently given to a Wadiyar monarch in 1699 by the Mughal emperor Aurangzeb.

A city of palaces

There are three other palaces, apart from the old fort which sequestered the previous Mysore Palace within its moat before it burned down in 1897. Two of them function as luxury hotels, **Lalitha Mahal** at the foot of the Chamundi Hill and **Rajendra Vilas** at the top. The former was built in the 1930s for those of the Wadiyars' guests who, unlike their indulgent but abstemious hosts, drank alcohol and were not vegetarian. White colonnades surround its two storeys and a staircase of Italian marble sweeps up from the foyer where today's guests of the Indian Tourist Development Corporation register into the five-star hotel.

Rajendra Vilas, with its echoes of the Italian style this dynasty seems to have favoured, was formerly the summer palace, also used at other times of the year as a devotional retreat.

The third palace is the **Jaganmohan** Ⓑ, just over a kilometre to the west of the main palace, housing the **Sir Jayachamarajendra Art Gallery** (open 10am–4.30pm). It was built in 1861 for the king's wedding, after which the members of the family, compulsive collectors all, began to store their many antiques and curios there, eventually opening it to the public.

A tour of the museum affords an examination of the assortment of trifles that amused royal minds: a set of medieval playing cards, carvings on rice grains, a French clock with toy soldiers to mark the time. Apart from such curiosities, the museum also has interesting Mughal and Rajput art, paintings by Raja Ravi Varma and a commendable collection of sculpture and brassware.

Further still to the west is the **Folklore Museum** Ⓒ (open Mon–Sat 10am–5pm, closed every second Sat in the month), an engrossing storehouse of implements, dolls, costumes, furniture and articles of daily use, their shapes, surfaces, colours and textures reflective of centuries of local craftsmanship. Among the objects of interest is a giant 200-year-old plough which probably needed the strength of a dozen oxen to pull it, a canopied pedestal festooned with scarab beetle wings for the elephant god Ganapati, and a cradle with a smart bamboo harness to secure its occupant around the waist.

At the **Oriental Research Institute** (http://namami.nic.in), India's art of the written word is manifest. Over 60,000 palm-leaf manuscripts in Sanskrit, Kannada and

RIGHT: the architectural melange of Mysore Palace.

the other major South Indian languages are kept here, some of them dating back to the 3rd century BC, and their texts range from dissertations on philosophy, literature and statesmanship to the sciences.

Similarly, the **National Archaeological Survey** has its epigraphical department in the city, with more than 10,000 inscriptions garnered from monuments all over India.

The **Railway Museum** (open Tues–Sun 10–1pm, 3–5pm, entrance charge) by the station offers a collection of rolling stock redolent of a dated grandeur, upholstered according to lavish regal notions of how travel was to be undertaken.

Mysore Zoo initially looks attractive with some large, open enclosures. However, like all Indian zoos this is more of a prison than anything else, with many of the animals being kept in a woeful condition in very cramped cages. Most of the inmates here display behavioral distress, including pacing, self-harm and tugging at the bars. In recent years a number of animals here have died in suspicious circumstances.

Chamundi Hill

Chamundi Hill Ⓓ towers more than 400 metres (1,320 ft) over the city and is named for the royal family's deity, who once delivered the people of the area from the buffalo-headed demon Mahisasura. The legend has it that after she killed him she took up residence on the hill. Having no desire to attract the evil eye once again, the inhabitants took the prudent step of naming the city they loved so much after the demon himself. Hence the name Mahisasura (which susequently became Mysore), referred to in the *Mahabharata* as Mahismati, and still elsewhere as Mahisamandala. His statue stands at a roundabout on the road to the **Sri Chamundesvari temple**, scowl in place, scimitar in one hand and an enormous cobra firmly gripped in the other. Just beyond is the temple, with its colossal pyramidal *gopuram* built by Krisnaraja Wadiyar III, who also made an endowment of a fabulous gold gem, carved with 30 Sanskrit verses, called the Naksatramalika.

BELOW: the huge Nandi on Chamundi Hill.

Maps:
City 246
Area 244

Descending the hill, either by road or down a flight of a thousand steps which has the virtue of being 9 km (5 miles) shorter – long-winded Mysoreans climb up and down it all the time on their way to the temple – you pass the 5-metre (16-ft) monolith of the seated **Nandi**, Siva's chosen carrier. A 17th-century work of devotional art in which the bull is carved from one enormous boulder with loving attention to detail, patent in everything from the bell around its neck to the anklets above each massive hoof. The statue is emblematic of Mysore; to Indians and to most travellers it remains the most enduring of the many images of the city.

Wildlife and gardens

Close to the city, near Srirangapatnam *(see below)*, is the **Ranganathittu bird sanctuary**, where hundreds of migratory birds swoop down onto ancient trees spread over the rocky islets dotting the Kaveri.

A halt made by many tourist buses is at the **Brindavan Gardens**, about 19 km (12 miles) outside the city. This is the site of the Krishnarajasagar reservoir, created when the adjoining irrigation dam, Karnataka's largest, was built across the Kaveri river. The dam is notable because it was constructed from stone and mortar, without the use of cement. The gardens, based on a Mughal design, have musical fountains complete with a coloured light display. The gardens descend in manicured terraces, fringed by water courses in the Islamic fashion. (Incidentally, inscriptions testify to Tippu's attempts to build a dam at the same spot.) In a niche beneath the ornate parapets on the rear face of the dam stands a statue of the river goddess, holding a pot from which water spills as symbol of prosperity and perhaps as a reminder that without the 1,245 million cubic metres (44,000 million cu ft) of water behind, the gardens might not be such a lush reality.

Srirangapatnam

Its strategic position as an island in the middle of a river has been to **Srirangapatnam's** ❸ advantage several times through its history. It has also worked against it, since this has brought it to the covetous attention of every ruler in the region. For a period of about three centuries, from the 15th century when the fort was first built until the end of the 18th century, Srirangapatnam suffered from the virtue of its location as various rulers strove mightily to oust whoever happened to be entrenched on it at the moment. The years from 1638 to 1799 in particular saw the island under siege seven times, the last by the British who finally vanquished its occupant, Tippu Sultan. Since then, this battle-fatigued island has been left more or less to itself.

It is odd that in this attractive town with its mausoleums, cemeteries (including the **British Garrison cemetery** and the graves of the troops of Tippu's French allies) and commemorative monuments (the obelisk in the Fort that marks where Tippu Sultan fell and the memorial to the soldiers who died in the final siege), the only ghost story you are likely to hear is the one concerning Scott's Bungalow.

Colonel Scott supervised a gun factory on the island when the British occupied it.

RIGHT: inlaid ivory at Tippu Sultan's palace.

One day he came home to his bungalow to find his wife and child dead from a sudden attack of cholera. Disconsolate, he threw himself into the river that ran outside the garden. For years, his ghost rose from the river at night and wafted forlornly up to the bungalow, looking for his loved ones.

Most of Srirangapatnam's buildings and monuments were constructed by Tippu Sultan, known as the Tiger of Mysore for his ferocity and tactical cunning. His insignia was tiger stripes, and everything, from his throne to his dagger, featured either a tiger's head, claws or teeth. (Apparently, tigers also functioned as summary dispensers of justice and he kept a cage of these beasts to punish the occasional miscreant, such as the tax collector who had come up short.) He proclaimed himself Sultan in 1782 after the death of his father Hyder Ali, a former commander under the Wadiyars who had wrested power from his employers.

Tippu was an inspired warrior and commander, his troops trained by the French whose revolutionary ideals he sympathised with to the extent that he referred to himself briefly, if whimsically, as Citoyen Tippu. He then proceeded to give the British, who had dismissed this as the mere antics of a temporary Francophile, a bad fright by inviting Napoleon, then in Egypt, to come to his assistance – an offer not taken up.

When the end did come, the British breached the Fort's southwest wall and demolished the Lal Mahal, Tippu's palace; most of the remaining fortifications have since crumbled away. The Elephant Gate, the dungeons where the river surged in to lap at the unfortunates who were chained there, and the obelisk on the spot where the great general fell: these are the only fragments of the fort left.

Daria Daulat

When not embroiled in conquest or defence, Tippu ruled his island capital well and built upon it with a fine aesthetic judgement. He indulged himself with a summer palace, built in 1784, called **Daria**

BELOW: the Daria Daulat Bagh interior.

Map on page 244

Daulat Bagh (open Sat–Thur 9am–5pm, antrance charge) – the Garden of the Wealth of the Seas. Made of teak, it looks exquisitely cool, an Indo-Saracenic structure painted forest-green and set in formal Islamic gardens. The restraint of the building's elegant facade nicely balances the extravagance of its interior.

Large wall murals, still vivid in hue, detail (with maybe a slight bias) the lives and times of the ruler and his family. There is one with the Mysore soldiers, French comrades in arms alongside, dashingly portrayed in contrast to their stodgily depicted British opponents. One room serves as a museum chock-a-block with personal trivia: a gold-embroidered tunic Tippu once wore, his coin collection and some Western paintings and engravings.

Temple and mosque

When Tirumalayya, a governor serving in the Ganga kingdom, built the **Sri Ranganatha temple** in AD 894 on an island in the Kaveri river, 16 km (10 miles) from Mysore, it was uninhabited and dense with jungle. Three centuries later came a chieftain Thimmanna, anxious to put to constructive use a cache of buried treasure he had unearthed. He built the island's fort with the temple structure and improved upon it. For this, as a gesture of secular stonework, he also used materials he had garnered from a stupefying pillage of 101 Jain temples.

These architectural efforts, three centuries apart, explain the melding of the temple's Hoysalan and Vijayanagaran styles. Representations of Visnu cover the pillars, ceilings and domes, and at the temple precincts is a juggernaut donated by Hyder Ali. In the sanctum, recumbent under the hood of Adisesa, the seven-headed serpent, is the image of the god after whom the island and its oldest structure were named.

Two hundred steps lead up to the top of each of the slender minarets on the Jama Masjid, both overlooking the fort area. Epigraphs in Persian record the 99 names of Allah and date the period of construction of the mosque to 1787. Tippu, a devout Muslim, offered *namaz* in the hall with its foil arches.

Gol Gumbaz

On Tippu's tomb in the **Gol Gumbaz** (open Sat–Thur 9am–5pm), the inscription says, "The light of Islam has left this world, a martyr for the faith of Muhammad." His father Hyder Ali is buried here, and his mother (born a Hindu) too. Splendid rosewood doors inlaid with ivory lead indoors, where Tippu's favourite tiger stripes band the walls. Glossy pillars of black hornblende offer a contrast to the cream walls and the superb dome, with its minarets in four corners. Traditional gardens define the approach to a mausoleum that has been inevitably compared to the Taj Mahal, though it is much smaller and more austere.

Somnathpur

Somnathpur ❹ is the site of the **Prasanna Chennakesava Temple** (open 9am–5pm, entrance charge), with the star-shaped base characteristic of Hoysala temple architecture. Of the three most famous Hoysala temples in Karnataka, this was the last to be built, in 1268 *(see also pages*

RIGHT: prayers at the mosque in Srirangapatnam.

255 and 257). It is situated in a village about 35 km (22 miles) from Mysore, a short distance and a trip well worth making to see the degree of sculptural and structural precision that the art of temple-building could attain.

The temple was the creation of Janakachari, perhaps the era's finest architect and sculptor, who is believed to have so excelled himself in its design and execution that the gods themselves were tempted to steal it. But as they caused the building to rise heavenward, the resourceful Janakachari disfigured some of the carvings on the outer walls. Seeing its perfection thus marred, the celestial ones coveted it no longer and let it go. The temple sank back onto the ground with a thud that dislodged its flagstaff, awry ever since – the one flaw in an edifice of perfection.

The diversions of legend aside, history relates that the temple was commissioned by Somnath, a minister of the Hoysala king, Narasimha III, from whom he received a handsome sum of 3,000 gold pieces for his many charitable works. A devoutly religious man, Somnath used the money to build the temple in homage to his family deities – Chennakesava, Janardhana and Venugopala – in the village that its elders named after him. Janakachari used soapstone in the construction of the building, since it is both easy to work with and hard-wearing.

Unusually for a Hoysala temple, there are three shrines, one for each member of the trinity. In the main one facing the entrance, the images of the sentries still stand guard, though the image of Lord Chennakesava it once housed disappeared long ago. The northern shrine still has its image of Janardhana, and the southern that of Venugopala. Both have haloes carved with the 10 incarnations of Visnu. The latter idol is particularly symmetrical: holding a flute, it stands with nose, navel and supporting foot in precise alignment.

Each shrine has its tower and multi-pillared hall that opens out onto a central square called the *navrang*, where devotional songs and dances were performed. Since the superstructure is not as tall as those of most South Indian temples, all the carving is at a comfortable eye level – marvellously articulate sculpture, with a variety of facial expressions minutely rendered.

The exterior walls are frescoed with narrative passages from the *Ramayana*, the *Mahabharata* and the *Bhagavata*, laid out so exactly that each segment ends at a door. Vivid with detail, no two frescoes are alike, and some extend right around the temple. The carvings ascend the temple walls in seven rows of distinct motifs. At the bottom, in symbolic support, is a row of elephants, and next, one of equine and floral forms, which support in turn the scenarios from the epics.

Row No. 4 is of the avatars of Visnu, and above that, a seated lion, emblem of the Hoysala dynasty. The second highest line has representations of Lord Narasimha and finally, a tier of swans and crocodiles. Stripped of ornamentation above this, the wedge-shaped shafts of the *gopurams* end in the Vysara style, derivative of both the Dravidian and the Orissan temple *gopurams*. (The latter ends in a point, unlike the former.)

LEFT: bands of friezes cover the exterior of the Chennakesava temple.

Map on page 244

The occasional contradictory detail presents itself in the decoration: a depiction from the *Bhagavata*, for instance, on the exterior of the middle shrine has a palace set in Mathura (the mythological birthplace of Krisna), framed by coconut palms. Another frieze from the *Mahabharata* has a row of camels, animals rarely seen in the South or in illustrations of the epic. These idiosyncratic touches were certainly deliberately introduced and left there, perhaps like the flagstaff, never straightened after that failed essay in divine larceny.

Hassan

Hassan is probably the most convenient point from which to visit Sravanabelagola, Belur and Halebid *(see below)*. There is little of interest in Hassan itself, but as it is the town with the most to offer by way of accommodation and transport, it would be logical to stay here. The tourist office here could assist in making reservations for Belur and Halebid, should you wish to spend the night there.

Sravanabelagola

The serenity that **Sravanabelagola** ❺ emanates derives from the simplicity of its ascetic inspiration and the grandeur of its scale (it is said to be the world's tallest monolithic statue).

The art historian Fergusson said of the monolith: "The statues of this Jain saint are among the most remarkable works of art in South India. One is astonished at the amount of labour such a work must have entailed, and puzzled to know whether it was part of the hill or had been moved to the spot where it now stands. The former is the more probable theory. The hill is one mass of granite about 122 metres (400 ft) high and probably had a mass or two standing at its summit – either a part of the subjacent mass or lying on it. This the Jains undertook to fashion into a statue 18 metres (58 ft) tall, and have achieved it with marvellous success. Nothing grander or more imposing exists anywhere out of Egypt, and even there, no known statue surpasses its height."

BELOW: the star-shaped plinth of the Somnathpur temple.

Sravanabelagola (158 km/99 miles from Bangalore) is wedged between two rocky hills called Indragiri or Vindhyagiri and Chandragiri. The translation of Sravanabelagola is "the white pond of the ascetic". This most probably refers to a pond that once existed where the present temple tank now is, at the base of the Indragiri hill. The ascetic is Bahubali, also known as the Tirthankar Gomatesvara, whose huge statue dominates this little village. This is the holiest of all Jain places of pilgrimage.

Note the simplicity of the carving at Sravanabelagola, and contrast it with the ornate and complex sculptural work in the temples of Belur and Halebid.

Indragiri looms as the visitor enters Sravanabelagola, and the steps leading to the summit are cut into the rock face. The visitor passes a temple as the climb begins, which is dedicated to Adinatha, father of the Jain saint whose monolith is at the peak of the hill. Climb yet higher, past another temple, and the town of Sravanabelagola is spread out below, with panoramic views of the surrounding districts and the azure Kalyani tank. The small hill of Chandragiri can be seen from here, crowned by a slender pillar and the tomb of the great emperor Chandragupta Maurya, a patron of Jainism. Climb past a stone gateway, and the head of the monolith is visible, silhouetted against the bright blue sky: serene, he seems to float in eternity.

The visitor then enters a court, where there are more shrines dedicated to Jain saints, and a beautiful sculpture of Kushmandini Devi with an oval cup in her hands. The visitor arrives at the base of the statue, its immense legs rising from a platform on which priests devoutly perform their rites, dwarfed by the mammoth monument. Jungle vines climb up around the legs of the saint, to signify the perfect concentration he attained during his penance.

Sravanabelagola has a history dating back to the 3rd century BC, when it is said that the emperor Chandragupta Maurya, having renounced his kingdom, came to this land with his guru, Bhadrabahu Svami. The emperor is believed to have died as a result of penitential starvation.

During the course of time, Bhadrabahu's disciples established Jainism all over the South. This religion found powerful royal patronage and reached its zenith between the 4th and 10th centuries. It was during the reign of the Ganga king Rachamalla that the statue of Lord Gomatesvara was erected, having been sculpted by Aristanemi in 981.

Bahubali and Bharata were the sons of Adi Tirthankara Vrisaba Deva, the Jain ruler of a kingdom in northern India, who renounced his throne to become the first saint of the Jains. His renunciation sparked off a bitter succession war between his two sons. Bahubali emerged the victor after a long and bloody duel. In his moment of victory, Bahubali realised the futility of violence and worldly success, which inspired him to give all his worldly possessions away to his brother Bharata. So began his 1,000-year penance in the forest.

Thousands of Jain pilgrims from all over the world attend the *Mahamastakabhiseka* ceremony which is performed once every 12 years or so depending on the astrologi-

LEFT: the *Mahamastakabhiseka.*

Map on page 244

cal configuration. The most recent one was in February 2006 (delayed a year due to a bad drought). The culmination of this spectacular ceremony is the anointing of the statue by priests from a specially erected scaffolding above the image. They pour down thousands of pots of milk, curd, *ghi*, saffron, coconut milk, poppy seeds, almonds, gold coins and other items, each of which carries a special significance. The sight of the monolith's features being inundated and changing colours with every application is indeed a memorable one.

No single person can be credited with the building of Sravanabelagola. It was built over the period of a millennium and a half by saints, rulers, chieftains, merchants, artists, scribes and pilgrims, who gradually developed it into the centre of pilgrimage that it is today.

In no other Digambara Jain centre in India are there as many temples covering as wide a time span as at Sravanabelagola. The earliest dates back to the 9th century AD, while the most recent was built less than 100 years ago.

The carving of the Tirthankaras is an art that follows the strictest rules and regulations. No ornamentation of any kind can be attributed to the sculpture, whose entire demeanour has to follow the strictest codes of simplicity, in keeping with the Jain ethos. The face must not turn to the left or right, though the figure may be depicted sitting or standing. The rigid, sitting yogic posture is called *Paryankasana*; the standing, meditative posture is called the *Kayotsarga*. All the 24 Tirthankaras have identical features, though the first Tirthankara, Adinatha, is sometimes portrayed with long hair. Yaksas and Yaksis, attendants of the Tirthankaras, can be depicted in flexed postures and with attributes in their hands.

In addition to the main statue of Lord Bahubali are the Small Hill with archways and inscriptions at its summit, the Bhadrabahu Cave where many monuments are enclosed – the Chandragupta Basti, the Kattale Basti, the Bhandari Basti and the Akkana Basti which are built in the Hoysala style. There are well-preserved frescoes in one of the temples, documenting Jain history.

There is a large and valuable collection of old bronzes, some dating back to the 10th century, in the Basti temples in the Math. Observe the relief carvings on the pillars of this temple.

At the base of the hill is a long row of shops selling mostly religious tat, from fluorescent images of Lord Bahubali to plastic toys. A few stone carvings are the only worthwhile purchases.

Belur

In contrast to the grandeur and simplicity of Sravanabelagola is the small town of **Belur** ❻. Located on the banks of the river Yagachi, Belur used to be the capital of the Hoysala empire before it was shifted to Dvarasamudram, over 800 years ago. Today it is a sleepy little town with attractive countryside surrounding it, the memories of its past glory reflected in the **Chennakesava temple** (open sunrise–sunset). This structure was erected in 1116. It was built in observance of the victory of the Hoysalas over the Cholas in the great

RIGHT: a carving of Sarasvati at Halebid.

battle of Talakad. King Visnuvardhana commissioned this temple, and it took 103 years to complete. The facade of the building is intricately carved with sculptures and friezes. The interior panels and pillars are even more richly carved.

The Belur temple is one of the finest examples of Hoysala architecture. It was designed by Jakanachari, a notable sculptor of the period, though the signatures of other sculptors too can be discerned. Legend has it that Jakanachari left his wife and young son in quest of fame, and that when he had completed his most perfect work, an enormous Ganesa, its consecration was delayed by a young boy who pronounced the image unfit for worship. In front of a huge crowd, the distressed sculptor challenged the boy to substantiate his statement, saying that he would cut off his arm if proved wrong. The boy picked up a stick and struck Ganesa's navel which split open to reveal a frog squatting inside the damp stone. The stone was obviously defective, and it would have been a desecration, in Hindu tradition, to have allowed the image to be worshipped. The sculptor therefore cut off his arm, only to find that the boy was his own forgotten son, who had learned the art of perfection.

Legends aside, the temple was built in commemoration of the Hoysala king Bittiga's victory over the Cholas. The actual temple is built on a star-shaped plinth, reached by a short flight of steps. The first thing that strikes the visitor is the compact scale of the structure. In comparison with the towering edifices of most temples in India, the Belur temple is definitely small. It is when one gets close enough to notice the astounding wealth of detail in its sculpture that one realises its uniqueness. Around the base are 650 carvings of elephants, each one in a different configuration. Distinct themes embellish the rows above, mainly taken from the *Ramayana* and *Mahabharata*.

The Hoysalas did spend a lot of time on the battlefield, but that did not interfere with their avid interest in culture, as is apparent from the depiction of their music,

BELOW: the exquisite temple at Belur.

Map on page 244

dance and art. During times of peace and prosperity, they encouraged the arts, and talent was promoted. Competition flourished amongst artists, who were allowed to sign their creations – something not usually found in Indian art.

Rulers who commissioned the building of temples did so in fulfilment of a vow, or for the promise of victory on the battlefield. Their art was infused with an extraordinary complexity. Regard for the proportions and rules that governed the art of sculpture is apparent in every carving. If you were to insert a thread into the pupil of an eye on one of the sculptures, it would emerge through the nose. Suspend a taut string from the forehead of a dancer and it will fall straight onto an uplifted toe.

There is not a portion of the structure that has been left uncarved, and yet the effect is not overwhelming. There is a flow to the subject matter, like a story frozen in stone unfolding before you and coming to a definite conclusion. If you were to spend 10 hours a day studying the sculptures, it would take the best part of 2 weeks to complete your survey.

After studying the 38 ornamental figures, which range from the mythological to the erotic, you enter the temple. An inky blackness envelops you, and if the electricity has not failed you will see the hand-lathe-turned filigreed pillars, each distinct and astoundingly beautiful. It is said that the main Narasimha pillar once revolved on its own centre of gravity, but time has taken its toll. The jewellery on the sculptures is movable, and the delicate carvings are quite awe-inspiring in their perfection.

There is a sensuously smooth and polished platform where the Queen is said to have danced in praise of Krisna, Lord Chennakesava. The four bracket figures on the ceiling celebrate feminine beauty, and the model for each of these was the queen, Shantala Devi. Consort to King Vishnuvardhana, she was a woman of rare beauty and talent, and was considered responsible for the flourishing of art and culture during this period, as is discernible from these carvings. There was active participation by women in public affairs, and a high degree of sexual freedom.

The **Viranarayana temple** lies west of the main Chennakesava temple and is much smaller. There are exquisite carvings of various Hindu gods, and around the temple there are several small shrines dedicated to Kappe Chennigaraya, Soumyanayaki and Andal.

Halebid

The original name of **Halebid** ❼, the ancient capital of the Hoysalas, was Dvarasamudram, "gateway to the sea". After its sack by the Delhi Sultanate, it became known as Halebid, "old capital". There were many temples and palaces here, but very few of them survived the invasion.

The magnificent **Hoysalesvara temple** (open sunrise–sunset) is very similar to the temple at Belur, though different in its detailed work. It has two shrines, one dedicated to Siva and one to his consort, Parvati, also known as Santalesvara. It is set on the same star-shaped platform ascended by a short flight of steps. The palace once stood nearby, connected to the tem-

RIGHT: sculpture at the Chennakesava temple, Belur.

ple by a passage. A Nandi, the mount of Lord Siva, stands guard at the entrance. This temple is about 800 years old, although not wholly in ruins. Only one bracket figure remains, though the relief carvings on the walls are as profuse and complex as at Belur. The stellar base, with the emblem of the stylised lions and elephants which seem to support the temple, signifies stability.

Among the carvings are scenes of many historical battles, of the child Krisna's frolics, Siva and Parvati's embrace and Ravana hoisting Mount Kailas. Stories from the epics *Ramayana* and *Mahabharata* are depicted in the friezes: Krisna holding up the mountain Govardhana, Brahma on his vehicle, Hamsa, Visnu and various other gods and godesses. Even musicians and dancers are shown here. Queen Shantala also makes another appearance.

The Hoysalas, traditional enemies of the Chalukyas, ruled this part of the Deccan between the 11th and 13th centuries. They rose to prominence first under leadership of their ruler Tinyaditya and later under king Bittiga, better known as Visnuvardhana. It was during this latter period when the Hoysalas established their supremacy that the temples of Belur and Halebid were built.

The Jain faith had been predominant up to this time, under the patronage of the Chalukyas and the Gangas. Bittiga himself was a devout Jain until he came under the influence of the saint Ramanuja, who converted him to the Vaishnavite faith; he then took on the name Visnuvardhana. Bittiga encouraged one of his generals, Gangaraja, to rebuild the Jain temples that had been destroyed by the Chola invaders, adherents of the Saivite creed. There are records showing Visnuvardhana's tolerance for other religious sects, of grants made to temples of other faiths, and of pilgrimages undertaken to Sravanabelagola even after his conversion.

It is difficult to reconcile Halebid now with what it used to be in its days of glory; when it was the capital of the Hoysala empire, it was crowded with travellers and royal visitors from distant lands, and teeming with life and activity. The invasion by Alauddin Khilji's general in 1310 caused the city's decline.

The famous novelist R.K. Narayan tells of the legend of the curse which destroyed Halebid: "The extinction of Halebid or Dorasamudra was due to the curse of a woman. The king's sister had come on a visit to the capital, bringing with her two sons, who were handsome. One of the King's wives attempted to seduce the young men, and was repulsed. Enraged by her failure, she reported to the king that the boys had tried to molest her. The king immediately ordered his nephews to be impaled and their bodies to be exposed at the city gates. The mother, i.e. the King's sister, was cast out and the citizens were forbidden to give her shelter. She wandered the streets, maddened by all this injustice, cursing her brother and his kingdom. She was given help and admitted only in the Potter's street, and that is all that is left of the capital today, the only remnant of a grand empire. Although the human habitations of those times have

LEFT: the enchantress Mohini.

Map on page 244

disappeared, the temples built by Vishnuvardhana and his successor stand to attest once more to the grandeur of the Hoysala reign and their artists."

The detail of the friezes at the Hoysaleswara and Kedareswara are more complex than those at Belur. Fergusson says of this temple, "...From the basement to the summit, it was covered with sculptures of the very best class of Indian art. The Hoysaleswara temple is perhaps the building on which the advocate of Hindu architecture would like to take his stand. Unfortunately, it was never finished, the works having been stopped after they were in progress for more than 86 years. No two facets of the temple are the same; every convolution of every scroll is different. No two canopies in the whole building are alike, and every part exhibits a joyous exuberance of fancy."

The Archaeological Survey of India maintains a small **Museum** (open Sat–Thur 10am–5pm, entrance charge) within the temple with a collection of stone sculptures.

Kodagu

About 250 km (156 miles) from Bangalore, located in the Western Ghats, is the region of **Kodagu**, formerly known as Coorg. The British, with their propensity for nostalgia, dubbed it the Scotland of India, probably for its misty green slopes and lush forestation. Today, Kodagu is primarily an agricultural centre, with cash crops of coffee, rice and oranges supported by cardamom, pepper and other spices.

The Kodavas constitute the main population of Coorg, and have distinct cultural characteristics. The concept of the clan amongst them is a powerful institution that many credit with having preserved the Kodava culture for centuries. The clan or *okka* is an exogamous group: marriage within the same *okka* was considered tantamount to incest. Kodavas practise the cross-cousin marriage system, which is a distinct trait of Adivasi communities. Women occupy an exalted place in the family hierarchy, and remarriage from widowhood is encouraged. Many women

BELOW: the Hoysalesvara temple, Halebid.

run estates single-handedly, and local legends often have heroines occupying the central role.

Most explanations on the origin of the Kodavas are fairly colourful but have never been authenticated or proved. One such school considers them descendants of the Greeks. Alexander the Great, in pursuit of world domination, had sent his infantry down the west coast of India. Having travelled deep into the south, the Greek soldiers decided to settle where they were. These Mediterranean strangers are credited with the founding of the clans. Another story attributes Kodava ancestry to Arab migration, based on the similarity of the traditional costume, especially the head-kerchief and the long black robe worn to this day, known as the *kuppia* from the Arabic *kuffia*.

Kodagu's manicured neatness comes as something of a surprise to the traveller who has experienced the sometimes untamed landscapes elsewhere in India. It is a region of scattered hamlets and villages separated by distances varying between 5 km (3 miles) and 48 km (30 miles). The capital is **Madikeri** ❽, a picturesque little township at an elevation of over 1,525 metres (5,000 ft) above sea level. Access is by road, and bus services ply between Bangalore and different areas of Kodagu on a regular basis.

The township of Madikeri (previously Mercara) is itself worth a ramble. Streets dip and rise as they follow the hilly terrain. It is a charming, old-world town dotted with pretty cottages all around and panoramic views which come upon you unexpectedly. In the centre is the **Madikeri fort**, a 19th-century building of no particular distinction. Yet its red-tiled roof is typical of Hindu architecture in Kerala. Within its walls lie the local prison, a temple, a small museum and various government offices. **St Mark's Church** houses a small museum of British memorabilia, statues and ancient weapons.

Winding lanes meander off the main streets, and if you are fond of walking there are excellent prospects and mountain trails to follow. **Tadiyendamol**, the tallest peak in the area, is a beautiful climb and you can view the distant horizon of the Arabian Sea from the top.

The temples of Kodagu are also interesting, ranging from hero stones set up under banyan trees to multi-roofed buildings. There are three temples of particular interest. The **Omkaresvara** temple, dedicated to Siva and built by Lingaraja in 1820 in the centre of Madikeri, is an unexpected mix of Gothic and Islamic styles. It is built around a central pool teeming with fish that you can feed.

The **Bhagamandala** temple has been built at the confluence of three rivers, the Kaveri, Kanike and Sujyothi. It is built in the Keralan style and houses a variety of smaller shrines dedicated to various gods. Eight kilometres (5 miles) up the hill from Bhagamandala is the source of the river Kaveri with the **Talakaveri** temple built around it. In October, on Kaveri Sankaramana day, thousands of people gather at this little temple to witness the miraculous rise of the fountainhead, when water gushes up at a predetermined moment.

LEFT: a bus in the foothills of the Ghats.

Map on page 244

There are two attractive waterfalls in Kodagu. The **Abbey Falls**, near Madikeri, are an agreeable place for a picnic. The **Iruppu Falls** are where the Laxmanthirtha descends, and they lie on the route from Gonikoppal to Kutta.

Nagarhole and Bandipur

Magnificent natural forests stretch as far as the eye can see in **Nagarhole National Park**. Rosewood, teak, sandal, silver oak and other trees make up this thick jungle, teeming with the flora and fauna of the region. Jeeps and elephants are available for transport and guided tours. You can go directly to this reserve forest from Mysore or Hunsur. Forest lodges provide fairly decent accommodation and food. It is also possible to arrange treks through the Chief Wildlife Warden.

Bandipur National Park (open 6–9am, 4–6pm) to the south, is contiguous with the forests of Mudumalai in Tamil Nadu and Waynad in Kerala. Wildlife spotted here includes elephant, gaur and chital.

BELOW: Madikeri.

Mangalore

The Western Ghats have to be traversed if you travel to Mangalore from Bangalore, and the journey snaking down the hairpin bends is spectacular. As the descent begins, **Mangalore** ❾ becomes visible, ensconced on the coast. This maritime city has always been significant, for it was a major seaport and shipbuilding centre in Hyder Ali's time. Today it is a business and commercial centre and the major port of Karnataka for the export of coffee, spices and cashew. Mangalore has a turbulent history of conflict for possession of this important port. These influences are still apparent in the cosmopolitan attitude and diverse religions that exist here.

Places to visit include **Sultan's Bathery**, Tippu Sultan's old fort (6km/4 miles away), and the old lighthouse from where there are spectacular views. More views are to had from the **Kadri Hills** which are the location of the beautiful 10th-century temple to the goddess **Manjunatha**. Other temples worth visiting, of which there are many, include the **Sri Yogesvar Math**, and the **Dharmathsthala** and **Sringeri** temples.

Mangalore has a large Christian population and there are a number of fine churches in the city. These include **St Joseph's Theological Seminary**, the ancient **Church of the Most Holy Rosary** at Bolar, which was founded in 1526, and the **St Aloysius College Church**, which has a magnificent biblical fresco on the walls and ceiling painted in 1889 by an Italian Jesuit.

Among the remarkable mosques are the **Jama Masjid** in the Bunder, built centuries ago by the Arabs, and the **Idgah** mosque at Lighthouse Hill whose construction is attributed to Tippu Sultan at the end of the 18th century. The saint Shah Amir is entombed at the **Shamir Mosque** at Dongerkerri.

Mangalore is a good base for a trip down coastal Karnataka. Inviting beaches easily reached by a good coastal road dot the area both above and below Mangalore, although the beach in the city itself is indifferent and polluted. Seafood enthusiasts will appreciate the variety available in local restaurants. Local cuisine is spicy, with a lot of coconut gravy used in the preparation. Good vegetarian food is available from a host of Udupi cafeterias. Try also to catch a performance of the local theatre form *Yaksagana*, a stylised and elaborate dance that tells the stories of the ancient epics.

Around Mangalore

Within easy reach of Mangalore are a number of interesting sitghts. **Dharmastala** has the impressive Manjunatha temple, Jain *bastis* (temples), and a 14-metre (45-ft) high statue of Lord Bahubali. The ruins of a Mahadeva temple canb e found at **Venur**. Also here is a statue of Lord Bahubali 11-metres (35-ft) high on the banks of the Gurupur (erected 1604), and Jain *bastis*. **Mudbidri** has 18 *bastis*, the oldest of which is the Chandranatha temple with its 1,000 richly carved pillars. **Karkal** is an ancient and venerated religious township with a statue of Lord Bahubali, installed in 1432.

BELOW: red-tiled roofs are characteristic of the region.

Udupi

Up the coast from Mangalore lies the 13th-century seat of Madhavacharya, the great religious leader. The temple at **Udupi** ⓾ is an impressive institution with a beautifully bejewelled statue of Lord Krisna. The elaborate religious rites performed at each day's *puja* have remained unchanged through the centuries. Several festivals are held here throughout the year. Under the patronage of the *svamis* of the eight *maths*, religious centres, Udupi is a centre for higher learning through all the educational institutions and colleges that were opened under their sponsorship, and funded by their educational trusts.

A whole school of South Indian cuisine takes its name from this town. Today, in the most far-flung corners of India you will see the inevitable "Udupi Tiffin Room" or "Udupi Brahmin Hotel", a name synonymous with vegetarian food.

While in the town you should sample the *masala dosai*, a crisply fried pancake of fermented rice stuffed with a mix of spicy potato and onion, which has its origin here. Try the *idli*, a steamed rice cake that can be eaten with lentil and mint chutney or *sambar*. Other dishes to ask for are the *rava dosai*, *puri palya*, *uthapam*, *vada sambar* and the paper *dosai*, which is an outsize *dosai* with the crisp consistency of paper.

Coastal towns and beaches

The southern Konkan coast has a number of attractive beaches. **Malpe**, 10 km (6 miles) from Udupi, has beautiful silvery beaches. **Ullal**, 5 km (3 miles) to the south of Mangalore, is a pretty place set among casuarina groves. **Maravanthe**, just over 9 km (5 miles) from Kundapura between the river and sea coast, has good swimming. From here you can also travel down the river and explore the hinterland.

North of here, 125 km (78 miles) from Udipi, is **Bhatkal**. This used to be the major port of the Vijayanagara empire. There are Portuguese ruins to explore and old temples from the Vijayanagara period to visit.

Heading inland from here brings you to **Jog Falls**, about 45 km (28 miles) from the coast, where the Birur railway lines from Bangalore and Mysore terminate. Jog Falls are the highest waterfalls in India. The river Saravati makes a spectacular drop of 253 metres (810 ft) in four distinct cascades known locally as the Raja, Rani, Rover and Rocket. The dry season detracts from the grandeur of the falls, while during the monsoon, mist totally obscures the view. They are at their best just after the monsoon, when the arching rainbows are beautiful.

The pilgrimage town of **Gokarna** is not only known for the sacred *lingam* in its **Mahabalesvara temple**, but also the spectacular beaches nearby. The most popular of these is **Om Beach** (so-called because of its similarity in shape to the sacred syllable), now very crowded in high season. About 520 km (325 miles) from Bangalore, almost on the Goa border, is **Karwar**, a beautiful seaside town that Vasco da Gama is reputed to have visited. The fort at Sadasivgad, Devgad island and the lighthouse are of some interest. The nearby coastal villages of Binaga and Araga have good beaches. ❑

RIGHT: the golden chariot of the Udupi Math.

Maps:
Area 244
City 266

HAMPI

The ruined Vijayanagara city of Hampi, with its wonderful temples, is one of the most beautiful and spectacular sites in India

Perhaps the most beautiful and evocative of all the ruins in Karnataka is **Hampi** ⓫ (open: Vittala Temple 8am–4pm; Royal Enclosure 6am–6pm; entrance fee). There is a brooding, mystical ambience to the landscape – bleak, barren and strewn with boulders, the desolation offset by the magnificent remnants of a once-powerful empire.

The Vijayanagara empire was one of the largest in the history of India. Though there are diverse opinions on the founding of the empire, most historians agree that the Sangamas were the first ruling dynasty of this kingdom. The Telugu princes Harihara and Bukka in the 14th century extended their kingdom from the Tungabhadra right up to Tiruchirappalli in the south. A hundred years later, the empire reached its zenith under Krisnadeva Raya, who controlled the whole of the peninsula south of the Krishna river.

For two centuries the glory of this kingdom was boundless. According to Nicolo Conti, the Italian merchant, the city of Vijayanagara was just 13 km (8 miles) in circumference and its ruler was the most powerful in India. In another instance, the Portuguese traveller Paes who visited Vijayanagara in its golden age described it as being as large as Rome, with the palaces of its kings being larger than the castles of Lisbon. He recorded that it was the most flourishing city in the world and had more than 100,000 dwellings.

A Muslim envoy, Abdul Razaq, visited the capital in 1443 and wrote, "Vijayanagara is such that the pupil of the eye has never seen a place like it and the ear of intelligence has never been informed that there existed anything to equal it in the world. The audience hall of the king's palace is elevated above all the rest. In the long bazaars, flowers are sold everywhere. The people could not live without flowers and they look upon them as quite as necessary as food. The jewellers sell publicly pearls, rubies, emeralds and diamonds. In this agreeable locality, as well as in the king's palace, one sees numerous streams and channels formed of chiselled stone, polished and smooth."

The notable rulers of this dynasty were Devaraya II (early 15th century), Krisnadevaraya and his successor Achyutadevaraya (early 16th century). Krisnadevaraya (1509–29), brother of Vira Narasimha, was the most successful ruler of Vijayanagara. He dominated the Bahmanis and contained the threat from the king of Orissa, another traditional enemy. His army advanced further to the north and his empire stretched from Konkan in the west to Waltair in the east

LEFT: the 6.7-metre (22-ft) statue of Narasimha. **RIGHT:** Hanuman.

and Kanniyakumari in the south. Some islands in the Indian Ocean also came under his influence.

The Vijayanagara kings were great promoters of culture. As is apparent even from these ruins, the arts flourished under their patronage and they gave equal attention to the development of new techniques in agriculture, warfare, waterworks and civic building. Textile production and mining flourished. Craftsmen and merchants' guilds played an important role in the economic system. There were 300 ports in different parts of the empire and trade relations were maintained with Burma, the Malayan Peninsula, China, the Arabian peninsula, Ethiopia, Portugal and islands in the Indian Ocean. The chief exports were textiles, rice, iron and sugar, while the imports included horses, elephants, pearls, copper and Chinese silk. Ships built in the Maldives were used for carrying cargo overseas.

Although Vijayanagara was essentially a Hindu kingdom, the rulers permitted the practice of other religions and they themselves following a variety of Hindu deities. The better known are the gods Virupaksa, Krisna, Vittala, Rama and Venkatesvara. Thus, Hampi had a diverse population with a rich blend of cosmopolitan cultures. By 1565, the Muslim Sultanates had declared war and defeated the Vijayanagara military commander. The king, together with his court and treasury, escaped southward and the abandoned city was sacked. Left in smouldering ruins, Vijayanagara was never to be occupied again.

The splendour of Vijayanagara has never been entirely lost, for even in the ruins you can glimpse its past glories. Ruins of ancient temples are found to this day in towns and villages around Hampi. The ruined city has been recognised as a World Heritage Site by UNESCO and is under the protection of the Archaeological survey of India. However, they have not been the most vigilant of guardians. The site has been placed on the List of World

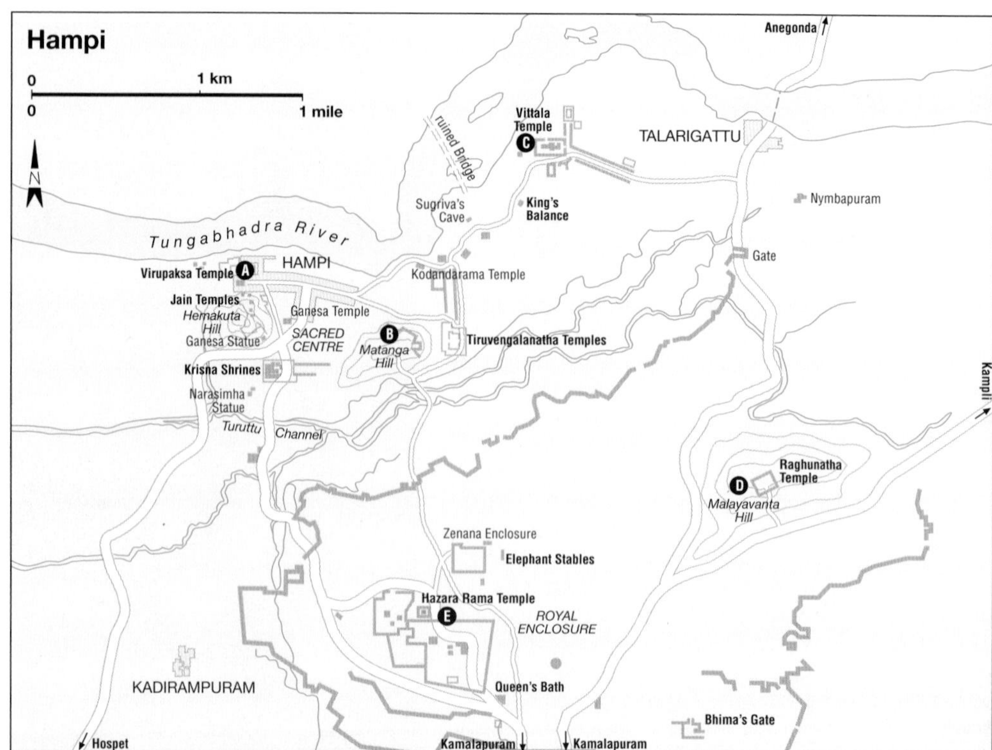

Map on page 266

Heritage in Danger register due to the construction of a road bridge across the Tungabhadra linking Hampi with Anegonda which would increase traffic near the site. A settlement appears to have been reached with the government agreeing to build a bypass around the most sensitive areas before completing the bridge.

The natural setting of Vijayanagara offered protection from invaders, since the capital had rocky ridges on three sides and the river on the fourth. The Tungabhadra flows through a rocky gorge which dominates the north, and extensive plains stretch to the Sandur hills towards the southwest. On the south bank of the Tungabhadra, on rocky outcrops overlooking the ravine, are the majority of the main temples. This, the sacred axis of the city, is said to have existed before the founding of the kingdom. The urban core of the city was fortified from invasion, and was separated from the sacred centre by an irrigated valley, through which ancient canals and waterways still run. There is evidence of habitation at the urban core, with temples, gateways, tanks and wells, most of which are in ruins or buried under the earth. It was probably here that the majority of the city's population lived, with different areas being assigned to the Jains and Muslims.

In the southwestern section of this core are structures enclosed by high granite walls. This was obviously the royal enclosure, because of the wealth of architecture associated with the court and military activity. The Mahanavami festival was the most important annual event and the Vijayanagara rulers celebrated its rituals here.

In the plains towards the southwest were the suburban areas of the city. Fragments of earlier fortifications are in evidence here, which indicate that the city itself was guarded by a series of concentric protective walls. These walls had gateways set into them that led to the centre of the city.

The elaborate defence system around Hampi suggests that the capital was planned as a gigantic fortress. The natural

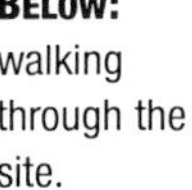

BELOW: walking through the site.

granite ridges have granite fortifications built upon them. Doorways and entrances are set into the fort walls and roofed with beams or corbelled brackets. **Bhima's Gateway**, one of the best preserved arches from this series, has beautiful ornamented corbels. An alternative design seems typically Islamic, with four archways raised high to form a dome. The gateways were fronted with courtyards enclosed by thick walls. All traffic passing through to the city was monitored here.

Hemakuta Hill

To the southern side of the village of Hampi, in the sacred centre, are the temples on Hemakuta Hill. These temples predate the Vijayanagara empire, and it is thought that they are from the 9th and 10th centuries. This was the first seat of power of the Vijayanagara kings, who built the later fortifications. These are constructed in the medieval Deccan style, using granite as the main material. This style is distinguished by unembellished exteriors, towers resembling stepped pyramids and terraces with gallery seating. Two or three temples were grouped together. Legends inscribed on the temples indicate that these shrines were dedicated to the god Siva.

The Virupaksa Temple

Pampa, a goddess symbolising the Tungabhadra river, and her consort Virupaksa, also known as Pampapati (another aspect of Siva), were the original divinities of the area, well before the establishment of the Vijayanagara empire. They appear to have postdated the empire as well as predated it, because the **Virupaksa Temple** Ⓐ is the only shrine at Hampi still to be used as a place of worship. An annual festival is held here to commemorate the marriage of Virupaksa and Pampa which attracts several thousands of pilgrims from all over the country.

The structure of the complex attests to its growth over the centuries, with ancient Chalukya and Hoysala shrines forming

BELOW: the Virupaksa Temple.

Map on page 266

the heart of the layout, and later additions forming the periphery. There are two main courtyards here, both accessible through towered gateways, one of which is over 50 metres (160 ft) high. The hall leading up to the principal sanctuary has finely detailed columns with carvings of animals, while the ceiling is painted with the legends of Siva. A colonnaded street leads out of this temple, which ends in a badly damaged monolith of Nandi.

Towards the south are two granite boulders carved with images of Ganesha, the elephant-headed god. One of these is enclosed in a temple with very tall columns while the other stands within an open hall. Further south is the notable Narasimha sculpture that has been carved out of a single boulder. There is a monolithic *lingam* in a chamber to the north.

The Krisna Temples

Krisnadeva Raya is said to have worshipped at the assembly of **Krisna shrines**. They date back to 1513 with the installation of a Balakrisna (the infant Krisna) image. The 16th-century standard layout has been followed here, with the sanctum sanctorum surrounded by colonnades and set within a large enclosure. There is an unusual Islamic-style granary in the south court. Yet another feature of interest is the plaster figures which feature along the east gateway.

Climb up **Matanga Hill** **B** for an imposing panoramic view of the city of Hampi. It is named after a sage who is believed to have protected the monkey gods Sugriva and Hanuman. However, in spite of these associations with the *Ramayana*, the temple on the hill is dedicated to a fierce aspect of Siva. (In the epic, Hampi is mentioned as Kiskindha, the domain of the monkey chiefs with whom Rama planned the crusade to rescue Sita from the demon king Ravana.) Immediately beneath the hill, on the south bank of the river, is the Kodandarama temple, dedicated to Rama and still popular with followers.

The Tiruvengalanatha Temples

The **Tiruvengalanatha temples** are set within a double-walled enclosure with two sets of towered gateways. Erotic sculptures decorate the columns within the open halls near the main gateway. Unfortunately the temples which make up the central part of this complex have been badly damaged and the original chariot pathway leading out of the temple is now a field for paddy cultivation.

Close to the temple complex is a site overlooking the river, where a crevice between two colossal rocks is believed to be the cave where Sugriva hid Sita's jewellery after she was kidnapped by Ravana.

The famous 16th-century South Indian musician Purandaradasa, whose works are performed even today, is associated with a columned hall on the river bank. You will see the stone pylons of a bridge that once connected the two banks of the river Tungabhadra.

The Vittala Temple Complex

Experts consider the **Vittala complex** **C** to be among the finest examples of existing sculpture from the Vijayanagara pe-

RIGHT: the Lotus Mahal.

riod. The Vittala temple has been designated a World Heritage Monument by UNESCO. Dated to the 16th century, this exquisite group of temples stands within the main courtyard. Built on a low elevation, the temples form an elegant pattern, while the tower is constructed out of brick and plaster. The hall in front has superb carvings of animals, while the detached columns are carved out of a single slab of granite. Some of the pillars, which give a ringing tone when tapped, are said to be tuned to the Indian *svaras* (musical notes). The brackets are intricately carved and support beams of immense spans. The ceiling is sumptuously carved with floral and geometric designs. To the east of this hall is the famous **stone chariot** of Hampi, styled as a miniature shrine. Close by is another columned hall with intricately carved sculptures which was probably used on ceremonial occasions.

Along a path by the river is an interesting structure known as the **King's Balance**. In the past ruling kings were weighed against grain, gold or money for distribution to the poor, usually on their birthdays.

The Ragunatha Temple

Malyavanta hill Ⓓ, associated with the Ramayana epic, is a shrine dedicated to Rama, Sita and Laksmana. Two shrines and a colonnaded hall are set within high walls entered through gateways that blend into the granite outcrop. Images of the deities are carved on a large boulder inside the temple that also projects through the roof, forming a sort of natural tower. As well as the Vaisnaivite temples there are also several Saivite shrines here. Behind the Ragunatha temple are two rows of *lingams* and Nandis cut into the rock face of a natural crevice.

The Royal Enclosure

The **Hazara Rama** Ⓔ, also known as the Ramachandra temple, was the state temple for the ruler and is situated significantly between the royal court and

BELOW: the Vittala Temple and stone chariot.

Map on page 266

residence. It dates from the early 15th century and is finely detailed. Within the central hall are superbly carved basalt pillars that display the various incarnations of Visnu. There are three rows of sculptures around the exterior walls that vividly tell the story of the *Ramayana*. There are two gateways outside with continuous friezes on the outside walls of the enclosure. They depict elephants, dancing girls, soldiers and horses which were probably the kind of images viewed by royalty during ceremonial worship.

Remains of civic buildings, the basement of a huge 100-column hall which might have served as a hall of justice, stepped stone platforms from which the king might have viewed the *Mahanavami* festival and other structures probably linked with the religious rituals and administrative functions of the court can be seen here. The state treasury is believed to have been situated here. Several wells, aqueducts and tanks with stepped stone sides have been discovered here, leading to the conclusion that the royal bath was an important ceremony. The **queen's bath** is located here, built in the Islamic style, a square water basin surrounded by a vaulted corridor. Beautiful filigreed balconies are cantilevered over the water.

Close to the Ramachandra temple is the *zenana* or women's quarters. A variety of Islamic inspired structures stand here, the most famous of which is the **Lotus Mahal**. This is thought to best represent the Vijayanagara courtly style which was a skilful blend of Hindu and Islamic architectural forms. Eastward of this enclosure are the famous **elephant stables**, a row of 10 chambers with high vaulted entrances in different styles centralised around a two-storey pavilion. A nearby arena might have been the site of military and athletic tournaments.

Recent excavations, which show that this was the area where large palaces once stood, are of particular interest as they fill in the gaps in the history of Indian architecture. Only stone basements, plaster floors and rubble walls now remain. Many Islamic-style gazebos and watchtowers are to be seen in this area.

There is also a Virupaksa temple, very similar to the one at Hampi, which was probably a private shrine for royalty. After the sack of Hampi, this temple was almost buried and has been wrongly assumed to have been underground, whereas recent excavations show that it was definitely within the precincts of the royal residence.

Anegonda

Across the Tungabhadra from Talarighat is the village of **Anegonda**. A bridge is soon to connect the two sides of the river *(see page 267)*, but the more traditional way to cross is by one of the coracles paddled by local villagers.

The small settlement predates the Hampi site, and was used after the sack of the city as the seat of the local ruler. In the village is a 17th-century palace and the bathing ghats, but about 1 km (½ mile) to the west are the impressive Vijayanagara fortifications. The large walls and gates surround a ruined complex of military buildings. ❑

RIGHT: the pillared dance *mandapam* of the Hazara Rama.

Map on page 244

THE NORTHERN DECCAN

Northern Karnataka has some superb Muslim buildings and is also home to the "cradle of Indian temple architecture" at Badami, Aihole and Pattadakal

Beyond the Western Ghats is the northern plateau, where the Malaprabha, the Ghataprabha, the Krishna and the Doni rivers vein the boulder-spiked landscape as they make their way to the east. This is where the early Islamic empires of Karnataka established themselves, creating in the span of their existence the superb examples of Deccani architecture that command such universal regard. These are the great buildings whose design came from the cultured synthesis of the Delhi and the Persian schools of Islamic architecture. The Islamic approach brought innovations: the use of the arch, the employment of mortar. Muslim mathematical and scientific building formulae were often applied by Hindu craftsmen, which resulted in more flexible interpretations of the original Persian traditions, no less memorable for being responsive to local inspiration. In fact, what happened sometimes, as in the case of the Karim-al-Din Mosque in Bijapur, was that old temple pillars were reused.

Belgaum

Like so many other South Indian towns before post-Independence industrialisation altered their profiles and demographics, **Belgaum** ⓬ had two main areas. There was the old quarter where the cotton and silk weavers still live, and the British-built spacious, tree-lined cantonment, the other main section of the city.

Belgaum's history followed much the same pattern as other towns of the region, submitting as a matter of course to different Hindu and Muslim rulers and then to the British. The reminders of dominion are few and scattered; the **fort** near the heart of the city where Mahatma Gandhi was incarcerated and the **Masjid-Sata** mosque are worth visiting, as are the two **Jain temples** and a **watchtower** with a view which has not yet been obscured by the fast-changing skyline. Local history celebrates the story of Rani Chennamma of Kittur, a nearby village. She was one of India's first freedom fighters, a ruler whose resolute opposition to British domination made her a heroine, still commemorated locally in song and story.

When the ruler of Kittur died, leaving the Rani childless, she sought to nominate a nephew to the throne. The British collector Thackeray (a relative of the 19th-century author), who had his eye on this wealthy principality, used this as an excuse to march on the fort. This was a mistake: the Rani and her troops held the British off; Thackeray was shot dead and his head impaled on a spear and paraded in triumphant procession.

LEFT: Durga defeating Mahisasura, Aihole. **RIGHT:** a Karnatakan smile.

Determined more than ever to get their hands on the fort and, more importantly, its treasury, and goaded by their recent defeat, the British attacked again, led by Sir Walter Elliot. This time they won and the Rani was taken prisoner. She lived the rest of her life in captivity, dying five years later at the age of 50.

Bijapur

The story of the Adil Shahi dynasty began in the 15th century with the death of the Sultan of Istanbul. It was a time when one male heir in each generation was deemed sufficient. The Sultan's widow, knowing this full well, had the second son Yusuf spirited away out of his brother's reach, and the young boy's long journey brought him to India. He was 17 years old, resourceful and adventurous. Sold to a minister in the powerful Bahmani kingdom, Yusuf rose above his circumstances to become the Adil Khan, the Governor of Bijapur, a Bahmani territory in the northwest of Karnataka.

The Bahmani dynasty was in decline, and in 1489 Yusuf asserted his independence of it to pronounce himself Adil Shah. For the next two centuries, the Adil Shahis reigned from **Bijapur ⓭**, a succession of rulers whose legacy was the architectural tradition that inspired so many generations of master builders, its influence unmistakeable too in the Indo-Saracenic style of the Raj.

Yusuf Adil Shah set about fortifying Bijapur with a wall 10 km (7 miles) in circumference, one that still stands in good repair, with its expansive moat and crenellated battlements. You can see how commanding its reach was over the arid, arduous environs, and how well the great ordnances must have guarded the approaches. On a bastion named for its ornamental stone lions is the **Malik-e-Maidan**, "the Lord of the Plains", reputedly the largest medieval cannon in the world. Ten elephants, 400 oxen and much manpower were needed to draw it all the way from Maharashtra. It is shaped like a lion's jaws and throat devouring ele-

Map on page 244

phants. A small tank of water would be nearby so gunners could immerse their heads and spare their eardrums when the gun was fired. In reassuring contrast is the legend which holds that if you touch the gun and make a wish, it will come true.

While the remnants of armaments and fortifications confirm dynastic prowess, the city of Bijapur affords proof (very little of it in perfect repair) that Deccani architecture was an elegant art under the Adil Shahis. You could spend days wandering around these buildings, over 30 in number, their austere silhouettes detailed with the precise mathematics of the Islamic style. The most distinguished of these are the Gol Gumbaz, the Ibrahim Rauza, the Jami Masjid, the Anand Mahal and the Mehtar Mahal.

The Gol Gumbaz

If is fitting that the dynasty's last principal structure should be a mausoleum, and it is equally appropriate that it is the most visible. The massive rotundity of the **Gol Gumbaz** (open 6.30am–5.30pm, entrance charge) dominates the eastern skyline near the station, the first silhouette the rail-borne traveller sees. In 1626 its builder, Muhammad Adil Shah, inherited from his father a kingdom with such factional instability that, perhaps presciently, he devoted much time and resources to building his own mausoleum. It is surmounted by a dome built in 1659 that is second to none but St Peter's in Rome, being a mere 5 metres (16 ft) smaller in diameter. It rests on intersecting pendentive arches over an enormous square hall, the largest floor space in the world covered by a single dome.

Four octagonal towers buttress the structure, each seven storeys tall and with its own small dome. They open on top onto the Whispering Gallery that runs round the inside of the central dome, all but invisible from below. Its acoustics are incredible: no matter how hushed the voice, the sound will echo, on and on. Entombed below with Muhammad Adil Shal in conjugal impartiality are his wife and his favourite courtesan.

LEFT: a prayer wall, part of the Muslim legacy on the Deccan. **BELOW:** the Ibrahim Rauza, Bijapur.

Across the town to the west is the **Ibrahim Rauza**, built by Ibrahim II, the sixth ruler of the dynasty who ascended the throne in 1580. He built it for his wife, though he died before her and is buried here too. With its enclosed garden containing a mosque, it provoked much emulation and envy: the architects of the Taj Mahal studied it before embarking upon their own task, and the Gol Gumbaz was another attempt to surpass it. Adjectives are rendered superfluous by an inscription on a wall which says, "Heaven stood astonished. When [the Ibrahim Rauza] rose from the earth, another paradise was created. Its every column is as graceful as the cypress tree in the Garden of Purity." Within the citadel Ibrahim II also built the **Anand Mahal**, the Palace of Joy, and the **Taj Baori** in the *zenana*, the ladies' quarter, named for his wife Taj Sultana.

The **Mehtar Mahal**, to the east of the citadel, is not a palace as its name would lead you to expect. According to one source, it was built for the sweepers of the regal household. The relief work around the doorways, on the balconies and the ceilings, proclaims a pride in workmanship that was as much the patron's as it was the artisan's.

The years after Yusuf's reign were tumultuous. When Ali Shah (Ibrahim II's predecessor and uncle) came to rule in 1557, he achieved a stability of sorts only after defeating the Vijayanagara empire in 1565 in alliance with three other splinter states from the erstwhile Bahmani kingdom. In thanks for his victory, he began to build the **Jama Masjid**, a mosque whose magnificent proportions are balanced by its understated ornamentation, the exception being the *mihrab* festooned with gold-leaf calligraphy, and stunning niches with *trompe l'oeil* books, censers and floral arrangements.

The comparative tranquillity of Ali Shah's reign also afforded him the time to build himself an enormous durbar, the **Gagan Mahal** or Sky Palace, and the **Mecca Masjid**, a miniature mosque for the women of the court, both within the

fortress walls. He also strengthened the city's defences and implemented its waterworks, the latter a far more important undertaking in that parched area.

In 1686, the Adil Shahi empire succumbed after an 18-month siege by the Mughals, the last in the series of assailants the dynasty had had to fend off throughout its life. With no food or ammunition and his forces decimated, the 19-year-old Sikander, the last of the Adil Shahis, opened the citadel gates to Aurangzeb.

Gulbarga

Gulbarga ⓮ features the burial place of a Muslim saint, and a temple dedicated to a Hindu savant, both of them scholars whose humanity attracted thousands of adherents to their philosophy. Khvaja Bande Navaz was from Delhi, a disciple of the religious teacher Hazrat Khvaja Pir Nasiruddin Mahmud Chirag. Fleeing from orthodox persecution in the north, he was invited to Gulbarga by the Bahmanis, the royal house that ruled the Deccan from the 13th to the 15th century. Scholastic deliberation was encouraged at their court, and respected astronomers and mathematicians taught at the schools and colleges these rulers started. The state coffers paid teachers' salaries and students' stipends, and Sultan Muhammad Shah II himself delivered regular lectures following a timetable that allotted particular days for logic, mathematics and rhetoric. Unlike his predecessors and successors, he could afford to do this since his 19-year reign was the most peaceful, as well as the longest.

Muhammad II spoke fluent Arabic and Persian, apart from Dakhni (Deccan) Urdu, the language of the new Islamic aristocracy of the South. Arabic came to India through commercial trade between its west coast and the Middle East and the founder of the empire claimed Persian ancestry in the more nebulous reaches of his family tree.

Like Khvaja Bande Navaz, Persian scholars flocked to the Bahmani court, disarmed perhaps by a ruler like Muhammad II with his intellectual attainments and

LEFT: the Gol Gumbaz. **BELOW:** the great mosque at Gulbarga.

inclination to teach. The saint-scholar lived in Gulbarga for over 20 years, and among the 100 or more books he wrote are the first essays in the new Dakhni Urdu. His belief in peace and brotherhood drew thousands of followers; today, on the *urs*, his annual feast, many flock to his brocade-bedecked tomb on the eastern side of Gulbarga. In the adjacent mosque is a venerable library of works in all the three languages this devout man had mastered. Today it is the temple cart procession in April from the temple dedicated to Basavesvara that attracts 100,000 pilgrims to its precincts near the Gulbarga Tank. The philosopher's name endows several colleges, and in this city the teaching of medicine and history, of the sciences and the arts continues.

The most majestic place of learning was the **Madrasa** in the nearby town of **Bidar**, where the Bahmani kingdom shifted in 1428. Though ravaged, the architectural and decorative details of its ruins are sufficient to explain why the architectural historian Percy Brown wrote that it "might have been bodily moved from Samarkhand". Founded by the Persian Muhammad Gavan, a minister at the Bahmani court, the original institution contained lecture halls, a library and a mosque, and dormitories and rooms for at least 300 students of Islamic theology and the arts. It rises within the 15th-century sandstone fort, strategically placed to monopolise the landscape. In its precincts activity bustles around the new buildings juxtaposed chock-a-block with charmingly timeworn *mahals* and mosques.

Enter its sprawling fort to see the **Jama Masjid**, a superb 14th-century mosque designed by a Moorish architect. His references are obvious: the 3,420 sq. m (38,000 sq. ft) building is based on the mosque in Córdoba. What is remarkable is that the roof spans the entire courtyard, something never before accomplished in South Asian Muslim architecture. Dome after dome crowns the prayer hall, and arched columns are so placed that the pulpit is seen from every angle, and the

BELOW: the ruins of Bidar, one of the Deccani Sultanates.

Map on page 244

acoustics so keen that everything said from it is just as easily heard.

The cradle of temple architecture

The rocks from which the temples of Badami, Aihole and Pattadakal have been hewn are part of the oldest land formation on earth, the Gondwana Plate. The lava from volcanoes cooled into rock formations which geologists say are a thousand million years old. Along the Malaprabha river on the northern Karnataka plateau, the land is red sandstone, planed and contoured into cliffs and gorges. Five kilometres (3 miles) from its banks is the town of Badami, earlier known in Sanskrit as Vatapi. Just as Mysore derived its name from the demon Mahisasura, Badami is named after the demon Vatapi who met his end when he was eaten by a ravenous sage. Eight kilometres (5 miles) from Badami is Pattadakal, and about 13 km (8 miles) down the river Aihole – three towns whose stone temples stand testimony to the great architectural heritage of the Chalukya dynasty.

Like many dynasties, the Chalukyas had a mythological explanation for their name and origin, recounted by Bilhana, the court poet of Vikramaditya, the fifth Chalukyan emperor. The god Indra once came to Brahma in supplication, while he was at his morning devotions. The world, he said, had become so wicked that there was no man left to make offerings to the gods or perform any of the Brahmanical sacrifices. Could Brahma not create a godlike being, righteous and valorous enough to rid the world of its sinfulness? In response, Brahma caused a valiant warrior to spring forth from the cupped hollow of his palm, a *chaluka* – a man endowed with the power to protect the three worlds – and it is to him that the Chalukyas traced their ancestry.

The extent of the Chalukyan empire originally defined the area of Karnataka. Their name was known throughout India: some authorities say that a cave painting at Ajanta testifies to their being known as far away as Persia. The Chalukyan predominance spanned two centuries, from about AD 547 to 753. According to the Chinese traveller Hieun Tsang, who visited Karnataka in AD 641 during the reign of Pulakesin II, the Chalukyas were a proud and martial race. A ten-line poem lauding their valour is inscribed on a large boulder near the nearby village of Tattukute. Hieun Tsang also observed that the great Chalukyan commanders and their warriors went into battle well intoxicated, with their elephant-mounts similarly primed for combat. The penalty of defeat was to be made to wear women's clothing, a dishonour deemed worse than death.

On the whole, the Chalukyas were enlightened, tolerant and actively concerned with their subjects' welfare. Prolific builders, they oversaw a major transition in medieval religious architecture – the shift from brick and wood construction to stone and rock. Though Badami, Pattadakal and Aihole bear the mark of empires and rulers who came after the Chalukyas, from the Rastrakutas who ousted them up to the Marathas of

RIGHT: a carved pillar, Pattadakal.

the 15th century, it was the Chalukyan accomplishments in excavated and structural temple architecture that gave these monuments their identity. The first ruler, Pulakesin I, proclaimed his supremacy over the region with an Asvamedha – the traditional rite of sending forth a riderless horse arrayed in royal colours and insignia, to roam where it wished; those who let it wander unchallenged through their territory were presumed to have acknowledged its master's sovereignty. He then set about building fortifications and excavating the rock-cut temples.

Badami cave temples

The cliffs of **Badami** ⓯ (open sunrise–sunset, entrance charge) have four rock-cut **temples**, three Hindu and one Jain. The former follow a plan which influenced the design of many structural temples built in Karnataka. A flight of steps leads up to a pillared verandah, behind which is a hall, with the *garbha griha* carved into the back wall. The exteriors of the temples are unadorned, save perhaps for a row of figures along the plinth beneath the verandah. Inside, figures from religion and myth, carved in relief, cover walls, pillars and ceiling. The felicity of execution captures in stone live movement with all its energy and grace.

The largest and most ornamental is **Cave No. 3**, dedicated to Visnu, with an inscription that testifies to its excavation by Pulakesin I's second son, Mangalesa, for his older brother who ruled before him. The verandah at the top of the steps has at one end a four-armed figure of Visnu, seated on the Ananth Naga, the serpent whose five hoods spread protectively over his crown. At his feet is the bird Garuda, his mount. This is the Vaisnavite avatar of Chaturbhuj. Another incarnation shows him as the cosmic boar, Varaha, four-armed also, a lotus in one of his hands bearing the earth goddess Prithvi, "relaxed in charming and complete resignation", as the art historian Zimmer described it in *The Art of India and Asia*. At the veran-

Map on page 244

dah's other end is Visnu in his avatar of the eight-armed dwarf Vamana. Barely discernible on the ceilings are what are probably Karnataka's first Hindu paintings, now very faint. The other caves are smaller, though equally arresting: the transition from daylight to near-darkness as you enter is dramatic, as the wealth of sculpted imagery becomes perceptible through the gloom. The Jain temple on top of a cliff is more modest than the rest, merely an early essay in rock architecture.

The structural temples at Badami represent the second developmental stage of Chalukyan architecture after Aihole. The **Malegitti Sivalaya** on the northern hill and **Mahakutesvara temple** at Mahakuta 5 km (3 miles) away are in the Dravidian style, while those at Aihole and Pattadakal are an amalgam of the Dravidian and North Indian Nagara styles. To the east, more structural temples fringe the **Agastyathirtha tank**, believed to have curative powers. In the monsoon, water plunges from a rocky ledge into the tank named for the sage Agastya Muni who once meditated by a sacred pool on the cliffs above and was revered for curing a king's leprosy. The man-made lake is also called Bhuthanath after Siva, Lord of the Spirits. His appropriately forbidding visage regards the worshipper from within the confines of the temples' inner sanctums. Stylistically they are distinguished by towers and finials derived from the technique of the antecedent Kadamba empire. There is an historical fort at Badami 5 km (8 miles) from the railway station. The fort enclosure consists of granaries, a treasury, watchtower and temples.

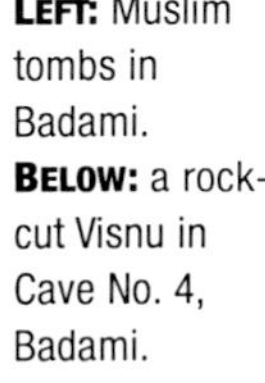

LEFT: Muslim tombs in Badami. **BELOW:** a rock-cut Visnu in Cave No. 4, Badami.

Aihole

An attractive village on the banks of the Malaprabha River, **Aihole** ⓰ (open sunrise–sunset, entrance charge) is referred to as the "cradle of Indian temple architecture". There are over 100 temples scattered around the village, their silhouettes and layouts anticipating the complexity of the later constructions at Belur and Halebid. Culled from contemporary northern and southern styles, the temples nonetheless exhibit the hallmarks of the Chalukyan style – its lavish doorframes and plinth mouldings, octagonal finials and roofs.

The **Lad Khan temple** is possibly the earliest, having been built in the 5th century. Its name comes from a Muslim noble who once inhabited it. Originally used for royal weddings and assemblies, it is a low, flat-roofed building with a porch on its eastern side. The river goddesses Ganga and Yamuna, popular icons of the 4th-century Gupta dynasty, flank the entrance. Over the cella at the back is a square, flat-roofed superstructure, in effect forming a two-storey sanctum. The roof itself echoes the earlier wooden structures, though the influence of its jointing technique of grooved stone slabs can be seen in subsequent Chalukyan design.

The **Durga temple** exemplifies another stage of architectural development. Sculpturally resplendent, it is notable for its semicircular apse, elevated plinth and the gallery that encircles the sanctum. However, its *shikhara* or roof, again in the northern Nagara style, seems to have been an architectural afterthought. It was not named after the goddess Durga, as is often thought, but because of its proximity to the fort (*durg*) wall. The interior abounds with images of Siva and also of Chamundi, the patron goddess of Mysore, in the process of dispatching the buffalo-headed demon.

The sculpture of Visnu on top of a large cobra in the **Hutchimalli temple** depicts him seated in a posture much like that of the Chalukyan kings. The structural innovation in this temple is the vestibule (*antarala*) that connects the *garbha griha* and the main congregational hall.

The **Ravalphadi cave** is Aihole's only excavated temple, again dedicated to Siva. Though similar in layout to the Badami caves, the representations of Visnu and Siva (such as the depiction of Ardhanarisvara, the dual aspect of Siva and his

BELOW: the Ravalphadi temple, Aihole.

Map on page 244

consort Parvati) are somewhat more delicately detailed.

Compared with the voluptuousness of Hindu temple craft, the two Jain and Buddhist temples of Aihole are ascetic. The roof still standing over the remains of the austere **Megutti** (or hilltop) **Jain temple** covers the sanctum within which Mahavira sits. The temple affords a view of the sleepy village below. A little way down is the Buddhist temple, its desolation highlighted by bats that occasionally swarm into flight under a ceiling carved with the image of the Enlightened One.

Pattadakal

Pattadakal ⓱ (open sunrise–sunset, entrance charge) was the last Chalukyan capital before the empire was supplanted by the Rashtrakutas, a feudatory family that rose to become the next major dynasty. It is where the Chalukyan kings were crowned, and the temples they built here express the complete maturity of their craft. Temples are found clustered at the foothills, built in both the Dravidian and the Nagara manner, with the Virupaksha, Mallikarjuna, Sangamesvara and Galaganatha temples in the former style.

In front of the **Virupaksa temple** is an independent Nandi *mandapa*, carved from green stone. The temple itself was built in AD 740 by Queen Lokamahadevi, its *vimana* (the tower over the sanctum) an eminent example of Dravidian design. The building's plain and fine proportions indicate just how much the discipline had progressed from the constructions at Badami. Sculpture narrating epic and myth has been employed here to lavish effect.

The earliest in the Nagara group is the **Papanatha temple**, though much of the Dravidian influence is discernible in its elevations. Two axial halls precede the *garbha griha*, the first with an open porch for the congregation, and the second an *antarala* controlling access to the sanctum.

The cumulative impact of these myriad forms and details can be overwhelming. The Hindus saw the temple as a metaphor for the human body: the tower symbolising the head, the sides the arms, the pillars the legs and the sanctum the womb. Associations of daily routine add resonance to the significance of handed-down legend. For instance, on the way between Pattadakal and Badami is **Mahakuta** where the devout come to wash away their sins in the Kashi Tirtha spring.

Outside the temple at nearby **Banasankari**, named after the local goddess, is the hallowed tank into which she was transformed. Inside the temple, her eight-armed form, borne by a gold lion with jaws ferociously open, confronts her devotees with a compelling stare.

Pulakesin I built the **fort** on the hill overlooking Badami, using not merely the location to advantage but also the huge boulders that lay around. This building material was pliable enough to work upon but strong enough to provide durable shelter, not merely for their builders but also for the objects of their veneration. It must have been formidable, back-breaking work; it certainly would have been a lot easier to have them built on the plains, though posterity would have been the poorer for it. ❑

RIGHT: conversing in the mosque.

ANDHRA PRADESH

Andhra is fantastically diverse, from Hyderabad, a bastion of Muslim culture, to Hindu temples and early Buddhist sites

The northernmost state of South India, Andhra Pradesh is the largest of the four states with an area of 275,600 sq km (106,000 sq miles) and a population of 76.2 million. The official language is Telugu, though Urdu is widely spoken in the capital, Hyderabad, and in the neighbouring Telengana district. Andhra Pradesh was formed by amalgamating the princely state of Hyderabad with the Telugu-speaking parts of the Madras Presidency.

Geographically it consists of the semi-arid Deccan plateau and fertile coastal plains irrigated by the Krishna and Godavari rivers. Andhra Pradesh has considerable topographical variations, with dense forests in the northeast, flat paddy lands in the coastal plains, several noteworthy beaches along the Bay of Bengal (particularly Bhimunipatnam near Waltair) and the stark boulder-strewn region around Hyderabad relieved only by several man-made lakes. The main crops of the state are paddy, millets, sugar cane and tobacco.

Andhra Pradesh has absorbed all the vital elements of India's past. It is historically linked with India's neighbours: from its ports Indian culture spread to Sri Lanka, Indonesia, Cambodia and Thailand. Buddhism, brought here by the Mauryan emperor Asoka's missionaries, took root under the Sathavahanas around the beginning of the first millennium AD and inspired some of its finest artistic expression. Under them, and later the Pallavas, the Chalukyas and the Kakatiyas, Andhra made important contributions to the classical Indian repertory of sculpture, architecture, Hindu law, music and dance. The era of the Bahmanis and the Qutb Shahi Sultans brought about a flowering of Indo-Islamic architecture, miniature painting and the Urdu language.

Traces of this rich heritage remain, at the Buddhist sites of Amaravati and Nagarjunakonda, in the early Chalukyan temples at Alampur, at the Kalinga capital of Mukhalingam, and in the temples of the Vengi Chalukyans at Draksharama and Bikkavolu. These and the Kakatiya edifices in the north of the state, the Vijayanagara in the south, and the Qutb Shahi architecture around Hyderabad, all flourished in the varied terrain of Andhra.

PRECEDING PAGES: a clear line to Visakhapatnam.
LEFT: a Lambadi woman, Hyderabad.

Maps:
Area 302
City 290

HYDERABAD

This city is one of the great centres of Indian Muslim culture, with the iconic Charminar, wonderful mosques, palaces and bazaars, and the superb fort at Golconda

Hyderabad ❶, the capital of Andhra Pradesh, is the creation of the Qutb Shahis. In 1512 Sultan Quli, powerful feudatory of a weak king, followed the example of his neighbours and took over the territory he governed. The Qutb Shahis were patrons of art and literature, and fostered the culture and language known as Dakhni – the culture a synthesis of Indo-Persian and South Indian elements, the language a forerunner of Urdu. The Deccan again became the great trading centre it had been since Roman times, when Pliny complained that India was draining Rome of gold. Kunasamudram steel, diamonds, beautiful painted cloths, glimmering gold brocades and fine muslins were exchanged for gold, silver, horses, spices, silk and wine.

The Qutb Shahis were of Turkoman origin. There were seven rulers of the line. Their greatest rulers are said to have been Ibrahim Quli and Mohammad Quli. In 1687 they were conquered by Aurangzeb, and the last of the Qutb Shahis, Abul Hasan Tana Shah, died in Aurangzeb's prison. The rule of the Asaf Jahis which followed saw the gradual increase of British influence. In return for his help in their wars with Tippu Sultan the British conferred the title "Our Faithful Ally" on the Nizam of Hyderabad. In the 19th century a determined effort was made to curb this influence, and Hyderabad managed to remain in control of its own affairs until it became part of independent India in 1947.

In the reorganisation of the states, prompted by Telugu activists for a linguistic division of the South, part of the Nizam's dominions were merged with neighbouring states, and part, with the addition of some coastal districts and Rayalseema, became what is now Andhra Pradesh. In recent years, under the direction of the controversial ex-Chief Minister Chandrababu Naidu of the TDP, the city has gained a reputation for promoting neoliberal economics and also for selling itself as an IT centre, the latter giving rise to the nickname "Cyberabad". Whilst there have been high levels of investment in the city – to the detriment of the rest of the overwhelmingly rural state – this has been targeted at a very small population. The city has a large number of urban poor, particularly in the old Muslim areas, and these disparities in wealth occasionally lead to communal and social unrest.

The Qutb Shahi legacy

The architecture of the Qutb Shahis is a form of the Deccan style, which is derived from the Pathan with Persian and Hindu influences. Early Deccan architecture can

LEFT: the Charminar. **RIGHT:** perfumes for sale in the bazaar.

be seen at Gulbarga, and later developments with regional variations throughout the Deccan Sultanates. The characteristics of this distinctive regional style are lofty proportions, bulbous domes of relatively smaller volume not covering the whole roof, prominent minarets and pointed arches. It is based on sound building principles and a high level of technical skill and often faced with cut plaster decoration and brilliant encaustic tiles, a style in which provincial charm wins over classical severity.

In 1589 Mohammad Quli laid out a new city 10 km (6 miles) from Golconda, on the east bank of the river Musi. Crossing the river had been made easier by the construction, 11 years before, of the **Purana Pul**, which in 1645 the French traveller Tavernier compared to the contemporary Pont Neuf in Paris. The **Charminar** Ⓐ is the hub of Mohammad Quli's city and the masterpiece of Qutb Shahi architecture.

The monument is built of stone with stucco plastering and decoration, square in plan, each side measuring 30 metres (100 ft). Each face is pierced with a large pointed arch with a string course, a lotus bud above the point, and decorative medallions on each side. At the corners is a row of vertical arches, and above it a prominent cornice supported on brackets and carried around the minarets above a lotus-petal capital. The upper storey of the main square consists of a row of arches and capitals matching in height the first double-storey gallery of the minarets. Above this is a prominent decorated band, also supported on brackets, and again extended round the minarets. Then comes a screen with smaller arched openings, and another screen which stylistically seems to be of a later date.

The minarets rise to a height of 55 metres (180 ft) from the ground. There are two more single-storey galleries after the first. The two lower sections are polygonal, the next plain and the last arched, each section smaller in diameter than the one before. They are topped with domed finials rising out of lotus-petal bases. Inside the central part, there are shallow arched alcoves in the

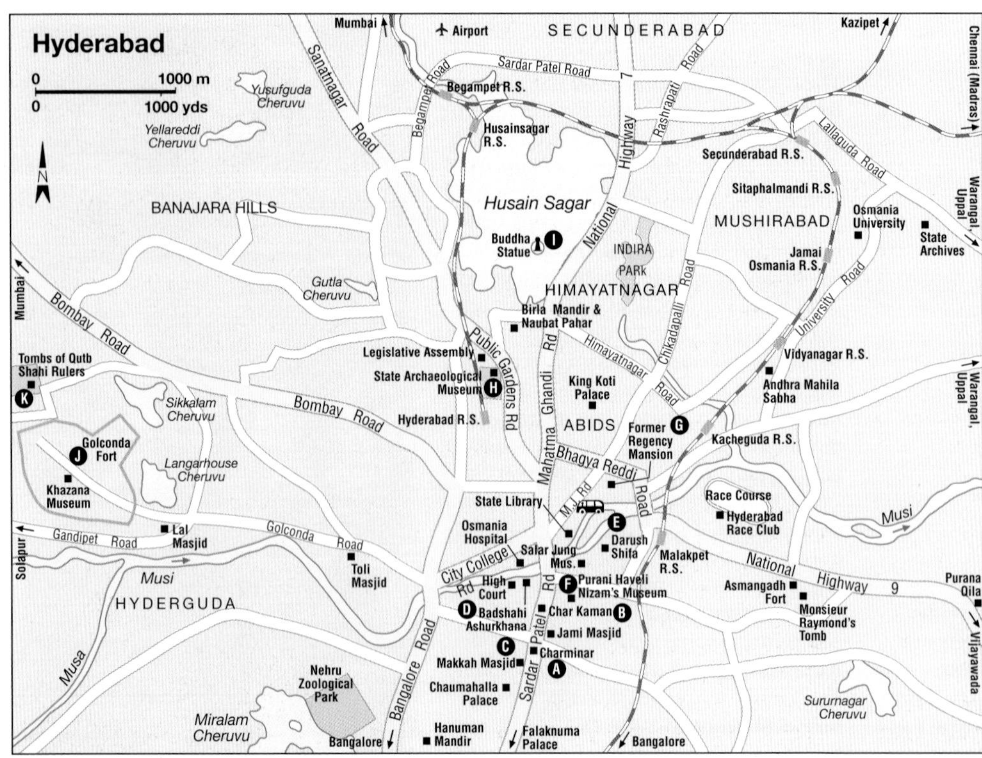

Map on page 290

thickness of the large arches, a balcony at first-floor level, and representations of Shia *alams* (battle standards) in cut plaster.

The whole is of graceful proportion and fine workmanship. It was built in 1591, two years after the foundation of the city. De Thevenot, who visited Hyderabad 65 years after it was built, said, "Nothing in this town seems so lovely as the outside of that building, and nevertheless it is surrounded with ugly shops made of wood, and covered with straw, where they sell fruit, which spoils the aspect of it."

Part of the upper floor housed a school, and part a beautiful mosque. Unfortunately, access to the upper floor is not allowed. There are various legends about the Charminar's origin and purpose: that it was built to celebrate deliverance of the city from plague, or that it was meant to be in the form of a religious symbol.

The bazaars

About 65 metres (225 ft) north of the Charminar are the four huge arches, the **Char Kaman** Ⓑ, between which the royal guards were stationed by the Qutb Shahis. If you go through the western arch, known as Mitti-ka-Sher – a corruption of Sihir-i-Batil (Land of Dreams) – you'll find shops selling old *saris* and brocades. This whole area up to the river is where the Qutb Shahi palaces used to be; inside the Sihir-i-Batil was another gateway with doors of ebony and sandalwood studded with gold.

The streets in this area are lined with shops selling gold and silver, pearls, paper kites, rough glasses and cheap chinaware. Near the little wayside shrine guarded by a plaster tiger is the entrance to a square of silversmiths and jewellers where you can buy old silver jewellery. **Lad Bazar**, a narrow street, is the traditional centre for bridal accessories and bangles, and leads to the **Chowk**, traditional hunting ground for antiques. The **Jami Masjid**, close to the Charminar, is the oldest mosque in Hyderabad. It was built in 1597 and is pleasingly simple and free from decoration. There is a fine chronogram over the entrance, and the prayer-hall facade is interesting.

The **Makkah Masjid** Ⓒ close by is the largest mosque in South India. It is built of stone with two domes. Fifteen arches in three bays support the roof, and the prayer niche is carved out of a single slab of granite. It was completed by Aurangzeb, and Hyderabadis like to say that it is because of his parsimony that the minars are so short. The Asaf Jahis are buried here. Musa Khan, supervisor during Abdullah Qutb Shah's reign of the long-drawn-out building of the Makkah Masjid, levied a *damri* for every rupee spent, and with this built the beautiful **Toli Masjid** on the Karwan, the old high road between Purana Pul and Golconda.

Of the other Qutb Shahi buildings near the Charminar, the **Badshahi Ashurkhana** Ⓓ and the **Darush Shifa** are the most interesting. The first, which houses the religious symbols of the Shias, still has its original encaustic tile decoration in the earlier parts of the building, the central niche and the western wall. These tiles with their beautiful calligraphy and geometric designs remind one of what the facades of other Qutb Shahi buildings must have looked like in their original state.

RIGHT: selling bangles near the Charminar.

The **Darush Shifa** Ⓔ (1595) is one of the most important buildings remaining, though now in a poor condition. It was a hospital and medical school. High doors lead to an imposing courtyard surrounded on three sides by a double-storey building with large rooms on both floors. Unani (Greek) medicine was taught and practised here, and all expenses met by the state. The baths have disappeared, but on the outside are the remains of the caravanserai, where the relatives of the sick could stay. The nearby mosque has fine tiled medallions.

Salar Jung Museum

The **Salar Jung Museum** Ⓕ (open daily 10am–5pm, entrance charge), on the southern bank of the Musi River, is the largest single-person collection of art and artefacts in the world. Salar Jung was a minister at the court of the Nizams and his collection of over 43,000 objects and 50,000 rare books and manuscripts includes a marble statue, *The Veiled Rebecca* by Italian sculptor Benzoni (1876), and the interesting double statue of Mephistopheles and Margaretta made of sycamore wood. The large Mughal jade collection in the museum is outstanding. There are several beautifully carved and inlaid pieces, including gem-studded boxes, animal-headed daggers and knives and delicate translucent leaf-shaped drinking bowls. The museum also has exceptional collections of manuscripts, miniature paintings, arms and armour, Chinese porcelain, Indian textiles and *pichwais*, ivory, Indo-Persian glass and Bidriware.

The Western collections are curious rather than beautiful: Salar Jung's taste, exquitite in Indian items, was florid where Western art is concerned. The development and different styles of Indian miniature painting can be followed from the comprehensive collection shown here. It ranges from early Jain Kalpasutras and vibrant 17th-century Malwa *raga-ragini* paintings to the first impact of Persian artists, European influence and finally to superb examples of the Mughal, Deccan, Rajput and Pahari schools, *siyah qalam* (pen and ink) drawings and illustrated Deccan manuscripts. The Children's section contains some wonderful period toys from Europe and India.

The arms gallery has an interesting collection of different styles of swords and daggers, some made of Kunasamudram steel, of which the chisels of the Egyptian pyramid-builders is said to have been forged. There are historic Mughal weapons and a resplendent diamond-encrusted ceremonial sword of Salar Jung. The Arabic and Persian manuscripts include a 9th-century Koran in Kufic script, an original Diwan of Hafiz, the great Persian poet, calligraphic masterpieces and royal autographs.

The Neoclassical **Falaknuma Palace**, about 4 km (3 miles) south of the Charminar, served as the royal guesthouse for the nizams. Built in 1884, it is an imposing structure (set on a hill to maximise its impact) with an opulent interior. At present the palace is being turned into a luxury heritage hotel by the Taj Group and there is no access to the site until its opening.

Hyderabad Zoo, or the **Nehru Zoological Park**, to give it its full name, is a sprawling area (300 acres), some of which has been left wild. A number of the ani-

LEFT: in the Falaknuma Palace.

Map on page 290

mals inhabit large moated spaces rather than cages. Even though this is said to be one of the better zoos in India, the condition of the animals is depressing and the management of the institution leaves a lot to be desired. In recent years poachers have even broken into the zoo to kill the tigers.

New Hyderabad

There is little of architectural interest in the modern public buildings of the city, the latest additions to the skyline being of the corporate glass-and-concrete variety seen the world over. However, the buildings of the early 20th century are definitely worth a look. **Osmania University** at Tarnaka, the **High Court** and **Osmania Hospital** facing each other across the river Musi, with the State Library nearby, are built in a style of Islamic pastiche; but they have an undeniable grace and convey the flavour of the last glorious fling of the old order in Hyderabad, the high Edwardian period between the two World Wars, which the great photographer Raja Deen Dayal so faithfully recorded.

An addition to Hyderabad during the days of the East India Company is the **Regency Mansion** Ⓖ, just off Bhagya Reddi Road and now the Osmania University College for Women. It was built in 1803 by James Kirkpatrick, resident at the court of the second Nizam, to replace the much smaller villa used by the previous incumbents. It was built on land donated by the Nizam and its construction was also paid for by him: "Nizzy will pay!" declared the Resident, and the Nizam did, including inflated prices for some discards from the Brighton Pavilion.

Designed by an officer of the Royal Engineers, the Residency is full of architectural solecisms. The main facade has a six-columned portico in the Corinthian style, the pediment still bearing the arms of the East India Company. A pair of lions flank the granite steps, replacing the original sphinxes. The Durbar Hall is well proportioned with a gallery, Ionic columns, a beautiful painted ceiling and chandeliers and mirrors acquired from the Prince Regent.

BELOW: the Salar Jung Museum.

Kirkpatrick, a favourite of the Nizam, was an unusual man who spoke fluent Urdu and Persian. He caused a scandal by sheltering and later marrying a girl from a good Hyderabadi family, a relative of the Prime Minister, who took refuge in his house from an enforced marriage (now the subject of a book, *White Mughals*, by William Dalrymple). To prove his love, he built the suite of rooms in Indian style known as the **Rang Mahal**. Also of interest in the Residency grounds is the architect's model of the building and the cemetery, last resting place of some of the English of the time.

North of the Regency Mansion is **King Koti Palace**, another late 19th-century Neoclassical residence of the Nizams. Part of it is now home to a hospital, while the rest is used for official functions. The **Purani Haveli**, close to the Salar Jung Museum, was previously a residence of the Nizam's ministers. It has now been turned into the **Nizam's Museum** (open Sat–Thur 10am–5pm) showing, among other items, his collection of vintage cars.

In the **Bagh-e-Aam** or Public Garden is the **Legislative Assembly** building, also date from the early 20th century, some charming pavilions still being used for public receptions, and the **State Archaeological Museum** ⓗ (open Sat–Thur 10.30am–5pm). Space is cramped and treasures from Andhra's past can be seen scattered about the gardens of the Archaeological Department. The museum has a superb Chalukyan Mahavir, dating from the 12th century, in polished black basalt. The Buddhist gallery has a 4th-century standing Buddha from Oppokondur, and some pieces from Amravati. There are also Kakatiya sculptured columns and roof slabs in the garden of the museum, reassembled as a little pavilion, some Islamic inscriptions in black basalt, and a good collection of ancient weapons.

Opposite the Bagh-e-Aam is **Naubat Pahar**, an imposing 91-metre (300-ft) high natural feature from where the Mughal *firmans* (edicts) were broadcast in the 17th century. The **Birla Planetarium and Science Museum** (open daily

Map on page 290

10.30am–8.30pm, entrance charge) is also here. On the twin peak of Kala Pahad is another contribution to the city from the family of industrialists, the white marble **Birla Mandir**. This temple, dedicated to Lord Ventaktesvara, has become one of the city's landmarks, particularly noticeable when illuminated at night.

Secunderabad

Secunderabad, 5 km (3 miles) to the north of Hyderabad, originated as a British cantonment under British law in 1806. Its military past and present-day commercial activity make it somewhat more orderly, if less colourful, than chaotic Hyderabad. It is often referred to as the "twin" city of Hyderabad. The main railway station for the city is located here.

LEFT: the Birla Mandir.
BELOW: the Hyderabad region is famous for its grape vines.

Husain Sagar, a large 17th-century reservoir, separates Secunderabad from the older city of Hyderabad. The "bund" or retaining wall dates back to the reign of Ibrahim Qutb Shah and was built by his brother-in-law Husain Shah Wali, after whom it is named. The statues on the bund date back to 1986. Tankbund Road, which runs along the shoreline of Husain Sagar, gives lovely views over the lake, and also the huge **Buddha Statue** ❶ on the island in the middle. Carved out of white granite and erected in 1985, standing at 22 metres (72 ft) high, it is one of the largest monumental statues in the world. It is possible to visit the island on one of the launches run by the state government. On the shore of the lake are **Lumbini Park** and **NTR Gardens**, a park named after the long-serving chief minister, with play areas, cafés and a monorail. Close by is the British Council Library.

The outskirts

On the edge of the twin cities are a number of modern developments. Most prominently among these is **Hitec City**, the newly-built district that has attracted a number of software development companies (putting the "cyber" in "Cyberabad"). While there is not much of tourist interest here, the gleaming, glass-clad buildings give an insight into how the other one percent live. More interesting, perhaps, is **Ramaji Film City**, centre of the Telugu film industry and the largest production complex in the world. It is possible to visit on guided tours (open 9am–5.30pm, tel: 040-2323 5777). Elsewhere are the new **Botanical Gardens**, covering 48 hectares (120 acres) and opening in stages, and the **Shilparamam Crafts Village** out in Madhapur. The latter has stalls and workshops of craftworkers from all over India.

Golconda

Built on the site of an earlier Kakatiya fort, 13 km (8 miles) from Hyderabad, **Golconda** ❶ (open daily 10am–4.30pm, entrance charge, daily Sound and Light Show in English, Nov–Feb 6.30–7.30pm, Mar–Apr 7–8pm) rises 122 metres (400 ft) above the plain. It was built by Quli Qutb Shah and during Qutb Shahi rule gained an aura of riches and romance. It was their capital until the end of the 16th century.

The outer wall, 15–18 metres (50–60 ft) high, encloses houses, shops, water reservoirs and fields. It is massive, built of blocks of local granite weighing more than a ton each. There are 87 semicircular bastions or *burj*, some still with their armaments. The Petla Burj looks out to the west. The Musa Burj, a three-storey bastion to the southeast, was built after the first Mughal invasion by Musa Khan, the builder of the Toli Masjid, and has an inscription with an account of a battle with the Mughals in both Telugu and Persian.

There are eight gates, four of which are in use. The road from Hyderabad winds through the Fateh Darwaza, through which Aurangzeb's army entered, led by his son Prince Muazzam in 1687. That was the only time Golconda was ever captured, and even then it was by treachery. Invited to attack Golconda by Mir Jumla, a powerful Deccan noble out of favour with the king, Aurangzeb had to raise the siege in 1656 on orders from his father Shah Jahan. The second time he came, so he said, to put down heresy, but he returned to Delhi laden with the fabled treasure of Golconda, including the Koh-i-noor diamond. Even so, the fort had held out for eight months until he managed to bribe one of the defenders to open the gate. The name of Abdulla Khan Pani is remembered for his treachery, as is that of Abdul Razak Lari for his gallantry in the same siege.

Golconda at this time was the centre of the world trade in diamonds. There were mines in the south of the kingdom, and a large part of the royal revenues came from taxes levied on their working. Stones over a certain size were the prerogative of the rulers and there was a skilled cutting and polishing industry. Pearls were also imported and drilled here, and continue to be worked in Hyderabad to this day.

The **Bala Hissar gate** is the only entrance to the fort. It is a huge doorway protected by a curtain wall and teak-wood doors studded with metal spikes, and leads into a large inner porch. On the right are mortuary baths, straight ahead are the guards' barracks and Nagina Bagh, and on the left is the three-storey armoury. Looking up, you can see the innermost wall of Golconda; it is an imposing sight, the huge

Map on page 290

blocks of cut stone butting onto natural outcrops of granite. Turning left past the armoury, **Taramati's mosque** is on the right. It has a small platform in front supported on arches, attractive parapet and wall treatment and no dome or minarets. Taramati was Abdullah Qutb Shah's companion, and is buried in the royal tombs.

On the left, near the outer wall, are the camel stables and Hall of Justice, and straight ahead are the remains of the royal palaces. These are the most interesting ruins in the fort. From the huge pointed arches and massive walls with cut plaster decoration, rectangular and arched niches, and the traces of mother-of-pearl inlay and polychrome tiles, they appear to be of early Qutb Shahi origin. Some of the buildings are two or three storeys high, and there were once gardens with fountains, Turkish baths and mirror-tiled dressing rooms. In their original carpeted, silk-hung and lamplit state they must have been magnificent.

Three stone stairways lead up to the **Baradari** at the very top of the fort. As you go up, you can see the pipes for the water system along the side walls. A series of Persian wheels took the water from reservoirs to the top, from where it was piped into baths and flush cisterns. On the way up there are superb views, with the tombs to the northwest. Halfway up the hill there is a well, baths, the remains of Abul Hasan Tana Shah's garden, a small jail, a grain store and a mosque. An inscription at the grain store reveals that it was erected by Abdullah.

At the top, aside from the view which takes in the mosque of Pemamati and the pavilion of Taramati, the Qutb Shahi tombs and the Banjara Hills, is a temple and the double-storey Baradari. The large hall on the first floor is finely proportioned, and may have been used as a durbar hall. Steps lead to a terrace and stone *takht* (throne). On the western side, the outer wall is protected by earthworks; the projecting bastion is the Petla Burj.

Mir Alam reservoir is nearby, with the hill of Falaknuma rising beyond it, and the army parade grounds are to the southeast.

LEFT: the Vidhan Sabha, or Legislative Assembly.
BELOW: Golconda Fort.

Down towards Bala Hissar gate, near the guard lines, is the two-storey building known as the office of Akanna and Madanna, the ministers of Abdullah Qutb Shah, though this is pure speculation. The Nagina Bagh, because of its Mughal layout, is presumed to be a later addition.

Outside the Bala Hissar gate are two huge arches known as Habshi Kaman. The rooms above housed the Naubat Khana (ceremonial musicians) and the Ethiopian guard. As you approach Banjara gate, towards the Tombs, the road winds between the walls of the fort, and carvings of mythical animals can be seen. On the right is the Katora Hauz, built by Ibrahim Quli and used by Abul Hasan Tana Shah for bathing.

The Qutb Shahi tombs

Close by is the burial ground of the Qutb Shahi rulers. The **tombs** Ⓚ (open Sat–Thur 9am–4.30pm, entrance charge) are remarkable for the unity of their design. Unlike the mosques, they all have a central dome, more or less onion-shaped, rising from a lotus-petal calyx, a small dome, minarets and stucco decoration. Most graves are of black basalt with calligraphic inscriptions. At the centre of the enclosure is the **hamam**, the baths built by Sultan Quli. The simple interior space is impressive, with a beautiful inlaid platform.

To the west is the earliest tomb, **Sultan Quli's**, contemporary with the hamam. The style shows Bahmani derivation in its simple outline and limited surface decoration. The outer walls of the chamber are divided into three arched panels on each face, and the interior is octagonal in shape. There are inscriptions in Naskh and Tauqi style.

Facing the hamam is the impressive tomb of **Mohammad Quli**. It stands on a double terrace, and the facade, differing from the others, is in pillar and lintel style, the slim octagonal columns rising to 6.6 metres (22 ft). The end bays on each face are closed with arched recesses. The octagonal columns at the corners become small domed minarets above a broad decorative band; in between the columns is an arched

BELOW: the Qutb Shahi tombs.

Map on page 290

and crenellated parapet. In Qutb Shahi days these tombs were carpeted, curtained and lit. Tavernier reports, "At the tombs of the Kings about four in the afternoon there is a dole of bread and *pilau* to all the poor that come. If you would see anything that is fayre you must go to view these tombs upon a festival day for then from morning till night they are hung with rich tapestry." Aurangzeb's army camped here in 1687, and much of the polychrome decoration was destroyed at that time.

Beyond Mohammad Quli's tomb is **Ibrahim Qutb Shah's**, on a high plinth with black basalt doorways and a double row of arched recesses. Some of the original tilework still remains. In a smaller dome on this terrace lies the tomb of his son Mohammad Amin, and both tombs evidently have fine calligraphic inscriptions; Mohammad Amin's has the only Kufic inscription in Golconda or Hyderabad.

Jamshed Quli was second in the Qutb Shahi line, and his seven-year stewardship was a sort of interregnum between the great reigns of his father and brother. He is supposed to have been responsible for the murder of his 93-year-old father in the Jami Masjid. The tomb said to be his (though there is no inscription) is perhaps the most architecturally satisfying, a double-storey facade of octagonal plan, with arched recesses at both levels, a decorated balcony supported on brackets, a matching crenellated cornice with small minarets at each angle and an almost hemispherical dome.

Just inside the gate to the right is the tomb of **Hayat Baksh Begum**. This remarkable woman was the only child of Mohammad Quli, the founder of Hyderabad, and was educated to rule by her father. She shared the duties of kingship with her husband Sultan Mohammad, whose tomb is nearby, and was the regent and virtual ruler of the kingdom during her son's long minority. The tiny mosque in front of her tomb is known as Aurangzeb's mosque; he is said to have built it here out of regard for Hayat Baksh. The mosque behind and to the left of this tomb has been restored, and is said to be one of the finest in Hyderabad.

Outside the enclosure is the tomb of **Abdullah Qutb Shah**, the sixth in the line, set on a large terrace. The five-arched upper storey is set back from the seven-arched lower part, a technique also deployed on the tombs of his parents Sultan Mohammad and Hayat Baksh. The stucco decorations of this tomb are particularly fine, and traces of the glazed tilework remain.

The Asaf Jahi era began in 1724 when Nizam-ul-Mulk, the Mughal governor of the Deccan, declared independence of the declining Mughal dynasty. His successors saw the struggle for supremacy between the Marathas, French, and East India Company, and allied themselves in a most pragmatic fashion. Raymond, a French adventurer who arrived in Pondicherry in 1775, rose to command the Nizam's troops and later to direct his ordnance factories. The **tomb of Monsieur Raymond** on a little hill in Sarurnagar is marked by a simple obelisk of black granite with the initials, "J.R." He became very popular with the local people, and on the anniversary of his death an *Urs* (festival) was held for Musa Ram or Musa Rahim, as he was known. ❑

RIGHT: an apple seller.

Map on page 302

THE DELTA AND THE NORTH

Northern Andhra Pradesh contains the fertile deltas of the huge Krishna and Godavari rivers, the temples of the forested Eastern Ghats, and the inland region of Telengana

One of the most beautiful stretches of the Andhran coastal plain is formed by the delta of the twin rivers Krishna and Godavari, two of the longest in the country. The rich silt makes this one of the most fertile regions in South India, producing two crops a year of high-yielding varieties of rice and sugar cane. The elaborate system of canals and dams is the result of the works of Sir Arthur Cotton, started in 1847 following several years of famine. These calmed the destructive force of the river and provided extensive irrigation to the surrounding area. The works, finished by April 1850, involved 3,054,413 workers, five times the population of the area at the time. Not surprisingly, Sir Arthur Cotton is an extremely popular figure locally. His statue – adorned with *kumkum* powder like a temple image – can be seen in many villages across the region.

To the north lie steep, forested hills that fall to the coast. Among the hills are some fine temples and the caves at Borra, while the major settlements along the coast are Srikakulam and, to the south, the pleasant port city of Visakhapatnam.

The northern inland reaches of Andhra Pradesh are some of the poorest areas of the country and comprise the Telengana region, which has long campaigned for separate statehood, claiming that it has been neglected by politicians from the richer coastal and southern regions. With the success of the Telengana Rashtriya Samiti in the 2004 elections this seems more likely than ever. As an extremely poor region there has been a significant level of support for left-wing Naxalite insurgents who continue to wage a battle against the local police and landlords. Recent overtures have been made between the state government and the Naxalites and these may lead to a reduction in the violence on both sides.

LEFT: three *apsaras* from the Ganesvaralayam, Muluru, Warangal.
RIGHT: a village school, Mulathanda.

Vijayawada

The Krishna, one of India's great rivers, dominates the bustling commercial town of **Vijayawada** ❷. All is calm and peaceful on its banks, while the town itself, impressive in extent, is an important railway junction on the Chennai–Howrah and Chennai–Delhi routes, and a busy complex of unmarked, unplanned and crowded streets with very few trees, parks or green spaces. Vijayawada's importance as a commercial centre stems from its location on the river, and it was particularly prosperous as a port under the Qutb Shahi rulers of Hyderabad. The railway and road cross the river at this point over the enormous, 1 km (⅔ mile) long Prakasam Barrage, constructed in 1855.

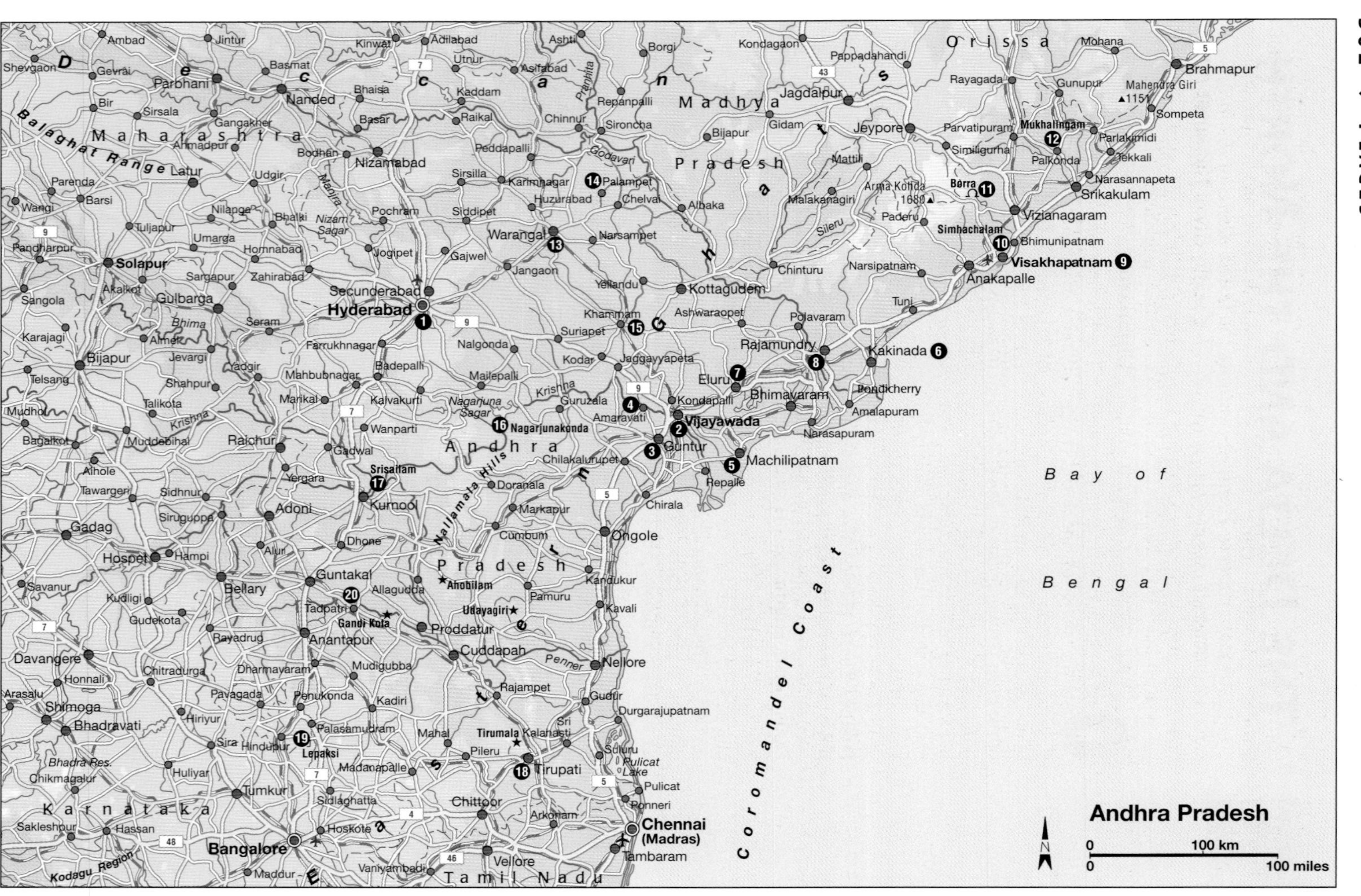
Andhra Pradesh
0 100 km
0 100 miles
N
Bay of Bengal
Coromandel Coast
Orissa
Madhya Pradesh
Maharashtra
Andhra Pradesh
Karnataka
Tamil Nadu
Balaghat Range
Nallamala Hills
Brahmapur
Mahendra Giri
1151
Sompeta
Tekkali
Narasannapeta
Srikakulam
Parlakimidi
Mohana
Gunupur
Mukhalingam
Palkonda
Vizianagaram
Bhimunipatnam
Visakhapatnam
Anakapalle
Simhachalam
Borra
Rayagada
Parvatipuram
Similiguma
Arma Konda
1680
Paderu
Jeypore
Pappadahandi
Jagdalpur
Kondagaon
Gidam
Mattili
Malakanagiri
Sileru
Narsipatnam
Tuni
Kakinada
Pondicherry
Amalapuram
Polavaram
Chinturu
Rajamundry
Narasapuram
Bhimavaram
Machilipatnam
Eluru
Vijayawada
Repalle
Guntur
Chirala
Ongole
Kottagudem
Ashwaraopet
Bijapur
Albaka
Chelvai
Palampet
Sironcha
Repanpalli
Borgi
Pranhita
Godavari
Narsampet
Warangal
Yellandu
Khammam
Jaggayyapeta
Kondapalli
Amaravati
Suriapet
Kodar
Guruzala
Krishna
Nagarjunakonda
Chilakalurupet
Kandukur
Kavali
Nellore
Gudur
Durgarajupatnam
Sri Kalahasti
Sulluru
Pulicat Lake
Pulicat
Ponneri
Chennai (Madras)
Tambaram
Tirupati
Tirumala
Arkonam
Vellore
Chittoor
Pileru
Rajampet
Cuddapah
Penner
Pamuru
Udayagiri
Markapur
Cumbum
Doranala
Ahobilam
Proddatur
Allagudda
Kurnool
Srisailam
Nagarjuna Sagar
Mailepalli
Nalgonda
Hyderabad
Secunderabad
Jangaon
Huzurabad
Karimnagar
Peddapalli
Chinnur
Asifabad
Ashti
Adilabad
Utnur
Kaddam
Raikal
Sirsilla
Siddipet
Gajwel
Jogipet
Pochram
Nizamabad
Bhaisa
Basar
Bodhan
Kinwat
Nanded
Basmat
Jintur
Parbhani
Gangakher
Ahmadpur
Udgir
Nilanga
Bhalki
Nizam Sagar
Manjira
Homnabad
Zahirabad
Umarga
Latur
Tuljapur
Solapur
Barsi
Parenda
Bir
Sirsala
Gevrai
Ambad
Shevgaon
Wangi
Pandharpur
Sangola
Akalkot
Gulbarga
Sargapur
Seram
Farrukhnagar
Badepalli
Mahbubnagar
Kalvakurti
Wanparti
Gadwal
Manikal
Raichur
Yergara
Adoni
Alur
Dhone
Guntakal
Gandi Kota
Tadpatri
Anantapur
Mudigubba
Kadiri
Mahal
Madanapalle
Vaniyambadi
Hoskote
Sidlaghatta
Bangalore
Lepakshi
Hindupur
Penukonda
Palasamudram
Dharmavaram
Rayadrug
Pavagada
Bellary
Hampi
Hospet
Siruguppa
Sidhnur
Kudligi
Gudekota
Chitradurga
Hiriyur
Sira
Tumkur
Huliyar
Maddur
Hassan
Sakleshpur
Chikmagalur
Bhadra Res.
Bhadravati
Shimoga
Honnali
Davangere
Arasalu
Savanur
Gadag
Tawargeri
Aihole
Bagalkot
Mudhol
Muddebihal
Talikota
Shahpur
Jevargi
Yadgir
Bhima
Almel
Bijapur
Telsang
Karajagi
Kodagu Region

Map on page 302

Bandar Road is the main shopping and commercial street, and here the **Victoria Jubilee Museum** (open Sat–Thur 10.30am–5pm) is a fine example of a small local museum, set in a shady garden of old trees. In its open verandahs it has a small but good collection of sculpture, among them an important white stone early Siva, two-armed and seated with a Nandi, one of the earliest Pallava sculptures from the Krishna valley. Inside are prehistoric finds, local crafts and coins. The Buddhist gallery, though small, has some rare pieces from nearby sites.

Though the town is modern, it has ancient roots and its ritual geography is not confined to ghats from which people bathe in the Krishna. The **Kanakadurga temple** (or Vijayesvarasvami, from which the city gets its name) dominates Vijayawada from its hilltop position and is an important pilgrimage site (the image in the main shrine is said to *svayambhu* or "self-manifest").

Other important places of worship include the **Mallesvarasvami temple** and the **Mogalrajapuram cave temple** with an early but badly disfigured representation of Siva Nataraja, thought to be one of the oldest statues in South India. The **Akanna-Madanna temple** is cut into two levels of the hillside, and in the grounds have been re-assembled some capitals and beams from a 9th-century Vengi Chalukyan temple from Jammidoddi, with delightful smiling *ganas* (dwarfs) holding up the ceiling. They seem to bridge a gap of three centuries, faint reflections of an earlier tradition. The city also has two **Jain temples** dating back to the 10th century, and the **Hazratbal mosque**.

The **Ondavalli caves** are at a pleasant riverbank site on the other side of the river from the town. These cave temples, dating from the 6th and 7th centuries, with the remains of sculpted columns and wall niches for sculpture, foreshadow the free-standing temples of the 8th century.

Twenty-five kilometres (15 miles) north of Vijayawada is **Kondapalli**, a village famous for its painted wooden figures. Its rural charm has been eroded by the thermal power station nearby, but Kondapalli fort is worth the short, stiff climb. It was built by the Reddi kings of Kondaviddu in the 13th century and has later additions by the Qutb Shahis.

The nearby city of **Guntur** ❸ (31 km/20 miles) to the southwest of Vijayawada is another important railway and commercial centre. While there are few monuments of historical interest in the city, there is a small **museum** with more Buddhist artefacts from the surrounding region (open Sat–Thur 10.30am–5pm). Guntur is the most convenient place from which to take the bus to Amaravati.

Amaravati

At **Amaravati** ❹ (35 km/22 miles northwest of Guntur), in the 2nd century AD, the Buddhist art of the Krishna valley achieved its highest point. Andhra, through the influence of Buddhism and trade with Rome, was already emerging from its seclusion, when in the 1st century AD it came under Satyavahana rule. They had already been great patrons of art in the

RIGHT: winnowing rice.

western Deccan, and they brought with them a tolerant, liberal and cosmopolitan culture that fostered art and learning.

Buddhism at this time was in a state of flux, reflected in the art of the time: Buddha is now shown in human form for the first time, whereas before he was represented only by symbols. In these iconic figures the influences of Mathura and Gandhara in the North are evident.

In the sculpted medallions and panels of Amaravati, all these influences come together: the physical characteristics of the local people and their worldly and unmystical approach to life, the ideals of Buddhism, the sophistication of the Satyavahana civilisation, the derivations from Mathura, Gandhara and West Asia, all put down with a sureness of touch attained by the Amaravati sculptor after 300 years of practice. Coomaraswamy describes the Amaravati style as "the most voluptuous and the most delicate flower of Indian art".

Today only a low mound remains of the stupa, with a paved path around it. A few of the slabs from the stupa find themselves in the **Amaresvara temple** nearby. The temple itself, though of respectable antiquity and originally Eastern Chalukyan in style, has been extensively restored and renovated. Most of the damage to the ancient structure was done at the end of the 18th century, when a local landowner systematically raided the site for the building materials he needed for a new town. However, the temple is in a fine position on the banks of the Krishna river and it remains a lively and interesting pilgrimage site.

The excellent **Museum** (open Sat–Thur 9am–5pm) at the site houses some important pieces from the various phases of Amaravati's development and from other nearby Buddhist sites (the rest of the finds from the excavation of the stupa are now in the British Museum in London or the Government Museum in Chennai). An early stele carved in low relief from the 2nd century BC shows scenes of contemporary life at Dhanyakataka. A *yaksi* (female guardian) from the 2nd or 1st

Map on page 302

century BC wearing heavy jewellery is very much in the style of Sanchi and Barhut. From the mature phase, the presentation of Rahula to the Buddha and the story of the serpent king, both on parts of the railing, are outstanding. The life-size image of Buddha in the first gallery was found here, and the small bronzes are among the earliest in South India. The Padampani figures in Gallery 2 are also very fine. Some reliquaries and a gold necklace from Gummadidurru are in the reserve collection.

Machilipatnam

On the coast, north of the mouth of the Krishna, is what was one of the principal trading posts of the East India Company. **Machilipatnam** ❺ (previously Masulipatnam) is easily reached directly by road from Vijayawada (70 km/44 miles) or train via the bustling town of Gudivada. It has long been a centre of textile production and this continues today, although the town's importance as a port has drastically declined since the 19th century. It is a centre of Kalamkari work *(see page 90)*, the famous painted cloths that have been exported from here for over a thousand years. It was to collect and export these that the first English and Dutch factories were established in the 17th century. The Kalamkari process involves 14–15 stages after the preparation of the dye, including fixing the colour with mordants. Although there is little to see of Machilipatnam's colonial past, there is a wide stretch of beach nearby, which is used by the local fishing communities.

The Godavari

West Godavari District to the north is exceptionally fertile and the network of canals, and paddy and sugar-cane fields is beautiful. It is separated from East Godavari by the huge Godavari river, seen to its best advantage from the 6.4 km- (4 mile-) long series of barrages at Daulaisvaram close to Rajamundry. On the northern bank, close to the barrage, is the house

LEFT: the Ondavalli caves.
BELOW: fishing boats, Visakhapatnam.

of Sir Arthur Cotton *(see page 301)*, now a small museum dedicated to the history of the irrigation works. Inside is a garlanded marble statue of the engineer.

The area around Rajamundry and the port of **Kakinada** ❻ is strewn with remains of Eastern Chalukyan architecture. This was the kingdom of the Vengi Chalukyans who ruled coastal Andhra for 400 years from AD 625. Their capital may have been **Eluru** ❼, which today is a pleasant small town. The once thriving carpet industry here, which in the 17th and 18th centuries produced among the finest carpets in India, is in the doldrums, though attempts are being made to revive it.

The reign of the Vengi Chalukyans was a time of wars, upheavals and chaos, but two powerful rulers, Gunaga Vijayaditya and Chalukya Bhim in the late 9th century, were great temple builders and their works can be seen at **Bikkavolu**, **Draksharama**, **Chebrolu** and **Bhimavaram**.

Most of the temples are in use and have suffered from later renovations, additions and much whitewashing. Probably the one that has suffered least is the Bhimeswara at Chebrolu, untouched except for the *vimana*. The doorways are sculpted with figures of *dvarapalas*, dancers and musicians, and the Buddhist *purnaghata*, the vase symbol denoting the birth of the Buddha, reappears as a decorative motif. The glossy black stone torso of Kumara already shows Kakatiya influence.

During this period the architectural importance of sculpture was established; it began to dominate rather than decorate the temple wall. This tendency grew even further during Kakatiya times, and became quite overwhelming during the Vijayanagara period. In Vengi sculpture, an element of folk art combines with the earlier tradition of vigorous naturalism. To this idiom belong the delightful musicians and dancers of the panels from Jammidoddi, now in the grounds of the Akanna-Madanna temple at Vijayawada, and the Mahisamardini from the same source, unique in the South for its detail.

Map on page 302

Rajamundry ❽ is a busy town on the northern bank of the Godavari. A series of ghats (bathing places) lines the river front from where devotees can take a ritual bath. These are the site of the 12-yearly Godavari Pushkaram festival which draws pilgrims from all over the state. As well as having one of India's longest railway bridges, the town is also the place from which to take a trip upriver to the **Godavari gorges** where the river forces its way through the Eastern Ghats amid spectacular scenery.

The northeastern coast

The coastline along the stunning **Visakhapatnam–Bhimunipatnam road** is one of blue sea, curving white sandy beaches, palm trees and feathery araucaria plantations. On the other side are the forested foothills of the Eastern Ghats. Outside of the monsoon sea appears deceptively calm, but like the rest of the eastern coast the currents here are treacherous, and swimming is dangerous.

LEFT: Dutch tombs at Bhimunipatnam near Vizag. **BELOW:** the Tapu Rapu Valasa bridge, Vizianagaram.

Visakhapatnam

Visakhapatnam ❾ ("Vizag"), in spite of its large dockyard, oil refinery, steel plant and other industries, is a pleasant town, perhaps the nicest in Andhra today. It has a splendid natural harbour and is one of India's largest naval bases. Built on a sweeping bay with a wide beach, the city (the second largest in Andhra) is overlooked by hills to the north (Kailasagiri) and south (Dolphin's Nose), both of which have wonderful views over the city and ocean. On Beach Road is VUDA Park, with play areas for children and a musical fountain display. Slightly more unusual, and also on Beach Road, is a decommissioned Soviet submarine, now a museum.

The Vaishnavite temple at **Simhachalam** ❿, 20 km (12 miles) away, once belonged, with the villages around, to the Raja of Vizianagram. It is situated in a commanding position about 240 metres (770 feet) above the plain, with wide views of the surrounding countryside. The temple dates from the 11th century, and is

built in the Orissan style. Though it has suffered from later additions and renovations, the original reliefs on the walls are very fine, including several variations of the Krisna and *gopis* theme. In the courtyard is a large stone chariot with horses.

About 25 km (15 miles) towards Bimanipatnam the remains of a Buddhist monastery have been discovered. This is the hilltop site of **Bavikonda**. Very little now remains except the water reservoirs cut into the red laterite and a few sculpted pillars in the same stone, but the site itself is enjoyable for its calm and natural beauty. Near Anakapalle, at **Sankaran**, there is a remarkable complex of Buddhist stupas and *viharas* (monasteries) cut into the rocks.

Borra

The Eastern Ghats rise inland from Visakhapatnam. The road winds through thickly wooded hills with streams and waterfalls, the highest and scenically the most picturesque part of the state. There is a profusion of bird life and some wild animals, including panthers and a few tigers. There are coffee estates around Ananthagiri and Chintapalli, and the limestone **Borra caves** ⓫ with stalagmites, stalactites and an underground stream nearby. The forests here and at Araku valley are the home of Adivasi people, the original inhabitants of the state. A wildfowl sanctuary has been erected at **Pedda Cheruvu** near **Vizianagaram**, while at **Kondakarla Ava**, about 50 km (35 miles) from Vizag, migratory birds make their home during October and November.

Mukhalingam

There is a group of three small but beautiful temples at **Mukhalingam** ⓬, just 48 km (30 miles) north of **Srikakulam** on the Vamsadhara river. Mukhalingam was for a time the capital of the great Kalinga empire, which at its peak ruled all the country between the Ganges to the north and the Godavari to the south. The Eastern Ganga dynasty ruled here for over a thousand years, from the 5th to the 15th cen-

Map on page 302

tury. Their empire had links with neighbours to the south and west, the Vengis, Cholas and Kadambas, and was visited by Buddhist pilgrims. One of them, the Chinese traveller Hieun Tsang, left a description of the city as he saw it in the 7th century. He saw a peaceful and prosperous land and commented on the abundance of flowers and fruit, on the vast jungles and the many impressive Buddhist stupas, most already falling into disrepair with the decline of the faith.

The three temples, the **Somesvara**, **Madhukesvara** and **Bhimesvara**, were built in that order between the 6th and 12th centuries AD. The style is Orissan with local variations. They were probably built when the Saivite Eastern Ganga empire was well-established and show a confidence and maturity of style as in the contemporary temples at Bhubaneshwar, foreshadowing the great temple at Puri.

The Somesvara, the smallest of the three, is of simple design. The horizontal bands of stone are broken by niches on each side and by the doorway on the west. Above the lintel the banding continues in the *deul* and is crowned by the *phalaka*, *gala*, and *amlaka shikhara* resting on four seated Nandi bulls at the corners. The whole effect is of graceful proportion and fine detail. The sculpture of the doorway and the niches on the walls deserves detailed study. In the central niche on the north wall is a poetic Kartikeya with a peacock at his feet. The whole is interspersed with exuberantly curling leafy vines in bands and panels. The largest of the three is the Madhukesvara. Built on a rectangular plan, it has a courtyard, a central doorway facing east, and one central and four corner shrines.

The sculpted figures of Mukhalingam, though of somewhat exaggerated proportions, are characterised by a serene detachment of expression which is their great attraction. Warriors, kings and sages adorn the walls of the Madhukesvara. The south wall is a masterpiece, a series of beautiful units: the panels of elegant scrollwork, the

LEFT: planting out in a paddy field.
BELOW: a village tank.

niches with sculpted figures, the architectural details of the corner shrines, the southern doorway and seven miniature *vimanas* making up a magnificent whole. The figures of Kumara, Durga Bhuvaraha, Bhiksatana, Siva and Narasimha are outstanding, while it has been said that "the door facing east may well claim to be the loveliest entrance to a temple in the whole of India."

Telengana

Inland from East Godavari, from the districts of Khammam up to Adilabad on the Maharasthran border, and down to Mahbubnagar by Karnataka, is the Telengana region. Previously the domains of the Nizam of Hyderabad, the area was incorporated into the new state of Andhra Pradesh in 1956. Compared to the rest of the state, Telengana is undeveloped and its overwhelmingly rural population faces considerable hardship.

The virtues of the Kakatiyas, their patronage of art and letters, their bravery in battle and, above all, their happy knack of finding able and faithful servitors, shine even at a remove of 10 centuries. The dynasty became independent of its Chalukyan overlords about 1050, and ruled the Telengana region till 1323. Their name derives from their family deity, the goddess Kakati, possibly a local version of Durga.

The first Kakatiya capital was Anumakonda, modern Hanamakonda; later they moved to Warangal, originally known as Orugallu or Ekasila, from the massive rock-hill near Warangal fort. Here they fought off attacks by the Yadavs of Deogiri, the Tughlaqs from Delhi, predatory neighbours and disaffected vassals. While Ganapatideva was a captive of the Yadavs, Rudra held the kingdom for his master. Rewarded by a large fief, the loyal general built the reservoir of Palampet and the temple that stands on the bund. Ganapatideva's daughter Rudramma led her army in battle and is believed to have been killed in the field at the age of 80.

Map on page 302

During Rudramma's reign, Marco Polo, the Venetian traveller, landed at the port of Motupalli and commented on the fine cotton fabrics of Andhra: "In the Kingdom are made the best and most delicate and those of the highest price, in sooth they look like a tissue of spider's web." Literature, music and dance played an important role. The poetry of Tikkana vanquished the Jain religion, and Jain icons were broken and temples rededicated. Even the generals of the Kakatiya army were writers, notably Jaya Senapati whose *Nritta Ratnavali* is a classic work on dance.

Rudradeva, the first sovereign ruler of the line, built the Thousand-Pillar temple at **Hanamakonda** in 1162 in thanksgiving for victory in battle. The temple is in a walled enclosure, in two parts. The triple shrine or *trikuta* is connected to a *mandapa*, now roofless, by a platform on which there sits a beautiful monolithic Nandi in highly polished black stone. Like other Kakatiya temples, this is Chalukyan in style but with innovations. The *mandapa* has 300 pillars, while the "pillars" of the *trikuta* are vertical slabs with carved ends, arranged in a dentate pattern to look like pilasters. Half-metre (2-ft) wide projecting stone slabs make up the cornice, their heavy unsculpted ends balancing the overhang. The doorways are carved with figures and decorated with looped chain motifs in stone.

Warangal

Warangal ⓭ fort lies 141 km (88 miles) northeast of Hyderabad. Within its outer mud walls, the inner fortifications consist of large stones fitted together. The fort was begun by Rudradeva when the capital was relocated here, added to by his nephew Ganapatideva and finished by Rudramma, who ruled for 30 years. In 1323 it fell to Ulugh Khan, who later ruled Delhi as Mohammad Tughlak. Prataparudra, the last Kakatiya ruler, killed himself on the road to captivity. After this the fort changed hands several times until it was absorbed into the Qutb Shahi empire in the 15th century.

LEFT AND BELOW: coconuts, cotton and chillies, three important crops in Andhra.

Inside the fort are four massive *toranas*, the gateways of the **Sahasralinga temple**, destroyed at the time of Ibrahim Qutb Shah. The scattered fragments are clearly from the high period of Kakatiya art, the reign of Ganapatideva, the same period as the temples at Palampet and Ghanapur. A large *linga* has figures carved on four sides with the stoic Kakatiya faces. The triangular panel of Lakshmi and her attendants illustrates the curious contrast between the lively body movements and set, mask-like faces of Kakatiya sculpture.

The repetition of decorative motifs to form a pattern is brought to perfection in the perforated screen of the doorway, and in the friezes of elephants, lions and swans interspersed with foliage. The *toranas* themselves, standing at the cardinal points, are striking for their size and beauty. The columns, brackets and architraves are carved with the Kakatiya genius in a harmonious blend of animals, plants and jewellery motifs.

Palampet

The **Ramappa temple** at **Palampet** ⓮, 50 km (32 miles) northeast of Warangal, stands on the retaining wall of the Palampet dam. The reservoir is 12.5 km (8 miles) across, and is one of several irrigation works undertaken by the Kakatiyas. As Dr Yazdani said, "The titanic dykes and sluice-gates of Pakhal, Lakhnaram and Ramappa are object lessons even to the modern engineer."

The temple was consecrated in 1213 and is of pink sandstone with hard black basalt for the sculpted elements. It is cruciform in plan with porches to each side of the central *mandapam*. The horizontal banding along the outer face of the basement level and the parapet wall of the *mukhamandapam* is made up of plain and ornamented bands, of projections and recesses, of figures in movement contrasted with floral motifs. There is a frieze of elephants marching round the temple, full of playful tricks. Above this is a row of gods and goddesses, musicians and

Map on page 302

dancers, Jain Tirthankaras and soldiers – a glorious medley expressing the joy of life and release from convention.

Under the eaves of three of the porches, stretching from column to cornice, are 12 bracket figures of *madanikas*, women in graceful but strange dance poses. They are almost life-size, with long slender limbs carved in high relief. The simple modelling and restrained ornamentation are typical of the elegance of Kakatiya art. The Nagini figure is remarkable for its stylised simplicity. *Yalis* standing on elephants rear up on other brackets. The Kakatiyas scattered these mythical beasts throughout their temples and what are fanciful creatures in their hands, when translated into the Vijayanagara idiom, grow to threatening size and fearsome aspect. The southern and western outer faces of the beams of the *mandapam* celebrate the marriage of Shiva, the lower faces his great feats. Triangular panels in the ceiling depict Agni, Yama and Varuna with their attendant animals and consorts.

Another temple, at the east end of the same bund, has sculptures of dancers on columns and door jambs. At **Ghanapur**, 6 km (4 miles) east of Palampet, there are some ruined temples. The main shrine has female *dwarapalas* (door keepers) and *madanikas*.

The local interest in goldsmithing and metal work, which is evident in the sculptural motifs, continues to this day. Karimnagar is a centre for silver filigree work, and throughout Warangal district, notably around Pembarthi, there are clusters of metal workers.

Khammam

The little-visited district town of **Khamman** ⓯ lies in the east of Telengana. With its busy shopping streets and market (near the railway) it makes an interesting place for a short stop. The town's atmospheric and deserted **fort**, rising above the higgledy-piggledy Muslim housing below, is a fascinating place to explore and has good views over the town. ❑

LEFT: figures from the Ganesvaralayam, Muluru, Warangal. **BELOW:** Nandi at the Ramappa temple.

Map on page 302

CENTRAL AND SOUTH ANDHRA

Central and southern Andhra is home to the ancient Buddhist site at Nagarjunakonda, the world's busiest pilgrimage site at Tirupati and the wonderful temples at Lepaksi and Tadpatri

The central and southern parts of Andhra Pradesh are known as Rayalaseema. Hot and arid, the landscape is characterised by rocky outcrops and ranges of forested hills. Set amid these are some of South India's most holy pilgrimage sites, impressive forts and a number of important archaeological sites.

Nagarjunakonda

The original site of **Nagarjunakonda** ⓰ (166 km/104 miles south of Hyderabad), the Hill of Nagarjuna, is now under the reservoir of Nagarjunasagar. Before it was submerged, evidence was found of early settlements from the Stone Age up to medieval times, but its most brilliant period was the century of Ikshvaku rule, beginning in the second quarter of the 3rd century AD. At this time the valley was known as Vijayapuri – there is no known connection with Nagarjuna, the Buddhist philosopher of the 2nd century.

A valley on the banks of the Krishna river, Nagarjunakonda was protected on the other three sides by natural fortifications. Satyavahana culture had been established in the Godavari-Krishna basin since 200 BC, and thrived in the immediate post-Christian era.

According to the Roman historian Pliny, the country of the "Andrae" had 30 well-fortified towns. The economy that produced this wealth was based on crafts and trade more than on agriculture, and the civilisation was urban rather than rural. Trade flourished, especially with Rome but also with Southeast Asia, the most important product being the local muslin. More than a thousand years before the European "factories", the Romans had their trade emporia in coastal Andhra.

Buddhism was the religion of the people. At Nagarjunakonda the Ikshvaku rulers were Brahmanic, but their princesses inclined towards Buddhism, and were responsible for the building of many of the *chaityas* and monasteries. Chamtasri, sister of Chamtamula, the first of the Ikshvaku line, built the earliest of the Buddhist monuments found at the site, the Mahachaitya complex. Donors' tablets show that though there was royal patronage, the artisans and craftsmen, both individually and in guilds, were the backbone of the Sangha. Wealth was not concentrated in a few hands but distributed through society.

The Ikshvaku rulers were native to Andhra, and were inheritors of Satyavahana culture, though less refined. Under their rule the centre moved from Amaravati to Nagarjunakonda *(see page 304)*, perhaps the artists and sculptors too. The Nagarju-

LEFT: the Venkatesvara temple, Tirumalai. **RIGHT:** inside the Raja Mahal, Chandragiri.

nakonda reliefs have the same style and idiom, the same technique, but there is a certain naivety in facial types, and a simplicity in the attitudes of the figures when compared with those of Amaravati. Nature, both animal and plant, plays a larger part. The stone used for carving by the Buddhists in Andhra is always the same type, white limestone with a grey-green tinge. Like Greek sculpture, it was originally painted.

Nine important monuments from the Ikshvaku period have been rebuilt inside the medieval hill fort which is now an island lying on the eastern bank of the reservoir. The Brahmanic temples are the earliest found in South India. By far the largest number of monuments is Buddhist, and most of the sculpture is now contained in the museum.

From the ruins of secular buildings a fascinating picture emerges of a planned city with wide roads, drainage and sewerage, public baths, assembly rooms and inns for travellers. Sculpted reliefs depict games and entertainments such as wrestling, dancing and drinking, and there are stones engraved for dice games.

The only amphitheatre in ancient India was found here, with superb acoustics, suggesting a high regard for music and a connection with contemporary Rome. An impressive giant statue of the Buddha dominates the **museum** (open Sat–Thur 9am–4pm). Like the other Buddha statues of Andhra, this follows the conventions of Mathura (between Delhi and Agra). But in the carving of the panels and roundels the Nagarjunakonda and Amaravati sculptors not only carry on the tradition of Sanchi and Barhut in Madhya Pradesh and Mathura – the deep relief and varied planes to catch the light – but also echo Gandhara in the animation of the figures and the rhythmic lines of the composition.

The memorial columns are rare examples of secular art, commemorating the achievements of soldiers and artisans. The terracotta heads are witness to Hellenistic contacts, borne out by the numbers of Roman coins found here. The jewellery,

Map on page 302

ritual vessels and reliquaries are in precious metals, but it is the sculpted drum slabs, beams, cornices and pillars that are the treasures of Nagarjunakonda.

Srisailam

Srisailam ⓱, the Holy Hill, has been venerated as the abode of the gods since prehistory. It lies in the Nallamala range, once thickly wooded and full of wildlife and rare plants, now alas fast being denuded. The western approach to Srisailam for the pilgrim is from **Kurnool** and **Alampur**, the heart of "Chalukya Visaya", the country of the Badami Chalukyas from the 6th century until they were supplanted by the Rastrakutas in the middle of the 8th century. Badami Chalukyan art in Andhra began in the 7th century, and the style first seen at Aihole developed simultaneously at Pattadakal and Alampur, with its mature phase at Badami.

Within the walls of a moated fort on the south bank of the Tungabhadra river just before it joins the Krishna are eight temples and a museum. The architecture of the temples, with their curved and tapering *vimanas* crowned with *amlaka shikharas*, and the delineated sculpture niches on the temple walls, marks an important stage in the evolution of temple design. Unfortunately, much of the sculpture is missing or broken, but the museum houses a good collection.

The genius of the Alampur sculpture lies in the expression of abstract concepts in the curves and tensions of the human body. Half-closed eyes and serene smiles convey mystical ectasy, divine power is channelled through the taut dance pose of Siva Nataraja, and the Kumara and Devi and *mithuna* couples express the duality and interdependence of male and female. These are well displayed in the Archaeological Site Museum (open Sat–Thur 10.30am–5pm).

The pillars of Alampur often have *purnaghatas* at the base and lion masks at the top, while the sculpture niches are elaborately defined with columns, domed

LEFT: Nagarjunakonda. **BELOW:** devotees at Tirupati.

chaityas above and small sculpted panels below. The diagonal lines of the Shiva figures of Svargabrahma, the Nataraja on the north wall and the Tripuratankamurti on the south convey dynamic and powerful movement, while the figure of Parvati in the museum embodies serenity. There is a celestial airiness over the lintel of the *antarala* doorway of the Garuda Brahma. The largest temple of the group, the Balabrahma, has several notable icons, while the door panels of the Taraka Brahma are noteworthy.

Chirala

Further south along the coast is **Chirala**, one of the great centres of handloom weaving in Andhra, and of the *telia rumal*, a fabric woven from oil-treated and tie-dyed thread, recognisable by its distinctive design and the oily smell of the new cloth. It has been exported to Arab countries for centuries and was the traditional head-cloth of the Arabs, the oil treatment being said to keep off the sun's rays.

The southwest

This area was ruled by a branch of the Pallavas between the 8th and 10th centuries, and their capital **Hemavati**, now a small village near Hindupur, has evidence of their highly developed artistic sense. The **Mallikarjuna** and **Doddeswara** temples, incorporating a mix of Karnatakan and Andhran styles, are full of sculpture. In the Vijayanagara period this region was an important part of the empire; temples, forts and palaces can be found at Tadpatri, Lepaksi, Chandragiri, Gandikotta and Penukonda, and more temple art can be seen at Markapur and Pushpagiri.

In the far south of the state, at a height of 1,265 metres (4,150 ft), is the hill station of **Horsley Hills** (reached from **Madanapalle**). The APTDC runs a pleasant resort here (*see* www.tourisminap.com for details).

The towns of **Kalahasti** and Tirupati are full of crafts fostered by the patronage of temples and pilgrims. At the **Kalahasti temple**, hangings depicting religious and mythological themes are

Map on page 302

painted in vegetable colours using an elaborate technique involving 14 stages spread over three weeks.

Tirupati

Tirupati ⓲ is a phenomenon. It attracts vast numbers of pilgrims all year round, and offerings of money and jewellery pour in every day. Easily approached by road or rail from Chennai 170 km (106 miles) to the southeast, it is the richest and busiest pilgrimage centre in the world, even more than Makkah (Mecca) and Rome.

Tirupati is the town at the foot of the seven Tirumala Hills; the main temple site itself is on the last of these, reached by bus via a 22-km (13-mile) winding road; pilgrims walk up following a path through the forest. At the centre of Tirupati town is the impressive 17th-century Govindaraja temple, with its seven-storey *gopura* (gateway tower). Behind, in an old temple building, is the museum (open daily 8am–8pm) with a collection of temple art.

The **Tirumala temple** is dedicated to Lord Venkatesvara, a manifestation of Visnu, who is said to reside on the hill. The god is housed within a gold-clad sanctum at the centre of the temple, and his image, decorated with rubies and diamonds, is flanked by two manifestations of Devi; the god's eyes are covered, as it is believed his gaze would destroy the devotees.

The temple is efficiently run by the Tirupati Tirumala Devasthams (www.tirumala.org), who employ some 16,000 people to deal with the 60–70,000 pilgrims who arrive every day (rising to over 100,000 during major festivals). The temple operates 18-hour-a-day *darsan* (view of the deity) regulated by a token system: pilgrims receive a token from one of several offices which tells them which time to enter the queue, after which it takes about two hours to enter the temple. It is possible to pay for "special *darsan*" which gets you through the process quicker. Non-Hindu visitors are allowed to attend *darsan* but they must

LEFT: many devotees have their heads shaved at Tirupati.
BELOW: rickshaws at the Station.

sign a form declaring their faith in god and respect for the temple's procedures. As well as attending a *darsan*, many pilgrims have their heads shaved as an offering to Lord Venkatesvara; the hair – which brings in a considerable amount of revenue to the temple – is exported to be made into wigs.

Chandragiri

At **Chandragiri**, 11 km (7 miles) from Tirupati, are the Raja Mahal and Rani Mahal, late Vijayanagara structures of the 17th century. These palaces lie within a series of formidable battlements and a moat. The three-storey Raja Mahal is the larger, with a brick tower at the centre and small towers at each corner. The beauty of the structure lies in the repetition on each floor of the row of Indo-Persian arches, and the prominent brackets supporting each level. The first floor has fine stucco decorations on walls and ceiling. The Rani Mahal is a similar structure, also with good stucco decoration.

Lepaksi

Thirteen kilometres (8 miles) east of Hindupur (136 km/85 miles north of Bangalore, close to the border with Karnataka) is the temple town of **Lepaksi** ⓳. On a little hill is the **Virabhadra temple**, built in 1530 by a Vijayanagara governor, Virupanna. It was said that he misused state funds to build it and forestalled royal punishment by blinding himself. A monumental Nandi, the biggest in India, proudly raises its head 1 km (½ mile) away. The temple is in a walled enclosure, and on either side of the inner entrance are carved figures of the river goddesses Ganga and Yamuna with a background of foliage. Near the shrine is a huge Nagalinga carved out of a boulder.

The pillars of the *mandapas* have Vijayanagara capitals and carry figures of gods and goddesses, musicians or dancers. Some have single or double *yali* brackets. Sadly, these and the panels in relief on the walls of the *ardhamandapa* have been disfigured by layers of whitewash.

Map on page 302

The glory of Lepaksi is its beautiful frescoed ceilings. Painting on cloth must always have played a part in temple ritual, though being fragile they have mostly perished. Frescoes no longer had a place when temple forms evolved from the cave to the free-standing forms, until the flat stuccoed granite ceilings of the Vijayanagara style again provided a suitable background. Certainly, nine centuries later there is an echo in Lepaksi of the Ajanta frescoes – in the colour palette, the differing skin tones of a group of devotees, their long tapering fingers and the drooping moustaches of some of the men. A more direct influence is the palm-leaf Kalpasutras of the Jains, painted in the 14th and 15th centuries: groups of people are always ranged in rows, and they have the sharp noses and "further eye" of the Jain style. Here, too, the figures are flat and the poses stylised. But the Lepaksi painters make their own contribution in the lively line, the invention that makes the patterns of the clothes so rich and various, the realism that introduces unorthodox elements into conventional scenes and the feeling that breaks through the stylised forms.

The ceilings of the *mandapam* and *antaralas* and some of the shrines are painted. Each bay is separately treated. Vegetable and mineral colours, red and yellow ochre, black, blue and green were mixed with lime water and infused with the lime-mortar base. The background to most of the pictures is red, another Jain tradition. Gods, goddesses, groups of worshippers and donors are portrayed, as well as Puranic scenes. The *avatars* of Visnu are gracefully rendered. Bhairava is an expression of the painter's idea of the young Siva, and the painter himself stands humbly nearby with folded hands.

The hunting scenes are full of lively incidents, the wounded cheetah biting the hunter and a rushing wild boar terrorising man and beast. Worshippers and attendants are signified by the *kaivara* gesture of humility, one hand upraised. The temple

LEFT: a temple carved out of the rock at Lepaksi. **BELOW:** weeding in the fields near Anantapur.

donor Virupanna is shown with his brother, both in Vijayanagara caps, and groups of women, each in a distinctive *sari*, wear jewellery and flowers in their hair.

The barren landscape of **Penukonda** with its black gneiss rocks about 35 km (22 miles) north of Hindupur was the home of the defeated Vijayanagara king after his defeat in 1565 at Hampi. The fort here comprises a massive encircling wall and a pavilion on the hilltop. Nearby is the elegant Gagan Mahal (a royal pavilion), still in good repair.

Another spectacular fort can be seen at **Gandikota**, to the east of Anantapur. Poised above a gorge carved out by the Pennar river and surrounded by huge stone walls, this near-impregnable site was used by the Vijayanagara kings, but the ruins of the fort seen today date from Qutb Shahi times.

Northeast of Penukonda is the small, and seemingly insignificant, village of **Puttaparthi**. Its claim to fame, however, lies in it being the location of the *ashram* of the controversial god-man Sai Baba. Whatever your views on his divinity, the *ashram* is impressive in its organisation and the pleasant grounds and buildings are all spotlessly clean (*see* www.srisathyasai.org.in for more information).

Tadpatri

About 25 km (15 miles) on from Gandikota are the fabulous temples at **Tadpatri** ⓴. The **Ramalingesvara temple** was built in the 15th century and the **Venkataramana** in the early 16th. They are in the Chalukyan mode with Chola elements and the Vijayanagara stamp: a lavish use of monumental sculpture. The northern *gopuram* of the Ramalingesvara, though unfinished, is considered by many, including Fergusson, to be the greatest achievement of Vijayanagara art:

"The wonders of the place are two gopurams… One of these was apparently quite finished, the other… never carried higher than the perpendicular part. In almost all the gopurams of India this part

LEFT: gram drying in a field near Anantapur. **BELOW:** women picking beans near Madanapalle.

Map on page 302

is comparatively plain, all the figure sculpture and ornament being reserved for the upper or pyramidal part. In this instance however the whole of the perpendicular part is covered with the most elaborate sculpture, cut with exquisite sharpness and precision… and produces an effect richer and on the whole perhaps in better taste than anything else in this style."

The characteristic blending of figurative, architectural and decorative elements begins at the lowest level, and an excellent Mahisamardini and a mysterious bowman feature on the outer side. The southern *gopuram*, though damaged, is comparable to the other. On the inner face a figure with folded hands in Vijayanagara headgear is assumed to be Ramalinga Nayudu, the benefactor of the temple.

In the **Venkataramana** the artistic emphasis is on the walls and pillars of the *mandapam*. On the walls of the *ardhamandapa* are some beautiful Puranic reliefs. The 40 columns of the *mukhamandapa* support *surasundari* figures, the inner composite pillars bear riders on huge, rearing, mythical *yalis*. The mouldings are decorated with creepers, swans and elephants.

Ahobilam and Udayagiri

Further north, up in the hills about 45 km (28 miles) from Cuddapah, is the pilgrimage site at **Ahobilam**. The **Narasimha temple** celebrates Visnu in the form of a lion and dates back to the 16th century, although the worship of the god here predates that. Built by the Vijayanagara kings, it is impressive and ornate and bears a great deal in common with the Vitthala temple at Hampi.

The fort at **Udayagiri** lies to the southeast in the Velikonda hills. Surrounded by high crags, the hilltop is an excellent defensible site and this was taken full advantage of by the Reddis of Kondavidu who built the fort here. Their great rivals at Hampi occupied the fort in 1512, before it fell to the Qutb Shahis during their conquest of Vijayanagara. ❑

BELOW: the Raja Mahal, Chandragiri.

First to Fly
A38
In this ever changing world,
Singapore Girl, you're a great way to fly.
SINGAPORE AIRLINES
A STAR ALLIANCE MEMBER
singaporeair.co
JAKARTA · SEOUL · BRISBANE · ZURICH · JOHANNESBURG · LOS ANGELES · OVER 55 MAJOR CITIE

TRAVEL TIPS

Transport

Accommodation

Eating

Activities

A – Z

Language

Further Reading

TRANSPORT

GETTING THERE AND GETTING AROUND

GETTING THERE

By Air

The vast majority of visitors arrive in India by air. Mumbai and Delhi airports are the major entry points with fewer international flights using Kolkata and Chennai from Europe. Kolkata and Chennai especially have flights to and from East Asia.

Other international airports include: Thiruvananthapuram, with flights to and from the Gulf region, the Maldives and Sri Lanka; Hyderabad, with fewer flights to and from the Gulf region; and Dabolin (Goa), with charter flights from Europe.

Kozhikode, Kochi and Bangalore are airports with limited international air access and customs and immigration facilities, and are not international airports in the real sense of the term. Kozhikode and Kochi have a number of scheduled flights to and from the Gulf region.

Discounts are often available during the off-peak season, so it is worth making enquiries. Many long-haul flights arrive between midnight and 6am, apparently to suit the night landing regulations of European and East Asian cities but, in reality, to help a full plane taking off in the thin air of an Indian summer. Once you have bought a ticket, check with the airline to confirm your booking well in advance. **NB**: It is advisable to check in for flights to and from India as early as possible, as planes are often full and/or overbooked.

All airports have left-luggage facilities. Porters and licensed, pre-paid taxis are available. Airport banks are open 24 hours for currency change.

Cut Your Carbon

Air travel produces a huge amount of carbon dioxide and is one of the main contributors to global warming. Where possible, take the train to while in the country as this produces less CO_2 *(see page 328)*. Although nothing can repair the immediate damage of your flight out, it is possible to offset your "carbon load" by, for example, having trees planted as a "carbon sink". A number of organisations can do this for you and many have online "carbon calculators" which tell you how much you need to donate. In the UK travellers can try www.climatecare.org or www.carbonneutral.com, in the US log on to www.climatefriendly.com or www.sustainabletravelinternational.com

By Sea

A few cruise ships do call in at ports such as Cochin and Mumbai, but India is not a regular cruise destination. Some freighters offer passage to India and excellent accommodation is still available. Great Eastern Shipping (www.greatship.com), Lloyd Triestino (www.lloydtriestino.it) and the Shipping Corporation of India (www.shipindia.com) have sailings to and from Mumbai, Kolkata and Chennai.

Overland

It is theoretically possible to take the train from the UK to India. The Eurostar takes you from London to Paris, from there you can get to Istanbul via Vienna and Sofia. A train leaves once a week from Istanbul to Tehran, from where you can make your way to the Pakistani border at Quetta (the line between Kerman and Zahedan on the Iranian side is nearing completion, thus completing the last section of track between Europe and South Asia).

Land services have now resumed between India and Pakistan.The train from Lahore in Pakistan to Delhi in India crosses the Wagah-Attari border. The Samjhota Express to Delhi via Amritsar leaves Lahore at 11am (check in 8am) on Mondays and Thursdays. There is also a direct bus from Lahore to Delhi leaving at 6am from outside Faletti's Hotel on Egerton Road Tues–Wed, Fri and Sat. The new bus between Muzaffarabad and Srinigar is for Kashmiris only.

The border with Nepal is only open for non-Indian or Nepalese nationals at Birganj/Raxhal, Bairwa and Kakarbitta/Naxalbari.

GETTING AROUND

Air Travel

Indian Airlines (www.indian-airlines.nic.in), not to be confused with the international carrier Air India, has one of the world's largest domestic networks. The reservations system has been improved by the introduction of computers, and tickets can now be booked online. For travel during the peak season (September– March), try and make reservations in advance as flights are usually heavily booked.

With time-consuming check-in and security procedures, you must be at the airport an hour before departure time. Coach services from some city terminals are available. In-flight service is adequate. Alcohol is only available on international flights. Indian Airlines has a good safety record and its fares are often lower than those charged for comparable distances elsewhere. The baggage allowance per adult is 20kg, and 30kg in business class. Cancellation charges on tickets purchased locally are extremely high, but none is applicable for domestic sectors issued on international tickets.

The Discover India fare, valid for 21 days of travel all over the country, and the Tour India Scheme, valid for 14 days and limited to six flight coupons, must be purchased abroad, or paid for in India using foreign currency. For details, contact your travel agent or an Air India office abroad, or write to: Traffic Manager, Indian Airlines House, Parliament Street, New Delhi.

Air India (www.airindia.com) carries domestic passengers on its linking flights between Mumbai and Delhi, Kolkata, Chennai and Bangalore. These flights leave from the international terminals in the respective cities. The privately operated airlines Air Deccan (a low-cost and web-based carrier; www.airdeccan.net), Jet Airways (www.jetairways.com), which has a good reputation, and Air Sahara (www.airsahara. net) fly on many domestic routes.

Boats

Apart from the river ferries there are very few boat services in India. The Andaman Islands are connected to Kolkata, Chennai and Vishakapatnam by boat, as well as to each other. There is a catamaran service between Mumbai and Goa run by Samudra Link Ferries (www.sam-link.com).

Kerala operates a regular passenger boat system on its canals and lagoons. A number of services operate from Alappuzha and Kollam (formerly Alleppey and Quilon), including the popular backwater trip between the two. Boats run daily (by the Water Transport Department or Alleppey Tourism). The trip lasts up to eight hours depending on the route.

There is also a boat service to and from the Lakshadweep islands from Kochi (*see* www.lakport.nic.in).

Buses

Almost every part of the country is connected by an extensive and well-developed bus system with the railway stations being the natural hubs for both local and regional services. Some of the more rural routes are serviced by noisy dilapidated vehicles, but an increasing number of deluxe and air-conditioned expresses ply the trunk routes. Local, rural buses, however, can be a charming, if slightly bumpy, way of seeing the landscape and rubbing shoulders (literally) with local people. On most buses the front few rows of seats are reserved for women and couples may be expected to sit apart.

Many of the trunk routes are now operated by video coaches – if you have never been to an Indian cinema, a night bus journey, for better or (usually) worse, is a highly amplified introduction to the popular variety of Tamil, Telugu or other regional film.

There are many parts of the country where the bus service is the only means of public transport. On many routes, even local ones, reservations can be made. Most baggage is carried on the bus roof, so all bags should be locked and checked on at intermediate stops.

Almost all cities have a bus service; Mumbai's bus service is excellent, the one in Chennai is not too bad, and the service in Delhi is steadily improving. It is advisable not to use city bus services during rush hour when they become unbearably crowded.

In most cities, however, it is generally preferable to use taxis or three-wheeled "auto-rickshaws".

Regional road transport websites

Each state has a road transport executive responsible for regional bus services. Their websites *(below)* have general information and timetables for many useful routes.

Andhra Pradesh
www.apsrtc.net
Karnataka
www.ksrtc.org
Kerala
www.keralartc.com
Tamil Nadu
www.tn.gov.in/transport/stu.htm

Cars and taxis

Chauffeur-driven cars, costing around £10–15 a day, can be arranged through tourist offices, hotels, local car rental firms, or branches of Hertz, Budget or Europcar.

Taxis are both air-conditioned and non-air-conditioned (cheaper and sometimes more comfortable). Charges vary, ranging from Rs325 for eight hours and 80 km (50 miles) to Rs450 for an air-conditioned car. For out-of-town travel, there is a per km charge, usually between Rs2.30–Rs3 per km in the plains (in the hills this rate is often Rs6 per km), with an overnight charge of Rs100. Package tours, sold by travel agencies and hotels, include assistance, guides and hotel accommodation, in addition to taxi charges.

The local yellow-top black taxis are metered, but with constant hikes in fuel prices, charges may often be higher than indicated on the meter. If so, this will be prominently stated in the taxi and the driver will have a card showing the excess over the meter reading that can be legitimately charged.

When taking a taxi or bus into town from the airport, it is advisable to change money in the arrival hall. In Delhi, Mumbai and Bangalore, a system of prepayment for taxis into the city is operated by the traffic police. This saves considerable anguish when the occasional unscrupulous driver takes a long route or tries to overcharge. Elsewhere, enquire at the information desk for the going rate for a journey to your destination before getting into the taxi; and make sure the meter is "down" before you embark. It is alright to share a taxi even if the destination may not be the same (although in the same area). In some cities, for example Mumbai, taxis have fare charts which, when applied to the amount on the meter, give the correct fare. There is often a night surcharge of 10 percent between 11pm and 6am and a rate of Rs1 to Rs2 per piece of baggage.

The fare for three-wheelers is about half that of taxis. Do not forget to ensure that the meter in the three-wheeler is flagged down to the minimum fare.

Driving in India

The best advice to anyone who is thinking about driving in India is, don't. Roads can be very congested and dangerous and there are many unwritten rules which are only known to local drivers. It is much easier and safer to hire a car and driver.

However, if you do have to drive you will need your domestic licence, liability insurance, an international driver's permit and your vehicle's registration papers. Information regarding road conditions can be obtained from national and state automobile associations which periodically issue regional motoring maps, general information regarding roads and detailed route charts. Contact: the Automobile Association of Southern India, 187 Anna Salai, Chennai 600 006, tel: 2852 1162.

Railways

Rail travel is safe, comfortable and by far the best way to get around the country. Indian Railways has a number of different classes, of varying degrees of comfort. In descending order of price, they are:

- First class AC, very comfortable with lockable cabins of four berths each.
- AC II tier, partitions arranged in groups of 6 berths with curtains that pull across to provide privacy.
- AC III tier, partitions with groups of 9 berths, the middle berths fold down for sleeping.
- AC chair car.
- First class (unfortunately now rare), non-AC but with ceiling fans. Has lockable cabins of four berths each. There is one cabin of two berths halfway down each carriage.
- Sleeper class, partitions of 9 berths with ceiling fans.
- Second class, unreserved with no berths and hard seats.

Reservations are required for all classes other than second class. In the summer months it is best to go AC. When the weather is cooler then first class can be an excellent option as it is possible to see the passing countryside without having to stare through the darkened windows of AC.

All carriages have both Western and Indian-style toilets. If you are up to squatting on a moving train always use the Indian toilet as they are invariably cleaner and better maintained.

NB: Reservation as far in advance as possible is strongly recommended as services can get booked up very quickly. Over 400 stations now have very efficient computerised booking counters from where you can book any ticket for any route. Reservations may be made up to 60 days in advance and cancellations (for which you will need to fill in the same form as for a reservation) can be made with varying degrees of penalty depending on the class and how close the cancellation is made to the time of departure. In the larger cities, the major stations have tourist sections with English-speaking staff to reduce the queues for foreigners and non-resident Indians buying tickets; payment is in pounds sterling or US dollars (traveller's cheques or cash). If reservations are not available then certain trains have a tourist quota that may be available. Other options are to take a waitlisted ticket or the more assured reservation against cancellation (RAC); the booking clerk should be able to advise you on how likely you are to get a reservation. Tatkal trains (marked with a "T" in timetables) have a certain number of reservations held back, which become available one day in advance for an extra charge. It is also possible to make bookings from abroad through Indian Railways representatives. They will accept bookings up to six months ahead, with a minimum of one month for first class, three months for second.

Trains are slow compared to those in the West, so if you are in a hurry, stick to the expresses. Fares are generally low. The Indrail Pass, available to foreign nationals and Indians resident abroad and paid for in foreign currency, can cut down on time getting reservations and be good value if you plan on travelling nearly every day.

In the UK the pass can be obtained through the very efficient and highly recommended S.D. Enterprises Ltd, 103 Wembley Park Drive, Wembley, Middlesex HA9 8HG; tel: 020-8903 3411; fax: 020-8903 0392; www.indiarail.co.uk They can also book single-journey tickets in advance for you. The Indrail pass can be bought in India at Railway Central Reservations Offices in Chennai, Kolkata, Mumbai Central, Mumbai CST and New Delhi.

Tourist Offices at railway reservation centres are helpful in planning itineraries and obtaining reservations. Tourist Offices are available at New Delhi (tel: 2340 5156), Mumbai Churchgate, Kolkata Fairlie Place, Chennai Central, and some other popular tourist destinations. Railway timetables available at Indian Tourist Offices abroad also contain much useful information.

Each regional railway prints its full timetable in Hindi, English and the regional language. There is also the monthly *Indian Bradshaw*, which lists all services across the country, or the concise but comprehensive *Trains At A Glance*, probably the most useful timetable for foreign tourists. These publications should be available from railway stations but they are updated and reprinted regularly so are periodically unavailable. All this information (and more, including fares and details of special trains and passes) can be found on the Indian Railways websites: for general information www.indianrailways.gov.in; for timetables and the current status of trains and your ticket www.indianrail.gov.in; and www.irctc.co.in to buy tickets online (you will need to register, and delivery and collection of tickets is only available in certain cities; see the website for details).

Remember to check which station your train departs from (many cities have at least two mainline stations) and do allow at least half an hour to find your seat/berth. Lists of passengers with the compartment and seat/berth numbers allotted to them are displayed on platforms and on each carriage an hour before departure. The station superintendent and the conductor attached to the train are usually available for assistance.

Food can usually be ordered through the coach attendant. On Shatabdi and Rajdhani trains the fare covers food, drinks and snacks as well. Bedding consisting of two sheets, a pillow and a blanket is provided in first class AC, AC II tier and III tier, and is also available from the attendant for Rps 20 in first class. In theory, if they want bedding, first-class passengers should contact the Station Manager before travelling, but extra bedding is often available. If travelling sleeper class then it is a good idea to take a sheet sleeping bag (any Indian tailor will run one up for you).

Retiring rooms (for short-term occupation only) are available at over 1,100 stations on a first-come first-served basis, but these are usually heavily booked. All first-class waiting rooms have couches for passengers using their own bedding. At both New Delhi and Howrah stations, a Rail Yatri Niwas has been built for transit passengers. Rooms can be booked in advance.

Cloakrooms are available at most stations where travellers can leave their luggage, but bags must be locked, and don't lose the reclaim ticket. Check opening times of the cloakroom for collection.

Very useful pre-paid taxi and/or auto-rickshaw services are available at most large stations.

Reservation forms

To buy your ticket you must first fill out a Reservation Requisition Form, which will be available from one of the windows in the booking office. The form is in the local language on one side and English on the reverse. In addition to the obvious information such as where you wish to leave from and go to and when, to fill in the form you also need to know:

- The train number and name. You can get this from a timetable, or, if the train departs from the station you are booking from, it is usually displayed on a board in the booking office.

- The class you require and whether you require a berth (for overnight journeys, or any journey between 9pm and 6am), or only a seat.
- Whether you require a lower, middle or upper berth. An upper berth is a good idea as it can be used throughout the day, whereas the other two may only be used for sleeping 9pm–6am.

Foreign travellers should also fill in their passport numbers in the column that asks for your Concession Travel Authority Number, as it is needed if the ticket is issued under the foreign tourist quota.

Regions

Indian Railways is divided into a number of regional zones; those in the South are given below with, where applicable, their websites.

East Coast Railway
Konkan Railway, www.konkanrailway.com
South Central Railway, www.scrailway.gov.in/web/
Southern Railway, www.srailway.com
South Western Railway

Rajdhani and Shatabdi trains

The list below gives each train's starting and destination stations, the train's number and name, departure and arrival times (**NB**: many long-distance trains take longer than 24 hours to reach their final destination), and the days it leaves on. The trains given here are a guide to the fastest times. They are only the superfast Rajdhani or Shatabdi and Jan Shatabdi services; many, many more – slower – trains run on these and numerous other routes. Times do change periodically so check at the booking office when buying your ticket.

From Bangalore
To H. Nizamuddin (Delhi): 2429 Rajdhani, dept. 18.35, arr. 05.15, Sun–Mon, Wed, Thur
To Hubli: 2079 Jan Shatabdi, dept. 06.00, arr. 13.00, Wed–Mon

From Chennai
Chennai Central to H. Nizamuddin (Delhi): 2433 Rajdhani, dept. 06.20, arr. 11.25, Fri, Sun
Chennai Central to Mysore: 2007 Shatabdi, dept. 06.00, arr. 13.00, Wed–Mon
Chennai Egmore to Vijayawada, 2077 Jan Shatabdi, dept. 06.45, arr. 13.35, Wed–Mon

From Delhi
H. Nizamuddin to Bangalore: 2430 Rajdhani, dept, 20.50, arr. 17.50, Mon–Tues, Fri–Sat
H. Nizamuddin to Chennai: 2434 Rajdhani, dept. 15.30, arr. 20.05, Wed, Fri
H. Nizamuddin to Mumbai: 2954T Rajdhani, dept. 16.55, arr. 10.15, Daily
H. Nizamuddin to Secunderabad: 2438 Rajdhani, dept. 20.50, arr. 19.10, Sun
H. Nizamuddin to Thiruvananthapuram: 2432 Rajdhani, dept. 11.00, arr. 05.45, Tues, Sun
New Delhi to Mumbai: 2952 Rajdhani, dept. 16.00, arr. 08.35, Daily

From Ernakulam
To Thiruvananthapuram: 2075 Jan Shatabdi, dept. 17.40, arr. 21.15, Daily

From Mumbai
Mumbai Central to New Delhi: 2951 Rajdhani, dept. 16.55, arr. 09.55, Daily
Mumbai Central to H. Nizamuddin (Delhi): 2953T, dept. 17.40, arr. 10.55, Daily

From Mysore
To Chennai: 2008 Shatabdi, dept. 14.20, arr. 21.25, Wed–Mon

From Secunderabad
To H. Nizamuddin (Delhi): 2437 Rajdhani, dept. 06.55, arr. 05.15, Wed

Indrail Pass Fares in US Dollars

	First Class AC		Other AC and FC		Sleeper Class	
	Adult	Child	Adult	Child	Adult	Child
Half-day	57	29	26	13	11	6
1 Day	95	47	43	22	19	10
2 Days	160	80	70	35	30	15
4 Days	220	110	110	55	50	25
7 Days	270	135	135	68	80	40
15 Days	370	185	185	95	90	45
21 Days	396	198	198	99	100	50
30 Days	495	248	248	126	125	65
60 Days	800	400	400	200	185	95
90 Days	1060	530	530	265	235	120

From Thiruvananthapuram
To Ernakulam: 2076 Jan Shatabdi, dept. 06.05, arr. 9.45, Daily
To H. Nizamuddin (Delhi): 2431 Rajdhani, dept. 19.15, arr. 13.50, Tues, Thur

From Vijayawada
To Chennai: 2078 Jan Shatabdi, dept. 14.30, arr. 21.20, Wed–Mon

Hill trains

India has a number of charming "toy trains" which run from the plains up to certain hill stations. These include the narrow-gauge track up to Udhagamandalam (Ooty) in the Nilgiris and the track between Neral and Matheran near Mumbai.

Rickshaws

The most convenient, and classically Indian, way of getting around town is by rickshaw. These come in two types: a cycle rickshaw (a tricycle with a seat for two people on the back), and a motorised three-wheeler known as an "auto" (to cut down on pollution some oof these have now been converted to run on CNG, compressed natural gas).

Autos are, like taxis, supposed to use a meter. You should insist on this and get out if they refuse. Meter rates are subject to periodic changes, and extras for late-night journeys etc., which the driver should show you on a card. In popular tourist spots, during rush hour and bad weather, you may find it impossible to persuade the drivers to use the meter. A tactic that might work is to offer "meter plus five" (the cost plus Rs 5). If not, you'll have to negotiate the fare. After a short while in the country you will get a feel for what is acceptable and, given that as a relatively well-off foreign tourist you are expected quite reasonably to pay a little more, what is not.

In many places it is common for auto drivers to suggest that, for a fixed amount, they take you around the sites for a whole day. This can be convenient and, if you bargain well, good value. Make sure that both of you understand what the price is and where you want to go (i.e. not via endless shops) before you set off.

Cycle rickshaws are more convenient in some places, like the very congested streets of Old Delhi. With these you should negotiate the fare before you set off.

Note: rickshaws are not allowed into central Mumbai and the only options are to use either the well-developed bus service or the reasonably-priced taxis.

ACCOMMODATION

HOTELS

Where to stay

Accommodation in India is varied to say the least; it runs the full gamut from very cheap and rather unsavoury, to hideously expensive with every conceivable luxury. Between these two extremes are some lovely places to stay. The indigenous five-star hotel chains are extremely well run, but luxury does not come cheap; most charge well over £100 per night.

Perhaps the best, and certainly the most Indian, places to stay are small, cheaper hotels which provide basic but usually clean and sometimes attractive accommodation. It is always wise to ask to see the room first before committing yourself (there are some truly dreadful places as well as charming ones). It is also a good idea to ask if there are any discounts, especially out of season. Air conditioning will always cost more but you might find it a necessity during the summer.

As well as luxury, business and cheaper hotels, there is also a growing network of "Heritage Hotels", set in converted palaces, forts or merchants' houses. The facilities can, though not always, be luxurious and expensive, with marble swimming pools, beautifully decorated suites and well-maintained grounds. Food is usually available to guests. Although heritage hotels are mainly concentrated in Rajasthan and Gujarat, the concept has spread and there are some superb old buildings to stay in elsewhere in the country. For more information try the website of the Indian Heritage Hotels Association (www.indianheritagehotels.com).

ACCOMMODATION LISTINGS

ANDHRA PRADESH

Amaravati (08645)

Punnami Amaravati
Tel: 255 332
www.tourisminap.com
Just four non-AC rooms in a tiny government-run guest house. **£**

Hindupur (08556)

Palla Residency
Railway Station Road
Tel: 224 869
Fax: 228 759
A friendly, new hotel with large, clean and safe AC rooms. Well-run with a decent veg restaurant. **£**

Hyderabad-Secunderabad (040)

Taj Krishna
Road No.1, Banjara Hills, Hyderabad
Tel: 5566 2323
Fax: 5566 1313
www.tajhotels.com
Previously the Oberoi Krishna, this gorgeous hotel is designed to blend in with natural rocks and waterfalls. It has recently been glammed up even more, though the rooms have an anonymous feel. **£££££**

Taj Residency
Road No.1, Banjara Hills, Hyderabad
Tel: 2339 3939
Fax: 2339 2684
Close by the Krishna is another Taj luxury outfit with Lakeside views. (Taj seem to have a monopoly on posh accommodation in Hyderabad as they also operate the neighbouring Taj Banjara.) **£££££**

Baseraa
9/1–167/8 Sarojini Devi Road, Secunderabad
Tel: 2770 3200
Fax: 2770 4745
www.baseraa.com
Immaculate air-conditioned rooms and good restaurants make this hotel a comfortable base. **£££–££££**

Amrutha Castle
5/9–16, Saifabad, Opposite Secretariat, Hyderabad
Tel: 5563 3888
Fax: 5582 8222
www.amruthacastle.com
Fantasy Bavarian castle. Good rooms and all amenities including a 5th-floor open-air swimming pool. **£££**

The Residency
5/8/231–2 Public Garden Road, Hyderabad
Tel: 3061 6161
Fax: 2320 4080
www.theresidency-hyd.com
A comfortable, fairly pricey and plush hotel near to Hyderabad station. There is a popular restaurant, **Venue**, and a bar and coffee shop. **£££**

Parklane
115 Park Lane, Secunderabad
Tel: 2784 0466
Fax: 2784 0599
Roomy and clean, non-AC rooms also available. **££**

Hotel Sai Prakash
Station Road, Nampally, Hyderabad
Tel: 2461 1726
Fax: 2461 3355
An good option close to Hyderabad station. Clean, well–maintained rooms around a large atrium. Two good restaurants, the veg **Sukhasaghra**, and the non-veg **Rich'n'Famous**, which serves Mughlai food. **££**

Nagarjunakonda (08680)

Punnami Vijay Vihar
Nagarjuna Sagar
Tel: 277 361
www.tourisminap.com
A pleasant small hotel with AC and non-AC rooms, and a decent restaurant. **£–££**

Srisailam (08524)

Punnami Srisailam
Tel: 287 369
www.tourisminap.com
Good value, simple accommodation close the pilgrimage site, with a restaurant attached. **£**

Tirupati (0877)

Bhimas Residency
Renigunta Road
Tel: 223 7376
Fax: 223 7373
A newish hotel, run by the owners of the Bhimas Deluxe, and up to their high standards. **££–£££**

Hotel Bhimas Paradise
33–7 Renigunta Road
Tel: 223 7271–6
Fax: 223 7277
www.hotelbhimas.com
Not run by the same owners as the Bhimas Deluxe but well run with large rooms, restaurant and swimming pool. **££**

Hotel Bliss
Near Ramanuja Circle, Renigunta Road
Tel: 223 7770–6
Fax: 223 7774
Modern hotel with clean rooms and bathooms. Two restaurants, vegetarian and non-veg. **££**

Bhimas Deluxe
34–38 G. Car Street
Tel: 222 5521
Fax: 222 5471
A lovely, very well-run hotel just around the corner from the railway station. Friendly, helpful staff and management. The excellent **Maya** vegetarian restaurant is in the basement. Recommended. **££**

Vijayawada (0866)

Hotel Raj Towers
Congress Office Road, Governorpet
Tel: 257 1311–8
Fax: 556 1714
Good value and modern AC rooms in a well-run hotel. The two restaurants serve vegetarian and non-vegetarian food. **£–££**

Sree Lakshmi Vilas Modern Cafe
Besant Road, Govenorpet
Tel: 257 2525
Central rooms with or without bath. There is also a good veg restaurant. **£**

Visakhapatnam (0891)

The Park
Beach Road
Tel: 275 4488
Fax: 275 4181
www.theparkhotels.com
Good modern rooms with sea views. Two restaurants, swimming pool and direct access to beach. **£££££**

Taj Residency
Beach Road
Tel: 256 7756
Fax: 256 4370
www.tajhotels.com
Vizag's finest and most striking hotel. All rooms have a sea view. Two good restaurants and a pool. **£££££**

Hotel Meghalaya
10-4–15 Ram Nagar, Asilmetta Junction
Tel: 275 5141–5
Fax: 275 5824
www.hotelmeghalaya.com
Friendly hotel with a large range of rooms (AC and non-AC). It also has a good vegetarian restaurant (the **Vaishali**). **££**

Warangal (0870)

Punnami Warangal
Opposite R.E.C., Kazipet
Tel: 243 2312
www.tourisminap.com
Simple but clean accommodation (some AC rooms) and a restaurant. **£**

KARNATAKA

Bandipur (08229)

Bandipur Safari Lodge
Melkamanahalli
Tel: 633 001
www.junglelodges.com
Very well run basic accommodation in modern cottages (no air conditioning) close to the park entrance. The camp has knowledgeable staff and good jeep safaris for watching the wildlife can be arranged. Recommended. **£££**

Country Club Bush Betta
Mangala
Tel: 236 090
www.countryclubindia.net
Recently taken over and renovated this resort now has over 60 rooms and a large swimming pool. A little way from the park entrance but good for families. **£££–££££**

Forest Department Cottages
For reservations contact:
The Field Director, Project Tiger, Aranya Bhavan, Ashokapuram,Mysore 570 008
Tel/fax: (0821) 248 0901
www.karnatakatourism.org
Basic accommodation, some of it in very cheap dormitories, in good locations. **£–££**

Hotel Mayura Prakruti
Melkamanahalli
Tel: 233 001
www.karnatakatourism.org
Simple budget accommodation but one of the best options near the park. Good value cottages and a decent outdoor restaurant. **£**

Tusker Trails
Mangala
Tel: (0821) 263 6055
Basic (no air conditioning) but clean and comfortable accommodation in a nice forested setting. Good opportunities for wildlife spotting and safaris are conducted twice daily. **££££**

Bangalore (080)

The Oberoi
37–9 Mahatma Gandhi Road,
Tel: 2558 5858
Fax: 2558 5960
www.oberoibangalore.com
A very expensive but luxurious hotel with beautiful gardens. The rooms and suites all have private "sit out" areas overlooking the gardens. **£££££**

The Park
14/7 Mahatma Gandhi Road
Tel: 2559 4666
Fax: 2559 4029
www.theparkhotels.com
A very swish, modern hotel. The rooms are elegant and bright, and there is the excellent **Monsoon** restaurant. **£££££**

The Taj West End
55 Race Course Road
Tel: 5660 5660
Fax: 5660 5700
www.tajhotels.com
A beautiful old garden hotel, Bangalore's most attractive five star. The lawnside rooms and restaurants are lovely. The Taj Group also runs two modern business hotels in the centre, the **Taj Residency** on M.G. Road, and the **Gateway Hotel** on Residency Road (see the website above for details). **£££££**

Highgates Hotel
33 Church Street
Tel: 2559 7172
Fax: 2559 7799
Very central and well-maintained hotel. Comfortable, good-value AC rooms. Price includes breakfast. Recommended. **£££**

Hotel Infantry Court
66 Infantry Road
Tel: 2559 1800
Fax: 2559 6890
hotelic@vsnl.com
Modern, central hotel with comfortable rooms which

PRICE CATEGORIES

The rates below are for a double room (AC where available) in high season, including taxes:
£ = up to Rs 700
££ = Rs 700–1,700
£££ = Rs 1,700–3,000
££££ = Rs 3,000–4,500
£££££ = above Rs 4,500

are good value for Bangalore. The price includes breakfast but watch out for hidden extras. **££££**

Niligiri's Nest
171 Brigade Road
Tel: 2558 8401
Fax: 2558 2853
nilgrisnest@vsnl.net
A central hotel with large, clean AC rooms, reasonable value, and a restaurant. **£££**

Woodlands Hotel
5 Raja Ram Mohan Roy Road
Tel: 2222 5111
Fax: 2223 6963
wood@bgl.vsnl.net.in
A large but pleasant hotel, well established, with good-value rooms and a decent restaurant. **£££**

Hotel Ajantha
22A Mahatma Gandhi Road
Tel/fax: 2558 4321
bagilthay@vsnl.com
Excellent-value, large rooms, some with AC, in good location. There is also a good vegetarian South Indian restaurant. **££**

Kamat Yatri Nivas
4 1st Cross, Gandhinagar
Tel: 2226 0088
Fax: 2228 1070
www.kamatyatrinivas.com
Located towards the railway station, this is a modern budget hotel. The 4th-floor South Indian restaurant has exceptionally good North Karnatakan vegetarian food. **££**

YHA
65/2 Millers Road, Benson Town Cantonment
Tel: 2354 0849
bangalore_youthhostel@yahoo.co.in
A modern building with clean AC and non-AC rooms, and a very cheap dormitory. Popular so book ahead. **£**

Gokarna (08386)

Hotel Gokarna International
Kumta Taluk, Gokarna,
Tel: 657 368/656 848
A comfortable option and very good value for money, though on the main road at the entrance to the town and thus prone to traffic noise during the day. **£**

KSTDC Hotel Mayura Samudra
Tel: 256 236
http://kstdc.nic.in
Just three exceptionally good-value large, clean rooms. A little out of the way, there is a pretty garden and a basic restaurant. **£**

Nimmu's
Behind the beach
Tel: 656 730
Large budget guest house. The rooms are clean and have bathrooms. Only a stone's throw away from the temples and town beach, but a peaceful location nonetheless. **£**

Hassan (08172)

Southern Star Hassan
B.M. Road
Tel: 251 816
Fax: 268 916
www.ushashriramhotels.com
A well-run and clean hotel with decent rooms, most of which have AC. More expensive than some but with friendly and helpful service. **£££**

Hotel Suvarna Regency
97 B.M. Road
Tel: 264 006
Fax: 263 822
An excellent-value modern hotel with comfortable AC rooms. There is also a restaurant serving resaonable Indian food. **££**

Vaishnavi Lodging
Harsha Mahal Road
Tel: 267 413
Clean and roomy budget accommodation with a decent vegetarian restaurant attached. **£**

Hampi Bazaar (08394)

Hotel Mayura Bhuvaneshwari
Kamalapur
Tel: 241 574
Fax: 228 537
http://kstdc.nic.in
Good-value AC and non-AC rooms a little distance from the site. Good food is available in the restaurant. **£**

Shanti Lodge
Near Virupaksha Temple
Tel: 241 568
Spotlessly clean rooms with shared baths in a two-storey building with windows overlooking a shaded inner courtyard. If it is full, **Rahul** (tel: 0839 411648), south of the main bazaar, is also fine. **£**

Hospet (08394)

Hotel Malligi
10/90 Jambunath Road
Tel: 228 101
Fax: 227 038
Close to M.G. Road. A reasonably expensive but popular hotel, with a bar, pleasant restaurant and good pool (non-residents may pay to use the pool). **£££**

Hotel Priyadarshini
V-45 Station Road
Tel: 228 838
Fax: 24709
priyainn@vsnl.com
AC rooms with balconies, helpful and friendly service and a garden restaurant looking out over the sugar-cane and paddy fields. Hot water 6.30–9.30am. **££**

Hotel Shivananda
Beside KSRTC Bus Stand, College Road
Tel: 220 700
Cleanish, good-value rooms with attached bath, and a small restaurant. Hot water is available 6–9am. **££**

Mangalore (0824)

Manjarun Hotel
Old Port Road, Bunder
Tel: 566 0420
Fax: 566 0585
www.tajhotels.com
A little way out of town, this modern Taj-run hotel has good-value, comfortable rooms, some overlooking the sea. There is a pool and a restaurant serving Indian and Western food. **££££**

Hotel Poonja International
K.S. Rao Road
Tel: 244 0171
Fax: 244 1081
www.hotelpoonjainternational.com
Very good-value, clean rooms in a large modern hotel. Well run with excellent food in the restaurant. **£££**

KSTDC Maurya Netravati
Kadri Hills
Tel: 221 1192
http://kstdc.nic.in
Extremely good-value, large and clean rooms. There is also a decent restaurant. **£–££**

Mysore (0821)

ITDC Lalitha Mahal Palace Hotel
Siddhartha Nagar
Tel: 247 0470
Fax: 247 0555
www.theashokgroup.com
Palatial rooms with wonderful period bathrooms, in a neoclassical building sporting a dome modelled on St Paul's Cathedral. Excellent service, an impressive Wedgwood-blue restaurant, and a pleasant pool and gardens. **£££££**

Green Hotel
Chittaranjan Palace, 2270 Vinoba Road, Jayalakshmipuram
Tel: 525 5000–2
Fax: 251 6139
www.greenhotelindia.com
A charming palace conversion in own gardens a little way out of town. A remarkable project in sustainable tourism through energy-saving and equal-opportunity employment. Good-value, attractive rooms and superb food. Highly recommended. **£££–££££**

The Viceroy
Sri Harsha Road
Tel: 242 4001
Fax: 243 3391
A clean, modern hotel with well-appointed rooms. The **Pavilion** restaurant serves good North Indian food. **£££**

KSTDC Mayura Hoysala and Yatrinivas
2 Jhansi Lakshmibai Road
Tel: 242 5349
http://kstdc.nic.in
Extremely good-value large rooms. There is also a decent bar and restaurant and pleasant gardens. The **Yatrinivas** (tel: 242 3492) adjoining the Hoysala has a very cheap dormitory. **£**

Hotel Ritz
Bangalore–Nilgiri Road
Tel: 242 2668
Fax: 242 9082
Characterful little hotel with only four rooms around balcony with a guest's dining area. The rooms have mosquito nets and attached bathroom

with hot water. Good restaurant downstairs. Book ahead. Recommended. **£**

Nagarahole

Forest Department Cottages
Book through:
Conservator of Forests, Kodagu Circle, Aranya Bhavan, Madikeri 571 201, Karnataka
Tel: (08272) 225 708
www.karnatakatourism.org
Basic lodges with simple but clean rooms. food is available as are jeeps for safaris. **££–£££**

Jungle Inn
Veeranahosalli, Hunsur, Murkal–Nagarhole Road, Mysore District 570 011, Karnataka
Tel: (08222) 246 022
www.jungleinnnagarhole.com
Decent rooms in a well-run resort. The wildlife watching facilities are excellent and safaris within the park are accompanied by a knowledgeable naturalist. **£££££**

Kabini River Lodge
Karapur, Nissana Beltur, Mysore District 571 114, Karnataka
Tel: (08228) 264 402
www.junglelodges.com
One of the best wildlife lodges India. Comfortable accommodation, decent food and excellent advice from the resident naturalists. Very good value and highly recommended. **££££–£££££**

Water Woods
19 Karapur, Mysore District 571 114, Karnataka
Tel: (0821) 226 4421
www.waterwoods.net
Expensive but beautifully kept and comfortable accommodation overlooking the river. Decent buffet food and good access to the park by boat or jeep. **£££££**

KERALA

Alappuzha (0477)

La Casa del Fauno
Muhamma, Aryakkara
Tel: 286 0862
www.casadelfauno.com
A very classy homestay, about 8 km (5 miles) from Alappuzha. The rooms are spotless and attractive in a kitschy-minimalist sort of way. The facilities on offer include, among others, boat hire, Ayurvedic treatments and a swimming pool. **£££££**

Raheem Residency
Beach Road
Tel: 223 0767; mobile: 94470 82241
www.raheemresidency.com
A beautiful colonial villa dating from 1868 now converted into a chic and luxurious heritage hotel. The rooms are delightful, with period furniture. The staff are attentive without being pushy and there is a lovely pool. It is not far from Alappuzha beach. **£££££**

Kayaloram Heritage Lake Resort
Punnamada
Tel: 223 2040
Fax: 223 1871
www.kayaloram.com
A peaceful resort 4km (2½ miles) from Alappuzha (free transfer at 11am and 1pm). Individual Keralan-style wooden cottages, as well as a restaurant and pool. Stays can also be arranged in *kettuvallams* – traditional boats. **£££–££££**

Alleppey Prince Hotel
A.S. Road
Tel: 224 3752
Fax: 224 3758
www.alleppeyprincehotel.com
Decent, clean, air-conditioned rooms, restaurant and pool, in a long-established hotel. Kathakali dance performances are occasionally staged and backwater tours can be organised from here. **£££**

Emerald Isle Heritage Villa
Kanjooparambil–Manimalathara
Tel: 270 3899; mobile: 94470 77555
www.emeraldislekerala.com
A highly recommended, peaceful retreat. Four guest rooms with lovely 'outdoor' bathrooms in a traditional house set in idyllic tropical surroundings. Excellent traditional Keralan meals and considerate, friendly service. Twelve km (7 miles) from Alappuzha; call in advance so the boat is waiting for you at the jetty to take you over to the island. Evening boat trips can be arranged as well as cruises on *kettuvallams*. **£££**

KTDC Yatri Nivas
Motel Aram Compound, A.S. Road
Tel: 224 4460
Fax: 224 4463
www.ktdc.com
Good-value air-conditioned rooms (very cheap non-AC accommodation) in a government-run guesthouse. **£**

Athirapalli (0480)

Rainforest
Kannamkuzhy
Tel: 276 9062
www.avenuecenter.com
This peaceful resort has superb views over the waterfalls and surrounding forests. The rooms and facilities are rather basic but it is the location that counts. **£££**

Bekal (0467)

Gitanjali Heritage
Panayal
Tel: 223 4159
www.gitanjaliheritage.com
This is a wonderful place to base yourself. Mr Jagannathan and his family are very welcoming and their 70-year-old home, a traditional *kodoth* house, is beautifully maintained. It is set in a delightful garden and the food is excellent. Mr Jagannathan is also a mine of information on the local *Teyyam* dances. This is a highly recommended retreat. **£££**

Guruvayur (0487)

Vrindavan Tourist Home
Next to KSRTC Bus Stand, West Nada
Tel: 255 4033
A rather sweet and well-maintained budget lodge that mainly caters to pilgrims. The staff are welcoming and the rooms are clean and extremely good value. **£**

Kannur (0497)

Royal Omars Hotel
Thavakkara, opposite Bharat Petroleum
Tel: 276 9091
A flash, modern business hotel near the station. Remarkably good value comfortable rooms and facilities. **££–£££**

Kochi-Ernakulam (0484)

The Brunton Boatyard
Calvetty Road, Fort Cochin
Tel: 221 5461
Fax: 221 5562
www.cghearth.com
A luxury hotel in a splendid location, built in the style of early Portuguese and Dutch colonial architecture. Elegant and beautifully appointed rooms and bathrooms. A good restaurant serves local dishes recreated from historical recipes. **£££££**

Malabar House Residency
1/268–9 Parade Road, Fort Cochin
Tel: 221 6666
Fax: 221 7777
www.malabarhouse.com
One of the best luxury hotels in Kerala, set in a refurbished 300-year-old house within the fort area. The rooms are comfortable and furnished with antiques, there is an inviting plunge pool, and the food in the outdoor restaurant is excellent.

PRICE CATEGORIES

The rates below are for a double room (AC where available) in high season, including taxes:
£ = up to Rs 700
££ = Rs 700–1,700
£££ = Rs 1,700–3,000
££££ = Rs 3,000–4,500
£££££ = above Rs 4,500

ABOVE: looking out towards Kovalam beach.

Often booked up so make reservations well in advance. **£££££**

Taj Malabar
Malabar Road, Willingdon Island
Tel: 266 6811
Fax: 266 8297
www.tajhotels.com
One of the best hotels in the state; try and get a room in the old wing, which is more atmospheric. There are also good restaurants – especially the one where you sit outside on the point of the island overlooking the harbour – and there's a pool too. **£££££**

The Avenue Regent
39/2026 M.G. Road, Ernakulam
Tel: 237 7688
Fax: 237 5329
avenue@md2.vsnl.net.in
A modern business hotel with very comfortable rooms. The hotel restaurant is very good (try the buffet lunch) and the modern and chic **Loungevity** bar is one of the best in the state. **££££**

Casino Hotel
Willingdon Island
Tel: 266 8221
Fax: 266 8001
www.cghearth.com
Comfortable hotel with a highly recommended seafood restaurant. Very clean and tasteful rooms (nice touches such as cosmetics in small terracotta pots in the bathrooms), and a good pool. A little way from the centre of Ernakulam but convenient buses go to M.G. Road. **££££**

Abad Plaza
M.G. Road, Ernakulam
Tel: 238 1222
Fax: 237 0729
www.abadhotels.com
A good, modern hotel with clean rooms in central Ernakulam. There is a pool and a decent restaurant serving seafood. **£££**

Woodlands
M.G. Road, Ernakulam
Tel: 238 2051
Fax: 238 2080
woodland1@vsnl.com
A comfortable hotel with clean, excellent-value air-conditioned rooms (it's cheaper for non-AC rooms) and a good vegetarian restaurant. **£££**

Delight Tourist Resort
Parade Ground, Fort Kochi
Tel: 221 6301
www.delightfulhomestay.com
A quiet little guesthouse with spotless rooms right in the centre of Fort Kochi. Comfy beds, a lovely garden and an extremely helpful travel desk. **££–£££**

Adams Hotel
South Junction, Ernakulam
Tel: 237 7707
A good-value hotel above Pizza Hut, very convenient for the railway station. Clean rooms and efficient service. **££**

SAAS Tower Hotel
Cannon Shed Road, near Boat Jetty, Ernakulam
Tel: 236 5319
Fax: 236 7365
This good-value hotel has decent if smallish rooms. The attached restaurant has good Indian food. **£–££**

YHA
NGO Qrts Junction, Thrikkakra
Tel: 242 2808
Fax: 242 4399
www.yhaindia.com
A bit out of the way behind Ernakulam Junction, but clean, good value and quiet. Meals are available. **£**

Kollam (0474)

Hotel Sudarshan
Paramesvar Nagar, Hospital Road
Tel: 274 4322
Fax: 274 0480
www.hotelsudarshan.com
Clean, largish air-conditioned rooms with attached bath and hot water. There is also a restaurant and snack bar. **££**

Government Guest House
Ashramom
Tel: 274 3620
Formerly the British residency, on Ashtamudi Lake. Very atmospheric, it has five spacious rooms, and food, if ordered in advance. Backwater trips may be arranged from here (the boat will pick you up from the jetty across from the garden). **£**

KTDC Yatri Nivas
Ashramom, Guest House Compound
Tel: 274 5538
www.ktdc.com
This large, government-run hotel has good-value, basic rooms and is situated beside the lake (opposite the jetty). **£**

Kottayam (0481)

Coconut Lagoon
Vembanad Lake
Tel: (0484) 266 8221
www.cghearth.com
One of the finest resorts in Kerala, about 10 km (6 miles) from Kottayam and only accessible by boat. The facilities are first class, including the Ayurvedic treatments, and the rooms are tasteful and luxurious. **£££££**

Hotel Aida
Aida Junction, M.C. Road
Tel: 256 8391
Fax: 256 8399
www.hotelaidakerala.com
Good-value, comfortable rooms, all with bath and hot water. There is a restaurant serving Indian dishes. **££**

KTDC Aiswarya
Thirunakkara
Tel: 258 1440
Fax: 256 5618
Pleasant rooms in a government-run hotel, with optional air conditioning and cable TV. The hotel also has a decent restaurant. **££**

Vembanad Lake Resort
Kodimatha
Tel: 236 1633
Fax: 236 0866
Located 3 km (2 miles) from the town. Comfortable cottages in gardens by the lake. A good restaurant on a houseboat serves tanduri and seafood dishes. **££**

Kovalam (0471)

Coconut Bay
Vizhinjam
Tel: 248 0566
www.coconutbay.com
A well-run and quiet resort, just behind the beach, set out in small bungalows. The staff are discreetly attentive and the Ayurvedic package here is extremely good. **£££££**

The Leela Kovalam
Tel: 248 0101
Fax: 248 1522
www.theleela.com
Striking hotel complex (previously the Kovalam Ashok), designed in part by Charles Correa. The hotel now includes the Halcyon Castle, summer palace of the Maharajas of Travancore. Expensive but exceptionally luxurious, with a great pool and in a superb location. **£££££**

Surya Samudra Beach Garden
Tel: 226 7333
Fax: 248 0413
www.suryasamudra.com
An expensive and exclusive resort with accommodation in relocated traditional

houses. It's 8km (5 miles) from Kovalam in a wonderful, quiet location overlooking the sea. **££££**

Taj Green Cove Resort
G.V. Raja Vattapara Road
Tel: 248 7733
Fax: 248 7744
www.tajhotels.com
The Taj group doing what it does best, well run and with low-key luxury. Very comfortable rooms and cottages set in lovely grounds, and with a superb pool. **£££££**

Lagoona Davina
Pachallur
Tel: 238 0049
Fax: 238 2651
www.lagoonadavina.com
Peaceful resort, close to Pozhikkara Beach, run by Englishwoman Davina Taylor. The attractive rooms have four-poster beds, and there is good food, Ayurvedic massage and yoga classes. **££££**

Hotel Sea Face
N.U.P. Beach Road
Tel: 248 1835
Fax: 248 1320
www.hotelseaface.com
A popular hotel close to the beach. Pleasant, clean rooms, friendly staff, as well as a good restaurant and pool. **££££**

Hotel Neelakanta
Lighthouse Beach
Tel: 248 0321
Fax: 248 0421
www.hotelneelakantakovalam.com
This reasonably priced hotel is right on the beach front. The rooms have huge windows and balconies, all of which gives you a great view over the sea. **££–£££**

Hotel Rockholm
Lighthouse Road
Tel: 248 0306
Fax: 248 0607
www.rockholm.com
Pleasant hotel at the end of Lighthouse Beach. The spotless rooms have great views and there is a good restaurant. **££–£££**

Maharaju Palace
Tel/fax: 0031-(0)299-372 597
www.maharajupalace.nl
A Dutch-owned hotel (book through the Netherlands) close to the lighthouse. Very pleasant and quiet and only 30 m (100ft) from the beach. **££**

Kozhikode (0495)

Kadavu
N.H. Bypass Road, Azhinjilam
Tel: 283 0570
Fax: 283 0575
www.kadavuresorts.com
Beautifully located hotel, 14 km (8½ miles) from Kozhikode. The comfortable rooms and suites all have a spectacular view over the river, and there is good food in the restaurant. **£££££**

Malabar Palace
Manuelsons Junction, G.H. Road
Tel: 272 1511
Fax: 272 1794
www.malabarpalacecalicut. com
A modern hotel that is a comfortable mid-budget choice with good air-conditioned rooms. Friendly service and a very efficient front desk. There is also an excellent restaurant. **££**

Alakapuri Hotel
Moulana Mohamed Ali Road
Tel: 272 3451
Fax: 272 0219
An excellent-value colonial-style guesthouse. The large rooms with bath are full of character. The restaurant serves good Indian food. **£**

Munnar (04865)

The Windermere Estate
PO Box 21, Pothamedu
Tel: 230 512
www.windermeremunnar.com
Attractive, simple rooms in secluded planter's cottages with stunning views over the hills. It is beautifully quiet and very relaxing. **£££££**

The Olive Brook
In the Tata Tea Estate, Pothamedu
Tel: 230 588
www.olivebrookmunnar.com
These two bungalows set high above the town are a lovely retreat. The staff are great and there are cooking demonstrations in the evening. Highly recommended. **££££**

Blackberry Hills
Bison Valley Road, Pothamedu
Tel: 232 978
Fax: 232 965
www.blackberryhillsindia. com
A group of cottages 3 km (2 miles) out of town in an idyllic location. Well kept, with stunning views, the staff can also arrange treks in the surrounding countryside. **£££–££££**

Edassery East End
Temple Road
Tel: 230 451
Fax: 230 227
www.edasserygroup.com
This large hotel has comfortable double rooms in the main building, and a series of cottages in the well-maintained grounds. Good value for its location and facilities, this is one of the best hotels in the town itself. **£££**

Isaac's Residency
Top Station Road
Tel: 230 501
A comfortable, modern hotel close to the centre of town. The rooms are spacious and well maintained, and the ones at the front of the building have excellent views. The in-house restaurant is not bad. **£££**

Periyar (04869)

Lake Palace
Thekkady, Idukki 685 536, Kerala
Tel: 222 023
www.ktdc.com
Previously belonging to the Maharaja of Travancore, this small heritage resort is a great place from which to launch your wildlife spotting trips. **£££££**

Spice Village
Kumily Road, Thekkady 685 536, Kerala
Tel: 224 514
www.cghearth.com
Traditional-style thatched cottages in beautiful grounds. Very comfortable and excellent service. Forest walks and *ayurvedic* treatments are on offer. Recommended. **£££££**

Aranya Niwas
Thekkady, Idukki 685 536, Kerala
Tel: 222 023
www.ktdc.com
Set on the banks of the lake this somewhat dated but still comfortable retreat retains some of its colonial charm. **££££–£££££**

Bamboo Grove
Periyar Tiger Reseve, Thekkady 685 536, Kerala
Tel: 224 571
www.periyartigerreserve.org
Set right in the park itself, these simple huts are perfect for serious wildlife observation. Book in advance. **£££**

Periyar House
Thekkady, Idukki 685 536, Kerala
Tel: 222 026
www.ktdc.com
Good-value budget accommodation near to the park, Clean and comfortable rooms and friendly staff. **££**

Jungle Inn
Periyar Tiger Reseve, Thekkady 685 536, Kerala
Tel: 224 571
www.periyartigerreserve.org
A rare opportunity to spend a night in amongst the wildlife of the park. A small, secluded hut that is ideally placed for forest treks. **£–££**

Silent Valley

Forest Department Rest House
Mukkali
Book through:
Wildlife Warden, Silent Valley National Park, Mannarkkad, Palakkad, Kerala
Tel: (0492) 242 2056/245 3225
www.keralaforest.org
Basic accommmodation ranging from simple doubles to a dormitory. You must be accompanied by a forest guard to enter the sanctuary. **£**

Thiruvananthapuram (0471)

The Muthoot Plaza
Punnen Road
Tel: 233 7733
Fax: 233 7734
www.sarovarhotels.com
The city's top business hotel, with very comfortable rooms and good facilities. **££££**

The South Park
M.G. Road

PRICE CATEGORIES

The rates below are for a double room (AC where available) in high season, including taxes:
£ = up to Rs 700
££ = Rs `700–1,700
£££ = Rs 1,700–3,000
££££ = Rs 3,000–4,500
£££££ = above Rs 4,500

Tel: 233 3333
Fax: 233 1861
www.thesouthpark.com
A swish hotel with a flash lobby, aimed at the business market, with reasonable rooms that don't quite match up to the promise of the public areas. **££££**

Residency Tower
South Gate of Secretariat, Press Road
Tel: 233 1661
Fax: 233 1311
www.residency tower.com
A modern, comfortable hotel with good facilities. There are good restaurants and a rooftop pool. Good value for what's on offer. **£££–££££**

Mascot Hotel
P.M.G. Junction
Tel: 231 8990
Fax: 231 7745
www.ktdc.com
Pleasant, quiet, renovated hotel, originally built to house British officers during World War I. In a quiet location with a good restaurant. **£££**

Hotel Chaithram
Central Station Road, Thampanoor
Tel: 233 0977
Fax: 233 1446
www.ktdc.com
A clean, good-value KTDC hotel opposite the railway station. Some rooms have air conditioning and attached baths. There is a good restaurant on the ground floor. It is often full so book in advance. **££**

Hotel Highland Park
Manjalikulam Road, Thampanoor
Tel: 223 8800
Fax: 233 2645
A newish hotel with both AC and non-AC rooms at good rates. The rooms are well maintained and there is a decent vegetarian restaurant. **££**

Greenland Lodging
Aristo Road
Tel: 232 3485
A long-established and decent, budget hotel with clean rooms. Very convenient for the railway and bus stations if you are making an early start. **£–££**

Hazeen Tourist Home
Off Aristo Road, close to Aristo Junction
Tel: 232 5181
Clean, but very basic rooms in a quiet hotel not far from the railway station. **£**

Hotel Prathiba Heritage
Dharmalayam Road
Tel: 233 6442
Very central with clean and safe rooms in a friendly hotel. Filtered water available. **£**

Thrissur (0487)

Mannapuram Hotel
Kuruppam Road
Tel: 244 0933
Fax: 242 7692
A modern but attractive hotel with comfortable, well-priced and clean rooms. Efficiently run with a good restaurant attached. **££**

KTDC Yatri Nivas
Near Indoor Stadium
Tel: 233 2333
Fax: 233 2122
www.ktdc.com
A good budget option, government-run with clean rooms. Snacks are available. **£**

Ramanilayam Government Guest House
Palace Road
Tel: 233 2016
Strictly speaking for visiting officials only. Large suites with balconies in a colonial mansion. Food available to order in advance. Excellent value. **£**

Varkala

Taj Garden Retreat
Near Government Guest House, Janardana Puram
Tel: (0472) 260 3000
Fax: (0472) 260 2296
www.tajhotels.com
A luxurious resort hotel close to Varkala's superb beach. There are great views from its hilltop position. Good restaurants and pool. **£££££**

Villa Jacaranda
Temple Road West
Tel: (0470) 261 0296
www.villa-jacaranda.biz
Spotless and nicely designed rooms in a modern guesthouse. The surrounding gardens are quite beautiful and the views of sunset over the sea breathtaking. **££££**

Waynad

Green Magic Nature Resort
Book through:
Tour India
P.O. Box 163, near S.M.V. High School, M.G. Road, Thiruvananthapuram
Tel: (0471) 233 0437
Fax: (0471) 233 1407
www.tourindiakerala.com
Accommodation is in either a wonderful treehouse or cottages set in the heart of a pristine rainforest. This is an eco-resort in the true sense of the term (they use bio-gas and solar power, serve organic food and only natural cosmetics are allowed). Not cheap, but it is a unique experience. **£££££**

Jungle Park Resort
52a Vrindhavan Colony, Chevayur, Kozhikode
Tel: (0495) 552 1163
www.jungleparkresorts.com
Beautifully sited in the Fintser Hills, this eco-resort has traditional-style cottages set within the forest. **££££–£££££**

Forest Rest Houses
In Tholpetty, Muthanga, Kurichat and Thirunelly
Book through:
Wildlife Warden, Waynad Widllife Division, Sulthanbathery
Tel: (04936) 220 454
www.keralaforest.org
A series of simple huts and dormitories in the reserve. All of them have a cook and a guide. **£**

LAKSHADWEEP

Bangaram

Bangaram Island Resort
Book through:
Casino Hotel
Willingdon Island, Kochi
Tel: (0484) 266 8221
Fax: (0484) 266 8001
www.cghearth.com
A peaceful luxury resort. Visitors are transferred by boat from Agatti. The shallow lagoon is fabulously clear and clean, and perfect for swimming. All-inclusive board and lodging, but bottled water is extra and charged at a slightly shocking marked-up rate (make sure you have enough cash to cover extras at the end of your stay). Accommodation is in simple huts; although the water in the bathrooms smells strongly of sulphur, it is safe. Meals take the form of a buffet with lots of fresh fish. The friendly and helpful staff hold a barbecue on the beach one night a week. There are facilities for snorkelling and scuba diving, some of the best in the Indian Ocean (neither of which is included in the cost). There is a bar on the beach (again, drinks are not included in the price of the package). **£££££**

Kadmat

Kadmat Cottages
Book through:
Lacadives
Lakshmi Niwas, 43/2051 K Colony, Kochi
Tel: (0484) 220 6766
www.lacadives.com
A lovely, if simple, resort on a fabulous lagoon. Transfer is by boat from Agatti. Accommo-dation is in small cottages with AC and attached bathrooms. The price includes all meals, but alcohol is not allowed. There is a small shop selling basics such as toiletries, snacks and soft drinks. The swimming, and particularly diving, is excellent. Dive packages are available, including those for beginners, or you can book single dives by the day (for an extra fee). **£££££**

PONDICHERRY (0413)

Le Dupleix
5 rue de la Caserne
Tel: 222 6999
Fax: 233 5278
www.sarovarparkplaza.com
An elegant and chic heritage hotel set in an 18th-century French villa. The interior has been beautifully restored and the facilities are excellent. **££££**
Hotel de l'Orient
17 rue Romain Rolland
Tel: 234 3067
Fax: 222 7829
www.neemranahotels.com
An 18th-century neoclassical mansion, now turned into a heritage hotel. It has comfortable rooms and an excellent Creole restaurant. **££££**
Anandha Inn
154 S.V. Patel Road
Tel: 233 0711
Fax: 233 1241
www.anandhainn.com
A comfortable and good-value modern hotel with two restaurants serving Indian and continental food. Recommended. **£££**
Hotel Mass
152–4 Maraimalai Adigal Salai
Tel: 220 4001
Fax: 220 3654
www.hotelmass.com
Clean and good-value AC rooms in a friendly hotel near to the bus stand. It has a nice restaurant with good Chettinad food. **££**
Seaside Guest House
14 Goubert Salai
Tel: 233 6494
Fax: 233 4447
www.sriaurobindosociety.org.in
An Ashram guest house, kept spotlessly clean and with a magnificent view. There is also a cafeteria with decent vegetarian food. **£–££**
International Guest House
47 Netaji Subash Chandra Bose Salai
Tel: 233 6699
Fax: 233 4447
www.sriaurobindosociety.org.in
A well-kept, centrally located Ashram guest house with a vegetarian cafeteria. **£**

TAMIL NADU

Chennai (044)

Ambassador Pallava
53 Monteith Road
Tel: 2855 4476/2855 4068
Fax: 2855 4492
www.ambassadorindia.com
Largely a business hotel, it is, however, in a convenient location close to Anna Salai and the museum. Facilities include pool, a beauty parlour and a couple of decent restaurants. **£££££**
Taj Coromandel
37 M.G. Road, Nungambakkam
Tel: 2827 2827
Fax: 2825 7104
www.tajhotels.com
Luxurious but very expensive (well over £150 per night) with good service and four excellent restaurants, including the South Indian **Southern Spice**. **£££££**
Taj Connemara
2 Binny Road
Tel: 5500 0000
Fax: 5500 0555
www.tajhotels.com
One of the great hotels of India, deservedly popular and set in an Art Deco building. Excellent value (around £100 per night for a standard room) with wonderful service. It has a lovely pool and good restaurants, including the open-air **Raintree**, and **Hipasia**, as well as a chic cocktail bar. The newly renovated coffee shop is a great place for breakfast or lunch. **£££££**
The Trident
1–24 G.S.T. Road
Tel: 2234 4747
Fax: 2234 6699
www.tridenthotels.com
Part of the Oberoi chain (and therefore a little pricey), this sleek, modern and efficient hotel is out near the airport. It has an excellent coffee shop. **£££££**
Residency
49 G.N. Chetty Road, T. Nagar
Tel: 2825 3434
Fax: 2825 0085
www.theresidency.com
Recommended, with a range of rooms and good restaurant. Good value for what's on offer. Reserve ahead. **£££**
Hotel Kanchi
28 Ethiraj Salai, Egmore
Tel: 2827 1100
Fax: 2827 2928
www.hotelkanchi.com
Large and light rooms that are starting to show their age, but still with a certain charm. Good South Indian food downstairs, great views and OK North Indian dishes in rooftop **Geetham** restaurant. **££**
Hotel Himalaya
54 Triplicane High Road, Triplicane
Tel: 2854 7522
Fax: 2831 808
A good, central hotel. Very clean rooms with bath, helpful and friendly staff. Recommended. **££**
Hotel Pandian
9 Kennet Lane, Egmore
Tel: 2819 1010/2819 2020
Fax: 2819 3030
www.hotelpandian.com
Park-side rooms with nice views but no AC. The AC rooms on the other side are very cool but dark. It has a reasonable restaurant (the **Raj**) and a useful STD booth in grounds. Friendly staff and convenient for Egmore Station. **££**
Hotel New Woodlands
72–5 Dr Radhakrishnan Road, Mylapore
Tel: 2811 3111
Fax: 2811 0460
www.newwoodlands.com
A large hotel with excellent vegetarian restaurant. The large, clean rooms are popular, so book ahead. **££**
YWCA International Guest House
1086 E.V.R. Periyar High Road
Tel: 2532 4234
Fax: 2532 4263
ywcaigh@indiainfo.com
A safe place to stay near the Daily Tanti newspaper office. Rooms with attached baths, some with AC, and also camping facilities. The cost of the room includes breakfast. There is a temporary membership fee of Rs 20. Recommended. **££**
Hotel Mount Heera
287 M.K.N. Road, Alandur
Tel: 2234 9563/2233 0832
Fax: 2233 1236
Noisy hotel near airport, good if you have an early-morning flight. Price includes taxi to the airport. **£–££**
Youth Hostel
2nd Avenue, Indiranagar, Adyar
Tel: 2442 0233
Very cheap but quiet and clean accommodation. **£**

Chidambaram (04144)

Hotel Akshaya
17 East Car Street
Tel: 220 192
Decent rooms in a central hotel (close to the temple) with non-AC, and a few AC, rooms. **£–££**
Hotel Ritz
2 V.G.P. Street
Tel: 223 312–4
Good, clean rooms, some AC, in a friendly small hotel. **£–££**

Coimbatore (0422)

Heritage Inn
38 Sivasamy Road, Ramnagar
Tel: 233 1451
Fax: 233 3233
www.hotelheritageinn.com
Modern, comfortable and well-maintained rooms. A clean hotel with good

PRICE CATEGORIES

The rates below are for a double room (AC where available) in high season, including taxes:
£ = up to Rs 700
££ = Rs 700–1,700
£££ = Rs 1,700–3,000
££££ = Rs 3,000–4,500
£££££ = above Rs 4,500

ABOVE: bright colours in Kochi.

restaurants. **£££**

Nilgiri's Nest
739a Avinashi Road
Tel: 221 7132
Fax: 221 7131
nilgiris@md3.vsnl.net.in
Good and comfortable AC rooms. There is a great restaurant and useful shop. Convenient for the railway station. **££–£££**

Sree Annapoorna Lodging
47 East Arokiasamy Road, R.S. Puram
Tel: 254 7722
Fax: 254 7322
www.sreeannapoorna.com
Good-value rooms, some of them AC, in a well-established hotel. Tasty vegetarian food in the restaurant. **££**

TTDC Hotel Tamilnadu
Dr Nanjappa Road
Tel: 230 2176
Fax: 230 3511
www.tamilnadutourism.org
A quiet hotel near the bus-stand. Good-value clean rooms, some AC (non-AC **£**) with attached bathrooms. **£–££**

Coonoor (0423)

Taj Garden Retreat
Church Road, Upper Coonoor
Tel: 223 0021
Fax: 223 2775
www.tajhotels.com
Luxury cottages set in beautiful gardens. Excellent food in the restaurant (particularly the buffet). Surprisingly reasonable, with good discounts during off season. **££££**

Kanchipuram (04112)

Baboo Soorya Hotel
85 East Raja Veethi Street
Tel: 222 555
Fax: 222 556
Very clean rooms, both AC and non-AC, in a friendly hotel. There is also a very good vegetarian restaurant. **£–££**

Kanniyakumari (04652)

Hotel Singaar International
5/22 Main Road
Tel: 347 992
Fax: 347 991
singaar@sancharnet.in
A clean and modern hotel with some pricey AC rooms (non-AC a much better deal). There is a good pool and a restaurant. **£££**

TTDC Hotel Tamilnadu
Beach Road
Tel: 246 257
Fax: 246 030
www.tamilnadutourism.org
A wide range of cottages, rooms, dormitories, some AC, in a decent location. Good food available. **£–££**

Kodaikanal (04542)

The Carlton
Lake Road
Tel: 240 056
Fax: 241 170
www.krahejahospitality.com
A lakeside colonial house converted into an expensive luxury hotel with comfortable rooms. Good sports facilities and an excellent restaurant. **£££££**

Hilltop Towers
Club Road
Tel: 240 413
Fax: 240 415
www.indiamart.com/hilltoptowers
A good-value hotel near the lake, with comfortable, well-furnished rooms. There is also a decent restaurant and bakery. **££**

Hotel Jewel
7 Road Junction
Tel: 241 029
Fax: 240 518
glentravels@vsnl.com
Good-value, non-AC, comfortable rooms with attached bath and hot water, and a restaurant. **££**

Greenland's Youth Hostel
St Mary's Road, near Coaker's Walk
Tel: 241 336
Fax: 241 340
Probably the best budget option, though it can get crowded. Clean, but very basic, rooms and dormitories. Lovely views and nice gardens. **£**

Madurai (0452)

Taj Garden Retreat
40 T.P.K. Road, Pasumalai
Tel: 237 1601
Fax: 237 1636
www.tajhotels.com
Madurai's top hotel; based around an old company guest house dating from the days of the Raj. The rooms have lovely views, and there are pretty gardens and a pool. **£££££**

Hotel Chentoor
106 West Perumal Maistry Street
Tel: 235 0490
Fax: 235 0499
Modern and comfortable rooms, some AC, in a friendly hotel with a good vegetarian restaurant. **££**

Hotel Supreme
110 West Perumal Maistry Street
Tel: 234 3151
Fax: 234 2637
www.supremehotels.com
A modern hotel with a good rooftop restaurant with temple views. The rooms are clean and modern. **££**

Hotel Sree Devi
20 W. Avani Moola Street
Tel: 274 7431
Good-value, clean rooms (some AC, non-AC **£**) with attached bath. Great views of the temple gopurams from the roof. Filtered water available on ground floor. **£–££**

Hotel International
46 West Perumal Maistry Street
Tel: 234 1552
Fax: 274 0372
Good-value, non-AC rooms (some with views) in a clean and friendly hotel. **£**

TTDC Hotel Tamilnadu
Alagarkoil Road
Tel: 253 7461
Fax: 253 3203
www.tamilnadutourism.org
Quiet rooms (some AC) in a Government-run hotel. There is also a good restaurant. **£**

Railway Retiring Rooms
Good-value budget rooms on the first floor of the railway station. **£**

Mamallapuram (04114)

Fisherman's Cove
Covelong Beach, Kanchipuram District
Tel: 272 304
Fax: 272 303
www.tajhotels.com
Lovely, renovated beachside hotel, 8 km (5 miles) from Mamallapuram. Rooms with a sea view and beachside cottages. There is a great pool and a very good seafood restaurant. **£££££**

Mamalla Bhavan Annexe
104 East Raja Street
Tel: 242060
Fax: 242 160
Good-value budget rooms, some with AC, in a modern, clean hotel. There is also an excellent vegetarian restaurant. Recommended. **££**

TTDC Hotel Tamilnadu

Beach Resort
Tel: 242 361
Fax: 242 268
www.tamilnadutourism.org
AC and non-AC cottages, a bit run-down, in a lovely, quiet setting. There is a good pool and a restaurant. **££**

Mudumalai (0423)

Jungle Retreat
Bokkapuram, Masinagudi 643 223, Tamil Nadu
Tel: 252 6469
www.jungleretreat.com
An excellent, and very reasonable, place to stay. Straightforward and pleasant accommodation. Wonderful views from the grounds (which also have a pool). Friendly service and excellent wildlife watching. **££££**

Bamboo Banks
Masinagudi, Tamil Nadu
Tel: 252 6211
www.bamboobanks.in
A highly recommended place to stay. Well appointed cottages in wooded grounds. Good Parsi food using locally grown vegetables. Excellent value for the position and facilities. **£££**

Monarch Safari Park
Bokkapuram, Masinagudi 643 223, Tamil Nadu
Tel: 252 6250
www.hojoindia.com
Well-sited with some great views. Simple, raised huts with attached bathrooms. Decent food in the restaurant and good birdwatching from the grounds. **££–£££**

Jungle Trails
Masinagudi
Tel: 252 6256
Simple but clean and decent accommodation for the true wildlife enthusiast. The resort is run by the naturalist Mark Davidar who is a mine of information on the natural history of the surrouding area. **££**

Forest Rest Houses
Abhayaranyam, Kargudi, Masinagudi and Teppakadu
Book through:
ThWildlife Warden, Mahalingam Buildings, Coonoor Road, Udhagamandalam 643 001, Tamil Nadu
Tel: 244 4098
Simple accommodation in a number of locations. Catering is provided on request. **£**

Udagamandalam (0423)

Savoy Hotel
77 Sylks Road
Tel: 244 4142
Fax: 244 3318
www.tajhotels.com
Forty rooms, some in cottages evocative of the Raj. Fires are lit in the rooms for cold evenings. Lovely gardens, restaurant and coffee shop. **££££–£££££**

Hotel Nahar Nilgiris
52a Charing Cross
Tel: 244 2173
Fax: 244 5173
Good-value and comfortable rooms in a friendly, central hotel. Convenient and with a decent restaurant. **££**

YWCA Anandagiri
Ettines Road
Tel: 244 2218
Popular for its good-value rooms, dormitories and restaurant. Often full, so book ahead. **££**

TTDC Hotel Tamilnadu
Charing Cross
Tel: 244 4370
Fax: 244 4369
www.tamilnadutourism.org
Good-value rooms and dormitories in a friendly and cheap hotel. Good views and a decent restaurant. **£–££**

Ramesvaram (04573)

TTDC Hotel Tamilnadu
14 Sannathi Street
Tel: 221 277
Fax: 221 070
www.tamilnadutourism.org
Clean, sea-facing rooms, some AC (non-AC **£**), and a dormitory. Also has a good restaurant. **£–££**

Railway Retiring Rooms
Tel: 221 226
Good value and clean budget accommodation. **£**

Thanjavur (04362)

Hotel Parisutham
55 Grand Anicut Canal Road
Tel: 231 601
Fax: 230 318
www.hotelparisutham.com
A comfortable, modern hotel, with good rooms overlooking the canal. There is a decent restaurant and a great swimming pool. **£££££**

Hotel Sangam
Trichy Road
Tel: 239 451
Fax: 236 695
www.hotelsangam.com
Pricey, modern hotel with comfortable rooms. Good restaurants and pool in a nice garden. **£££££**

Hotel Gnanam
Anna Salai
Tel: 278 501
Fax: 235 536
www.hotelgnanam.com
Good-value, clean rooms in a central, pleasant hotel. There is also a good vegetarian restaurant. Recommended. **££**

TTDC Hotel Tamilnadu
Gandhiji Road
Tel: 231 421
Fax: 231 970
www.tamilnadutourism.org
Large and comfortable rooms in a good-value hotel, with a restaurant and garden. **£–££**

Hotel Ganesh
2905/3–4 Srinivasan Pillai Road
Tel: 231 113
Fax: 272 517
hotelganesh-97@hotmail.com
Simple but clean, good-value rooms close to the railway station. The hotel has a good vegetarian restaurant. **£**

Railway Retiring Rooms
Six, very popular and clean, double rooms on the first floor of the station. **£**

Tiruchirapalli (0431)

Hotel Sangam
Collector's Office Road
Tel: 241 4700
Fax: 241 5779
www.hotelsangam.com
A comfortable, fairly expensive hotel, but with good AC rooms. There is a pool, and a decent restaurant with tasty Indian food. **£££££**

Jenney's Residency
3/14 Macdonalds Road
Tel: 241 4414
Fax: 246 1451
jennys@satyam.net.in
A pleasant upmarket hotel, with good-value, large AC rooms. There is a pool and two good Indian restaurants. **£££**

Femina Hotel
109 Williams Road, Cantonment
Tel: 241 4501
Fax: 241 0615
try_femina@sancharnet.com
Comfortable AC rooms, some with balconies, in a good-value hotel. Good vegetarian restaurants and a pool. **££–£££**

Ashby Hotel
17a Rockins Road
Tel: 246 0652
chinoor@yahoo.com
Large, atmospheric rooms (non-AC much cheaper) with verandas around a courtyard. There is a good restaurant. **£–££**

TTDC Hotel Tamilnadu
Macdonalds Road, Cantonment
Tel: 241 4246
Fax: 241 5725
www.tamilnadutourism.org
A wide range of cheap, if a little shabby, rooms (AC and non-AC). There is also an attached restaurant. **£–££**

Railway Retiring Rooms
A good budget option. **£**

Vellore (0416)

Hotel Prince Manor
83 Katpadi Road
Tel: 222 7106
Fax: 225 3016
hotelprincemanor@vsnl.net
Good-value and comfortable AC and non-AC rooms in a well-run and friendly hotel. It has an excellent restaurant. **££**

Hotel River View
New Katpadi Road
Tel: 222 5251
Fax: 222 5672
A modern hotel with a few AC rooms. Good restaurants and pleasant gardens. **££**

PRICE CATEGORIES

The rates below are for a double room (AC where available) in high season, including taxes:
£ = up to Rs 700
££ = Rs 700–1,700
£££ = Rs 1,700–3,000
££££ = Rs 3,000–4,500
£££££ = above Rs 4,500

EATING

WHAT TO EAT AND RECOMMENDED RESTAURANTS

WHERE TO EAT

Decent food – though not necessarily local dishes – can often be found in hotel restaurants, particularly in the luxury hotels where it can be excellent. Where a hotel has a particularly good restaurant it has been mentioned in its description *(see also pages 330–339 for recommendations)*.

Don't get confused if you see an eating place described as a "hotel" (vegetarian and non-vegetarian), as this usually denotes a restaurant in South India. To taste the best of South Indian dishes, these small, rather shabby-looking "hotels", found throughout the area, are probably the best places to eat in.

Do be aware of the approach to food hygiene in these typically Indian places. Although they may look rather grubby, when preparing food for the locals, stricter rules regarding hygiene apply than is often the case in the outwardly clean international restaurants (where you can't see the kitchens). The owners of the sooty stalls cook over on open fire, which, when compared to the spotlessly clean cooking appliances back home, looks rather unappealing, but the food will taste better.

Most are open for lunch and dinner, usually from around noon–3pm, and then 6pm–10.30pm, though cheaper places are generally open all day. Booking is not usually necessary; though it might be wise to phone restaurants in the luxury hotels beforehand.

One of the biggest problems can be tracking down good, authentic local food. A number of restaurants rely on a menu of North Indian favourites; all of which can become very repetitive and heavy after a while. To find more unusual dishes, look for places full of locals, with a quick turnover to ensure freshly cooked ingredients.

In the South, local "meals" places are generally excellent, cheap and very clean. Look for places with a high lunchtime turnover (the traditional time for the day's big meal) to find the best food. "Meals' usually come in the form of a *thali*, literally a "tray" with a pile of rice in the middle and small pots containing different vegetable and *dal* dishes, as well as some curd, around the edge.

Street food from stalls, provided it is fresh and cooked in front of you, can be very good and tasty. Snacks range from *chana dal* and *puris*, to omelettes laden with green chillies, to freshly cooked *paratha*. As with most things, use your common sense and only buy from stalls that appear hygienic.

Regional Variety

Similar vegetarian food is served in most of Tamil Nadu, Pondicherry and Karnataka but is given added chillies in Andhra Pradesh and enriched with coconut flakes and coconut milk in Kerala. Kerala breakfast food, however, is different, *idiappam*, a thin rice noodle preparation steamed as "cakes", *appam*, a coconut-milk-based pancake with a thick soft centre and *puttu*, a rice dish steamed in a bamboo hollow. All are also favourites in the far south of Tamil Nadu and along coastal Karnataka.

It's in non-vegetarian dishes that marked differences emerge from area to area. The fiery hot Andhra chicken and mutton dishes are a far cry from the less hot, more subtly flavoured soup-like milligatawnys, thick gravies, dry curries and *kurumas* of Chettinad. In like manner, the tamarind-rich sea food preparations – the *molies* and *karimin* curries of the Malabar Coast in the west.

Desserts are not traditionally part of a South Indian meal, though there are numerous sweet snacks and festival specialities, including almond *payasam (badhamkeer)* or fruit *payasam* (both creamy and sweet dishes with vermicelli). If your visit falls during the mango season in late March to August – you should try feasting on the South Indian varieties; *Banganapalle* is particularly delicious. The smaller species of South Indian bananas are also very tasty.

Drinks

There's also nothing quite like South Indian coffee: freshly roasted seeds are ground at home and their "decoction" obtained by filtering the liquid drop by drop, the cup of coffee then prepared by blending one part of "decoction" to three parts of milk. Local tea is prepared in much the same way. Both are served sweet.

Fresh lime soda makes a good thirst quencher. The juice of fresh limes is squeezed into a glass and then topped up with soda water, with sugar or salt as possible additives. If you like it sharp, ask for plain lime soda. Alcoholic toddy *(kallu)* is produced from palm sap. The quick-fermenting toddy tastes best early in the morning fresh from the palm tree.

RESTAURANT LISTINGS

ANDHRA PRADESH

Hyderabad-Secunderabad

Kamat's
There are several outlets of this clean and inexpensive Udupi-style vegetarian chain in the city; in the Ramalaya and Alladin complexes on Sarojini Devi Road in Secunderabad, and on Secretariat Road and Station Road in Nampally.

Laxmi
Nampally, close to the railway station
Good value and tasty vegetarian and non-vegetarian North and South Indian dishes.

Paradise Cafe and Stores
Annexe Persis, M.G. Road, Secunderabad
A complex of stalls offering good Indian and Chinese food to eat in or take away. Very good biryani.

Utsav
221 Tivoli Road, Secunderabad
Excellent North Indian vegetarian food served in pleasant surroundings.

Nagarjunakonda

Punnami Ethiopothala
Punnami Vihar
A small eating place about 11 km (7 miles) from Nagarjuna Sagar, though many tour buses stop here. It is in a wonderful position beside a gorge with an impressive waterfall.

Tirupati

Punnami Srinivasam
Tirupati
A good vegetarian restaurant attached to a government-run hotel.

Vijayawada

Hotel Santhi
Near the Apsara Theatre, Governorpet
A clean restaurant with good vegetarian food.

Punnami
Berm Park
A riverside restaurant attached to a large government-run hotel. The food is decent and the position is lovely.

Vishakhapatnam

Dakshin
Hotel Daspalla, Suryabagh
Very tasty – and spicy – non-vegetarian Andhran food. The lamb dishes are particularly good.

Punnami Yatri Niwas
Opposite the Appu Ghar Site, Beach Road, M.V.P. Colony
A decent restaurant attached to a government-run hotel. The menu is wide-ranging and the food is well-prepared.

KARNATAKA

Bangalore

Barista Coffee House
M.G. Road
One of a number in the city, very popular with young Bangaloreans. Good for real *espressos* and *cappuccinos*, as well as cakes and snacks.

Casa Piccola
Devatha Plaza, 131 Residency Road
Fast food and good coffee. Imaginative, informal decor and sensible prices. Recommended.

Chalukya
44 Race Course Road
Good-quality Udipi dishes.

Chinese Hut
1st Floor, High Point 4, 45 Palace Road
Very good food, mainly Cantonese and Sichuan.

Coconut Grove
Spencer's Building, 86 Church Street
Pleasant restaurant with outdoor seating. Excellent Andhran, Malabar, Konkan, Kodagu and Chettinad dishes.

Crescent Avenue
2a–b Crescent Road, High Ground
Good-value and tasty Thai food in nice surroundings.

Gangotree
45 Palace Road
Excellent spicy vegetarian snacks, and even better sweets.

Kamat Yatrinivas
4 1st Cross, Gandhi Nagar
Excellent South Indian vegetarian meals and snacks.

Koshy's
39 St Mark's Road
A Bangalore institution and favourite meeting place. Relaxed surroundings and extensive menu of well-cooked food. Open all day.

Mavalli Tiffin Rooms
Lalbagh Road
Very good Udupi-style food. Opens very early, good for breakfast.

Megh Malar
80 Hospital Road
Good South Indian food; excellent dosas.

Nagarjuna Residency
44/1 Residency Road
Hot and spicy non-vegetarian Andhran food; excellent biryanis.

Orange Country
The Central Park, 47 Dickenson Road
Live jazz and decent Cajun and Creole dishes. Good service and fun cocktails. A good place for women to have a drink.

Prince's
9 First Floor, Curzon Complex, Brigade Road
Good-value with nice surroundings and good service.

Hospet

The Waves
Hotel Malligi, 10-90 Jambunath Road
Pleasant rooftop restaurant serving average Indian and Chinese dishes.

Manasa
Hotel Priyadarshini, V-45 Station Road
Garden restaurant looking out on sugarcane and banana plantations. Good vegetarian and non-vegetarian food, also serves beer.

Hassan

Hotel Suvarana Regency
B.M. Road
Excellent South Indian vegetarian meals and snacks.

Mangalore

Lalith
Balmatta Road
A decent restaurant with a good range of North Indian and Chinese dishes.

Surabhi
Near the KSRTC stand
Excellent North Indian meaty and vegetarian *tanduri* dishes.

Mysore

Hotel Dasprakash
Gandhi Square
Good vegetarian restaurant serving meals and Udupi cuisine, dosas a speciality.

Ilapur
2721/1 Sri Harsha Road
Andhran restaurant serving excellent vegetarian meals, and some non-vegetarian dishes.

Lalitha Mahal Palace Hotel
Siddhartha Nagar
Good food, try the *biryanis*, accompanied by live Hindustani music.

Shilpastri
Gandhi Square
Popular and central rooftop restaurant serving mostly North Indian food.

Kerala

Alappuzha

Arun Komala Hotel
Good vegetarian meals in a small restaurant attached to a hotel.

Indian Coffee House
Mullakai Main Road
Coffee and basic meals from the state-wide chain; a good place for breakfast.

Guruvayur

Indian Coffee House
Kizhakkenada
A dependable fall back in this town which is mostly given over to feeding pilgrims.

Kochi-Ernakulam

Bimby's/Southern Star
Sanmukam Road, Ernakulam
Bimby's is a great place for cheap Indian fast food. The Southern Star upstairs does very good and reasonably priced sit-down meals.

Canopy Coffee Shop
Abad Plaza Complex, M.G. Road, Ernakulam
Tasty continental and fast food – a good place for breakfast. Open all day.

Caza Maria
6/125 Jew Town Road, Mattancherri, Kochi
This restaurant on the first floor of a historic building has been beautifully decorated. The food is an imaginative mixture of Indian and European dishes on a menu that changes daily.

The Cocoa Tree
The Avenue Regent, M.G. Road, Ernakulam
A great modern coffee shop attached to the hotel. Good coffee, light meals and excellent pastries. Open until 1am.

Gokul Restaurant
M.G. Road, Ernakulam
An excellent place for South Indian meals and snacks, the dosas and uttapams are particularly good.

Indian Coffee House
Cannon Shed Road, Ernakulam, also at Darbar Hall Road, M.G. Road and at the Kerala High Court Campus
Good snacks and coffee in a somewhat run-down building not far from the main jetty.

Pandhal
M.G. Road, Ernakulam
A very clean restaurant that serves up good North Indian and tasty Keralan dishes.

Kollam

Indian Coffee House
Main Road, Chinnakkada
Decent snacks and coffee from this popular chain.

Sri Suprabathan
Clock Tower
A cheap and cheerful vegetarian place, with tasty food.

Kottayam

Indian Coffee House
T.B. Road, also at M.L. Road and the Medical College
The usual non-vegetarian snacks and good coffee. Convenient for the bus station.

Thali Restaurant
Homestead Hotel
Decent vegetarian meals served on the eponymous metal tray.

Kovalam

Kovalam has a plethora of eating places, most of them much of a muchness. They tend to specialise in grilled or fried fish, served with chips. You first of all choose your fish, making sure that it is fresh (check inside the gills and make sure the eyes are not too glassy). Some places to try include the **Sea View Restaurant** (at the northern end of Lighthouse Beach), the **Swiss Café Restaurant** and **Fusion** (both on Lighthouse Beach and both with decent views).

German Bakery
South End of Lighthouse Beach
Something of a Kovalam institution, the bakery-cum-restaurant sells strudel and bread, as well as dishing up a good selection of Thai and European dishes (mostly pasta).

The Lobster Pot
Above Ashok Beach
An excellent viewpoint on top of the cliff and under the coconut palms. Decent enough Indian food, but the location is better.

Kozhikode

Kalpaka Tourist Home
Town Hall Road
Reasonable Indian food. Conveniently near the railway station.

Sagar
I.G. Road
A very popular restaurant with locals, sometimes you have to queue to get a table. However, the wait is worth it as the Indian food is excellent.

Woodlands
G.H. Road
A good, and cheap, vegetarian meals hall in the centre of town.

Thiruvananthapuram

Annapoorna
Pazhavangadi, opposite the Ganesh Temple
A good meals place with an air-conditioned first floor "family room". The *dosas* and *uttapams* are particularly good and the fresh fruit juices (make sure you order without ice) are also worth a try.

Arul Jyothi
M.G. Road, opposite the Secretariat
A very clean meals hall with excellent food. This is some of the best vegetarian food in the city. Good for juices.

Casa Bianca
96 M.P. Appan Road, Vazhuthacaud
This lovely café and restaurant run by Ingrid, a Swede settled in Thiruvananthapuram, is a little out of the ordinary for the city. A well-designed interior is the setting for very tasty Italian and Indian food (the pizza is excellent). Open daily 11am–10pm.

Coffee Beanz
Magnet, Thycaud
A modern café, opposite the women's college, serving excellent coffee and snacks such as chips and sandwiches. A popular hang-out for students and young people. Open Mon–Sat 11am–10pm, Sun 9am–10pm.

Indian Coffee House
Maveli Café, Central Station Road, also at many other locations including M.G. Road, the Secretariat Campus opposite the Botanical Gardens, and Sanmukam Beach
City landmark, beside the bus stand. Great coffee and snacks served in spiral building designed by Laurie Baker. A good place for breakfast or a late-night snack.

Park Field Gardens
Cotton Hill, Vazhuthacaud
A pleasant restaurant serving good Indian and international dishes. The combination meals, with a wide variety of Indian dishes, are particularly good.

Hotel Sri Bhadra and Hotel Sree Padmanabha
Opposite the temple tank, Fort
A pair of decent vegetarian restaurants serving meals – dosas and the like – with not much to choose between them. They both have good views of the temple from the first floor and can be very pleasant in early evening.

Below: sorting chillies.

Thrissur

Hotel Anupam
The Round
Decent vegetarian meals, with plenty of tasty extras, not far from the north gate of the temple. "Meals" are served on the first floor.

Indian Coffee House
Round South, also at C.B.D., Kuruppam Road and K.A.U. Mannuthi
Another set of places from the Keralan cooperative. They all serve good coffee and reasonable selection of light meals and snacks.

Varkala

Like Kovalam, Varkala too has a whole string of restaurants lined up along the sea front. Most of them have great views out to sea and the food is all much of a standard (the usual combination of North Indian dishes, noodles and some seafood). Near the road try the **Somatheeram Beach Restaurant** or the **Sea Face** (both on Main Beach, Papanasam), or the slightly more upmarket **Marine Palace** just above.

PONDICHERRY

La Terrasse
5 Subbaiyah Salai
Excellent and good-value Continental dishes. Closed Wednesdays.

Le Club
33 rue Dumas
An expensive but excellent French restaurant, probably the best in India. Authentic food, wine and great service; also good for breakfast. Closed Mondays.

Rendezvous
30 rue Suffren
This is a popular Continental restaurant with a pleasant rooftop area. Especially good for breakfast.

Satsanga
13 Lal Bahadur Sastri Street
A very good restaurant serving European dishes. Lovely surroundings and good value. Closed Thursdays.

TAMIL NADU

Chennai

Annalakshmi
804 Anna Salai
Excellent Southeast Asian vegetarian food prepared by volunteers (all profits go to charity).

Buhari's
83 Anna Salai
Well-prepared and tasty tandoori food.

Chungking
67 Anna Salai
Reasonable Chinese food served in rather dark surroundings.

Cozee
By the beach, Besant Nagar
Excellent kebabs and other non-vegetarian offerings from a legendary open-air stall and restaurant.

Dakshin
ITC Park Sheraton, 132 T.T.K. Road
This South Indian restaurant is one of the best in the country, with unusual dishes from all 4 states and the Chettinad region. Recommended.

Dasaprakash
806 Anna Salai, next to Higginbotham's
Udipi fast-foods in an up-market environment but at reasonable prices.

Kaaraikudi
10 Sivasvamy Street, Mylapore
Excellent Tamil food, including non-vegetarian Chettinad dishes.

Kabul's
35 T.T.K. Road, Alwarpet
Expensive but very good NWFP and Mughlai food.

Mavalli Tiffin Room
G.N. Chetty Road, T. Nagar
The first branch of this long established restaurant outside of Bangalore serves up wonderful vegetarian dishes – you can also buy spices and pickles to take-away.

Midnight Express
T.T.K. Road
The only late-night eatery outside of the psh hotels. Good for a fix of *dosa* or *idli* when everything else is shut.

Sangeetha Vegetarian Restaurant
Ethiraj Salai, Egmore
One of a chain of decent vegetarian eating halls in the city. Clean with a wide range of tasty South Indian food.

Saravana Bhavan
many branches including Shanti Theatre Complex, 44 Anna Salai; Central Railway Station; 77–9 Usman Road, T. Nagar; 209 N.S.C. Bose Road, George Town
An excellent chain of clean, cheap and tasty South Indian vegetarian meals halls. Open all day.

The Cascade
15 Khader Nawaz Khan Road, Nungambakkam
Expensive but very tasty Chinese and Thai food.

Velu's Military Hotel
Valluvar Kottam High Road, Nungambakkam
You can't get much better than this long-standing institution for a superb binge on traditional Chettinad non-vegetarian food. It is possible to get a sample plate so you can try many of the different dishes.

Woodlands Drive-in
Agri Horticultural Gardens, 30 Cathedral Road
Set in a horticultural garden. Better on North Indian food than Udupi dishes. Open all day.

Chidambaram

Hotel Saradharam
19 V.G.P. Street
A run-down hotel with a popular restaurant serving a wide range of tasty dishes.

Kanchipuram

Saravana Bhavan
504 Gandhi Road; 66 Anna Indira Gandhi Road, near the Bus Station
Two branches of the excellent, cheap and very clean chain of South Indian vegetarian restaurants.

Kanniyakumari

Hotel Saravana
Sannathi Street
A good, clean "meals" place serving excellent *dosais*.

Madurai

Meenakshi Bhawan
West Perumal Maistry Street, near the Anna Bus Stand
Excellent and locally popular South Indian food, including a few Chettinad dishes.

New Arya Bhavan
241a West Masi Street
Good-value and tasty North and South Indian vegetarian food. Open all day.

Thanjavur

Ananda Bhavan
Gandhiji Road, close to the Hotel Tamilnadu
Clean with extremely cheap and very tasty vegetarian meals.

Coffee Palace
Eliamman Kovil Street
The best place in Thanjavur for real South Indian coffee and snacks.

Golden Restaurant
Hospital Road
Another vegetarian meals place, but with a good local reputation.

Udagamandalam

Nilgiri Woodlands
Ettines Road
This hotel serves up good value, and very tasty, vegetarian "meals" and snacks.

ACTIVITIES

FESTIVALS, NIGHTLIFE, THE ARTS, SHOPPING AND WILDLIFE SANCTUARIES

FESTIVALS

The main South Indian festivals are listed below:

Dussera

This 10-day festival in September/October is celebrated with the most gusto in Mysore. *Dussera* was once a festivity sponsored by royalty, but it is now a tourist extravaganza and a funfair for the public. Processions are led by caparisoned elephants, there are classical and traditional music and dance programmes, firework displays, and the public gardens in Mysore and at the Brindavan dam site are brilliantly lit. The car festival on Chamundi Hill is also spectcular.

Dussera is celebrated in most other parts of the South as *Navaratri* (Nine Nights), the highlight of these 10 days and 9 nights in September/October are the *golu* (doll) displays in homes, the *Ayutha Puja* in factories and homes when all implements of work are decorated and worshipped, and *Vijaya Dasami* when the implements are first put to use again and new ventures started.

Pongal/Sankranti

Pongal in Tamil Nadu, and *Sankranti* in Karnataka and Andhra Pradesh in mid-January, are harvest festivals, the bounties of the gods offered back to them for their blessings. *Pongal* in Tamil Nadu one of the most charming of these festivals in the South, lasting almost a week. During that time, houses are cleaned and bonfires made of all that's not needed; rice – with milk and jaggery – is cooked in the open on open hearths and the resulting *pongal* is offered to the gods, cows are decorated and worshipped for the bounty they provide. People dress in their best clothes and visit relatives and friends. In the far South, near Madurai, cattle fairs are part of the festivities, in several villages they include cattle races, cart races and cattle-wrestling.

People display dolls in the house during the three-day *Makara Sankranti* in Andhra Pradesh in mid-January.

Onam and the Elephant Parade

Like *Pongal* in Tamil Nadu, *Onam* is Kerala's harvest festival in August/September. Floral decorations are everywhere, but the greatest excitement is generated by the elephant procession in Thrissur, and the snake-boat races in Alappuzha, Kochi, Payipad and Aranumula. Traditional dances, music recitals and cultural shows are also part of this festival.

The Great Elephant Parade in Kerala is a major attraction. It begins in early January in Thrissur with a parade of over a 100 finely decorated bull elephants. Also part of the festivities are dancers in fantastic costumes, with drummers and trumpet players. During the next few days, about a half of the elephants form a colourful caravan and head south towards Thiruvananthapuram, where in the Backwater region the snake-boat races of Alappuzha take place.

Dipavali

Dipavali (the Southern version of *Divali*) is another major festive occasion in the South. In the weeks leading up to *Dipavali*, *sari* shops are packed with buyers. Visiting a *sari* shop at this time is an experience, not the least to marvel at the dazzling array of silks in a fantasy of colour and design. *Dipavali* in the South is mainly a religious occasion, with temple visits followed by calls on friends and relatives with an exchange of sweets and savouries. Fireworks are also an integral part of the two-day festivity. In parts of the South, where there are old settlements of people from the North, *Dipavali* is celebrated more riotously, with fireworks, dancing and feasts of sweets.

Ganapati Chathurti

The festival of Lord Ganesh in September/October is also an important celebration in the South. The image of Lord Ganesh, which gets grander by the year, is taken in procession through towns and villages before being immersed in the sea, rivers or tanks. Some of the most colourful celebrations are in Hyderabad, where *Ganesh Chathurthi* is preceded by the month-long *Batkamma* harvest festival.

Christmas

Christmas and New Year in Kerala among the Syrian Christians is different in its sobriety from the commercial Christmas celebrations in the West. No presents are given and Hindu influences are evident in the fireworks, torch-lit processions, nativity plays and singing which goes on until early in the morning

Secular Festivals

The festival of classical dance and music during the Chennai music season takes place in December/January. The southern capitals stage parades on 26 January (Republic Day) and 15 August (Independence Day). The highlights of these parades are the the traditional dances and the floats.

NIGHTLIFE

Outside of the sometimes dubious pleasures of Goa, India is not famed for its nightlife. However, things are slowly changing in the large cities as the young middle class adopt more "western" lifestyles. Many clubs are in the large, luxury hotels, many of which have strict admission policies. Visitors from abroad may well find Bangalore's famous "pub culture" over-hyped. Bars are still largely a male preserve and lone women may find them intimidating. For up-to-date listings check on the www.explocity.com site.

Bangalore

180 Proof, St Marks Road. A very popular bar with music and dancing; also has decent Southeast Asian food.
Pub World, 65 Residency Road. Basically lots of beer and cocktails; more comfortable than some.
NASA, 1–4 Church Street. Space Shuttle-themed pub – lots of metal – with very loud music.
Peco's, Rest House Road, off Brigade Road. Slightly "alternative" bar (well, pictures of Frank Zappa anyway) on two levels, less in-your-face than some.
Underground, 65 M.G. Road. A very popular bar disguised as a London tube station.

Chennai

EC41, 41 East Coast Road, Injambakkam. Open until dawn with a sprinkler system to cool things down. Opens 10.30pm.

MUSIC AND DANCE

Chennai

No music and dance festival in India is as popular as the Chennai "season". The Season started 65 years ago, when the Chennai Music Academy was founded and began organising annual conferences at which various aspects of classical Karnatak music and *Bharata-natyam* were the chief topics of discussion. The serious discussions were accompanied by day-long programmes comprising instrumental and vocal concerts and dance recitals.

That 3-week season from mid-December to early January still continues at the Academy and artists consider it an honour to be invited to perform at its concerts. Devotees of South Indian music and dance come from all over India every year to attend these concerts. But nowadays they get much more than the Academy's offerings alone.

Several other societies *(sabhas)* which promote the arts have sprung up in Chennai and now they all organise "Seasons" during the same period. Some of these societies are the Tamil Isai Sangam, Brahma Gana Sabha, Narada Gana Sabha, Krishna Gana Sabha and the Mylapore Fine Arts Club.

One of the highlights of the Season is the annual dance-dramas of the Kalakshetra Institute, a college that teaches the fine arts in traditional ways. Kalakshetra is where some of India's finest *Bharata-natyam* dancers learn their skills.

The many societies and academies of Chennai keep busy the rest of the year by organising concerts, dance recitals and even theatre and film shows to which the public are also welcome. Left-over tickets are available at the door; watch the newspapers for announcements. You can find a classical music recital or *Bharata-natyam* performance happening in Chennai every evening right through the year, but during the Season just keeping up with the variety offered can be trying.

Tiruvaiyaru

Later in January, there is the finest classical music festival in the South. It is held on the banks of the river Kaveri in a village called Tiruvaiyaru. The Tyagaraja Music Festival commemorates the greatest composer of Karnatak music and two other great composers, Syama Sastri and Muttusvami Diksitar, who were from neighbouring villages. All the great instrumentalists and vocalists of Karnatak music come to this festival to pay homage to the "Trinity" by playing for them and singing in their memory.

Kerala

Kathakali, the masked dance-drama, is one of Kerala's great contribution to the art forms of the South. Daily dance recitals, aimed at tourists, can be seen in Kochi. Two reputable companies are: the **Cochin Cultural Centre** (Carvetty Road, Fort Kochi; daily performances starting at 6.30pm); and the **Kerala Kathakali Centre** (off River Road, Fort Kochi; daily performances, make-up from 5pm, dance 6.30–8pm; www.kathakalicentre.com). Both places also run short courses in Keralan dance and music. Cheruthuruthi, 110 km/70 miles northwest of Kochi and near Thrissur, is Kerala's answer to Kalaksetra. Here, *Kathakali*, *Mohini Attam* and other Keralan dance and music forms are taught at the Kerala Kala Mandalam.

Elsewhere

What the Music Academy's auditorium is to Chennai, the Chowdiah Hall is to Bangalore and the Rabindra Bharati Hall is to Hyderabad. In Hyderabad scan the newspapers for announcements of *ghazal* concerts ("light classical"Hindustani music). Mysore is quite similar to Chennai with its sabhas, so keep a lookout for their varied programmes.

In Madurai, the Satguru Sangita Samajam stages regular dance and music recitals in its auditorium.

Most smaller towns have occasional recitals and classical dance performances, and the bigger hotels occasionally stage events.

Traditional dance

In the rural areas many local dances are found, especially at festival time. Dance forms such as *Karagam* (in which pots are carried on the head), *Kavadi* (in which feathered arches are borne on the shoulders), *Poikkal Kutirai* (in which the dancers dress as mock horses) and *Kolattam* (a rhythmic dance with sticks) are some of the more popular dances of the South.

Adivasi dances in the Arakku Valley in northern Andhra Pradesh, *Balakkatu* at Kodagu weddings in western Karnataka and other ritual dances in Karnataka, like the *Dollu Kunita* (drum dance) and *Pata kunita* (pole dance), are all fascinating. Karnataka and Kerala are also famous for dance exorcisms.

Websites

The following all have good listings:
www.kutcheribuzz.com
www.sangeetham.com
www.sruti.com
www.saintthyagarajar.com

CINEMA

Films are immensely popular in southern India and fans often deify popular stars and build temples in their honour. Hyderabad has now overtaken Chennai in terms of production, but the studios at Chennai remain at the heart of the South Indian industry. Several film stars have used their popularity to enter politics and have been

ABOVE: a *Kathakali* perfomer.

successful politicians. Three former film stars have been chief ministers in Tamil Nadu and Andhra Pradesh.

The consequence of this is that there are more cinema theatres in the four southern states and Pondicherry than the rest of the country put together. Every town has several theatres, some of them huge and opulent. In rural areas, there are smaller permanent cinema theatres or thatched roofed sheds, and if those are not available the empty space reserved for the weekly shandy (the market fair, yet another cultural experience) is likely to be taken over by a travelling cinema. Although film remains exceptionally popular, in some areas its audience is being stolen by television and a number of cinemas are finding it hard to keep up their theatres, and some have had to close down.

The films based on religious epics, the "mythologicals", and the Robin Hood-type action films are fewer now, and "social dramas" – with songs, dance and fights thrown in to stretch the entertainment to not less than 2½ hours – and musicals are the films most often made in the South. Experts prefer not to break up the South Indian film into such genres. A successful film must have everything: action, adventure, crime, love, music and dance.

Theatres vary from the luxurious to the seedy, but most good theatres are air-conditioned. Shows are fixed – usually four times a day and are advertised in the newspapers. Tickets are priced in three or four classes, the most expensive seats being about Rs 100 each.

TIt is also possible to visit some of the big studios, such as MGR Film City, and Vijaya, Prasad and AVM (all in the Kodambakkam area of Chennai), as well as the huge studios in Hyderabad.

SHOPPING

What to Buy

The assortment of goods is staggering, look around first and check out the differing quality and prices before you buy anything. Places selling handicrafts (of all kinds) are a good first stop. Carpets are available in different sizes and knot-counts. Unless you know a lot about carpets, shop at a Government Emporium. Less expensive are rugs and dhurries from all over the country. There is a huge assortment of precious and semi-precious gemstones, jewellery set in both gold and silver, traditional as well as modern, often much cheaper than in Europe. India is famous for its textiles which come in a bewildering array of natural and man-made fibres, textures, weaves, prints, designs and colours. Carved sandalwood figures and elaborately worked wooden panels are found in the South. There are also many objects in brass, copper and gun metal, inlaid, enamelled, worked or beaten. Marble inlay work and papier mâché items with intricate designs, reproductions of miniature paintings on paper or cloth, and leather wallets, shoes and bags are all good buys. Hand-painted pottery, and cane goods ranging from table mats to furniture, are popular, and so are ready-made clothes. Antiques and semi-antiques are governed by strict laws limiting their export; also beware of fakes. Export of skins, furs and ivory is strictly forbidden.

Emporia

All four southern states have government-owned (or backed) handicrafts corporations as well as councils. These organisations have shops in their own state capitals and in the capitals of other states, and in other towns and cities in the region. All of them have a splendid variety of handicrafts made in the state each represents. **Lepakshi** is the Andhra Pradesh shop, **Kairali** is the Kerala shop, **Kaveri** is the Karnataka shop and **Poompuhar** is the Tamil Nadu shop. In addition to these handicrafts and handloom emporia, there are **Khadi Gramodyog Bhavans** and **Khadi Kraft** shops in all the southern state capitals. These outlets sell handicrafts and handlooms manufactured according to the manually-intensive philosophy Gandhi propounded for rural India to supplement its economy.

Major credit cards such as Visa and Mastercard are now widely accepted in shops. Do be careful not to let your card out of your sight as fraud has been reported in India (sometimes multiple copies of card receipts have been made and charged later on). Most cities will now have a number of ATMS where cash can be withdrawn. Local bank ATMS may not accept international cards, so try and find one of the multinationals, or one of the larger national banks.

Where to Shop

Bangalore

M.G. Road and Brigade Road are Bangalore's main shopping streets, with the usual array of shops selling Lacoste and Adidas. For general shopping, the government emporium, **Kaveri**, is on Brigade Road.

Brigade Road has a post office and a Citibank ATM (there is another on Infantry Road). Just off Brigade Road is the **Premier** bookshop with a good selection of titles. Other bookshops are the **Select** on St Mark's Road, and the **Strand** in the Manipal Centre.

Thomas Cook are on M.G. Road and there is a branch of **Foodworld** at no. 86, with a good fruit stall outside (there is another fruit stall at the bottom of Brigade Road).

Chennai

Chennai is one of the best places in India to buy books. The following shops are all very helpful, have a good stock and will post books back for you: **Landmark Books** in Spencer Plaza is said to be Asia's largest bookstore, with a huge number of books and CDs; **Bookpoint**, 160 Anna Salai is helpful and worth a look; **Higginbothams**, 814 Anna Salai, is one of India's longest established bookshops; and **Giggles** in the Taj Connemara Hotel is highly recommended for its knowledgeable owner and eclectic stock.

Close by the Connemara is **Spencer Plaza**, a large, air-conditioned shopping centre. This has an American Express exchange on the ground floor (and a local rival with better rates opposite), some internet places and a **Foodworld** supermarket, where you can buy familiar food and toiletries, including Tampax.

Chennai is also a good place for clothes and fabrics, particularly Kanchi silks. Try the government shops (and others) at the top end of

Anna Salai, in particular the **Central Cottage Industries Emporium** at No. 476 and **Poompuhar** at No. 818. For ready-mades, **Naidu Hall** in Pondi Bazaar, T. Nagar is recommended.

Hyderabad/Secunderabad

Hyderabad is the pearl capital of India, and pearl jewellery and silver filigree work are the best buys in the city. Hyderabad is also framed for its glass and lacquer bangles and Lambadi silver jewellery. Venkatagiri and Pochampalli handloom saris, Dharmavaram silk fabrics, Kalamkari "painted" cloths, and carpets from Warangal and Eluru are good buys. Kondapalli wooden toys and inlaid bidriware are other well-known Andhran handicrafts. All these are available at **Lepakshi** in the Mayur Complex.

The **pearl market** is on Petherghati Road near the Charminar in Hyderabad. Nearby are the famed bangle shops. In this area too are numerous silversmiths and bidriware craftsmen.

Other good shopping areas are **Abid's** (particularly good for fabrics) and **Basheer Bagh** in Hyderabad and **M G Road** in Secunderabad.

Kerala

The state government emporium is known as **Kairali**, with branches in Ernakulam (on M.G. Road), Kozhikode (on M.M. Ali Road) and Thiruvananthapuram, where it is called the **SMSM Handicrafts Emporium** (just behind the Secretariat building).

One of Kerala's exports is items made from coir (coconut fibre), spun and made into all kinds of mats, carpets and bags. Alappuzha is the centre of the coir industry and is probably the best place to look.

All towns have their fabric shops. In Thiruvananthapuram try **Partha's** on Powerhouse Road (they also have a branch in Ernakulam on M.G. Road), which has a huge selection of dress fabrics and ready-made clothes, or **Alapatt Silks** in East Fort. In Kochi a lovely modern shop selling designer clothes and items for the home is **Cinnamon** (Ridsdale Road, by the Parade Ground; tel: 0484-221 7124).

Traditional gold jewellery can be exquisite, with delicate interwoven strands and characteristic small bobbles. It is generally sold by weight, and the day's gold price should be displayed in the shop. Don't expect jewellery to be cheap, especially if gems are included in the piece. Do make sure, as well, that you buy from a reputable jeweller. One of the largest chains in the state is **Alukkas**. They have branches in Thiruvananthapuram (East Fort), Ernakulam (M.G. Road), Alapuzzha (Boat Jetty Road) and Thrissur (Round East, by the temple). Another very reputable chain is **Josco**. They can be found in Thiruvananthapuram (East Fort), Kottayam (K.K. Road), Ernakulam (M.G. Road), Thrissur (M.O. Road) and Palakkad (G.B. Road).

Although the rules for exporting antiques from India are very strict, you can find some very fine items (all passed for export) at **Natesans** on M.G. Road in Thiruvananthapuram.

Other places in Thiruvananthapuram are the **Modern Book Centre** close to M.G. Road. Further up, opposite the South Park Hotel, is **Spencer's Supermarket**, handy for toiletries and bits and pieces to eat and drink.

Mysore

Mysore is famous for silk and sandalwood. An excellent place to buy fabrics is the **Mysore Silk Emporium** (3 Nethra Nivas, Hotel Sandesh Complex, Nazarbad Main Road). Check the purity of the silk by burning a strand or two. If the fibres burn away to ash that just crumbles in your fingers then it is pure silk, if there is a residue then the fabric is wholly or partly synthetic.

Sandalwood is found all over Mysore, but check that sandalwood oil comes in a metal bottle from the licensed factory just outside of town. **The Handicrafts Sales Emporium** (Ramson's House, opposite the zoo) has a good selection of sandalwood carvings, jewellery, bronzes and fabrics, all at fixed prices.

WILDLIFE SANCTUARIES

Andhra Pradesh

The largest of the four South Indian states, Andhra Pradesh, has a varied terrain with a rich and interesting population of birds and animals. Andhra also has a long and varied coastline with two great rivers (the Godavari and the Krishna) flowing west to east into the Bay of Bengal. There are mangrove forests along the estuaries, dry deciduous forest inland, and extensive open scrub stretching into the Deccan plateau. The southern half of the state, below the Krishna river, is largely thorn forest while the northern part is teak dominated. Lake Pulicat is one of South Asia's largest lagoons and an important centre for both resident and migratory water birds.

For details of accommodation and access contact: the Chief Wildlife Warden, Tuljaguda Complex, Mouzamjah Market, Hyderabad 500 001; tel: (040) 2460 0255; fax: 2460 0272. Information about the individual parks and sanctuaries can also be found on www.ap.nic.in/apforest

Kolleru Sanctuary

Established in 1963, this large bird sanctuary of almost 900 sq km (342 sq miles) comprises wetland and marsh in a natural shallow depression surrounding Kolleru Lake, between the Krishna and Godavari deltas. Water, after the northeast monsoon, extends over 600 sq km (228 sq miles). Many migratory ducks and resident water birds and the famous pelicanry at the village of Aredu use the lake for feeding.
Best time to visit: late October–February.
Nearest town: Eluru.

Papikonda Sanctuasry

Established in 1978. Covers 590 sq km (224 sq miles) of mixed forest on the banks of the Godavari as it cuts through the Eastern Ghats, with a core area of 221 sq km (84 sq miles). The many steep slopes of the Papikonda range give the sanctuary its name. Animals include tiger, leopard, chausingha and wolf and many water birds.
Best time to visit: November–June.
Nearest town: Rajamundry.

Pulicat Sanctuary

Established in 1976, the southeastern mouth of this large lagoon is in Tamil Nadu. Of the 580 sq km (220 sq miles), about 500 sq km (190 sq miles) are in Andhra. Large flocks of flamingo, many migrant shore birds, and local residents are visible.
Best time to visit: late October–March.
Nearest town: Sulurpetta.

Rollapadu Sanctuary

A 614 sq km (233 sq mile) sanctuary of gently undulating grassland at the northern end of the Erramala range of hills. Established in 1985 to protect the 60 resident Great Indian Bustard there. Another rare bird breeding in the sanctuary is the Lesser Florican. Animals that are found in the sanctuary and buffer include blackbuck, wolf, jackal, fox and the blacknaped hare.
Best time to visit: May–June for minor nesting, and August–December for major nesting.
Nearest town: Kurnool.

Srisailam-Nagarjunasagar Sanctuary (Tiger Reserve)

Established in 1978, this sanctuary of 3,568 sq km (1,355 sq miles) is India's largest tiger reserve, with a core area of 1,200 sq km (456 sq miles). The reserve spans the Krishna river with a dam forming the Nagarjunasagar reservoir. The area is dissected by deep winding gorges which cut through the Mallamalai hills. There's a range of forest types, from dry scrub and dry mixed deciduous forests on the plateau to the west and south to moist valleys with bamboo and tropical thorn forest to the east.

The range of animals includes the leopard, sloth bear, palm civet, wolf, striped hyena, in addition to the tiger. Also found are barking deer, nilgai, chinkara, chausingha, sambar, chital, langur, bonnet macaque and the Indian pangolin.
Best time to visit: October–June.
Nearest town: Machesla.

Sri Venkatesvara Sanctuary

A 507 sq km (192 sq mile) sanctuary of which the 300 sq km (114 sq mile) core area is now a national park. This is one of the few well preserved tracts of southeastern deciduous forests still remaining, with several endemic species of both flora and fauna such as the red sanders trees and the golden gecko.
Best time to visit: November–February.
Nearest town: Tirupati.

Karnataka

Southern Karnataka in what was once Mysore State is famous for its rich and distinctive wildlife and magnificent forests. The great tracts of forest that remain today as a legacy of the management and concern shown by the Mysore rulers are noted for elephant, gaur and other large mammals.

The forests of the Western Ghats contain many endemic birds and flora species. In the northern part, the dry thorn forests and scrub are home to different species. In the dry deciduous scrub of Ranebennur, the blackbuck and an increasing number of great Indian bustard are found. The bustard has also returned to the scrub areas north of Bijapur, near the Maharashtra border.

For information on access and accommodation contact: the Chief Wildlife Warden, II Floor, Aranya Bhavan, 18th Cross, Malleswaram, Bangalore 560 003; tel: (080) 2334 1993; fax: 2334 6389. Information about the individual parks and sanctuaries can also be found on www. karnatakawildernesstourism.org

Bandipur National Park & Tiger Reserve

Established in the early 1930s with an area of 60 sq km (23 sq miles), the area was expanded to 690 sq km (262 sq miles) in 1974 and is now a total of 874 sq km (332 sq miles). Bound on the northwest, west and south by the Nagarahole (Rajiv Gandhi National Park), Waynad and Mudumalai parks. It has one of the best road systems among the parks with excellent opportunities for game viewing, especially of elephants. The gaur population is also increasing. The park is bisected north–south by the Mysore–Udaga-mandalam road. The hilly landscape in the shadow of the Western Ghats is dissected by rivers and streams.
Best time to visit: March–July, September–October.
Nearest town: Gundulpet.

Bannerghatta National Park

Established in 1974 with 104 sq km (40 sq miles) of undulating terrain with valleys and hills, only 28 km (10½ miles) south of Bangalore. Mammal life is poor although the occasional leopard is seen, and also chital, wild boar and sloth bear. Zoo-born tigers have been introduced to a large enclosed area. A few elephants still traverse the area. There is also interesting scenery and fascinating birdlife. A popular attraction, especially during weekends.
Best time to visit: September–June.
Nearest town: Bangalore.

Brahmagiri Sanctuary

Established in 1974 in southern Kodagu near the border with Kerala. Borders Nagarahole National Park to the east. It is 181 sq km (69 sq miles) of hill country with moist and mixed deciduous forest. Animals which can be seen here are the elephant, gaur, tiger, mouse deer, chital and sambar.
Best time to visit: October–May.
Nearest town: Virajpat.

Nagarahole National Park (Rajiv Gandhi National Park)

Established in 1955 and expanded to its present size of 573 sq km (218 sq miles) in the mid-1970s. Extremely attractive situation with the Brahmagiri hills in the distance. The Kabini river has been dammed to form a large and attractive reservoir which separates the park from Bandipur National Park to the southeast. The viewing is excellent and well organised. Large groups of gaur, elephant, the occasional tiger and leopard, chital and sambar are seen. Over 250 species of birds recorded.
Best time to visit: October–April.
Nearest town: Kutta.

Ranganathittu Bird Sanctuary

Established in 1940 near Tippu Sultan's capital of Srirangapatnam on six tiny islands in the Kaveri River 16 km (10 miles) north of Mysore. Nesting starts as early as March for many species. Scenically beautiful. A few crocodiles, otters and flying foxes (fruit bats) seen.
Best time to visit: March– November.
Nearest town: Mysore.

Kerala

Flanked to the west by the Arabian Sea and along the east by the Western Ghats, Kerala is well endowed with dense vegetation supporting a rich and varied fauna. Forest still covers around 24 percent of the state and nearly 6 percent protected. The weather throughout the year is pleasant with the monsoon arriving in late May and the wet period continuing up to September.

For details of accommodation and access contact: the Chief Wildlife Warden, Forest Headquarters, Vazhuthacaud, Thiruvananthapuram 695 014; tel: (0471) 252 9241; fax: 233 8806. Information about the individual parks and sanctuaries can also be found on www.keralaforest.org

Eravikulam National Park

Declared a national park in 1978, this area was earlier established as a sanctuary to protect the Nilgiri tahr (the only wild goat south of the Himalaya) of which it has the largest population (approximately 550). The tahr are easy to spot near the park entrance. The park covers 97 sq km (37 sq miles) of beautiful rolling grassy hills and forests in the valleys. It also has the highest peak in South India: Anamudi (2,695 metres/8,853 ft). The tahr are often seen near the bordering Rajamalai tea estate. Elephant, tiger, leopard, dhole (wild dog), Nilgiri langur, lion-tailed macaque and giant squirrel are found.
Best time to visit: November–April.
Nearest town: Munnar.

Idukki Sanctuary

Established in 1976 with an area of 70 sq km (23 sq miles) above the Idikki arch dam. Sambar and elephant are usually seen and tiger, sloth bear and gaur occasionally.
Best time to visit: November–May.
Nearest town: Vazhathope.

Neyyar Sanctuary

Established in 1958, it has an area of 128 sq km (49 sq miles) with the Neyyar reservoir covering slightly more than 9 sq km (3½ sq. miles). Most of the sanctuary is wet tropical evergreen forest although in higher areas the grasslands have tahr. Agasthyadudam at 1,891 metres (6,203 ft) is the highest point. Rich bird and insect life. Lion-tailed macaque, Nilgiri langur, gaur, sloth bear and wild boar are seen. Occasional tiger sightings.
Best time to visit: Year-round.
Nearest town: Kattakada.

Periyar Tiger Reserve and National Park

Established in 1934 as the Nellikkampetty Sanctuary, it was enlarged in 1950. It now extends over 777 sq km (295 sq miles) of which 350 sq km (133 sq miles) is National Park. The lake covers 26 sq km (10 sq miles) and is 31 km (20 miles) long. Most of the sanctuary is undulating. The elephant viewing is excellent, although many tuskers have been poached. Tiger sightings are rare. Woodland birds are abundant.
Best time to visit: September–May (open all year).
Nearest town: Kumily.

Silent Valley National Park

Established in 1984 after a national campaign to protect the peninsula's last substantial area of primary tropical forest. The 90 sq km (34 sq miles) of park holds a valuable reserve of rare plants and herbs. A neighbouring area of 225 sq km (85½ sq miles) ranging from 300 metres to 1,554 metres (980 ft to 5,050 ft) has been proposed as the Karimpuzha sanctuary. Elephant, lion-tailed macaque and tiger are among the animals seen.
Best time to visit: September–March.
Nearest town: Mannarghat.

Thattekkad Bird Sanctuary

Established in 1983 as Kerala's first bird sanctuary. Mostly moist deciduous forest on 25 sq km (9½ sq miles) of land between branches of the Periyar river. Many water and forest birds including rarities such as the Ceylon frogmouth and the rose-billed roller. Also found are the lion-tailed macaque and flying squirrel.
Best time to visit: September–March.
Nearest town: Kothamangalam.

Waynad Sanctuary

Established in 1973 although a game reserve since the 1920s. Borders Nagarahole (Rajiv Gandhi National Park) and Bandipur in Karnataka and Mudumalai in Tamil Nadu. It has an area of 344 sq km (131 sq miles) with rich birdlife in remarkable and varied forests. Elephant, chital, gaur, sambar and sloth bear are fairly common. Good roads.
Best time to visit: December–April.
Nearest town: Sultanbathery.

Tamil Nadu

The parks of Tamil Nadu are little-known, although their range is extraordinary, mixed deciduous forests of the Western Ghats, through the hot, dry plains, to the coastal and marine parks. Two biosphere reserves have been established: one at the Gulf of Mannar and the other in the Nilgiris. Most of Tamil Nadu receives both monsoons, and the two rainy seasons limit wildlife viewing. November to February are pleasant months to travel through the state.

For details of accommodation and access contact: the Chief Wildlife Warden, 259 Anna Salai, IV Floor, DMS Compound, Teynampet, Chennai 600 006; tel: (044) 2432 1738. Information about the individual parks and sanctuaries can also be found on www.forests.tn.nic.in

Indira Gandhi Wildlife Sanctuary

Previously the Annamalai Sanctuary, it was established in 1976, covering 840 sq km (319 sq miles) of the northern end of the Cardamom Hills and abuts other sanctuaries in Kerala on its Western border (forming a protected area of over 200 sq km/76 sq miles). Rich, mixed deciduous forest with large rosewood and teak trees leading to temperate grassland at higher altitudes. Its main attractions are the lion-tailed macaque and the Nilgiri langur for which it offers a secure home, and both of which tend to stay in the evergreen sholas. Gaur can be seen near the Srichalippallam river. Elephant, chital, sambar, mouse deer and black bucks are all found here. Extensive birdlife,
Best time to visit: February–June.
Nearest town: Pollachi.

Kalakad-Mundanthurai Tiger Reserve

Formed in 1987 by linking the Kalakad and Mundanthurai sanctuaries to create a single area of 800 sq km (304 sq miles) under Project Tiger. The tiger reserve is the southernmost range in India and has an extraordinary range of habitat. Dry teak forest merges into moist mixed deciduous forest and at lower levels tropical evergreen. The Mundanthurai area receives almost 300 cm (117 in) of rain and there are still pockets of virgin rainforest. Excellent primate viewing with the bonnet macaque and common langur found throughout the sanctuary; the Nilgiri langur at Tarucvattamparai and the lion-tailed macaque near the top of Valaiyar Hill. Tiger, leopard, sloth bear, sambar, gaur, slender loris, dhole and chital can also be seen.
Best time to visit: January–March.
Nearest town: Ambasamudram.

ABOVE: a thatched hut, Yelagiri.

Mudumalai Sanctuary

Established in 1938 and now expanded to cover 322 sq km (122 sq miles) of mixed and moist-deciduous forests. The sanctuary is bisected by the road from Mysore to Udagamandalam and bounded to the north by Bandipur National Park in Karnataka and to the west by the Waynad Sanctuary in Ke-rala. Excellent birdlife at the base of the Nilgiris at Masinagudi.
Best time to visit: March–June, September–October.
Nearest town: Gudalur.

Point Calimere Sanctuary

Established in 1967, protecting 17 sq km (6½ sq miles) of shoreline and hinterland that surround a saline lagoon. Part of the area is tidal swamp. Dolphins are occasionally seen in the lagoon. There are numerous shore birds and waders, large flocks of both greater and lesser flamingoes. Blackbuck, chital, feral pig and bonnet macaques are some of the land mammals which visitors can see in the sanctuary.
Best time to visit: November–January.
Nearest town: Vedaranyam.

A – Z

A HANDY SUMMARY OF PRACTICAL INFORMATION, ARRANGED ALPHABETICALLY

Arrival

Once through customs the visitor is often besieged by porters, taxi drivers and others. Choose one porter and stick to him. There is a system of paying porters a fixed amount per piece of baggage before leaving the terminal: a tip of Rs5, once the bags are aboard the taxi or bus, is sufficient. If a travel agent or a friend is meeting you, he or she may be waiting outside the building.

Some major hotels operate courtesy buses, and a public service known as EATS (Ex-Serviceman's Transport Service) operates an airport bus service in Delhi, Mumbai and Kolkata with stops at hotels and major points en route to the city centre. There are also offical, pre-paid taxi and coaches.

Begging

Visitors to South India will encounter people asking for alms, especially in the cities, around holy shrines and on railway journeys. Many of these beggers are physically disabled and they have few other options for survival. Although you should use your discretion, giving small amounts of money (one or two rupees) will be gratefully received and will generally be helping someone out. Try and give discretely as you might attract unwanted attention. If you are unsure about whether to give or not, it is fine to follow what other people around you are doing.

Children

Indians love children and are very tolerant and indulgent with them, making India a very easy place to travel with children, and children will find the sights and sounds just as rewarding as adults. The problem is that children can be more easily affected by the heat, unsafe drinking water and unfamiliar food seasoned with chillies and spices. In case of diarrhoea, rehydration salts are vital. Keep the child away from stray animals, especially dogs and monkeys. To avoid the risk of rabies, it may be safer to give children an anti-rabies vaccine. For infants, it is difficult to find nappies and places to change them. Consider bringing a supply of disposables, or changing to terries which, after rinsing, can be given to the hotel laundry or *dhobi*. A changing mat is essential, as is powdered milk of a brand that your child is familiar with. For touring, walking and hiking, a child-carrier backpack is well worth its weight.

Climate

The South is warm throughout the year, except in the hill ranges of the Nilgiris, the Anamalais, the Cardamom Hills, the Western Ghats and the Shevaroys. But the region can also be very wet, especially if the monsoons are good.

Average temperatures in the plains range from 23°C–32°C (73°F–90°F) in Tamil Nadu and Pondicherry, 23°C–29°C (73°F–85°F) in Kerala and Lakshadweep, 19°–31°C (66°F–88°F) in Karnataka and 21°C–33°C (70°F–92°F) in Andhra Pradesh. Hill station temperatures tend to range from about 10°C–18°C (50°F–65°F).

The hottest part of the year is from April–June, just before the southwest monsoon. Temperatures on some days can reach 50°C (130°F) in Tamil Nadu and Andhra Pradesh and over 40°C (110°F) in

Annual Temperature and Rainfall Chart

		Jan	Feb	Mar	Apr	May	June	July	Aug	Sep	Oct	Nov	Dec
Bangalore	Max/Min °C	28/15	31/16	33/19	34/21	33/21	30/20	28/19	29/19	28/19	28/19	27/17	27/15
	Rainfall mm	4	14	6	37	119	65	93	95	129	195	46	16
Chennai	Max/Min °C	29/20	31/21	33/23	35/23	38/28	37/28	35/26	35/25	34/25	32/24	29/23	28/21
	Rainfall mm	24	7	15	15	52	53	83	124	118	267	309	139
Hyderabad	Max/Min °C	29/15	31/17	35/20	37/24	39/26	34/24	30/22	29/22	30/22	30/20	29/16	28/13
	Rainfall mm	2	11	13	24	30	107	165	147	163	71	25	5
Tiruvanantha-puram	Max/Min °C	31/22	32/23	33/24	32/25	31/25	29/24	29/23	29/22	30/23	30/23	30/23	31/23
	Rainfall mm	20	20	43	122	249	331	215	164	123	271	207	73

Karnataka and Kerala. Both Kerala and Tamil Nadu are very humid. The monsoons begin around 10 June and can last well into October. Kerala, Lakshadweep and the Karnataka coast, as well as the western hills of Tamil Nadu, are lashed by seasonal monsoon rains, but the rest of the South gets only scattered showers or drizzles in bright sunshine.

From October to February/March the weather is mainly dry in many parts of the South, with temperatures ranging from 18°C–24°C (64°F–75°F) and hill stations like Udagamandalam and Kodaikanal even registering a low of 4°C (39°F). Kerala, Tamil Nadu and the Andhra Pradesh coast, however, are the only parts of India that get rain at this time of the year; the northeast monsoon being most active from mid-October to early December.

Kerala, Lakshadweep and Tamil Nadu in the monsoon are experiences in themselves, but sea-bathing is ruled out by rough seas at this time of the year. The Tamil Nadu and Andhra coasts are also prone to cyclonic storms from October to December. But the rains notwithstanding, the best time to visit the southern coasts is from October to March and also April and May if you can bear the heat. The hills and plateau-cities of Bangalore, Mysore and Hyderabad and their environs are year-round destinations.

Customs

Customs procedures have recently been simplified. Visitors fill in declaration forms on the plane, and then proceed to the relevant red or green channels. Keep the slip in your passport for when you disembark. Tourists seldom have any trouble. Occasionally, customs officials ask to see one suitcase at random and make a quick check.

Currency declaration

At present, forms for bringing in amounts of cash in excess of US$10,000 must be completed at customs on arrival.

Duty-free imports

These include 200 cigarettes (or 50 cigars), 0.95 litres (1 pint) of alcohol, a camera with five rolls of film and a reasonable amount of personal effects, including binoculars, laptop, sound recording instruments, etc.

Professional equipment and high-value articles must be declared or listed on arrival with a written undertaking to re-export them. Both the list and the articles must be produced on departure. As this formality can be a lengthy process, allow extra time, both on arrival and at departure. For unaccompanied baggage or baggage misplaced by the airline, make sure you get a landing certificate from customs on arrival.

Exports

Export of antiques (over 100 years old), all animal products, and jewellery valued at over Rs2,000 (in the case of gold) and Rs10,000 (in the case of articles not made of gold) are banned. When in doubt about the age of semi-antiques, contact the office of the Archaeological Survey of India in Delhi, Mumbai, Kolkata or Chennai.

Prohibited articles

These include certain drugs, live plants, gold and silver bullion, and coins not in current use. All checked luggage arriving at Delhi airport is X-rayed before reaching the baggage collection area in the arrival hall.

Departure

It is absolutely essential to reconfirm your reservations for all outward-bound flights at least 72 hours before departure, especially in the peak season, when most of the flights are overbooked. Security procedures can be intensive and time-consuming, so allow at least two hours for check-in.

An airport/seaport tax is charged on departure and must be paid prior to check-in (check the cost with your airline at the time of booking). Ensure that the name of your outward-bound carrier is endorsed on the tax receipt.

For visitors with entry permits, exit endorsements are necessary from the office where they were registered. Should a stay exceed 180 days, an income tax exemption certificate must be obtained from the Foreign Section of the Income Tax Department in Delhi, Mumbai, Kolkata or Chennai.

Remember before you leave that there is a departure tax of Rs750 (Rs550 for neighbouring SAARC countries) for all international departures. This should be included in your ticket, but make sure you check with your airline or on your ticket, where it should be marked.

Disabled Travellers

Although disability is common in India, there are very few provisions for wheelchairs and special toilets. The roads are full of potholes and kerbs are often high and without ramps. If you have difficulty walking, it may be hard to negotiate street obstacles, beggars, or steep staircases. On the other hand, Indians will always be willing to help you in and out of buses or cars, or up stairs. Taxis and rickshaws are cheap and the driver, with a little baksis, will probably help. You could employ a guide who will be prepared to help with obstacles. Another option is to go with a paid companion.

In the UK, Holiday Care, 7th Floor, Sunley House, 4 Bedford Park, Croydon, Surrey CR0 2AP (tel: 0845 124 9974; www.holidaycare.org.uk), could put you in touch with someone. Some package holiday operators cater for travellers with disabilities, but first ensure that your needs have been understood before making a booking. Contact an organisation for the disabled for further information.

Electricity

The voltage system in India is 220V AC, 50 cycles. DC supplies also exist, so check first. Sockets are of the two round-pin variety normally, but do vary. Take a universal adaptor for British, Irish and Australasian plugs. American and Canadian appliances will need a transformer.

Much of the electricity comes from hydro-electric projects and the low water levels during the dry season coupled with a greater demand for supply due to air-conditioning means that electricity supplies may be particularly irregular in summer. Power being switched off at local distribution points is known as "load shedding".

Entry Regulations

Tourist visas for all nationalities are issued for three or six months from the date of issue (not entry). It is preferable to take a multiple-entry visa, in order to have the option of visiting a neighbouring country. Get a visa is from the embassy or high commission in your country of residence, rather than risk the complications and delays involved in applying for one in neighbouring countries.

Tourist visas cannot be extended; you must leave the country and re-enter on a new one. It may be difficult to apply for a new visa from neighbouring countries. Five-year visas are also issued to businessmen and students. In addition to visas, special permits are required for certain areas, while other areas are out of bounds to foreigners altogether (see Restricted and Protected Areas below).

If you stay for more than 180 days, before leaving the country you must have a tax clearance certificate. These can be obtained from the foreigner's section of the income tax department in every city. Tax clearance certificates are free, but take bank receipts to demonstrate that you have changed money legally.

Restricted and Protected Areas

The country is generally open to tourism, apart from sensitive border regions (essentially those with China and Pakistan) certain areas of the Northeast and some of the islands.

Lakshadweep: only Agatti, Bangaram and Kadmat are open to foreign tourists. Kavaratti may be used as for transiting.

Embassies, Consulates and High Commissions

In Chennai

British Deputy High Commissioner
24 Anderson Road, Nungambakkam
Tel: 2827 3136–7
Fax: 2826 9004
Consulate of Canada,
Chamber 2, Business Centre, The Residency Towers, Thyagaraja Road
Tel: 2815 1445
Fax: 2815 7029
US Consulate
220 Anna Salai
Tel: 2827 3040

In Delhi

Australian High Commission,
Australian Compound, 1-50G Shantipath, Chanakyapuri (P.O. Box 5210)
Tel: (011) 5139 9900
Fax: (011) 5149 4491
British High Commission
Shantipath, Chanakyapuri, New Delhi
Tel: (011) 2687 2161 (24 hrs)
Fax: (011) 2687 0065
Canadian High Commission
7–8 Shantipath, Chanakyapuri, New Delhi (P.O. Box 5207)
Tel: (011) 2687 6500
Irish Embassy
13 Jor Bagh
Tel: (011) 2462 6714
New Zealand High Commission
50N Nyaya Marg, Chanyakapuri, New Delhi
Tel: (011) 2688 3170
US Embassy
Shantipath, Chanakyapuri, New Delhi
Tel: (011) 2419 8000
Fax: (011) 2419 0017

Indian Missions Abroad

Australia
High Commission of India
3–5 Moonah Place, Yarralumla, Canberra ACT-2600
Tel: (616) 273 3774/273 3999
Fax: (616) 273 3328/273 1308
www.highcommissionofindiaaustralia.org
Canada
High Commission of India
10 Springfield Road, Ottawa, Ontario KLM 1 C9
Tel: (613) 744 3751–3
Fax: (613) 744 0913
www.hciottawa.ca
Great Britain
High Commission of India
India House, Aldwych, London WC2B 4NA
Tel: (0891) 880 800 (24-hours recorded visa information); (020)7836 0990 (specific visa enquiries); (020) 7836-8484 (general)
www.hcilondon.org
US
Embassy of India
2107 Massachusetts Avenue NW, Washington DC 20008
Tel: (202) 939 7000
Fax: (202) 939 7027
www.indianembassy.org

Emergencies

Generally speaking, India is a safe place to travel, but a tourist is a natural target for thieves and pick-pockets, so take the usual precautions and keep money, credit cards, valuables and passport in a money belt or pouch well secured with a cord around your neck. A protective hand over this in a crowded place could save you a lot of heartache and hassle.

Do not leave belongings unattended, especially on a beach. Invest in good strong locks (available in India) for your bags. Chaining luggage to the berth on a train, or to your seat on a bus, is another precaution that travelling Indians often take. Watch your luggage carefully, especially during loading and unloading.

Credit card frauds do exist so make sure that shops and restaurants process your card in front of you.

Another sensible precaution is to keep a photocopy of your passport and visa, traveller's cheque numbers and receipts, ticket details, insurance policy number and telephone claims number, and some emergency money in a bag or case separate from your other cash and documents. If you are robbed, report the incident immediately to a police station (be patient, this can take hours).

Etiquette

● Removing one's shoes before entering someone's house, temple or mosque is essential. Overshoes are provided in some places of worship at a nominal cost and stockinged feet are usually permissible.

● The *namaskaram* greeting with joined hands, is the Indian form of salutation and its use will be appreciated, though men, especially in the cities, will not hesitate to shake hands with you if you are a man. A handshake would even be appreciated as a gesture of special friendliness.

Most Indian women would be taken aback at the informality of interaction between the sexes common in the West and physical contact between men and women is to be avoided. Men should not shake hands with a woman (unless she first offers to).

- Avoid taking leather goods of any kind into temples as these can often cause offence.
- Always walk around religious shrines clockwise.
- Photography is prohibited inside the inner sanctum of many places of worship. Do obtain permission before using a camera. Visitors are usually welcome to look around at their leisure and can sometimes stay during religious rituals. For visits to places of worship, modest clothing is essential. In mosques, women should cover their head and arms and wear long skirts. A small contribution to the temple donation box *(hundi)* is customary.
- In private, visitors are received as honoured guests and your unfamiliarity with Indian ways will be accepted and understood. When eating with your fingers, remember to use only the right hand.
- Avoid pointing the soles of your feet towards anyone as this is considered a sign of disrespect. Don't point with your index finger: use either your extended hand or your chin.
- Central Government has passed a law banning smoking in all public places, and this has now been enacted by most State governments.

Gay and Lesbian Travellers

Homosexuality is still a taboo subject for many Indians. Sexual relations between men are punishable with long prison sentences and cruising in public could come under public disorder laws. There is no similar law against lesbians.

While general attitudes are discriminatory, things are changing slowly, and at least the issue of gay and lesbian rights is starting to be discussed, due in no small part to Deepa Mehta's 1998 film *Fire*, which depicted an affair between two married women, and the 2004 film *Girlfriend*. Attacks on cinemas by the religious right brought counter demonstations onto the streets of major cities.

However, gay and lesbian travellers should be discreet and avoid any public displays of affection (as should heterosexual couples). On the plus side, hotels will think nothing of two men or women sharing a room.

More information can be found on the male-oriented www.bombay-dost.com website, or, for women, from Sangini (c/o The Naz Foundation, P.O. Box 3910, Andrews Gunj, New Delhi 110049). Sangini run a helpline (Tues and Fri 6–8pm, tel: (011) 2685 1970). Alternatively, contact the Campaign For Lesbian Rights, P.O. Box 3526, Lajpat Nagar P.O., New Delhi 110024.

Health

Diarrhoeas

Traveller's diarrhoea

Usually caused by low-level food poisoning this can be avoided with a little care. When you arrive, rest on your first day and only eat simple food; well-cooked vegetarian dishes, a south Indian thali and peeled fruits are perhaps best. An upset stomach is often caused by eating too many rich Indian meat dishes (usually cooked with vast amounts of oil and spices) and failing to rest and let your body acclimatise.

Drink plenty of fluids but never drink unboiled or unfiltered water. When in doubt, stick to soda, mineral water, or aerated drinks of standard brands. Avoid ice as this is often made with unboiled water. All food should be cooked and eaten hot. Don't eat salads and always peel fruit.

With all cases of diarrhoea, including dysentery and giardia described below, it is not a good idea to use imobilising drugs such as loperamide (Imodium) and atropine (Lomotil) as they prevent the body ridding itself of infection. These should only be used if you have to travel. The most important thing to do in cases of diarrhoea and/or vomiting is to rehydrate, preferably using oral rehydration salts.

Dysentery and Giardia

These are more serious forms of stomach infection and should be suspected and treated if the diarrhoea lasts for more than 2 days.

Dysentery is characterised by diarrhoea accompanied by the presence of mucus and blood in faeces. Other symptoms include severe stomach cramps and vomiting. Bacillic dysentery comes on quickly and is usually accompanied by fever. It may clear up by itself but its usual treatment is with 500mg of ciprofloxacin or tetracycline twice daily for 5 days. Do not take the powerful antibiotic chloramphenicol as it can have dangerous side effects. Amoebic dysentery has a slower onset and will not clear up on its own. If you suspect you have amoebic dysentery you should seek medical help as it can damage the gut. If this is not available then self-treat with 400mg of metronidazole (Flagyl) three times daily with food for 7 days. You must not drink alchohol when taking metronidazole.

Giardia is a similar infection caused by a parasite. Like amoebic dysentery it comes on slowly and its symptoms include loose and foul-smelling diarrhoea, feeling bloated and nauseous, and stomach cramps. Giardia will not clear up on its own and will recur; its treatment is the same as for amoebic dysentery.

Fungal infections

Prickly heat is a common complaint caused by excessive perspiration. Try to keep the skin dry by using talcum powder and wearing loose-fitting cotton clothes. Fungal infections are also common, especially during the monsoon, and can be treated by exposure to the sun and/or by the application of Caneston cream.

Hospitals

Delhi

All India Institute of Medical Sciences, Ansari Nagar
Tel: 2686 4851
Kripalani Hospital, Panchkuin Road
Tel: 2336 3788
Safdarjang General Hospital, Sri Aurobindo Marg
Tel: 2616 5060

Hyderabad/Secunderabad

General Hospital, Nampally
Tel: 2234 344
Newciti, Secunderabad
Tel: 2780 5961

Mumbai

Prince Ali Khan Hospital, Nesbit Road
Tel: 2375 4343

Malaria

This moquito-borne disease is very serious and potentially fatal. There are two common strains in India, *P. falciparum* and *P. vivax*, both carried by the Anopheles mosquito. Symptoms are similar to acute flu (including some or all of fever, shivering, diarrhoea and muscle pains) and an outbreak may come on as much as a year after visiting a malarial area. If malaria is suspected then medical attention should be sought as soon as possible. Prophylaxis is essential for all areas except those above 2,500m (8,200 ft). The usual anti-malarial protection for India consists of a combination of daily proguanil (Paludrine) and weekly chloroquine (Avoclar, Nivaquin). These are now bought across the counter in the UK, and your pharmacist will advise you on the correct dosages (usually 200 mg of proguanil daily and 300 mg of chloroquin weekly). This is at present the only safe prophylaxis during pregnancy. However, the combination is at best 70% effective and it may be that medical advice will change soon.

An alternative drug is mefloquine (Lariam), taken weekly. However, this should not be taken by people with a history of epilepsy or mental illness and there has been much anecdotal evidence of long-lasting and serious side effects (although medical evidence suggests that these are no more likely than with the proguanil/chloroquin combination). In the UK mefloquine is only available as a private prescription. A newly approved drug is the atavoquone-proguanil combination marketed as Malarone. This is recommended for areas of chloroquine resistance (such as Assam) and is taken once-a-day. It is expensive and at present only some Health Authorities offer it as an NHS prescription. Other drug regimes are not effective against both strains of the disease.

The best, and only certain, protection against malaria is not to get bitten. Sleep under a mosquito net impreganted with permethrin, cover up in the evenings and use an effective insect repellent such as DEET (diethyltoluamide). Burning mosquito coils, which are easily obtainable in India, is also a good idea.

Medical supplies

Bring along a personal medical kit to take care of minor ailments. This should include anti-diarrhoea medication, a broad spectrum antibiotic, aspirin, clean needles, and something for throat infections and allergies would be a good idea. Take your regular medications, tampons and pantyliners, contra-ceptives and condoms, as these may be difficult to find.

BELOW: a snack stall, Kochi.

Also include plasters, antiseptic cream and water purification tablets. All cuts, however minor, should be cleaned and sterilised immediately to prevent infection. Locally available oral rehydration powders (such as Vijay Electrolyte) containing salts and dextrose are an ideal additive to water, especially when travelling in the summer months or when suffering from diarrhoea. If oral rehydration salts are not available then one teaspoon each of salt and sugar in 500 ml of water is a useful substitute.

Sun exposure

The dangers of sunburn are now well-publicised. Cover up and use a high factor sunscreen, even if it is cloudy. The power of the sun is obvious on the plains and in tropical India, but also be careful in the mountains, where thinner air makes the sun very powerful, even if it feels cooler. Overexposure can also lead to the two conditions below:

- Heat exhaustion is common, indicated by shallow breathing, rapid pulse, pallor, and is often accompanied by leg cramps, headache or nausea.

The body temperature remains normal. Lying down in a cool place and sipping water mixed with rehydration salts or plain table salt will prevent loss of consciousness.

- Heatstroke is more serious, and more likely to occur when it is both hot and humid. Babies and elderly people are especially susceptible. The body temperature soars suddenly and the skin feels dry. The victim may feel confused, then pass out.

Take them quickly to a cool room, remove their clothes and cover them with a wet sheet or towels soaked in cold water. Call for medical help and fan them constantly until their body temperature drops to 38°C (100°F).

Vaccinations

No inoculations are legally required to enter India, but it is strongly advised that you get inoculations against typhoid (Typhim Vi gives protection for 3 years), hepatitis A (Havrix gives immunity for 1 year, up to 10 years if a 6-month booster is given; the combined hepatitis A and typhoid injection gives immunity for 10 years), polio, diptheria and tetanus (a booster of Revaxis will give immunity for 10 years). India has recently had serious outbreaks of meningitis and you should get an inoculation against meningitis A, C, W and Y. You may need to show proof of a yellow fever inoculation if arriving from an infected area. Other diseases against which vaccinations might be considered, particularly for longer trips, include rabies and Japanese B encephalitis. There is no vacccination against Dengue fever, occasionally contracted in India. The only protection is to avoid being bitten *(see also Malaria)*.

Maps

Obtaining good maps of India can be difficult; the government forbids the sale of detailed maps in border areas, which includes the entire coastline, for security reasons; those which can be bought may not be exported.

Some good maps to bring along are: Bartholomew's 1:4,000,000 map of South Asia; Lascelles map of the same scale and Nelles Verlag maps. Tourist offices can supply larger scale city maps. State and city maps are also published by the TT company, 328 G.S.T. Road, Chromepet, Chennai, Tamil Nadu 600 044, or the Survey of India, Janpath Barracks A, New Delhi 110 001. Other highly recommended maps are the Eicher series of detailed city maps, including those of Chennai and Bangalore. Many of these maps are available from www.indiamapstore.com

Media

Newspapers & Magazines

The English language newspaper *The Hindu* (www.hinduonnet.com), established well over a hundred years ago, is published simultaneously in five regional editions and covers the entire South. A serious, well-edited newspaper with a national slant to the news, *The Hindu* is one of the best English-language newspapers in Asia. The local editions carry regional news, and it carries a comprehensive diary of events every day. It also publishes the exemplary fortnightly news magazine *Frontline* (www.frontlineonnet. com). The *Indian Express* (www.indian express.com), another daily also published in the four southern states, has a lighter style than *The Hindu* but still well written and with good reports.

Despite their regional editions, both these papers are basically Tamil Nadu newspapers, being headquartered in Chennai. The other English daily in Chennai is the evening *News Today* (www.newstodaynet.com) that has strong coverage of local politics. Other regional English-language titles are Karnataka's *Deccan Herald* (from Bangalore; www.deccanharald.com) and

Andhra Pradesh's *Deccan Chronicle* (from Hyderabad; www.deccan.com). Mumbai's leading daily, *The Times of India* (www.timesofindia.com), has Bangalore and Hyderabad editions.

The most literate part of India, Kerala, does not have an English daily of its own, though its Malayalam language dailies are among the newspapers with the highest circulation in the country.

As well as *Frontline*, other news magazines with a national reach include *India Today* (www.india-today.com), *Outlook* (www.outlookindia.com) and *The Week* (www.the-week.com). There are also excellent general-interest magazines such as *Sanctuary* (www.sanctuaryasia.com), which specialises in South Asian natural history, and the travel magazine *Discover India*. Magazines like *Travel Links* and city magazines such as *Hallo! Madras* give current information on internal travel and local cultural events. There are several glossy women's magazines in English, including *Femina* (www.feminaindia.com) and Indian editions of *Cosmopolitan* and *Elle*. The two cinema magazines with the widest reach are *Cineblitz* and *Filmfare* (www.filmfare.com).

Television & Radio

Doordarshan is the government television company and broadcasts programmes in English, Hindi and regional languages. Local timings vary, but generally the news in English can be heard daily at 7.50am and 9.30pm.

Satellite television is available almost everywhere, including the Star TV's network incorporating the BBC World Service and MTV. NDTV is a local 24-hour news channel that provides good coverage of Indian news and politics. Other stations include Channel V (a local youth-orientated music channel) and Zee TV (Hindi). There are channels showing sport, American soaps and sitcoms and English-language movies. Up to 50 channels can be picked up, given the right equipment.

All India Radio (AIR) broadcasts on the short-wave, medium-wave and in Delhi, Mumbai and Chennai on FM (VHF). The frequencies vary, so check with your hotel.

Money

All encashments of traveller's cheques and exchange of foreign currency used to have to be recorded on a currency declaration form, or receipts kept as proof of legal conversion. The laws have eased, but some businesses and hotels may still insist. Visitors staying more than 180 days will have to produce proof of encashment of traveller's cheques or exchange of currency for income tax exemption and show they have been self-supporting.

Indian currency is based on the decimal system, with 100 paise to the rupee. Coins are in denominations of 10, 20, 25 and 50 paise and 1, 2 and 5 rupees. Notes are in 10, 20, 50, 100 and 500 rupee denominations. Indian rupees may not be brought in nor taken out of the country. Exchange rates fluctuate against other currencies.

Traveller's cheques should be well-known brands such as Thomas Cook, American Express and Visa. A slightly better exchange rate is offered by banks, but not all banks will accept traveller's cheques.

Credit cards are increasingly accepted by hotels, restaurants, large shops, tourist emporia and airlines. It is preferable to have a well-known card such as American Express, MasterCard or Visa. A number of banks will now issue rupees against a Visa card and Amex issues rupees or traveller's cheques to cardholders against a cheque at their offices. More conveniently, ATMS that issue cash against a variety of cards are found in many places. The ATMs of local banks may only issue cash against their won cards so try and find a machine on an international bank. Changing money on the black market is illegal and not worth the premium.

Opening Times

Banks

Open from 10am–2pm weekdays, 10am– noon Saturday for most foreign banks and nationalised Indian banks (of which the State Bank is the largest). Some banks operate evening branches, while others remain open on Sunday and close on another day of the week, and some open 9am–1pm. In larger cities many banks now have 24-hour atms, often guarded, which are very convenient and safe. All banks are closed on national holidays, on 30 June and 31 December. Most businesses close on public holidays.

Government offices

Officially 9.30am–6pm Monday to Friday, but most business is done between 10am and 5pm with a long lunch break.

Post Offices

Open from 10am–4.30pm Monday to Friday, and until 12 noon on Saturday. However, in most of the larger cities, the Central Post Office is open until 6.30pm on weekdays, 4.30pm on Saturday. On Sunday some open until noon. Major telegraph offices are open 24 hours.

Restaurants

Usually open until 11pm. A few nightclubs and discoteques close very much later. Hotel coffee shops are often open around the clock.

Shops

Open from 10am–7pm. Some shops close for lunch. Although Sunday is an official holiday, different localities in major cities have staggered days off so that there are always some shopping areas open.

Place names

Some places have changed their names, in many cases away from Anglicisations, including the following:

Alleppey (Alappuzha)
Bombay (Mumbai)
Calicut (Kozhikode)
Cannanore (Kannur)
Cochin (Kochi)
Capecomorin (Kanyakumari)
Madras (Chennai)
Mahabalipuram (Mamallapuram)
Mercara (Madikeri)
Ooty (Udagamandalam)
Palghat (Palakkad)
Quilon (Kollam)
Sulthan Battery (Sulthanbathery)
Tanjore (Thanjavur)
Tellicherry (Thalassery)
Trichur (Thrissur)
Trichy (Thiruchirappalli)
Trivandrum (Thiruvananthapuram)

Post

The internal mail service is efficient in most areas. It is advisable to personally affix stamps to letters or postcards and hand them over to the post office counter for immediate franking rather than to post them in a letterbox. Indian stamps do not stick very well so make sure you use the pot of "gum" (glue) that is almost always available.

Sending a registered parcel overseas is a complicated and time-consuming process. Most parcels should be stitched into cheap cotton cloth and then sealed (there are people outside major post offices offering this service). Two customs forms need to be completed. Once the parcel has been weighed and stamps affixed, make sure it is franked and a receipt of registration is issued. Important or valuable material should be registered.

Many shops offer to dispatch goods, but not all of them are reliable. It is usually only safe when handled by a government-run emporium.

Airfreighting purchases is possible but can be equally time-consuming. You will need to produce the bill and receipt, encashment certificate, your passport and onward airline ticket. There are many airfreight agents throughout India and most travel agents can provide assistance

Generally poste restante works well, but make sure your name is clearly written.

Courier services

Most of the major international courier networks have agency agreements with Indian companies. DHL, Skypak and IML all work under their own brand names while Federal Express operates as Blue Dart. These companies have offices in the major towns and operate both international and extensive domestic networks. NB. The government's **Speedpost** service delivers quickly at a similar price.

Public Holidays

Sunday is the official weekly holiday throughout the South, but a few private establishments might close on Friday. Other compulsory holidays are:

26 January (Republic Day)
1 May (May Day)
15 August (Independence Day)
2 October (Mahatma Gandhi's Birthday).

Other holidays generally follow the individual State Government's list, though many business establishments work during several of these holidays.

The main holiday seasons in the South are the week-long *Pongal-Sankranti* period in mid-January, *Dussera* (ten days in September/October) and *Dipavali* (a few days in October/ November).

Repairs and Tailors

Traditionally, India's use of resources is very efficient, reflected in the way almost everything can be recycled and/or repaired. Since travelling around India can be hard on your shoes, baggage and clothes, this is very useful. Chappal-wallahs, shoe repairers, can be found everywhere, usually sitting by the side of the road with their tools in a wooden box. For an embarassingly small charge, they will be able to glue, nail or stitch almost any pair of shoes or sandals back into shape.

Indian tailors are very skilful and can run up a set of clothes quickly. Although they can do fair copies of Western fashions, they are, obviously, much better at stitching sari blouses or shalwar kamiz. The process of buying fabric is one of the great pleasures of visiting India, and if you want it made up, most shops will be able to recommend a good tailor.

Tailors will also be able to repair your existing clothes, even badly torn ones, and – just as useful – can stitch up rucksacks which are on the point of collapse.

Telephones

India's telephone system is steadily improving and international calls can now be dialled direct to most parts of the world or booked through the operator. Calling from hotels can be extremely expensive, with surcharges up to 300 percent, so check rates first. Mobile telephones are widely used in India and your own phone may well work while you are there.

Privately run telephone services with international direct-dialling facilities are very widespread. Advertising themselves with the acronyms STD/ISD (standard trunk dialling/international subscriber dialling), they are quick and easy to use. Some stay open 24 hours a day. Both national and international calls are dialled direct. To call abroad, dial the international access code (00), the code for the country you want (44 for the UK, 1 for the US or Canada), the appropriate area code (without any initial zeros), and the number you want. Some booths have an electronic screen that keeps time and calculates cost during the call. Prices are similar to those at official telecommunications centres.

To call India from abroad, dial the international access code, followed by 91 for India, the local code less the initial zero, then the number.

Indian telephone numbers change often and although those in the book have been checked carefully they may well change in the future. NB. Indian telephone numbers are now all 10 digits long (including the area code minus the initial zero). The vast majority of numbers now start with a "2", if you encounter an old-style number (i.e. eight digits long) add a "2" to the beginning and it should work.

Home country direct services are now available from any telephone to the UK, US, Canada, Australia, New Zealand and a number of other countries. These allow you to make a reverse-charges or telephone credit card call to that country via the operator there. If you cannot find a telephone with home country direct buttons, you can use any phone toll-free by dialling 000, your country code and 17 (except Canada, which is 000-167). US international access codes are: MCI 000 127; Sprint 000 137; and AT&T 000 117.

Many privately run telephone services have fax machines and most large hotels have a fax.

E-mail and the internet are now very popular and widely available. All large cities, and many smaller places, have internet cafés or similar places where you can surf the net or send e-mails. Charges are usually by the minute or hour, and are usually around 60 Rs per hour.

Time Zone

India is 5½ hours ahead of Greenwich Mean Time.

Tipping

There is no harm expressing your appreciation with a small tip. Depending on services rendered and the type of establishment, this could range from Rs2–Rs10.

In restaurants, the tip is customarily 10–15 percent of the bill. Leading hotels add a 10 percent service surcharge and tipping in such places is optional.

Although tipping taxis and three-wheelers is not an established norm, it does not go amiss. Here again, 10 percent of the fare or leaving the change, if not substantial, would be adequate. Porters at railway stations would expect around Rs2 a bag. At airports, a rupee per bag in addition to the fee charged by the airport authority would be welcome.

If you have been a house guest, check with your host whether he has any objections to your tipping any of his domestic helpers (for instance, a chauffeur who may have driven you around) before doing so.

Tourist Information

The Ministry of Tourism has a good website (www.tourismofindia.com or www.incredibleindia.org) with a lot of useful information on obtaining visas, places to visit and tour operators.

Indian Tourist Offices abroad

Australia
Level 2 Piccadilly, 210 Pitt Street,

Sydney, New South Wales 2000
Tel: (02) 9264 4855
Fax: (02) 9264 4860
Canada
60 Bloor Street West, Suite 1003, Toronto, Ontario M4N 3N6
Tel: (416) 962 3787–8
Fax: (416) 962 6279
UK
7 Cork Street, London W1X 2AB
Tel: (020) 8812 0929 (24-hour tourist information); (020) 7437 3677 (general)
Fax: (020) 7494 1048
US
1270 Avenue of America, Suite 1808, New York 10020
Tel: (212) 586 4901–3
Fax: (212) 582 3274

Local Tourist Offices

Below is a list of government tourist offices in the major cities:
Bangalore
K.F.C. Building, 48 Church Street
Tel: 2558 5417
Chennai
154 Anna Salai
Tel: 2846 1459
Delhi
88 Janpath
Tel: 2332 0008
Hyderabad/Secunderabad
30-60-140, 2nd Floor, Netaji Bhavan, Liberty Road
Tel: 2326 1360
Kochi/Ernakulam
Willingdon Island
Tel: 266 8352
Mumbai
123 Maharishi Karve Marg, opposite Churchgate
Tel: 2203 3144
Thiruvananthapuram
Park View
Tel: 232 2517

State Tourism Websites

Andhra Pradesh
www.aptourism.com
Karnataka
http://kstdc.nic.in
Kerala
www.keralatourism.org
Lakshadweep
http://lakshadweep.nic.in
Pondicherry
www.tourisminpondicherry.com
Tamil Nadu
www.tourtamilnadu.com

Water

Many water supplies in India are contaminated and are a common source of disease for travellers who have no immunity to water-borne bacteria such as giardia. Bottled water is available. However, there is no guarantee that this is safe and, perhaps more importantly, it is extremely bad for the environment (India is accumulating an enormous plastic bottle mountain). It is much better to carry your own water bottle (those made by the Swiss firm Sigg are very tough and hygienic) and fill it from safe water sources (the best is boiled water). This is not always available and portable water filters are an excellent solution. Those made by Katadyn (www.katadyn.com) are considered the best.

Weights & Measurements

The metric system is uniformly used all over India. Precious metals, especially gold, are often sold by the traditional *tola*, which is equivalent to 11.5 grams. Gems are weighed in carats (0.2 grams).

Financial outlays and population are usually expressed in *lakhs* (100 thousand) and *crores* (100 *lakhs* or 10 million).

What to Bring

Clothing

Travelling in southern India it is best to wear cotton. Avoid synthetics. Cotton shirts, blouses and skirts are inexpensive and easily available in all towns and cities. Remember to bring underwear (especially bras) and swimwear.

In winter a light sweater might be necessary as the early mornings can be a little chilly. Comfortable footwear is essential. "Trekking" sandals are excellent for wearing in India as they are tough and provide good protection to your feet. Teva and Reef are good brands.

For their own convenience, women should not wear sleeveless blouses, mini skirts and short, revealing dresses. Cover up – it's a good idea in the Indian sun anyway – locally available *shalwar kamiz* (also known as *churidar* or a Punjabi suit), a long tunic top worn over loose trousers, are ideal.

Film

Colour print film, developing and printing facilities are available in all big cities. Colour slide film can only be found in major cities and it may be safer to bring your own.

There are few places where prompt and reliable camera servicing can be done, so photographic equipment should be checked before the trip. Protect your camera and film from excessive exposure to heat, dust and humidity.

There are strict restrictions on photography of military installations, bridges and dams, airports, border areas and Adivasi/restricted areas.

ABOVE: snake boat racers, Alappuzha.

Other Essentials

If travelling away from the major cities or big hotels, take a sheet sleeping bag, pillowcases and medical kit among other items. Sun cream and sun block are not readily available so they should be brought with you, along with cosmetics and tampons. A hat or scarf to cover your head is a sensible item, as is an umbrella. A mosquito net and a basin/bath plug are also useful in smaller hotels, which often do not have them.

It is always advisable to obtain good travel insurance to cover the worst possible scenario. Take a copy of your policy and keep it separately as a safeguard.

Women Travellers

"Eve-teasing" is the Indian euphemism for sexual harassment. Take the normal precautions such as looking out for yourself on crowded local public transport (crowds are a haven for gropers). Do not wear clothes that expose legs, arms and cleavage; *shalwar kamiz* are ideal, and a shawl is handy to use as a cover-all when required.

More serious sexual assaults on tourists are rare and tend to occur in popular tourist areas, but in case something should happen, call for help from passers-by.

On the up-side, there are "ladies-only" queues at train and bus stations, and "ladies-only" waiting rooms at stations and compartments on trains.

LANGUAGE

SOUTH INDIAN LANGUAGES

Introduction

With 18 official languages, hundreds of others and countless dialects, India can present a linguistic minefield. Luckily for the traveller, English is often understood and it is usually possible to get by. However, attempts to speak the local language are always appreciated. The language most widely spoken in the North is Hindi, while in the South Tamil has the highest profile (it is a source of considerable regional pride) and has recently been given official status as a classical language.

Of the other South Indian languages, Malayalam (a south Dravidian language spoken in Kerala) is closely related to Tamil, though with more influence of Sanskrit. The two central Dravidian languages, Telugu (spoken in Andhra Pradesh) and Kannada (spoken in Karnataka) are also both closely related and, again, display a greater influence of Sanskrit than is evident in Tamil. All the Dravidian languages, however, show distinct similarities and many basic words are common or similar across all four (for example, the word for "I", *nan/nenu*, or "milk", *pal(u)*).

Indian languages are phonetically regular, based on syllables rather than an alphabet. Important differences are made between long and short vowels, and reteroflex, palatal and labial consonants – listen hard to get a feel for the words below. There are various transliteration systems and you may see many of the words below spelt different ways in English. Where a consonant is followed by "h" this is an aspirated sound, "c" is usually pronounced "ch" (followed by "h", "chh"), and "zh" stands for a sound somewhere between a reteroflex "l" and "r".

Tamil

Basics

Hello *Vanakkam*
Goodbye *Poyvituvarukiren* (Reply *Poyvituvarungal*)
Yes *Amam*
No *Illai*
Perhaps *Oruvelai*
Thank you *Nandri*
How are you? *Celakkiyama?*
What is your name? *Ungal peyar yenna?*
My name is (John/Jane) *Yen peyar* (John/Jane)
Where is the (hotel)? (Hotel) *yenge?*
What is this/that? *Idu/Adu yenna?*
What is the price? *Yenna vilai?*
That is very expensive *Anda vilai mikavum adikum*
I want (coffee) *(Kapi) Vendum*
I like (dosa) *(Dosai) Pudikkum*
Is it possible? *Mudiyuma?*
I don't understand *Puriyadu*
Enough *Podum*
Toilet *Tailet*
Bed *Kattil*
Room *Arai*
Bedroom *Patukkai arai*
Train *Rayil*
Sari *Pudavai*
Dhoti *Vesti*
Towel *Tundu*
Sandals *Ceruppu*
Money *Punam*
Temple *Kovil*

Verbs

Come (imperative) *Varungal*
Go (imperative) *Pongal*
Stop (imperative) *Nillungal*
Sleep *Tungu*
Eat *Sappidu*
Drink *Kudi*
Buy *Vangu*
Pay (money) *Punam kodu* (literally "give money")
See *Par*
Wash (clothes) *Tuvai*
Wash (yourself) *Kazhavu*

Prepositions, adverbs and adjectives

Quickly *Sikkirum*
Slowly *Meduvaka*
A lot *Mikavum*
A little *Koncam*
Here *Inge*
There *Ange*
This *Idu*
That *Adu*
Now *Ippodu*
Same *Ade*
Good *Nalla*
Bad *Ketta*
Hot *Karam*
Cold *Kulirana*
Dirty *Acattam*
Clean *Cattam*
Beautiful *Azhakana*
Sweet *Inippu*
Big *Periya*
Small *Cinna*
Old *Pazhaiya*
New *Pudiya*

Days of the week

Monday *Tingal*
Tuesday *Cevvay*
Wednesday *Putam*
Thursday *Viyazhan*
Friday *Velli*
Saturday *Ceni*
Sunday *Nayiri*
Today *Inraikku*
Week *Varam*
Month *Matam*
Year *Varutam*

Numbers

1 *onru*
2 *irandu*
3 *munru*

4 *nanku*
5 *aindu*
6 *aru*
7 *yezhu*
8 *yettu*
9 *onpadu*
10 *pattu*
11 *patinonru*
12 *pannirandu*
20 *irupadu*
30 *muppadu*
40 *rarpadu*
50 *aimpadu*
60 *arupadu*
70 *alupadu*
80 *yenpadu*
90 *tonnuru*
100 *nuru*
100,000 *latcam*
10,000,000 *kodi*

Questions and "and"

How? *Yeppadi?*
What? *Yenna?*
Who? *Yar?*
Why? *Yen?*
Where? *Yenge?*
When? *Yeppodu?*

How much? *Yettanai/Yevvalavu?*
Questions in Tamil are usually formed by adding a long "a" to the last word of a sentence (usually the verb), e.g. *"Ningal venduma?"* "What do you want?". "And" is formed by adding *"um"* to the end of the nouns (with an extra *"y"* if the noun ends in a vowel), e.g. *"Kapiyum, dosaiyum"*, "Coffee and dosa".

Pronouns and relatives

I *Nan*
You *Ningal*
He/She/It *Avan/Aval/Avar*
We (including addressee)/(excluding addressee) *Nam/Nangal*
They *Avakal*
Man *Manidan*
Woman/Girl/Daughter *Pen*
Boy/Son *Paiyan*
Children *Pillaikal*
Baby *Pappu*
Mother *Amma*
Father *Appa*
Husband *Kanavan*
Wife *Manaivi*
Aunt *Mami*
Uncle *Mama*

Health

I am sick (vomiting) *Utampu cariyillai irukkiradu*
I have a pain Vali irukkiradu
I have diarrhoea "Motions" *irrukkiradu*
Doctor *Taktar*
Help! *Utavi cey!*

The English word "motions" is a common expression for diarrhoea.

Food (Sappadu)

Tunnir Water
Sadum Rice
Puzham Fruit
Kaykuri Vegetables
Pal Milk
Mor Buttermilk
Minakay (iilamal) (without) chilli
Tengay Coconut
Mampazham Mango
Valaippazham Banana
Kapi Coffee
Ti Tea
Iddli Steamed rice cakes
Dosai Pancake made from fermented dough
Vadai Deep fried snack made of dal
Rasam Thin, spicy soup
Sampar Thick soup made from dal
Poriyal Dry vegetable curry
Kolikarri Chicken curry
Attukkari Lamb curry
Mils "Meals", similar to a North Indian *thali*
Payasam Sweet milk-based dish served at festivals

Telugu

Basics

Hello/Goodbye *Namaskaram*
Yes *Avnu*
No *Kadu* (is not), *Ledu* (there is not)
OK *Sari*
What is your name? *Ni peru eni?*
My name is (Jane/John) *Na peru* (Jane/John)
Where do you come from? *Ni uru edi?*
I *Nenu*
You (plural) *Miru*
This *Idi*
That *Adi*
Those *Avi*
These *Ivi*
Come (imperative) *Ra*
Go (imperative) *Po*
Eat (imperative) *Tinu*
Drink (imperative) *Tagu*
Some/a little *Cancam*
Enough *Chalu*
Good *Manci*
Bad *Cedu* or *Cedda*
Mother *Thalli* or *Amma*
Father *Thandri*
Husband *Bharta*
Wife *Bharya*
Room *Gadi*
Bed *Mancamu*
Temple *Gudi*

Numbers

1 *okati*
2 *remdu*
3 *mudu*
4 *nalugu*
5 *aidu*
6 *aru*
7 *edu*
8 *enimidi*
9 *tommidi*
10 *padi*

An "o" sound at the beginning of a word will often be pronounced with an intial "w", hence *"w"okati*, for "one".

Questions

What? *Eni?*
Which? *Edi?*
Where? *Ekkada?*
When? *Eppudu?*
How? *Etlu?*
Why? *Enduku?*
How many? *Enni?*
How much? *Enta?*

Food

Bhojanamu Meals
Annamu Rice
Pappu Dal
Kayaguralu Vegetables
Masamu Meat
Guddu Egg
Mirapakaya Chillies
Tenkaya Coconut
Aratipandu Banana
Mamidipandu Mango
Uppu Salt
Chakkera Sugar
Perugu Curd
Majjiga Buttermilk
Palu Milk

Malayalam

Basic Phrases

Hello/Goodbye *Namaskaram*
Please *Deyavu Cheytu*
Thank You *Nanni*
OK *Sari*
Yes *Untu*
No *Illa*
Where is...? *Evide anna...?*
I would like... *Nan venam...*
Where is the toilet? *Tailet evide?*
I am from... *Nan... ninnu*
How much? *Enta villa?*
How are you? *Cukmano?*
What? *Enta?*
Where? *Evide?*
I don't understand *Mancilla illa*
What is your name? *Ninte peru entanu?*
My name is... *Enthe peru aanu...*
Right *Vallate*
Left *Edade*

Numbers

One *Onnu*
Two *Randu*
Three *Munnu*
Four *Nallu*
Five *Anch*
Six *Aru*
Seven *Ezhu*
Eight *Ettu*
Nine *Ompatu*
Ten *Pattu*

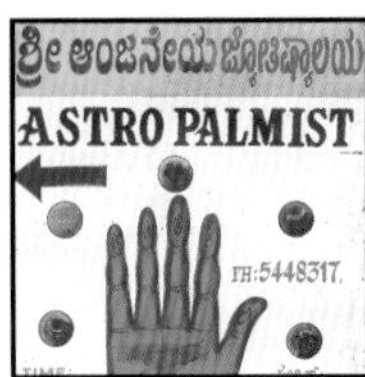

FURTHER READING

History

An Autobiography, or My Experiments with Truth, by M.K. Gandhi (Penguin, 1982). A translation from the original Gujarati which shows the complex and at times flawed nature of one of India's greatest popular leaders.
A Concise History of India, by Francis Watson (Thames and Hudson, 1979). Compact and thorough history in readable format, with illustrations and photographs.
The Discovery of India, by Jawaharlal Nehru (Asia Publishing House, 1966). Revealing history by India's first Prime Minister, which tells as much about the author as its subject.
Early India: From the Origins to AD 1300, by Romila Thapar (Penguin, 2002). The updated and revised edition of her acclaimed history, which forms part one of the Penguin History of India.
Freedom at Midnight, by Larry Collins and Dominique Lapierre (Tarang, 1975). Gripping popular history of the birth of the Indian nation.
A History of India, Volume II, by Perceval Spear (Penguin, 1996). Deals with the period from the Mughals to the assassination of M.K. Gandhi.
An Introduction to India, by Stanley Wolpert (Viking 1992). Informative account of India's complexities by an American academic.
India, by Barbara Crosette (University of Indiana Press, 1993). Contemporary Indian politics and international relations recounted by New York Times correspondent who was on the scene at Rajiv Gandhi's assassination.
India a History, by John Keay (HarperCollins, 2000), A new one-volume history by a well-respected writer. Also by Keay, **India Discovered** (Collins, 1998) documents the unearthing of India's past by British scholars and adventurers.
Liberty or Death: India's Journey to Independence and Division, by Patrick French (HarperCollins, 1997). Readable and well-researched account of the freedom struggle and Partition.
The Nehrus and the Gandhis: an Indian Dynasty, by Tariq Ali (Pan, 1985). A gripping account of India's famous political family. Now out-of-print but secondhand copies can still be found.
No Full Stops in India, by Mark Tully (Viking, 1991). Essays on modern political India by the BBC's ex-South Asia correspondent.
Tea: Addiction, Exploitation and Empire, by Roy Moxham (Constable, 2003). A fascinating history of the skullduggery and economics behind one of India's most valuable crops.
This Fissured Land, by Madhav Gadgil and Ramachandra Guha (Oxford University Press, 1993). Searching and thought-provoking ecological history of South Asia.
The Wonder that Was India, by A.L. Basham (Rupa, 1967). Learned historical classic in idiosyncratic, rapturous prose.

Society, Culture and Religion

A Book of India, by B.N. Pandey (Rupa, Delhi, 1982). A real *masala* mix of philosophies, traveller's notes, poetry and literary trivia, revealing a quixotic India. Recommended.
The Castes and Tribes of Southern India, by Edgar Thurston and E. Rangachari (1904, reprinted Asian Educational Services). This seven-volume work is still the best guide to the myriad castes of South India.
Conversations in Bloomsbury, by Mulk Raj Anand (Oxford University Press, 1986). In turns, amusing, scathing and enlightening account of an Indian author's meetings with 20th-century luminaries of the British literary scene.
Dravidian Gods in Modern Hinduism, by W.T. Elmore, and, **The Village Gods of South India**, by Henry Whitehead (Asian Educational Services, 1995 and 1999). Reprints of two classic studies of South Indian local religion and ritual.
Gods, Demons and Others, by R.K. Narayan (Heineman, 1986). Retellings of some of India's most popular religious myths by one of the country's greatest writers. Also worth looking out for are his retellings of **The Ramayana** (Penguin, 1977), based on the Tamil Kamban version, and **The Mahabharata** (Heineman, 1986).
The Idea of India, by Sunil Khilnani (Hamish Hamilton, 1997). An intellectual *tour de force* examines concepts about an ancient civilisation and its status as a relatively new nation.
India: A Literary Companion, by Bruce Palling (John Murray, 1992). Another compilation of impressions taken from literature, letters and unpublished diaries, skillfully presented.
India File, by Trevor Fishlock (John Murray, 1987). Witty observations of a resident British correspondent.
Indira: the Life of Indira Nehru Gandhi, by Katherine Frank (HarperCollins, 2002). An in-depth biography of one of post-Independence India's most charismatic leaders.
Intimate Relations: Exploring Indian Sexuality, Sudhir Kakar (University of Chicago Press, 1990). This study throws light on many aspects of Indian marital and family relations.
An Introduction to Hinduism, by Gavin Flood (Cambridge University Press, 1996). Perhaps the best general introduction to the complexities of this diverse religion. Recommended.
May You Be the Mother of a Hundred Sons, by Elisabeth Bumiller (Penguin, 1990). Women's issues tackled head-on, everything from dowries to infanticide, with dozens of poignant interviews.
A Million Mutinies Now, by V.S. Naipul (Heineman, 1990). The misanthropic scholar returns to seek his roots and finds a cast of characters not easily pigeon-holed. A more positive follow-up to his earlier, jaundiced, **India: A Wounded Civilisation** (Penguin, 1979).
The Mind of India, by William Gerber (Arcturus, 1967). Snippets from The Vedas, Buddhism, ancient and medieval commentaries and modern mysticism all help to understand a Hindu perspective.
Plain Tales from the Raj, ed. Charles Allen (Rupa, 1992). First-hand accounts from ex-colonialists.

The Remembered Village, by M. Narasimhachar Srinivas (Oxford University Press India, 1999). A reprint of the classic anthropological study of a South Indian village.
Savaging the Civilised: Verrier Elwin, his Tribals and India, by Ramachandra Guha (University of Chicago Press, 1999). Biography of the great champion of India's beleaguered Adivasis.
Subaltern Studies: Writings on South Asian History and Society, I–X, various eds (Oxford University Press India). An ongoing series of volumes dealing with Indian history, gender, class and violence. In turns fascinating, challenging and inspiring.
Temptations of the West, Pankaj Mishra (Picador 2006). An insightful account of modern India's encounter with global capitalism and the consumer society.

Fiction

The English Teacher, by R.K. Narayan (various editions). Narayan depicts infuriating and endearing characters which inhabit Malgudi, a composite South Indian village. Also in various editions, are **Malgudi Days**, a series of short stories.
The God of Small Things, by Arundhati Roy (Random House, 1997). The Kerala backwaters are evoked in a hauntingly personal novel set in a small village pickle factory in the 1960s. Recommended.
Kanthapura, by Raja Rao (Oxford University Press, 1947). A lyrical novel about a village in Karnataka which implements Gandhi's methods of non-violent resistance to British rule.
Kim, by Rudyard Kipling (Penguin Books, 2000, ed. by Edward Said). The wonderful adventures of a boy who wanders across North India in search of the Great Game.
Midnight's Children, by Salman Rushdie (Jonathan Cape, 1981). Rushdie burst onto the literary scene with this dazzling novel of post-Independence India. Sardonic. **The Moor's Last Sigh**, on Mumbai, also dazzles (Jonathan Cape, 1995).
Out of India, by Ruth Prawer Jhabvala (Morrow, 1986). A collection of strong short stories that amuse and startle.
A Passage to India, by E.M. Forster (Penguin, 2000). The classic novel of the misunderstandings that arose out of the East-West encounter. After a mysterious incident in a cave Dr Aziz is accused of assaulting a naive young Englishwoman, Adela Quested. The trial exposes the racism inherent in British colonialism.
The Raj Quartet, by Paul Scott (University of Chicago Press, 1998). Four novels – The Jewel in the Crown, The Day of the Scorpion, The Towers of Silence and A Division of Spoils – set during the last days of the British Raj and charting its decline and fall.
Red Earth and Pouring Rain, by Vikram Chandra (Viking, 1996). Acclaimed debut novel, quick-paced and audacious.
A River Sutra, by Gita Mehta (Viking, 1993). Gently wrought stories which linger in the imagination.
Samskara, by U.R. Anantha Murthy (Oxford University Press, 1976). Tale of a South Indian Brahman village in Karnataka, where one Brahman is forced to question his values. Beautifully translated by A.K. Ramanujan.
The Scent of Pepper, by Kavery Nambisan (Penguin, 1996). Wonderfully written family saga set in South India.
A Suitable Boy, by Vikram Seth (Phoenix Press, 1994). A huge and multi-faceted novel set during the run up to Independent India's first elections, which centres around a mother's search for a suitable husband for her daughter. Highly recommended.
Untouchable, by Mulk Raj Anand (Penguin, 1986). Grinding tale of poverty and discrimination.
Women Writing in India: 600 BC to the Present, ed. Susie Tharu and K. Lalitha (Feminist Press, 1991). Wonderful and eclectic anthology bringing to light the neglected history of Indian women. Volume 1 includes writings from 600 BC to the early 20th century, volume 2 concentrates on the 20th century alone.
Yaarana: Gay Writing from India, ed. Hoshang Merchant, and, **Facing the Mirror: Lesbian Writing from India**, ed. Ashwini Sukthankar (both Penguin, 1999). Anthologies of short stories, extracts from novels and poetry from gay and lesbian Indian writers.

Travel

Butter Chicken in Ludhiana: Travels in Small Town India, by Pankaj Mishra (Penguin, 1995). An urban Indian novelist casts a jaundiced eye over modern Indian life.
Exploring Indian Railways, by Bill Aitken (Oxford University Press, 1996). Highly informed and occasionally idiosyncratic tour of the Indian railway system written by a clear enthusiast.
A Goddess in the Stones, by Norman Lewis (Cape, 1991). The founder of Survival International travels among the Adivasis of Bihar and Orissa. Entertaining.
Leaves from the Jungle: Life in a Gond Village, by Verrier Elwin (Oxford University Press, 1992). Very entertaining account of this early anthropologist's stay with a central-Indian Adivasi group.
Sorcerer's Apprentice, by Tahir Shah (Penguin, 1998). A hair-raising travelogue of the author's attempts to learn the secrets of illusion and fraud of India's street magicians.

Food and Language

Dakshin: Vegetarian Cuisine from South India, by Chandra Padmanabhan (Angus and Robertson, 1999). An excellent guide to wonderful foods of South India.
Hanklyn-Janklin, or a Stranger's Rumble Tumble Guide to some Words, Customs and Quiddities Indian and Indo-British, by Nigel B. Hankin (Banyan Books, New Delhi, 1992). Lives up to its title and is a delightful reference work.
Hobson-Jobson (Routledge and Kegan Paul, 1968). This is the 1886 glossary on which Hankin modelled his modern etymology, if anything more charming than the later volume. The pair complement one another.

Feedback

We do our best to ensure the information in our books is as accurate and up-to-date as possible. The books are updated on a regular basis, using local contacts, who painstakingly add, amend and correct as required. However, some mistakes and omissions are inevitable and we are ultimately reliant on our readers to put us in the picture. We would welcome your feedback on any details related to your experiences using the book "on the road". Maybe we recommended a hotel that you liked (or another that you didn't), as well as interesting new attractions, or facts and figures you have found out about the country itself. The more details you can give us (particularly with regard to addresses, e-mails and telephone numbers), the better. We will acknowledge all contributions, and we'll offer an Insight Guide to the best letters received.

Please write to us at:
Insight Guides
PO Box 7910
London SE1 1WE
United Kingdom
Or send e-mail to:
insight@apaguide.co.uk

Art and Photo Credits

M. Amirtham back cover left, 160
Clare Arni 65, 154, 167, 208, 235, 238, 261, 315, 320
Pallava Bagla 217
C.H. Basapannavar 24/25, 32
David Beatty 19, 58/59, 103R, 152, 155, 194, 204, 205, 253
R. Belbin/TRIP 38
Berlitz 203, 286
Sharad Bhandari 26
Subhash Bhargava 161
M. Mahesh Bhat 260, 273
Uzra Bilgrami 40
Tibor Bognar/TRIP 9T, 48, 105, 159, 230, 233, 234, 239
Nick Bonetti/Eye Ubiquitous back cover top, 7L, 199, 201
Bridgeman Art Library 150
Dhiraj Chawda 84, 92, 278, 284/285
Meera Chatterjee 125
COP 61, 70, 129
Arvind Chenji 297, 298, 313
Gerald Cubitt 114
David Cumming/Eye Ubiquitous 36, 42, 110/111, 141, 151, 218, 346
Sujoy Das/Fotomedia 256
Bennett Dean/Eye Ubiquitous 62, 71, 72, 88, 112/113, 187, 338, 340, 342
Sue Dent/Hutchison 310R
B.N.S. Deo 324
Dinodia Picture Library 276, 306
DPL/LinkIndia 54L, 54R, 90, 107, 207, 216, 240, 267, 283
Chris Fairclough/Eye Ubiquitous 237
Laurence Fordyce/Eye Ubiquitous 192R
David Forman/Eye Ubiquitous 350
Dirk Frans/Hutchison 321, 322L
Carlos Freire/Hutchison Library 46
Andrew Gasson/TRIP 45
Getty Images 51
Nirmal Ghosh 23, 173
B. Gibbs/TRIP 182/183
Fiona Good/TRIP back flap bottom, 7T, 8T, 9L, 44, 64, 66, 73, 118, 121, 127, 143, 144, 146, 147, 148, 149, 166, 169, 171, 193, 195, 197, 198, 202, 211, 215, 317, 319, 326, 349
Richard Hammerton/TRIP back flap top, 56, 57, 69, 85, 178, 180, 181, 236, 241, 344, 360
E. Hanumantha Rao 29L, 30, 31
Blaine Harrington back cover centre, 1, 2/3, 6, 34/35, 98, 162, 190, 191, 270, 357
Maurice Harvey/Eye Ubiquitous 210
Maurice Harvey/Hutchison 123, 130, 214
Nick Haslam/Hutchison 132
John van Hasselt/Corbis Sygma 314
Jeremy Horner/Hutchison 89, 172, 247, 330
Walter Imber/APA Publications 99, 257
T.A. Jayakumar 27, 164
Koshy Johnson/Eye Ubiquitous 94, 157
Ravi Kaimal 124, 128
Alok Kavan 174/175
Ajay Khullar 135
Dariusz Klemens/LinkIndia 67
Bob Krist 68, 153
Lyle Lawson 16, 310L
R. Lingeshwar 93
Maria Lord 223
Ashwin Mehta 134, 165, 209, 296
Fayaz A. Mir 192L, 225
Pramod Mistry 131
Anna Mockford/Eye Ubiquitous 86, 354
V. Muthuraman 12/13, 60, 76, 91, 145, 168, 179, 219, 226/227
S. Nagaraj/DPA/Link India 33
Courtesy of the Nehru Memorial Museum New Delhi 50
Kevin Nichol/Eye Ubiquitous 4/5
Avinash Pasricha 102
Aditya Patankar 101
T.N.A. Perumal 274
Andrea Pistolesi 104, 126L&R, 133, 158
K. Prabhakar/Resource Foto 83, 300, 312L/R
V.K. Rajamani 79, 80, 97
Sudhir Ramachandran 108/109, 243
P.S. Rao/Resource Foto 305
K.T. Ravindran 176, 177, 224
Simon Reddy/TRIP 7B, 8B, 43, 63, 245, 255
Kamal Sahai 14/15, 20, 137, 139, 142, 184, 251, 263, 289, 295, 316, 318
Dave Sanger back cover bottom, front flap top, 29L, 100, 163, 186, 189, 311
Malini Saran 41
Shalini Saran 95, 213, 268, 271, 272, 279, 280, 282
T.S. Satyan 242, 249, 250, 258, 259, 262, 275, 277, 281
Peter Sayle 77
Geeti Sen 81, 82, 140
Pepita Seth 78, 96, 264, 265
Pankaj Shah 10/11, 52, 74/75, 103L, 106, 207, 228
Rajendra Shaw/Hutchison 308, 309, 322R
Toby Sinclair 39, 47, 231, 252
Paul Smith/Panos 55
Sean Sprague/The Image Works 301, 303
Ajay Sud/Fotomedia 304, 323
Barbara Swanson/TRIP 120
Jane Sweeney/TRIP 22, 156, 248, 269, 334
Larry Tackett 220/221
Luca Invernizzi Tettoni 87
Topham Picturepoint 37, 53R
TRIP 293, 294, 299
TRIP/Resource Foto spine, front flat bottom, 212, 288, 291
TRIP/Dinodia 254, 292 293, 294, 307
Hashim Tyabji/Fotomedia 28
Vijay/Fotomedia 53L

Map Production:
Mike Adams

INSIGHT GUIDE
SOUTH INDIA

Cartographic Editor **Zoë Goodwin**
Production **Linton Donaldson**
Design Consultant **Klaus Geisler**
Picture Research **Hilary Genin**

INDEX

U

V

W

Y

HotelClub.com Membership Discount Card

Register with HotelClub.com and get £15!

At ***HotelClub.com***, we reward our Members with discounts and free stays in their favourite hotels. As a Member, every booking made by you through ***HotelClub.com*** will earn you Member Dollars.

When you register, we will credit your account with ***£15*** which you can use for your next booking! The equivalent of ***£15*** will be credited in US$ to your Member account (as ***HotelClub Member Dollars***). All you need to do is log on to ***www.HotelClub.com/insightguides***. Complete your details, including the Membership Number and Password located on the back of the ***HotelClub.com*** card.

Over 2.2 million Members already use Member Dollars to pay for all or part of their hotel bookings. Join now and start spending Member Dollars whenever and wherever you want – you are not restricted to specific hotels or dates!

With great savings of up to 60% on over 20,000 hotels across 97 countries, you are sure to find the perfect location for business or pleasure. Happy travels from ***HotelClub.com!***

www.insightguides.com